From BOULANGER

---

to STOCKHAUSEN

BÁLINT ANDRÁS VARGA

From BOULANGER

to STOCKHAUSEN

INTERVIEWS AND A MEMOIR

UNIVERSITY OF ROCHESTER PRESS

First published 2013
Transferred to digital printing 2017

University of Rochester Press
668 Mt. Hope Avenue, Rochester, NY 14620, USA
www.urpress.com
and Boydell & Brewer Limited
PO Box 9, Woodbridge, Suffolk IP12 3DF, UK
www.boydellandbrewer.com

ISSN: 1071-9989
ISBN: 978-1-58046-439-0

Library of Congress Cataloging-in-Publication Data

Varga, Bálint András, author, interviewer.
    From Boulanger to Stockhausen : interviews and a memoir / Bálint András Varga.
        pages cm — (Eastman studies in music, ISSN 1071-9989 ; v. 104)
    ISBN 978-1-58046-439-0 (hardcover : alkaline paper) 1. Musicians—Interviews. 2. Composers—Interviews. 3. Varga, Bálint András. 4. Music publishers—Biography. I. Title. II. Series: Eastman studies in music ; v. 104.
    ML385.V373 2013
    780—dc23

                                                            2013019341

A catalogue record for this title is available from the British Library.

Cover image: *Deep Blue* by Caro Woods. Mixed media on paper, 20 cm x 20 cm, 1998. http://www.carowoods.co.uk/. Caro Woods is an artist who lives and works in Cornwall, UK. She has exhibited widely throughout Europe and Africa.

To my family:

My brother, Peter
My wife, Kati
My daughters, Fanni and Flora
And my grandson, Leon, born in 2012

CONTENTS

FOREWORD

After I'd finished reading Bálint András Varga's text, I dug out the copy of Schoenberg's *Sechs kleine Klavierstücke* (Universal Edition, 1913) that I'd bought as a schoolboy in 1953. At that distant time, the bold capitals and wide spaces on the front cover and the seven challengingly complex yet startlingly economical pages of music within stood for just about everything that was not central to mid-century musical life and education in my part of the world. Sadly, I failed to make it as a composer of music worthy to follow on from Schoenberg (and therefore to be published by Universal Edition), turning instead to academic, analytical exposition and explanation. But the sense of awe and excitement that came from that particular purchase and from the process of learning to play and think about those pieces has never diminished.

Such a frankly confessional tone is not normally the métier of the musicologist, still less of the music theorist. But this book is both frankly confessional and unusually illuminating about a musical life, in ways refreshingly different from what academic musicology can offer. During its author's time—the second half of the twentieth century and first part of the twenty-first—classical music has survived, despite the explosion of activity and interest in various kinds of commercial, popular, and ethnic musics, developed by artists who view creation and composition very differently from the composers Schoenberg admired, or the composers he taught; yet most of what has survived of classical music is to be found in concerts, recordings, and scholarly studies that give pride of place to compositions from earlier times.

Proclaiming the apparent immortality of Bach, Beethoven, and others is an important and valuable enterprise, but it does rather tend to marginalize and to highlight the ephemerality of those more recent kinds of music, which have sought to transform and even on occasion to contradict the principles on which that earlier music was based. As both parts of this book reveal, the quixotic desire to make possible a degree of permanence for Berio, Boulez, or Birtwistle within such a generally alien world involves the establishment of relationships—epic, comic, and with all intermediate shades of thought and feeling—between a great variety of often oversized egos: the egos of performers and of the artistic directors of concert-giving organizations at one extreme; of composers, in the middle; and (at the other extreme) of agents, publishers—even, occasionally, of critics or scholarly writers—who seek to promote certain compositions on the grounds that they need to be heard: ideally, heard frequently over many years.

In his earlier books, Varga offered the results of his intriguing encounters with many different contemporary musicians and composers, and although his own presence, in the form of questions and comments, was always scrupulously subordinate, he was fortunately unable to suppress completely the personality and professional expertise that helped to make possible such contacts and undertakings in the first place. Now, as well as supplementing his collection of interviews to take in some eminent figures not particularly involved with the new in music, he has been persuaded to add a first-person memoir that fills out the human identity and values behind those questions and comments. His progress from Budapest to Berlin and Vienna, from piano playing to broadcasting to publishing, is outlined in a wry narrative that should be of absorbing interest—not least to academic musicians impatient with the cliché that they inhabit ivory towers from which the real world is effortlessly excluded. Varga's real musical world has been constructed with insight and determination from the recalcitrant clay of commercial as well as political, cultural and—yes—musical concerns. And in counterpoint with this professional odyssey is a personal narrative about family and friends that is as moving in content as it is concise in expression. It would betray the spirit of this narrative, and the life and work it sketches so vividly, to elaborate further. To read—and reread—this story, and to meet this diverse, demanding, and sometimes disturbing cast of musical characters, is a rare and enlightening pleasure.

Arnold Whittall

ACKNOWLEDGMENTS

This book owes its existence to Professor Ralph Locke of the University of Rochester Press. He was muse and midwife; his encouragement, suggestions, and corrections had a major part in making the book what it is.

I am also grateful to my friend Paul Griffiths, who established contact on my behalf with the Press, which has led to the publication of three of my books, and who read and commented on most of my chapters the moment they were mailed to him.

I received much appreciated help from Professor Arnold Whittall who generously anglicized some Magyar turns of phrase, rooted out the many typos that had escaped my attention, and questioned what I had taken to be facts, which encouraged me to double-check them.

I am indebted to Antal Boronkay, managing director, and Tünde Szitha, head of promotion (Editio Musica Budapest), Marion von Hartlieb, former managing director, Astrid Koblanck, current managing director, and Eric Marinitsch, head of promotion, Jonathan Irons, head of the Web Department (Universal Edition), Louise Duchesneau, György Ligeti's assistant of many years, Dr. Werner Grünzweig, director of the Music Archives of the Academy of Arts, Berlin, Therese Muxeneder of the Arnold Schönberg Center in Vienna, Professor László Somfai, former director of the Bartók Archives in Budapest, Suzanne Stephens of the Stockhausen Stiftung in Kürten, László Vikárius, director of the Bartók Archives in Budapest, and my friend Professor Stephen Walsh of Cardiff University.

PART ONE

INTERVIEWS

PREFACE TO

THE INTERVIEWS

I n a way, these interviews are a form of memoir. They are written records of oral documents. For documents they are: of the ideas and opinions of major figures of international musical life, committed to tape decades ago.

Their own memories of conversations with significant personalities of a previous generation are for me particularly valuable. Stravinsky's words to William Glock on a train in the 1930s, Richard Strauss talking to Neville Cardus and Hans Swarowsky, Béla Bartók to the child Tibor Varga, Alois Hába to Franz Schreker, Pierre Monteux's comments to Neville Marriner—all of this would probably be lost if it had not been recalled at a given moment during the course of our interviews.

My own impressions, prefixed to the conversations by way of introductions, are also memoirs in their own way. (A fuller memoir of my life experiences and my interactions with *la vie musicale* and notable musical artists forms part 2 of this book.)

In the 1970s, I published three collections of interviews in Hungarian: the harvest of my single-minded devotion to what I describe later on in this book as an obsession.[1]

They have been slumbering within the covers of those books ever since. Thanks to the interest of the University of Rochester Press, I have

---

1 *Zenészekkel zenéről* (Musicians on music) was published in 1972 by Minerva in Budapest, jointly with Hungarian Radio where most of the interviews had been broadcast (with Arthur Rubinstein, Joseph Szigeti, Neville Cardus, and others). *Muzsikusokkal Amerikában* (With musicians in America), my account of the US tour of the Hungarian Radio Symphony Orchestra also included interviews (such as the one with Eugene Ormandy) and was published by Editio Musica Budapest in 1974. I have drawn the conversations with Ernest Bour, Hans Swarowsky, William Glock, and others from *Muzsikusportrék* (Portraits of musicians). It was published once again by EMB, in 1979.

awakened some of them and translated the texts back into English, for many of the cassettes were either stolen or lost in moving from one apartment and one country to another. I have been able to transcribe the interviews with Ernest Bour, William Glock, Sylvia Goldstein, Neville Marriner, Isaac Stern, and Walter Susskind from the original tapes.

The section titled "Snippets" is a compromise. If I were to include all my published interviews, the book would be forbiddingly thick, demanding unfair space on any bookshelf. The other extreme—omitting all but those I can identify with today in their entirety—would be an exercise in painful self-mutilation.

"Snippets" allows selected extracts of conversations with remarkable musicians to survive into the twenty-first century. If I have decided against including them as they appeared some forty years ago in Hungarian, it is because I am not happy with my own contribution as an interviewer—it is certainly no reflection on the interviewees.

I hope you will agree that these brief flashes round out the picture of some of the personalities evoked in the full-length interviews (Neville Cardus and Antal Doráti on Menuhin, for instance, Abbado on Toscanini, Doráti and Szigeti on Bartók, and so on). Other excerpts allow a glimpse of artists who, in talking of others, actually sketched a self-portrait—such as Ralph Kirkpatrick.

The interviews I did in the 1960s and early 1970s were the outcome of my urge to talk to great musicians, but in many cases I did not have a chance to properly prepare for them. I took my tape recorder on my travels, just in case, and used whatever opportunity offered itself. Hence my repeated apologies for some of my questions, which appear to me today as naive or beside the point. In fact, the first interview I prepared for properly did not occur until March 1973 when I met Witold Lutosławski in Warsaw and talked to him for nine hours on five consecutive days. It appeared in English as *Lutosławski Profile* in 1976.[2]

Sometimes, though, the originality or the probing nature of questions is of no particular consequence. You can make an indifferent comment on the weather and it may trigger a fascinating range of associations in your interviewee that retroactively justifies the insipidness of the comment. It really depends on the person you talk to.

Interviews are a psychological experiment or even adventure. Does a give-and-take come about as a result of mutual sympathy and the inspiration of the moment? On the few occasions I have myself been interviewed,

---

2   Bálint András Varga, *Lutosławski Profile* (London: Chester Music, 1976).

I have experienced waves reaching me from the person holding the microphone, waves that made me unwind and actually enjoy our exchange.

I hope you will derive some pleasure from eavesdropping on these conversations that took place between 1966 and 2008, in Budapest, Prague, Warsaw, London, Manchester, Zurich, Paris, Vienna, Dubrovnik, Amsterdam, Leeds, Philadelphia, and New York.

COMPOSERS

GEORGES AURIC

1 8 9 9 – 1 9 8 3

T he International Confederation of Authors and Composers Societies held its annual meeting in Budapest in 1971. France was represented by Georges Auric. I felt a tremendous thrill on hearing the news that a member of Les Six, that legendary group of French composers, was in Budapest. I remember I was beside myself with excitement, grabbed my tape recorder and dashed to the Hotel InterContinental, scene of the conference.

"I am looking for Georges Auric," I said, hardly believing what I was saying. "There he is, coming out of the hall."

I immediately felt affection and friendship toward the jovial elderly gentleman standing in the hotel's lobby. I sensed an inner youth, an amiable, teasing irony with which he appeared to be observing the world around him. Auric had not changed much since the photograph taken of Les Six in 1952. (In an earlier photo, of 1925, he was represented by Cocteau's drawing.) His hair had grown whiter, but the parting was still in the same place, toward the middle of his forehead. His face was slightly drawn, and he moved rather clumsily. He did not have much time for an interview; eventually, we met twice for ten minutes each. See the result below.

o

Bálint András Varga (BAV): The Théâtre du Vieux-Colombier was the scene, on January 18, 1918, of a concert which is supposed to have marked the beginnings of what came to be known as the Groupe des Six.[1] What are your memories of that concert and of the events leading up to it?

---

1 The Théâtre du Vieux-Colombier was founded in 1913 by Jacques Copeau.

Georges Auric (GA): Some of us who had studied together at the Conservatoire before World War I, met up at regular intervals in the 1910s. The idea came up at one point that we might join forces to give concerts of our music. The one you mentioned, at the Théâtre du Vieux-Colombier in 1918, was the first such event. I was nineteen years old and my friends, Poulenc, Honegger, Tailleferre, Durey, and Manuel were equally young, or perhaps one or two years older.[2]

In the years following the peace treaty, our concerts were held in a small hall in the Rue Huyghens on the Montparnasse. The venue served also as an artists' atelier and housed exhibitions of painters who were unknown at the time but have since come to be recognized as great masters.

We were young, full of enthusiasm and got together frequently to discuss problems that we regarded as important for the future of French music. I believe that our first concert of 1918 should also be viewed in this light. It was an adventure, the adventure of passionate young musicians, fueled by the desire to create something new that would be radically different from the music of the preceding era. We rebelled against our masters and wanted to compose music that was new and genuinely French.

I am more and more convinced that if composers are to address an international public, they have to write national music. Béla Bartók is a good example. His compositions are heard and admired all over the world precisely because they are recognizably Hungarian. If he had stuck to following in the footsteps of Richard Strauss whose art had made a strong impact on him in his youth, he would never have become the great composer we know. Sadly, we were not as significant, but were also guided by the goal to speak in a characteristically French idiom, because we hoped that our music would talk to music lovers the world over.

To return to our concerts in the Rue Huyghens: one of them was attended by the journalist Henri Collet.[3] He was the one who first referred to us as Les Six. It would never have occurred to us to call ourselves in this way. However, it proved a success because immediately people would call us Groupe des Six, a moniker which accompanied us all our lives. None of us protested against it, for that was what made us known.

Let me remind you, however, that our group was primarily that of six friends and, contrary to what Collet wanted to discern in our music, we

---

2 I expect the mention of Roland-Manuel (1891–1966) was a slip of the tongue, for the music critic and composer, a close friend of Ravel, was not a member of the Groupes des Six. Auric will have meant Darius Milhaud.

3 Henri Collet (1885–1951), French composer and music critic. His review of a concert in 1920 introduced the phrase "Groupe des Six."

were not linked by any common aesthetic. The music of Arthur Honegger, for instance, was different from Poulenc's or mine. Darius Milhaud also composed differently from Honegger.

It is true, however, that Poulenc and I shared the same goal: we wanted to break with the kind of traditional, romantic music which characterized the work of Honegger. He was no doubt a great musician, but he was romantic; perhaps I might even say that he followed a Germanic trail. Poulenc and I, on the other hand, were of an altogether different mold. We wanted to compose music that was pure, clear, and precise, in certain moments even aggressive, without any compromise.

What singled us out as a group was the fact that we were friends. We never fought with one another, we held together even if we pursued different ideals in music.

BAV: What exactly did you rebel against in the art of Debussy and Ravel? After all, they also wrote genuinely French music; on that count, there was nothing you could have taken exception to. And there is another thing: many of your pieces have a jazz element, a feature that cannot be described as French.

GA: It is difficult to reply to this question in a few minutes. In rebelling against Debussy, we were not protesting against the French traits of his art. In our eyes, he represented in music the same aesthetic as impressionism in painting. We, however, were vehemently against anything that smacked of impressionism. You know what I mean: sunset on the Seine, night, mist, clouds. The clouds are of course exquisitely beautiful in Debussy's *Nocturnes*, but we were dreaming of sunny, clear, pure art, even though sunlight and clarity are admittedly not always pleasant. Our means of expression also differed from tradition.

Many years have passed since, and I do not hesitate to admit that Debussy was a composer of genius. I maintain to this day, however, that his music was alien to our concepts. In contrast to his subtle art, enveloped in a veil, so to speak, we were out to be brutal, sometimes even vulgar. Chabrier was closest to us (he is rarely played today but in those years he was as much admired as Ravel); of the old masters, we loved Jean-Philippe Rameau and Couperin.

Jazz would also require a lengthy discussion: it has developed a great deal since the 1910s and today's jazz has nothing to do with what I understood by this term when I was nineteen or twenty.

Jazz interests me as a musical form, but I do not believe its influence has been beneficial as far as the greatest composers are concerned. Stravinsky, for instance, wrote several pieces which were strongly influenced by the rhythm of jazz, but they are hardly among his best. Ravel's only failed composition, *L'enfant et les sortilèges* has a foxtrot in it: it is very poor jazz and very poor Ravel.[4] As for me, I dislike all my works written under the influence of jazz. I consider them weak.

BAV: Do you agree with the opinion that your compositions are midway between serious and light music?

GA: I have endeavored to write clear, precise, sometimes ironical, witty, and entertaining music, no doubt under the impact of Stravinsky. However, I would not call it light music. I have composed several ballets, for instance *Phèdre*, which you could not describe as merry or light; also because of its subject matter.[5] I have also composed sonatas, orchestral works, opera, and much, perhaps too much, film music. I have written music for at least 150 films, because I found the genre interesting and novel; I felt it lent itself to experiment. Of course, you do have situations in films which require music in a light vein. As a result, even though I am a serious composer, I have had to solve some unusual assignments.

To cite just one example: it must have been around 1950 that John Huston asked me to write music for a film he was about to shoot. He called it *Moulin Rouge*.[6] I was intrigued by the plot—the life of Toulouse-Lautrec—and took on the commission. At a particular point, a three-minute song was needed (the score runs to forty or fifty minutes). I composed it to the best of my abilities and soon enough forgot about the whole thing. The film was then duly shot and was premiered in New York. One day I learned, much to my surprise, that those three minutes had been lifted out of the fifty and (perhaps it is odd that I should be saying a thing like this) it had scored a resounding success in the United States. The film was then introduced in Europe and the little song which had taken me thirty minutes or one hour at the most to write, became an international hit. Perhaps that is my best-known music. The success of *Moulin Rouge* came out of the blue, and I am pleased about it, for it shows that I am capable of writing music that is popular and on a high professional level. However, it is not the kind of music I had set out to compose, and I attach far more significance to my other compositions.

---

4   Ravel described this opera, written between 1917 and 1925 to a libretto by Colette, as a "lyric fantasy."
5   *Phèdre* was composed and premiered in 1950. The choreographer was Serge Lifar; the costumes and the sets were designed by Jean Cocteau.
6   John Huston directed *Moulin Rouge* in 1952.

BAV: Early on in your career, you and your friends represented what was new in music at the time. Now that you belong to the older generation of composers, what do you make of what the young generation of today is up to?

GA: This is a very complex issue—we could talk about it for hours. A great deal is being written about contemporary music; it is the subject of much debate. I would prefer to use a more precise description and talk of music composed in the past few years. We must not forget that an old gentleman of ninety is as "contemporary" as a twenty-year-old.

To answer your question: I am basically interested in everything that is happening in music. I observe every phenomenon even if I do not always agree with what I find. Sadly, I am not young anymore, but I hold it is the duty of the elderly to follow with interest what young people are doing. It would be sinful not to keep my ears open to the latest music.

Undoubtedly, we are living in an age of transition. I regret I shall not live to hear the kind of music that will be written in ten years' time. I am sure it will continue to develop; after all, the music being written today, in 1971, is different from what it was twenty years ago. The youngest composers have turned away from the Second Viennese School, which exerted such a huge influence on French music, indeed, on European music as a whole. They are looking for something wholly different. Their search is perhaps not devoid of confusion, but I hope that in ten or twelve years—of course, it could also be in five years or tomorrow, I do not know—there will appear a young musician who will lend music a new face.

Budapest, 1971

ALOIS HÁBA

1893–1973

A s I look back, Alois Hába's figure emerges through the mist of time, as he entered the room in Prague where I was waiting for him. He was seventy-nine but looked older. A pale, gray figure in a shabby coat, with a kindly, friendly, and shrewd look in his eyes. He rather looked like a village schoolmaster, which, as it turned out, he had been in his youth.

Our interview had an ABA form: it began as a tale, turned into an impassioned tirade with his fist landing on the table to add emphasis to the point he was anxious to bring home to me and ended, with an unexpected and abrupt change of voice, as peacefully as it had begun.

A few years later, I told Pierre Boulez of Hába's critical remarks. He said Hába was wrong because it is not the intervals you use that make your music "modern" but rather your thinking. Hába's music (Boulez continued) was just as rooted in tradition as Ivan Wyschnegradsky's, another pioneer of microtonal music.[1]

o

Alois Hába: I attended teachers' training college; that's where I obtained my degree. Thanks to my music teacher who had studied with Vitězslav Novák, I had the privilege of receiving a high-level education in music theory.[2]

I found employment as a teacher for two years in Eastern Moravia, which brought me in touch with Moravian and Slovak folk music.

---

1   Ivan Wyschnegradsky (1893–1979), Russian composer, primarily of microtonal music.
2   Vitězslav Novák (1870–1949), Czech composer.

Sometimes I would cross the border into Hungary to study the folk songs of the Slovak minority there.

In 1915 I was admitted to the class of Novák himself and it was there that I acquired the ins and outs of composition, even though I only stayed for a short time: I was called up in the army and was transferred to Vienna. I did not lose touch with music, however, for I was seconded to look after the collection of military songs within the Institute of Music History. The department was headed by Dr. Bernhard Paumgartner, who proved to be kindly and empathetic in his dealings with us, young men.[3]

Béla Bartók came by once in a while to study the collection—that is how we met, in 1916. From then on we would be seeing each other at various music festivals and have a cup of coffee together. We became friends. I was happy to develop a close relationship with that taciturn man who talked little of himself or of others. I respected his discretion, his power of concentration. Surely you remember his eyes: they had a searching look, lively and affectionate.

On one occasion, I was bold enough to pose the question as to why he was not teaching composition. He declined to give a straight answer. Rather, he said something to the effect that it was Kodály's responsibility. (I did not learn until later that they were friends.) I regret that composition in Hungary was not taught by Bartók: the education of the young generation ought to have been in the hands of someone who was playing an active role in the development of new music. Failing that, young people had to look for guidance elsewhere.

As you can see, my contact with Hungarian music goes back a long way. It began with Bartók, continued with Jemnitz and even younger people whom I would see at festivals.[4]

In Moravia, I listened to folk singers with keen attention and interest. On and off, I would notate some folk songs but I never collected them with anywhere near the single-mindedness of Bartók. What intrigued me more than anything else was the way the singers would be intoning above or below the correct pitch. I was thinking: well, that is certainly no ordinary half-tone music! It was wholly unknown in serious music and it suddenly struck me that I might use quarter tones in my own works as well.

3   Bernhard Paumgartner (1887–1971), Austrian composer, conductor, musicologist, teacher, one of the founders of the Salzburg Festival, of which he acted as chairman (1960–71). He also wrote books on Bach and Mozart.

4   Sándor Jemnitz (1890–1963), Hungarian composer, conductor, and music critic. He was a pupil of Max Reger and Arnold Schoenberg as well as of Arthur Nikisch. He was an influential music critic in postwar Hungary.

I proceeded to write my String Quartet op. 7—that was in 1920. Further quarter-tone compositions were to follow.

The music of Dvořák, Janáček, and Smetana exerted hardly any influence on my development as a composer, simply because I did not know them. Young people today easily forget that in my time there was no radio, neither did we have ready access to scores. Rarely did we have occasion to hear a recent piece at a concert. I remember traveling in my time as a village schoolmaster to Brno to listen to Novák's cantata *The Dead Man's Bride*. It was a revelation. However, I had to return to the village that very night to appear in my class at eight in the morning. In Moravia, then, I was isolated from music, nor did Prague musical life spoil me later with novelties. I am sure my life would have taken a different turn if I had not been called up in the army in 1915, for in Vienna I made the acquaintance of Schreker, Schoenberg, Paumgartner, and others.[5]

I continued my composition studies with Franz Schreker and it was to him that I showed my String Quartet op. 7 to find out what he thought of it. He was lying on his bed in tails, for he was conducting that evening.

"Well, what have you got for me?" he asked.

"Pro-pro-professor, I— I— I want to show you a qua-quarter-tone . . ."

"What?" he interrupted me, impatiently.

"A quarter-tone string quartet."

"Are you out of your mind?"

"No, professor, I have indeed composed a quarter-tone quartet."

"Let me have a look."

He leafed through it and asked meanwhile, "What signs are you using here? Anyway, I have no time now, but bring it along tomorrow morning, I shall take a look at it."

The next day he played the piece through on the piano but of course one had to bear in mind that in fact different notes were sounding. Schreker approved and recommended the piece to his publisher, Universal Edition. If it had not been for him, I might have had to wait twenty years for it to appear; after all, I was unknown. It was thanks to Schreker that I could present my work to the public.

Meanwhile, Schreker had been appointed director of the Music Academy in Berlin and we, his pupils, followed him, rather like students in the Middle Ages who would move wherever their professors went. There was of course no question of scholarships—we lived from hand to mouth.

---

5   Franz Schreker (1878–1934), Austrian composer, conductor, and professor of composition.

A violinist by the name of Havemann was on the staff of the academy and on Schreker's suggestion he put my piece on the repertoire of his string quartet.[6] In fact, they played the world premiere. The concert was attended by critics from all over Europe. My name became known overnight. It was all an accident.

I had a tremendous stroke of luck with my opera, *Mother*, as well: Hermann Scherchen conducted it in Munich, in 1931.[7] I coached the singers myself. As far as the instruments were concerned, string players had no difficulty in finding the quarter tones, and of the winds, flutes, clarinets, trombones, and horns could also "overblow" without any problem. Quarter-tone music is not more difficult, it just requires a purer intonation. You have above all to play the half tones properly. It is not against tradition—rather the other way round.

I have also composed with a system based on fifth tones. Actually, it is quite simple. If we regard the difference between C$\sharp$ and D$\flat$ as the basic interval, we are in fact having to do with a fifth tone. If we progress downward to D$\sharp$ and D, we have been moving in fifth intervals. Upward, too, two intervals lead to E. If we take a conscious note of this, we can easily find our bearings in the traditional system of intonation, i.e., enharmony. We note, for instance, that acoustically, E$\flat$ is higher than D$\sharp$. Violinists, incidentally, play E$\flat$ lower than D$\sharp$. The fifth-tone system restores the proper proportions.

In the early 1920s, I put forward a proposal to the Ministry of Culture in Prague that they approve the setting up of a quarter-tone class in the conservatory. My suggestion was accepted and I held the chair from 1923 right up to 1953. I also taught twelve-tone music and more recent novelties in music. Mine was the first quarter-tone class in music history.

I have composed in the half-tone system as well, I have never been dogmatic. Why confine myself to the quarter-tone system? I am unique in that I am thoroughly independent from any one system. Wagner was a prisoner of his invention. I am equally at home in the half-tone, quarter-tone, third-tone, and sixth-tone systems. I can choose freely; freedom for me is real. For the first time in history, it has become possible to freely select the musical material. This is true!

As far as young people today are concerned—let us forget about whether I like what they are doing or not. Likes and dislikes are emotional categories.

---

6 Gustav Havemann (1882–1960), German violinist and professor at the Berlin Music Academy (1921–45). In the 1920s, the string quartet he founded championed a great deal of new music.

7 *Matka* (Mother), op. 35 (1927–29), an opera in quarter tones. Libretto by the composer, based on the eponymous novel (1906) by Maxim Gorky (1868–1936).

I'd rather say something else. These colleagues—Boulez, Stockhausen, and the rest—have been bogged down in the half-tone system. Boulez uses quarter tones only sporadically. I have got farther. Right from the start, I have used scales in twenty-four divisions. And not just in individual tones, like those colleagues. They have a great deal to catch up with! I know precisely the right place of everything in history and in development. In the field of harmony, they have not reached the highest peak. My system has more to offer than the half-tone system. Only they do not know this!

As far as form is concerned, I decided already a quarter of a century ago that I would seek not to compose in a thematic style. I want to avoid repetition. I wish to create each voice freely in the genuine sense of the word. Such ideas do not even occur to the others. Those moderns! They advertise something that in reality is nothing new! For me, theirs is no new music!

Was that all? Then I want to thank you very much for your interest. I wish you much success in your work and hope you will be as openhearted with other people as you have been with me. I wish you all the very best.

Prague, 1972

GYÖRGY KURTÁG

b. 1926

The interview I did with György and Márta Kurtág, in November 2007, was our longest: we talked for some four hours. The text subsequently underwent corrections and additions and we got together again in April 2008, when I read out the text so that they could double- and triple-check every detail. The definitive version was published, together with our interviews of 1982–85 as well as 1996, in György Kurtág: Three Interviews and Ligeti Homages (2009) by the University of Rochester Press. It appeared in Hungarian and French in the same year as well as in German in 2010.

In April 2008, we also recorded a short interview on an activity that has been central to György Kurtág's life: teaching. On reading it, he said: "Well, that's all I could think of," generously taking the blame for what he judged to be not quite up to the mark.

It was consequently not included in the book and has been slumbering in my drawer, waiting to be brought to Kurtág's attention again, in the hope that he might change his mind about its merits. The moment has now arrived, with this collection of interviews waiting to see the light of day.

o

Bálint András Varga (BAV): You have said in the past that one must be able to play *dolce* even on a piece of wood. That seems to be a basic principle of your teaching: whatever composition one happens to be playing, the approach to it, the musician's *Haltung*, must be the same—the *dolce* as well as all other aspects of the music, must come from within.

György Kurtág (GK): Yes, that is true, but there is something else as well. *Dolce* means for me the transparency of sound. *Dolce* ensures that even in a *fortissimo* full of dissonance and friction, you can "see" through the chord. Just think of the beginning of the recitative in Beethoven's *Ninth*. In my music, there is *forte dolce* and *fortissimo dolce*: they are different from real *fortissimo* which could be *passionato* or something like that.

BAV: I believe you profit from teaching just as much as your pupils do: in putting ideas in words, you formulate them for yourself as well.

GK: That's right. In teaching a composition, I can *feel* it better than when I am analyzing it at the piano.

BAV: Teaching also confronts you with compositions you did not know thoroughly before, and, in preparing them, you may change your mind about them. I am thinking of Bartók's *Contrasts*, for instance, which I think you were of two minds about before learning it properly so that you could teach it.

GK: I admit I am still unsure about *Contrasts* and prefer not to teach it. On the other hand, whenever I am about to teach one of Bartók's string quartets, I learn it anew, again and again. This process might take weeks. And each time, I discover new interrelationships that escaped my attention in the past.

BAV: Each time, it is an encounter with Bartók, or indeed with whichever composer you are teaching.

GK: Yes, of course. On one occasion, I was teaching Beethoven's String Quartet op. 127. Márta found that I had not quite unraveled the slow movement for myself. I wanted to make good and learned it properly. (Now I would need to address myself to it yet again, to master it. I forget. And, perhaps because I forget, it retains its freshness.)

BAV: Just like when you are composing.

GK: Just like when I am composing. I coached the Ebène Quartet in that movement in Budapest and when they played it from beginning to end, they made us cry, it was so beautiful. (They went on to win a prize in Munich but by then they had forgotten much of what we had achieved together; their playing no longer satisfied me.)

BAV: You would take a chord from a piece in hand and by changing a few notes you would turn it into a Beethoven chord. Those are revelatory moments.

GK: I am also fond of citing *Tristan*. I shall, I am afraid, have to find some new passages to quote, for Márta says people might think that's all I know about it (I would be playing just the first few bars of the Prelude).

BAV: You quote from it to spotlight what?

GK: Well, for instance, to call attention to a literal quotation in Bartók's String Quartet no. 2 from the beginning of the Prelude, hidden in the harmonies. If the quartet is not aware of it, they are simply playing a neutral accompaniment, for the thematic material is different.

BAV: I also remember a talented pianist in Wiesbaden who thundered his way through Bartók's Opus 14. You then made him realize that each tone, each harmony had a meaning to it. By the end of class, he was playing a completely different piece of music. I believe he now knows how to approach a composition.

GK: I am devoting more and more attention to large phrases and their relationships. It all boils down to a basic principle: in speaking, sentences grow "tired" as they come to rest at the full stop. The same happens with musical phrases: they appear to exhaust themselves as they are nearing the phrase's end but before they do, they are immediately attached to the next one. You cannot end the phrase completely, for it would also end the whole piece. It is all a ceaseless concatenation of associations.

We have been talking of the beginning of the [Mozart] "Haffner" Symphony (*sings it*).[1] Those who are conscious of what is happening in the music partake of a unique human experience. Those who are not are just bureaucrats or post-office employees stamping letters. In the past, musicians—heirs to nineteenth century tradition—were aware of these moments in music as a matter of course: pianists like Edwin Fischer, Artur Schnabel, or Wilhelm Backhaus, violinists such as Bronisław Huberman, George Enescu, or Sándor Végh, cellists like Casals.

BAV: It seems to me that working with young musicians you are bound to have drawn rather negative conclusions regarding the standard of music education on an international scale.

GK: I am. But then I also come across encouraging examples such as the Norwegian pianist Leif Ove Andsnes. Artists like him do emerge; tradition does not vanish altogether.

---

1 Kurtág is referring here to our interview of 2007.

BAV: How much does your method of teaching owe to Leó Weiner, András Mihály, and Sándor Végh?

GK: They gave me a great deal, and so has László Dobszay, who is very important for me.[2]
To give you just one example: the second movement of Beethoven's Sonata in G Major, op. 30, for violin and piano. Weiner taught us to accent the *sforzato* by using the sustaining pedal, striking the key slightly stronger and giving just a bit more dynamics. If you are economical in your use of those elements, the effect will be staggering. Agogics: a conservative use of retardation. (Retardation also plays an important role with Dobszay.) Thereby, the tone receives an accent. I myself write lots of such syncopes— they render the music tauter.

BAV: In other words, the instruction you were given by Weiner and Dobszay has affected your composition as well.

GK: Absolutely! The Viola Concerto is a case in point. It started out as a particular exercise for performers and morphed gradually into a composition. I remember playing the first movement for Mihály (it was all in my head, I had not yet put it to paper) and he said: "But this is just one half of a theme!" That comment and many more helped me to improve on the first version and find the definitive shape of the movement. The pianist Mihály Bächer looked at the concerto from an interpreter's point of view.[3] For months on end, we would talk about development, transition, crescendo, and things like that. It took me a whole year to arrive at the final version. I allow performances of the first movement, but I am unhappy with the second one, so I have suppressed it.
At IRCAM, our son uploaded a Mozart piano sonata on a computer. The sounding result was unbearable as far as rhythm was concerned. He then added a thirty-second note rest to each bar and that, by itself, turned the music a little bit easier to take. In other words: an accurate rhythm will only sound like music if we add to it, however mechanically. His was in a way a study in the meaning of agogics.
Interestingly enough, agogics do not deprive the music of its basic pulsation. Even the strictest kind of music allows of all sorts of freedom, if the sense of basic pulsation is retained. If it is lost, so is the performer.

---

2   László Dobszay (1935–2011), highly respected musicologist, professor, and choral conductor in Hungary. In 1976 and 1977, Kurtág sang in Schola Hungarica, the chorus Dobszay founded together with Janka Szendrey.
3   Mihály Bächer (1924–93), Hungarian pianist.

Márta Kurtág (MK): You have been praising musicians of the past, but as far as Bach is concerned, we owe much of what we understand about him to the young generation.

GK: I have not been able to digest all that new information—perhaps I cannot digest it to this day. I am not sure whether the young generation of musicologists is right about Bach, but I am just as uncertain of their predecessors' approach. As a result, for decades I did not have the courage to teach Bach.

Let us jump back in time. I was sixteen when Magda Kardos entrusted me with the coaching of her pupils.[4] She kept a check on what I was doing, of course. It was then that I realized I had a pedagogical talent. In the beginning, I was something of a sophist: I could prove anything, whatever I thought of was true, even though I was often in the wrong.

My talent, then, consisted in convincing, torch in hand, anyone of what I believed in at any particular moment. I caused Márta a great deal of harm in the past through that.

MK: Old age has dampened the flame of that torch . . . As a young man, he came up against a hell of a resistance. Indeed, it is no different today but his pupils respect his age and do not dare to put up resistance so blatantly. I have frequently felt as though he was like the Christian martyrs of the past: some of his pupils would dearly like to cut his throat; they simply cannot accept what he is trying to teach them. And he, instead of giving up, keeps to his convictions and carries them through.

GK: One ensemble that rebeled in a spectacular manner was the Auryn Quartet. Brennecke had persuaded them to study with me but they told me point-blank: we do not like your teaching at all.[5]

MK: What they said was: "We like what you write but dislike the way you teach."

GK: In Webern's *Canon*, for instance, I suggested that the same motif be played by the different instruments in the same way. They asked: "Why?" I cannot work with people like that. "Why? Why not play it differently?" I was completely helpless. It is exactly the same category Schoenberg

---

4   Magda Kardos was Kurtág's piano teacher at Temesvár (Timişoara) beginning in 1940. Volumes 1–4 of *Játékok* are dedicated to her memory.

5   Wilfried Brennecke (b. 1926) was artistic director of the Witten Festival of New Chamber Music (1969–89). He was among the first musicians in Western Europe to recognize Kurtág's significance and commissioned a number of compositions from him, which he then premiered at his festival.

referred to in his introduction to Webern's *Bagatelles*, op. 9: "If faith can move mountains, the lack of faith makes them nonexistent." If they have no faith in what I tell them, so be it. There is nothing I can do. Incidentally, my son did not like my teaching either.

MK: He could not understand why Gyuri makes the musicians stop after two notes.

GK: I remember telling someone to stop just as he was about to start playing: he was supposed to be performing an *adagio dolcissimo* and set about it with tremendous élan. He could not have meant the same piece.

MK: In the early years at the Budapest academy, it took him three months, sometimes, to teach the exposition of a composition.

GK: That was partly due to anxiety. I was afraid of getting on with the piece. In those early years, I used not to prepare for classes as thoroughly as I do now. I would just improvise when commenting on whatever students brought to study.

BAV: You used to say you could only teach if you found something to hang on to, something to criticize. A perfect performance slips from your hands.

GK: Yes, the interpretation needs to have the kind of shortcomings that I can respond to.

   If it is spick and span, I cannot work on it. I cannot touch a competition-ready performance. It does not happen. It has no features I can hang on to. It has no weak points.

o

I typed this interview without knowing whether Kurtág would permit me to publish it. He finally telephoned me in February 2012 to say that while he still thought it was of minor interest, I might go ahead and use it. He suggested publication after his death but I pointed out that he might well survive me, so we left it at that.

The composer added a few details and made some corrections, thereby putting the stamp of authenticity on the text. I am aware that the ending appears incomplete. The reason is that the original interview was a meandering dialogue—or trialogue, rather—and the topics had to be brought into a logical sequence, with some details omitted altogether. At the end of the process, I was left with the dilemma of whether to include Kurtág's remark about needing to find "something to hang on to" in order to work on a piece, or to omit that part altogether. I have decided to keep it at the expense of a rounded form.

The interview has some of the hallmarks typical of György and Márta Kurtág: the composer's relentless self-criticism and his wife's critical remarks, with Kurtág immediately acting on them, in a rueful gesture of atonement. In fact, Kurtág admitted in the course of a telephone conversation that the only detail he really liked in the text was the exposure of his failure in his early years at the Budapest Academy of Music to properly prepare for his classes.

I am also intrigued by the revelation that for all Kurtág's prestige as a composer and teacher, his suggestions are sometimes questioned by his pupils causing classes to end in a deadlock.

Ill health and slow progress on his Beckett opera initially induced Kurtág to cancel his concerts and turn down invitations to teach. Indeed, I had the impression after his joint recital with Márta in November 2010 at the Opéra Garnier in Paris that it was their farewell to the concert podium. Not surprisingly, however, they decided to appear at a week-long festival given in Kurtág's honor by the Cité de la Musique in September 2012. The only other featured composer was Johann Sebastian Bach.

Gyuri and Márta are a unique couple. I think of them with great affection as they toil away, day in and day out, at endgame. Gyuri always uses the first person plural when he tells me on the telephone of the opera's progress. Márta says they are past worrying when it is going to be finished, even if it will be finished at all. What matters is that notes are put to paper, and that Gyuri keeps on discovering new harmonies and novel dramaturgical solutions.

Composing for the stage has been on Kurtág's mind for several decades. Plans were made and dropped; pieces were written for concert performance that revealed underlying dramatic qualities and were in some cases actually put on stage. The discovery of Samuel Beckett's world—his one-act plays directed by Peter Brook in Paris—gave Gyuri and Márta what they had been looking for. Well into his late eighties, György Kurtág is writing his first opera.

GYÖRGY LIGETI

1923–2006

L igeti has left behind a sizable legacy for the reader as well as for the listener. His collected writings were published in two volumes running to 876 pages, one year after his death.[1] They comprise his program notes on his compositions—a wonderful source of information for the musicologist, the concertgoer, and the CD collector. Also included are his admirable analyses of works by other composers, such as Boulez's Structures Ia, first published in 1958: an object lesson in erudition and clarity.[2]

The innumerable interviews he gave over the decades have to be traced down elsewhere. He was an ideal interviewee, including when he was answering his own questions.[3]

I did at least five interviews with Ligeti: one on his first visit to Budapest since his defection, in 1970, one for the Three Questions book in 1979, another one on his decoration with the newly created Bartók–Pásztory Prize in Budapest in 1984 (I did a short report for Hungarian Radio; I remember his first sentence: "I was a Bartók epigone"), and one each on his seventieth and seventy-fifth birthdays, in 1993 and 1998.[4]

That first conversation, in 1970, was followed by an exchange of letters initially to do with the text (he made fifty-five comments and

1 György Ligeti, Gesammelte Schriften, ed. Monika Lichtenfeld (Mainz: Schott Music, 2007).
2 György Ligeti, Pierre Boulez: Entscheidung und Automatik in der Structure Ia, Die Reihe (Vienna: Universal Edition, 1958).
3 György Ligeti, Ligeti in Conversation (London: Eulenburg Books, 1983). Ligeti's interview with himself first appeared in the German magazine Melos, in December 1971, under the title "Fragen und Antworten von mir selbst." I have used the English translation by Geoffrey Skelton, published in 1983 by Ernst Eulenburg Ltd. London, under the title "Ligeti in Conversation."
4 Bálint András Varga, Three Questions for Sixty-Five Composers (Rochester, NY: University of Rochester Press, 2011).

corrections) and in later years to report on his efforts to help me get out of Hungary. Ligeti's touching interest in my future sprang in part from his passionate rejection of communism. He was convinced that I would be better off in the West and did his best to find me a job. His initial efforts bore no fruit, but I know from Universal Edition (the Vienna-based music publisher that invited me to join its roster in 1992) that Ligeti had been consulted and that his recommendation had played a role in the decision in my favor.

Thanks to my new job with the Hungarian music publisher Editio Musica Budapest beginning in 1971, I was a relatively frequent visitor to Hamburg where Ligeti was spending most of his time and I would stop by at his Möwenstrasse apartment. When I moved to Vienna in 1992, we would meet once in a while at his house in the Himmelhofgasse.

Here is an entry from my diary, recorded on August 14, 1995:

Visiting Ligeti on 12th. (He had rung to tell me he was in Vienna and would gladly meet me.)

On arriving at his house at half past two, I heard him playing the piano—as I told him, it sounded rather like Brahms. He smiled and said: "It will be different when played in tempo." Although "officially" at work on Alice, he was still writing some Études while the impetus kept him going.[5] He was looking worn, his face unshaven, his back bent. An arthritic bone in his back was causing constant pain; it needed to be operated on. The doctor, however, wanted to wait until it was ready for operation—that is, Ligeti commented, until the pain had become unbearable. He was also feeling pain in his prostate but preferred not to talk about it.

In his study, we listened to all the Études available on CD. I sat in an armchair with Ligeti lying on the floor at my feet: that position appeared to be best for his shoulders. He announced the titles one by one and I commented on each piece when it was over. There was one I could not understand—as it turned out, he was unhappy with it, too (sadly, I cannot remember the title). His goal was, he said, to find something different from the obsolete avant-garde and the neo-trends which he also rejected—something between them.

The listening session over, we went downstairs where he and his wife Vera were drinking coffee and I was treated to a cup of tea. Ligeti also gulped down an inordinate amount of sweets.

We talked about composers and compositions: Ustvolskaya he thought highly of, Schnittke and Gubaidulina he had little time for. In his view,

---

5   Ligeti planned a music theater work based on *Alice in Wonderland*. He did not live to compose it.

Schnittke's "polystylistic" was nothing but eclecticism. Nevertheless, he declared himself ready to listen to the Concert for Chorus *and the* Viola Concerto, *which I hoped would change his mind. He had looked at the score of the opera* Gesualdo *but did not like it. He bore a grudge against Xenakis: in the early 1960s, in Darmstadt, he had analyzed one of Xenakis's works as a gesture—recently, however, Xenakis had given some interviews where he claimed that Ligeti was imitating him. I promised to give him a copy of my Xenakis book as proof that no such claim was made there.*

Ligeti expressed the view that Gruppen *and* Marteau *had a historical significance but* Hymnen *he could not stand. In fact, he had left the hall during a performance. He admired the integrity of Lutosławski's personality but was less happy with his music. He loves Janáček, especially* Makropoulos *and the* Glagolitic Mass. *He knows little of Szymanowski but knows and likes the violin concertos and the string quartets.*

Ligeti sensed a plot being hatched by left-wing Austrian concert organizers against his music and for Nono's. He was hurt that so little of his output was being programed in Austria.

He asked me if I ever missed Budapest. I had the impression that he was keeping his fingers crossed for the new regime and sometimes asked himself if leaving Hungary in 1956 had really been unavoidable.

My apartment having being conveniently close to Ligeti's house (a ten-minute drive from the Auhofstrasse to the Himmelhofgasse), the Hungarian music monthly Muzsika *asked me to record conversations with him to be published in time for his seventieth and seventy-fifth birthdays. This is their first publication in a language other than Hungarian.*

o

Seventieth Birthday Interview, 1993

Bálint András Varga (BAV): What would you be doing if we weren't recording this interview?

György Ligeti (GL): I would be asleep: I finished a work for the viola during the night.[6] Otherwise, I might be making a start on a new piano piece.

BAV: In other words, if composing is going well, you prefer to stick to it regardless of the hour of the day or night. Unlike, say, Thomas Mann who

---

6   The title of the solo viola piece was *Facsar*. After the interview, we drove to the nearest shopping mall, where Ligeti had several photocopies made of the manuscript. He inscribed one for me, at my request. *Facsar* was to become the third movement of his Viola Sonata.

kept to a strict daily schedule. Have you developed a working method over the past forty years?

GL: I work entirely as it comes, there is no regimented daily schedule.

BAV: Do you work when you feel "inspired" or when you have time?

GL: When I have time. My full-time job is to write notes and I do not just do it when it is going well: it must go well. But I do not want to appear conceited. There are always deadlines to meet, usually set not by myself but by performers. One makes light-minded promises to excellent musicians years ahead and one must not disappoint them. The violinist Saschko Gawriloff, for instance, waited for a concerto for ten years.[7] I said all right, I'd write one but he then organized a commission and that meant there was a date by which the piece had to be ready.

BAV: What I meant was whether over the years you have come to know the nature of the creative process as far as your biological makeup is concerned. Lutosławski told me, incidentally, that he had trained himself to think creatively even if he was not composing, to keep his brain in form.

GL: Questions like that do not interest me at all. You ask me if I have developed a biological rhythm or a working method. I do not know if I have. I simply do my job.

BAV: You never have any crises?

GL: I do not like the word "crisis." I have had problems, of course, mainly of a stylistic nature: it was a shock to realize that over the decades, the avant-garde and experimental approach had become obsolescent. I do believe that both atonality and the return to tonality—in other words, both the "avant-garde" and "postmodern" or "retro"—have become irrelevant.

BAV: Early on in your career, you also counted as avant-garde. At your level, however, a composer does not distance himself from his "old" pieces. They are just as valid now as at the time of their composition. However, today they may sound different, because so much has happened in music since the early 1960s. I read a review of *Atmosphères* the other day. The critic says it now sounds like romantic music. How do you view the time when you wrote *Apparitions* or *Atmosphères*? Was it your goal to create something radically new, like so many of your colleagues?

---

7   Saschko Gawriloff (b. 1929) played the world premiere of Ligeti's Violin Concerto in 1992.

GL: I can only speak of myself. I was never out to attract attention. There does exist an attitude like that, not so much in music as in art. I am thinking of Marcel Duchamp, or Dadaists like Tristan Tzara.[8] Their wish to create a scandal, *épater le bourgeois*, was very much part of their preoccupations. I have nothing to do with that.

Cage and Feldman as well as other American composers around them were marked by an experimental approach; their thinking was akin to Duchamp's. Cage, however, never endeavored to scandalize or to make a sensation. What he and his friends wanted to do was to define the role of music, of art in general, in the rather tangled and volatile American society. As a result, Cage has often been misunderstood and misinterpreted in Europe, I believe. As far as I can judge, culture in the United States exists in a different context (I lived there for some time). In any case, what I have done has nothing to do with sensationalism.

BAV: I have been reading several of your interviews and have discerned in them a desire to be different. They are characterized by an attitude of negation more than anything else. If you found that something was being negated already, then you proceeded to negate negation. Le Grand Macabre, for instance, is a negation of Kagel's antioperas.

GL: It is rather that I do not wish to belong anywhere: mine is a case of extreme individualism. After the war, at the Budapest Academy of Music, those of us who were studying together (Kurtág was one of them) knew Bartók and a little bit of Stravinsky. Our first impulse was to try and take our cue from Bartók, but proceed in a different direction. Then, slowly, I felt (this was still in Budapest, in the early 1950s) that I was actually turning against him. I have not repudiated Bartók to this day, I acknowledge the tremendous significance of his work, but felt at the time that I had to do something completely different. Bartók was the father and I revolted against him.

I settled in Cologne in 1956. The choice of the place was no accident, for although I had left Hungary to escape from communism, once I was free to go anywhere, I wanted to live in a city where new music was being written. I knew precious little of it, needless to say. So I went to Cologne, the place where Stockhausen was working, indirectly Boulez as well, to name only the two most important composers.

---

8   Marcel Duchamp (1887–1968), French artist, creator of "concept art," also played a role in
     founding the surrealist and Dadaist movements. Tristan Tzara (1896–1963), Romanian writer,
     cofounder of Dadaism.

BAV: Koenig was also important for you.[9]

GL: Whatever I learned, I learned mainly from Koenig but I do not think as highly of him as a composer. I experienced all over again what I had gone through in Budapest with regard to Bartók: I respected Boulez and Stockhausen, and continue to respect them today, I am interested in what they are up to, I have studied and analyzed their music, I made friends with them, but I did not take over their styles. What I did do, for instance in my first two orchestral compositions, *Apparitions* and *Atmosphères*, was a follow-up on what I had begun in Budapest. I had written a work under the title of *Víziók*; I still have its score. It was never published and it is better to leave unperformed, for it is a less successful predecessor of *Apparitions*.

Atmosphères may strike one as new, or different from what was being written in Cologne and Paris. In actual fact, however, you can find its model in two works: directly in the Prelude to *The Wooden Prince*, in the static sonority of the big acoustic overtone scale. The Prelude, which is in C major-Mixolydian-Lydian mode, refers back to the stationary E-flat major chord in the Prelude to *Rheingold*. In Budapest, I had not heard the third ancestor, Schoenberg's *Farben*, but I was of course familiar with the other two.[10]

I was captivated by this music: immobile, with no rhythm and no melody. I had to take one step further and renounce harmony as well. That is how I arrived at constructing clusters. I have moved away from that since, however. If you take a look at *Atmosphères* of 1961 and then listen to my piano études of the 1980s, it is as if you were dealing with two different composers altogether. And: if you go piece by piece following upon *Atmosphères: Volumina, Requiem, Lontano,* String Quartet no. 2 and so on, in other words, if you consider the individual pieces, you will realize that the change occurred by tiny steps.

In the 1980s, I was preoccupied with complex rhythms. My thinking switched angles, so to speak, partly under outside influences, such as African music, Nancarrow, and fractal geometry. I believe those three influences brought about a decisive change, not so much in my basic attitude—that remained the same—but in my language.

BAV: In talking about your tendency to negate accepted norms, I was also thinking of the statement you made in an interview with Josef Häusler in

9 Gottfried Michael Koenig (b. 1926), German composer. He worked in the electronic music studio in Cologne between 1954 and 1964.
10 Schoenberg's Five Pieces for Orchestra, op. 16, no. 3.

the late 1960s:[11] "When in 1962 I came to the frontier district represented by *Volumina*—the total destruction of the interval—I did not go any
further, but began to look for another frontier. I asked myself, how can I
work with intervals or with specific fixed pitches without returning to tonal
music?"

Well, that is what I had in mind in bringing up the subject of negation.
Having turned your back on a particular aspect of music, you looked for
another area you could negate. I have the impression as though you are irritated by particular aspects of music and in rejecting them, you arrive at
certain solutions which will then determine your music.

GL: My opera *Le Grand Macabre* is an outright negation of the aesthetic
represented by *Atmosphères* and *Volumina*. On the other hand, it does not
negate what I had done in *Aventures* but develops it further.

I want to make two remarks here. One concerns my work. Although
I am an artist, my working method is that of a scientist active in basic research rather than in applied science. Or of a mathematician working on
a new mathematical structure, or of a physicist looking for the tiniest par-
ticle of the atomic nucleus. I do not worry about the impact my music will
make or what it will turn out to be like. What interests me is to find out the
way things are. I am driven by curiosity to discover reality. Of course, there
is no reality in art the way there is in science, but the working method is
similar. Exactly as in basic research where the solution of a problem throws
up innumerable new ones, the completion of a composition raises a host of
new questions to be answered in the next piece.

That is why I have changed my language. The gesture has remained the
same but the idiom has changed. I started out from modal music on the basis
of Bartók and Stravinsky and arrived at a kind of chromaticism. That was still
in Hungary. My first string quartet is absolutely in the style of Bartók, it follows the modally centered chromaticism beautifully described by Lendvai.[12]
I proceeded to change that and followed in Webern's footsteps. When I arrived in Cologne, I came under the influence of Boulez and Stockhausen, but
instead of following them, elaborated chromatic and static spaces.

The reaction came in the mid-1960s: down with chromaticism, back
to or further on to the diatonic system. In *Lontano*, for instance, form remained static but the harmonic language was diatonic. I was not happy

---

11 György Ligeti, Péter Várnai, Josef Häusler, and Claude Samuel, *György Ligeti in Conversation*,
    trans. Geoffrey Skelton (London: Eulenburg Books, 1983), 95. The original interview with Josef
    Häusler was conducted in 1968/1969, translated into English by Sarah E. Soulsby.
12 Ernő Lendvai (1925–93), Hungarian musicologist. His research concerned, among other things,
    the implementation of the golden section and the Fibonacci series in Bartók's music.

with that. Why think in terms of chromaticism or diatonic, why keep to the tempered twelve-tone system of the piano? So I said: down with rhythm, there is no rhythm any more! Then again: why should there be no rhythm, but of a different kind? That is how, mainly in the early 1980s, I arrived at highly complex rhythms in my Horn Trio, for instance, and then in the piano études.[13]

My études may have indirectly to do with Chopin, Liszt, Rachmaninov, and Debussy, in essence; however, they reflect a different way of thinking and have little in common with romantic and impressionist piano music. That thinking absorbed influences from various kinds of sub-Saharan African polyphonic and polyrhythmic music. I do not quote African folklore; rather, I use polyrhythmic complexity as a compositional method. You see, I not only negate; I also conceive of new ideas once some problems have been solved.

My other remark may appear pessimistic. A composer born in the first third of the twentieth century and still alive in its last quarter, finds himself in a world less friendly than the one in which Haydn and Mozart lived. Haydn and Mozart inherited a valid syntax: the tonal, functional system. In Bach's time, periodicity had been far more complicated, but his sons and the Mannheim composers developed a very simple one: the eight-bar question and answer. Out of that, Haydn, Mozart, and of course Beethoven developed a fantastically great style of the highest order, but they did not have to devise a new language. Today, composers have to devise a new language all the time.

I have one more remark to make within that remark: in static cultures, such as traditional Chinese or Japanese court music, or that of the so-called primitive peoples in Africa and Oceania, the language of music, just as spoken language, develops at a slow pace. European music on the other hand—at least since the late Middle Ages—honors a cultural convention whereby each new generation has to produce something other than their predecessors. Machaut did something different from Perotinus; Ciconia did something different from Machaut; Dufay other than Ciconia. Debussy turned against Wagner and while Bartók did not turn against Debussy, he did something completely different, just like Stravinsky. And then came the generation of Boulez and Stockhausen, of Kurtág and myself. So that I actually expect of myself to be constantly doing something different.

I was once engaged in a dispute with Popper.[14] He was a highly significant science-theoretician and attacked me rather vehemently: "Ligeti, why

---

13 The Horn Trio was composed in 1982, the first piano études emerged in 1985.
14 Sir Karl Raimund Popper (1902–94), Austrian-born British philosopher.

don't you compose in the style of Haydn and Mozart? The tonal system has so much to offer yet in the way of beautiful music. Innovation is no criterion." I was too young to think of a fitting reply there and then, and I respected Popper far too much anyway. The right answer only occurred to me later: "And why did Haydn not compose in Palestrina's style?"

BAV: You said earlier on, "the gesture has remained the same." By "gesture" I believe you mean "personality" and, of course, much could be written about what constitutes that. It is striking that you not only refer time and again to different figures and periods of music history but also of the visual arts. For instance, I have been intrigued by the fact that a composition by Webern should have reminded you of Alexander Calder's mobiles. You have also referred to Klee and Botticelli and, during the course of our conversation, to Duchamp. It is also natural for you to include literature and science in your sphere of references.

GL: The same is true of politics, indirectly of course, for I do not write political music. However, my profound hatred of the extreme right and left indirectly determines what I do.

BAV: In other words, you have at your disposal the entirety of the human experience and heritage and you filter out from it whatever suits your personality and interest.

GL: It is nothing conscious. In writing a score, no conscious thinking is involved.

BAV: But it is all there in what you call gesture. Everything becomes part of it.

GL: It becomes part of a receptacle without my having a notion of its content. I draw from it without meaning to.

BAV: In another interview (I believe your interviews should also be numbered), you talked about a cauldron permanently on the boil. Various ingredients are added to the material in it which lend it different flavors: a graphic image of personality nurturing creation.

GL: The collecting of ingredients happens at random.

BAV: Why do you stress the unintentional aspect?

GL: Because it is wrong to assume that I consciously look for influences in science or the fine arts which I then apply in composition. It all happens randomly.

BAV: Like Debussy, you have turned to gamelan music; Messiaen studied Indian rhythms. It is as if some European composers have felt they have absorbed everything European music has to offer and look for inspiration elsewhere.

GL: I think the receptacle metaphor is less apt than the one with the cauldron. All sorts of things are boiling in there, a mixture of many ingredients. But it is certainly not true that with Europe "covered," I turn to Southeast Asia instead. Now with the release on disc of a wide range of ethnic traditions, we realize that our own continent has unsuspected treasures waiting to be discovered. There are so many kinds of fantastic folk music in Europe we were not aware of before, only because they were not available on record. The other day, I heard yodeling and alphorn playing from Switzerland—a wonderful and complex art. Or, Norway as well as the Shetland and Orkney islands possess an ancient, rich polyphonic music culture. There is also Corsican polyphony that surprised and delighted me recently. Did you know that folk polyphony on Corsica is very much alive today? It has been influenced slightly by nineteenth-century tonal music, but only on the surface. Or, there exists an Istrian and Dalmatian diaphony (I knew about it from Bartók's Dalmatian collection) with smaller and larger parallel seconds. This is an extraordinary two-part sound where the parts are linked rhythmically. Now that I have heard several recordings, I have realized that the Balkans are, independent of language (that is, whether they are singing in a Slav language, Albanian, or Romanian) full of "islands," each with a music culture of its own. Then there is the music of the Aromanians, a people coming from Macedonia whose language is similar to Romanian. They were resettled by the occupying Nazi troops in Dobrudja, that is, Romania. Those musics were related in various ways to Byzantine tradition. They are often marked by a long sustained drone (*ison* in Greek): it plays an important role in Romanian and Bulgarian church music. There is a village southwest of Sofia where women sing polyphonic music. We have known of wonderful Russian polyphony for a long time but now it is more readily available. Needless to say, I do not mean the pseudo-folklore falsified in the Soviet Union. I am interested more than anything in polyphony, like the fascinating one in Georgia which I found some ten years ago.

In other words, Europe is full of great folk musics we did not know about because they were submerged under nineteenth-century German romantic music. I agree with Bartók and Kodály who called for the elimination of the *Liedertafel* style and the exploration of genuine folk music.

Real folk polyphony is present in Corsica and Albania and Norway and many other places in Europe.

BAV: Does your enthusiasm for folk music derive from your need to find new sources of inspiration?

GL: My enthusiasm is not limited to music. Right now, I am bowled over by two of the world's most beautiful books. I am reading them side by side. One is Proust. I read *In Search of Lost Time* in Hungarian translation when I was young but never reached the end. I am now reading it in French, and a world is opening up before me: one that is lost forever but where human psychology was no different from ours. (Perhaps you will eventually find it in the material boiling in the cauldron.) The other book bears the title *What Is Mathematics* and was written by two American mathematicians, Courant and Robbins.[15] I hit upon it by chance and have since found out that, ever since its first publication in 1941, many people have become mathematicians because they read the book as young people.

It does not make allowances for the general public; you have to be well informed in order to appreciate it. I am no mathematician but know enough about it to understand, or rather, to more or less intuit what mathematics is all about as well as about the way mathematicians think. Quite apart from the book, I have over the past ten years devoted considerable attention to a new branch of mathematics, fractal geometry. My interest was awakened in 1983 when in a popular French color magazine I saw for the first time fractal computer images. Those chance meetings do not come about because I want to learn something new but because I find something by chance, without looking for it. It can be a recording of Central African polyphonic music, a book on mathematics or history. Each opens a new world and its discovery eventually appears on some level in my music.

BAV: It is interesting that you should be laying so much stress on spontaneity or chance. After all, your approach to music can be highly conscious—the way you analyze your own music or pieces by others. Recently, at the Vienna Konzerthaus, I heard you analyze the music of the Romanian composer Niculescu, and all the composer could do was nod in agreement: he had nothing to add.[16] It appears that a conscious approach exists side by side in you with a carefully guarded spontaneity.

---

15 Richard Courant and Herbert Robbins, *What Is Mathematics? An Elementary Approach to Ideas and Methods* (London: Oxford University Press, 1941).

16 Ştefan Niculescu (1927–2008), Romanian composer. Along with Harry Partsch and Claude Vivier, Niculescu was a composer whose music fascinated Ligeti, who did what he could to promote it.

GL: This kind of thinking is mainly subconscious. In composing, I imagine music in a wholly naive manner. With hindsight, I realize that here and there I employed such and such a construction. As far as analysis is concerned, the *Österreichische Musikzeitschrift* asked for an article to mark the bicentenary of Mozart's death. I replied that I was not going to write some superficial appreciation (anniversary celebrations are inane exercises in any case), but that I was going to take a close look at one of his compositions. And then, for the first time in my life, I examined thoroughly one of my favorite pages of Mozart, the slow introduction to the first movement of the C-Major String Quartet K. 465, dedicated to Haydn. Based primarily on what I had learned from Lajos Bárdos, I took a close look at this section—absolutely mad with its cross-relations and Neapolitan sixths, the swap of the A♭ and the A.[17] I wrote my analysis, but was absolutely certain that Mozart's thinking did not work that way. Rather, he was aware of the contemporary technique, a chromatic tradition inherited from Monteverdi through Buxtehude and Bach. Mozart did not mull over the way he would be making a big modulatory detour through the subdominant of the subdominant's subdominant or that he would use the dominant of the dominant as a means of maintaining tension; he simply wrote what he did. Mozart is of course a quite exceptional example. My own far more modest working method is similar.

Over the past three days, I composed a viola piece. Sándor Veress died in Switzerland in March last year and his former pupils, including Kurtág, Heinz Holliger, and myself have composed works in his memory.[18] Kurtág's has already been performed in Bern, as far as I know. Now I have composed this viola piece, which I have given a title in Hungarian: *Facsar*.[19] It is about remnants of completely tonal elements turned inside out but with constant cross relations and multiple stops that change all the time. If in a double-stop one string is open, then the violist cannot but change shift very fast on the other string. I have in the past composed a virtuosic viola piece (*Loop*), with exaggerated shifts. *Facsar* is my second work for viola solo and while composing it I had no idea what I was doing. During the night when I was

---

17 Lajos Bárdos (1899–1986), Hungarian composer (mainly of choruses) and professor of harmony, theory, and music history at the Academy of Music in Budapest. As a teacher, he was held in high esteem, among others, by Kurtág and Ligeti.

18 Sándor Veress (1907–92) Hungarian composer. Before settling in Switzerland in 1949, he taught composition at the Budapest Academy of Music. Veress turned eighty-five on February 1, 1992, and died on March 4 of that year. The works written to celebrate his birthday were then dedicated to his memory. Kurtág composed a piece for two basset horns and two pianos: *Életút/Lebenslauf/ Curriculum vitae*, op. 32, premiered on April 26, 1992, at the Witten Festival.

19 *Facsar*, to wring, to squeeze.

making a fair copy of the score, I realized what sort of structure the piece has, that this is actually a ten-bar sentence repeated again and again in variation. But while writing it, I was unaware of this.

BAV: Two things come to mind. One is your interview with yourself in which you say:

> However, the initial impulses that set the act of composition going tend to be naïve in character. I imagine the music in the form in which it will later be heard and hear the piece from beginning to end in my inner ear. To a certain extent what I hear in this way corresponds with what will be heard in performance after the completion of the score—but only to a certain extent.[20]

I believe this mirrors the image of a composer in the public mind: he hears the music in his head, born out of a divine spark, and puts it to paper.

There is also the example of Arnold Schoenberg who is said to have listened to one of his string quartets in rehearsal with total astonishment and in a state of great excitement because he could no longer recapitulate the compositional process: while writing the piece, ideas had come at such pace that he could not consciously deliberate on them. Does it work the same way with you? You hear the music, write it down, and then look at the result?

GL: With me, it is different. When I hear the piece for the first time, it corresponds more or less to what I imagined while writing it. What I am unaware of is its formal structure: that is, its constructive aspect. I do not have the kind of experience you mentioned in connection with Schoenberg. Because I work very slowly and also because I have an exact picture of what the piece is going to sound like. If it sounds different from what I had imagined, I make corrections.

BAV: To change the subject: what conclusions have you drawn from the way your works have fared? Some have obviously become part of the repertoire, others, like *Clocks and Clouds*, are played more rarely. Programming them could be costly, or it is difficult to find a suitable soloist. As a result, the piece figures less prominently in people's minds. *Le Grand Macabre* gathered dust for seven or eight years, until Alexander Pereira, general secretary of the Konzerthaus, put on a concert performance. Later, as director of the Zurich Opera House, he programmed it again, and that in turn led to further productions. Once again: in looking

---

20 Ligeti et al., *Ligeti in Conversation*, 124.

at the performance history of your works over the past thirty years, what conclusions do you draw for yourself?

GL: I think performances occur by chance, rather like self-organization in biology, sociology, culture, or national economy. In the early 1960s, the US meteorologist and mathematician Edward Lorenz used a beautiful metaphor: the flap of a butterfly's wing in Brazil has a bearing on whether there will be a storm in New York the day after.[21] In other words, a little plus or a little minus somewhere suffices to trigger . . .

BAV: . . . a chain reaction.

GL: To return to your question: The fate of musical works is not a compositional question but one of reception. What is it that determines whether an artist—a composer, a writer, or a painter—succeeds in making their names? Why are a composer's pieces played or not? I am not talking of myself but of music history.

If you take a look at the fourteenth and fifteenth centuries, you will see that only those composers' music has survived who lived long enough. If Machaut had died of the plague in 1348, we would know nothing of his compositions. However, he did live a long life, from 1300 until 1377, and took care that his manuscripts were copied in high quality, complete with illustrations. Dufay lived to be seventy-four (ca. 1400–1474) and left behind a wonderful oeuvre. (True, Mozart, Schubert, or Chopin died young, but the sociological situation in the nineteenth century was different from the fourteenth and fifteenth.) Medieval composers, who were not lucky enough to have been born in Paris or in Burgundy, survived as a matter of chance.

I first heard of Gesualdo as a student at the Budapest Academy. In those years, his pieces were not yet available on record. Now there are plenty and they reveal what a great composer he was. There may well be other equally significant musicians who have yet to be discovered.

I lived in Vienna between 1960 and 1970, but flew regularly to Sweden. I saw, I knew, I felt that the year 1960 had changed musical culture, thanks to the appearance of jets. Famous conductors, instrumentalists, singers, and of course concert organizers realized that they could fly nonstop to New York or Buenos Aires. As a result, musical life as a whole became shallower. The musical establishment has grown superficial. Concert organizers tell artists where they are to play and the artists obey. Air travel by jet planes has narrowed down the repertoire to a narrow range from

---

21 Edward Lorenz (1917–2008) coined the term "butterfly effect."

Bach to Richard Strauss. Debussy, Bartók, and Stravinsky might also be included. Of course, those born before and after them also get played but only in small cultural reservoirs. Earlier music appears to have been banished to zoos [i.e., specialized performing groups, not mainstream orchestras], and contemporary composers exist in small cages [i.e., new-music ensembles]. We get by all right, we have our cozy little corners but what happens beyond depends on the network of a few famous conductors, singers, instrumentalists, managers, and powerful record companies. This is a vicious circle: the insidious narrowing down of the repertoire means that the so-called educated public in Europe, the United States, or Japan, hear the same pieces all the time—actually, they no longer listen to the compositions themselves, but to Karajan's Wagner or Bernstein's Mahler.

To return once again to your question, as to what decides whether a particular work by a particular composer becomes part of the repertoire— the answer is that the repertoire is made up exclusively of what Haydn, Mozart, Beethoven, Schubert, and Brahms composed [so actually no new music becomes part of that repertoire].

BAV: Even in their case, only a fraction of their oeuvres is programmed as a matter of course.

GL: If you push a swing when and where the push is in resonance with its swaying, it will gather momentum. In other words, a piece of some fame will become even more famous. If it is unknown, it will stay that way, unless somebody happens to give it a "push" for some reason. My most played work is *Six Bagatelles* for wind quintet, which I wrote in Budapest in 1950–53, that is, at the age of twenty-seven to thirty, initially for the piano. I was a young teacher at the Music Academy and arranged them at the request of the Budapest Wind Quintet. They performed it in mid-October 1956, when none of us guessed what we were in for on the 23rd.[22]

BAV: But only the first five Bagatelles were actually played.

GL: That's right. There were too many minor seconds in the sixth one. The quintet is played more than any other of my compositions because it is rewarding for the wind players, and it is not atonal but modal. In every orchestra you will find five wind players who gladly join forces and play quintets.

Let me tell you an anecdote. Some eight years ago, I read a review published in New York. It said the *Six Bagatelles* had been performed in the city and Ligeti who had so far written indigestible music, had at last produced

---

22 The Hungarian uprising against Soviet occupation broke out on October 23, 1956.

some beautiful stuff. The critic had no idea when the quintet had been composed. If my *verbunkos* arrangement *Old Hungarian Ballroom Dances* (1949) were to be played again, it could easily become my most popular composition, even though it is but the arrangement of pieces by Lavotta, Bihari, and Csermák.[23] I am that skeptical about what may survive me.

BAV: I do not think you need to be that pessimistic. One usually cites Beethoven's late string quartets as instances of classical compositions which appeal to the select few, because of the concentration and some background in music required to properly appreciate them. The same is true of contemporary pieces which have not made it among the accepted repertoire.

GL: The situation is indeed not that discouraging, for we do have our reservations.[24] The fate of our compositions is influenced by practical sociological and economic factors. Let me give you an example. At the time I moved to Germany, orchestras used to rehearse contemporary pieces for a whole week, sometimes twice a day. Much the same applied also to Paris and Stockholm. That is why, in the 1950s and 1960s, I composed more works for orchestra, with or without chorus; the *Requiem* for instance. Nowadays, two rehearsals are the norm, three are an exception. As a result, I am reluctant to write for large orchestra because I know what to expect of lack of rehearsals. A very famous conductor, with a very famous orchestra, recording for a very famous company, released a disc with two of my pieces written in the 1960s, along with those by other composers. The disc has been promoted with a vengeance, it is on sale all over the place. I, however, cannot recognize my music. The recording had been made at a concert. I was there and protested vehemently on realizing in the interval that my works (*Atmosphères* and *Lontano*) were to be recorded. The company assured me that the tape would only serve documentary purposes—but then it was released nevertheless. One cannot protest against practices like that, only in an indirect manner like this. But what happened after that was even more interesting. The two publishers that owned the rights of the compositions, sent me the reviews. I was amazed that the interpretations which distorted my music out of all recognition were praised to the skies. The prestige of great names did the trick.

---

23 *Verbunkos* (from the German *Werbung*, that is, the recruitment of soldiers) is an eighteenth-century Hungarian dance and a music style. János Lavotta (1764–1820), Antal Csermák (1774–1822), and János Bihari (1764–1827) were popular composers in the verbunkos style.

24 Elsewhere in the interview, Ligeti finds other ironic descriptions for the areas of cultural life reserved for contemporary music, such as zoos and cages. Clearly, he wanted his compositions to be an integral part of the repertoire.

Here is another example. There is a great Russian pianist by the name of Yevgeny Korolyov, who lives in Hamburg. He is not well known. I have bought the *Kunst der Fuge* in his interpretation because I heard it praised. I have listened to it literally three or four hundred times. I am not exaggerating.[25] I listened to it in the evenings before going to bed. I cherish it as much as Michelangeli's Debussy or Serkin's Brahms. It is music-making of the highest order; no one has ever played Bach quite like him. I have purchased several copies of the CD (brought out by a small label) and given it away as a present. Naturally, I have checked why Korolyov's name is so little known and found out that while he had played all over the Soviet Union, he had not been allowed to travel for political reasons. He was born into the wrong family. Somehow he managed to reach Yugoslavia where he married a local pianist and never returned to the Soviet Union. Korolyov should be fifty-five or fifty years old; he has never won an international competition, was not the blue-eyed boy of Soviet or Western artists' agents, he has not made it. He may now have made the best Bach recording in the world, but people ignore him because he is over forty. You have to be young to make a career and you must attract the attention of a major international label. Sometimes they push absolute amateurs. Of course, quality wins out in the long run in the sense of Darwin's "survival of the fittest." But a great many excellent artists and a great many excellent compositions never become famous. Paintings may be different, because their true value can be recognized in a matter of seconds. However, books must be read, plays have to be seen, a piece of music must be performed to have a chance of making their way. I am sure that we do not know a great deal of good music simply because it has not become part of the circulation.

BAV: I know you detest dogma as much as you hate pompousness and self-importance. I am not going to ask what it feels like being seventy. But I do want to know if you feel you have accomplished what your talent has destined you for. You managed to leave Hungary when you were still reasonably young; you have followed your own path and the signs are that you have done so with some success. Is there any bitterness in you because you feel you could have done better?

---

25   Whereas Korolyov's recording of the *Kunst der Fuge* is listed on the Internet as one of the most remarkable discs available, there is no Wikipedia entry on him. TFODE, The Free Online Dictionary and Encyclopedia (www.tfode.com) does provide the information that Korolyov was born in 1949; his *Kunst der Fuge* record appeared in 1990 and again in 2008. He won the Leipzig Bach and the Van Cliburn Competitions as well as the Clara Haskil Grand Prix. The site quotes Ligeti as saying: "but if I am to be allowed only one musical work on my desert island, then I should choose Korolyov's Bach, because forsaken, starving and dying of thirst, I would listen to it right up to my last breath."

GL: To start with: there is no bitterness in me. Neither am I satisfied. I do my thing, as far as possible, without compromise. You say I got out of Hungary in time. I must add: alas, I had to leave. After all, my mother tongue has remained the same, even though back home some people may not regard me as a "true" Hungarian, because I am also a Jew. I hate this chauvinistic, nationalist, irrational absurdity, with Hitler, Stalin, Milošević, and in any other form.[26] We have had enough of that. I left home reluctantly, regretting that Hungary was not in a different part of the world with a normal, functioning democracy. Normal democracy will one day become reality; it is a matter of ten or fifteen years. It takes at least as long as that, wherever the chances of democracy were destroyed by communist dictatorship.

To return to your question: I am not satisfied with what I have accomplished. To explain: in the time of Bartók and Stravinsky, and before them of Debussy and Ravel, past the age of tonal music, Stravinsky did something odd—he performed the rite of resurrection, turning lifeless tonality into a "living" mask. Bartók did something completely different: modal, polymodal music. [I wonder] whether the process initiated by Schoenberg with twelve-tone music, for all the initial admiration it received, did not in the long run have the same fate as socialist utopia? I belong to a generation in Hungary, with Kurtág, Szőllősy, and some other composers, who set out with Bartók and Stravinsky and later absorbed the influence of the Viennese School, then the Cologne, Darmstadt, and the New York group: that is, Stockhausen, Boulez, Cage, and Feldman, to mention those who have been important for me.[27] I think it was all rather one-sided. To quote a relevant remark of Kurtág's son that has struck me as rather apt: "That music was ugly."

Ever since my youth, right up to the present day, I imagine the situation of composers in the following manner: we are sitting onboard a plane, flying quietly under the blue sky until we reach a cloudy patch and find ourselves in a milky, gray half-light. Then we leave the patch behind and can once again see the blue sky above the clouds.

After World War II, music as well as the visual arts reached a cloudy patch like that: with hindsight I realize that many of us wrote ugly music for a long time. That is why I am not satisfied. It is not "beautiful" music

---

26 Slobodan Milošević (1941–2006), president of Serbia and of Yugoslavia. Yugoslavia broke up into its constituent republics during his term of office, with the resultant Yugoslav wars. He was accused of war crimes and crimes against humanity by the International Criminal Tribunal for the Former Yugoslavia, but died before a sentence was passed.

27 András Szőllősy (1921–2007), Hungarian composer and professor at the Budapest Academy of Music. He prepared the catalogue of Bartók's oeuvre bearing his name.

that I am missing, because beauty would be a fake one. Rather, we ought to be doing something else: leave chewing-gum chromaticism behind.

You see, "avant-garde" music on the whole was a gesture of political resistance. The Nazis proscribed modern art and so did the communists, the latter for a time anyway, then left it in peace but did not support it. My youth was dominated by hatred for Hitler and Stalin and I became an avant-garde, or modern, or experimental composer, for it meant turning against both Nazi and communist cultural policies.

Incidentally, if I now think of the years 1908–10 and then World War I, I see the whole modern artistic trend in a strongly political light, as a manifestation of would-be left-wing, would-be "revolutionary" tenets. What it all led to was demonstrated by Lenin and Stalin's liquidation of most constructivist, formalist, and other "-ist" artists in the Soviet Union. Hitler's Germany committed much the same crimes. Fascist Italy was the only one—despite the sins of the system—which not only tolerated modern art but to a certain extent supported it as well.

My resistance was directed against Communism. Now that there is no Communism any more, I am against nationalism. Representatives of modern music and modern art, the futurist, constructivist, and surrealist movements were associated with some kind of social utopia. In France, for instance, most avant-garde artists were members of the Communist Party.

The socialist utopia, however, has collapsed. Not in 1989—it happened a long time ago: in Hungary in 1956, for me in 1945. It depended on when you woke up to reality. Up to 1945, I was also a half-hearted believer, a naive socialist. It was, briefly, a utopia.

BAV: Are you sure you became disillusioned as early as 1945?

GL: You are right. It happened in the winter of 1948–49. I even composed my VIT-Cantata; true, I did not know at the time that the VIT was a creation of the Party.[28] I was taken in. I did, however, resist the temptation of joining the Communist Party, even though my professors Sándor Veress and Endre Szervánszky told me in 1945 that every decent person ought to do so. It was somehow suspect and luckily I said no, although it would have opened doors for me. With the advent of dictatorship—that is, with the arrest of Mindszenty—the scales fell from my eyes, once and for all.[29]

---

28 VIT is the acronym for Világifjúsági Találkozó (World Youth Meeting). Organized by the Democratic World Youth Association beginning in 1947, VIT was a means of communist propaganda during the years of the Cold War. The latest meeting took place in Johannesburg in 2010.

29 Cardinal József Mindszenty (1892–1975) was Primate Archbishop of Hungary. A vocal opponent of communism, he was arrested, tortured, and sentenced in a show trial to life imprisonment in 1949. Mindszenty was liberated during the 1956 revolution and after its suppression by the Soviet

BAV: Your comment on new music makes me speechless. Do you really mean that its development is rooted in political rather than inherently musical reasons? Does this imply that it was Frank Martin or Britten or Shostakovich who wrote music in the genuine sense of the word, whereas Ligeti, Boulez, and Xenakis did not? That they used their music as a means of political protest?

GL: No, I did not say that. It is all genuine music, but "ugly genuine music." I would never claim that so-called modern music or abstract pictures are not valid but I do hold that modernism and the avant-garde have a strong socialist-utopian connotation (the word "avant-garde" is a military term). At the beginning of the twentieth century, modern arts were linked to socialist utopia and all the artists and writers who were involved in those movements were staunch left-wing utopian socialists. The Italians eventually converted to fascism but Mussolini himself started out as a socialist; the ideals of fascism and communism are, as we know, closely related. Thanks to real socialism, this utopia has since collapsed (I used to call it "surreal socialism" rather than "real socialism"). It collapsed actually far earlier than 1989.

I have a picture to go with that. There stands in Africa a giant baobab tree with aerial clinging roots. It is a hundred meters high and a hundred meters broad, but inside it has been eaten away by termites. The utopia of communism, this phantasm, had already been hollowed out by termites by the time Lenin appeared on the scene, but many people refused to admit it. Those inside the tree were shot dead, those outside (in Paris or in the Central Committee of the Italian Communist Party) paid lip service to communist ideals and were under the delusion that the tree was in the best of health. Even though it had long been dead.

BAV: You are not satisfied because you feel that the political situation forced you to compose ugly music? If only you had lived in an ideal democracy with nothing to protest against, you would have composed so-called beautiful music . . .

GL: I disagree with this interpretation. The past has no alternative. I do not place "beautiful" music next to "ugly" music. If I were to say that avant-garde music is ugly and there is also something like beautiful music, then I would need to be postmodern or retro or what have you. This is not true. Postmodern and retro are also lies. I do not believe the lovely

---

army, was granted asylum by the US Embassy in Budapest where he spent fifteen years. He was allowed to leave in 1971 and died in Vienna in 1975.

tonal and modal compositions of John Adams or dear, devout Arvo Pärt, because they have nothing to do with today's world, the way we feel about our world. Look at nationalism, look at new migration, the absolutely mad chaos all around us; look at our world inundated by Japanese microelectronic gadgets: this is no longer the nineteenth century!

We cannot go back to functional and modal music in the form Mahler used it, however fractured it was. We cannot go back to Debussy, Bartók, and Stravinsky, we cannot return to the avant-garde of the 1950s. I can only talk about what I am doing. Scylla and Charybdis are separated not by straits but by an infinite number of passages.

I am trying to do something in my own way which is neither avant-garde nor "experimental" and yet new. I do not look back. Some German music publicists have accused me of having betrayed the avant-garde. They were right: I will have no truck with that kind of art, but I do not turn against it by going back to an old, bearded, Brahmsian manner of music-making.

What I am now looking for is a new kind of rhythm. It learns from the African rhythmic system but makes no use of it; instead, it takes the system as a starting point and thinks in terms of geometry, spaces, and forms. As I said early on, the viola piece I finished during the night is called *Facsar*—i.e. wringing something out, creasing a smooth surface, twisting it: this is a topological idea.

Also, I have been trying for quite some time now to free myself from the twelve-tone tempered system. I want to write microtonal music, I am feeling the need to have unlimited sway over intonation. Two instruments, such as a violin and a viola, properly retuned, produce the fifth overtone (two octaves plus a perfect major third) and the seventh overtone (two octaves plus a minor—that is, perfect seventh). In other words, on a small orchestra, I can mix a harmonic spectrum with perfect overtones. I shall have to do without large orchestras because they could never do justice to this different intonation. There remain good string quartets and specialized ensembles, such as the Ensemble Modern in Frankfurt, ASKO in Amsterdam, or the Ensemble Intercontemporain in Paris. With their help, I shall be able to realize the iridescent harmonic world which I first tried to create in my Violin Concerto. In that work, I succeeded to a certain extent in freeing myself from the tempered system. It is far from perfect. In my next compositions, I shall attempt to progress in that direction.

Vienna, 1992

❍

For some reason, Ligeti preferred not to name in the interview the outstand-
ing conductor and the no less prominent orchestra who had recorded and
released Atmosphères *and* Lontano *despite his protests. He was so incensed*
by what he regarded as an act of vandalism against his music that he men-
tioned it to me again and again over the years and actually asked me to
actively spread word that Claudio Abbado and the Vienna Philharmonic
misrepresented his compositions.[30] *He was particularly worried because he*
felt that the fact that they were released during his lifetime could, in the eyes
of some people, lend authenticity to those interpretations, not to speak of the
tremendous prestige of conductor and orchestra. In revealing their identity, I
am acting in Ligeti's spirit.

Ligeti was rightly concerned that his music should be available for fu-
ture generations in performances that accurately reflected his intentions. The
offer around 1994 by the art patron Vincent Meyer to finance a recording
project covering his entire oeuvre, including works yet to be written, was an
unhoped-for windfall. The label was to be Sony, the conductor Esa-Pekka
Salonen, the orchestra the Los Angeles Philharmonic—a wonderful chance
that ended in bitter disappointment.

I remember a call from Hamburg: Ligeti told me the story in a deluge
of words lasting for over two hours. Vincent Meyer was generous, he said,
but the money made available did not suffice to cover the costs of adequate
rehearsal time. He was bitter and disappointed that an excellent musician
like Salonen was ready to compromise and allowed the release of record-
ings that were underrehearsed, and therefore misrepresented Ligeti's music.
The composer also railed against Peter Gelb, head of Sony Classical Records'
American division who refused to see Ligeti's point and insisted on putting
the CDs on the market. As a result, the Sony project was canceled. Warner
was found eventually to replace it and Jonathan Nott was engaged, who con-
ducted the orchestral works to the composer's satisfaction.

The story is summed up in Vincent Meyer's Foreword to a book on Ligeti
published in 2011.[31] *The composer's predicament and his vociferous protests*
are described in the following brief paragraph: "Over a period of ten years we
succeeded in recording his complete works for Sony and Warner. The proj-
ect was ambitious, conflictual and sustained throughout by Ligeti's persistent
search for perfection."

---

30 The CD was released in 1990 by Deutsche Gramophone. It also included works by Nono, Boulez, and Rihm.
31 Louise Duchesneau and Wolfgang Marx, eds., *György Ligeti: Of Foreign Lands and Strange Sounds* (London: Boydell Press, 2011), viii–ix.

A persistent search for perfection, I might add, also characterized his work as a composer. Only he knew how many times he had attempted to find a fitting beginning for his piano concerto, how many abortive starts found their way to the wastepaper basket. I do not know if he was really ever truly happy with works he allowed to be printed and performed. Once in a while, I would tell him how much a particular piece meant to me. He would be silent for a few seconds on the telephone and say, almost with animosity: "I do not like it if my works are praised." His reaction was so sensitive that I never asked the reason. On one occasion, he was prepared to admit: "I am a famous old composer." We left it at that.

o

Seventy-Fifth Birthday Interview, 1998

GL: I began to compose at the age of fourteen or fifteen, in a wholly naive fashion. I had not yet heard Bartók; interestingly enough, the same composition left an indelible mark on me as had also impressed Bartók in his youth: Richard Strauss's *Zarathustra*. I chanced upon a broadcast once and it stunned me, for I had never come across anything like it. We only knew the usual repertoire: a great deal of Liszt was on the air, as well as Romanian and French composers (but very little Debussy). Later on, I did hear more Debussy but by the time I had turned eighteen or so, Bartók's music had assumed supreme significance.

If you take a look at my early choruses and folk-music arrangements, you will discern the influence of Kodály. I was studying at the time with Ferenc Farkas at the conservatory of Cluj. Later on, in Budapest, I became a pupil of Veress, Járdányi, and once again Farkas, and as a result, came in touch with the circle known as the Hungarian school of composition.[32]

Bartók remained my primary influence until 1950, I think. We hardly knew Stravinsky, with only *Petrushka* on the repertoire of the State Opera House in Budapest. I once heard some fragments of *Sacre* on the radio, it was never played live. As a result, I lacked a horizon. It is well-known that we lived through very hard times politically between 1949 and 1953.

---

32 Ferenc Farkas (1905–2000). A pupil of Respighi, Farkas was a composer and a successful teacher of composition at the Budapest Academy of Music, with György Kurtág and György Ligeti among his pupils. Pál Járdányi (1920–66), Hungarian composer, ethnomusicologist, and professor at the Budapest Academy of Music.

One evening in 1950, I was sitting in a café with Endre Szervánszky.[33] I was infinitely fond of him, just like everyone else who knew him and we talked at some length, moaning of course over the hard times. After we parted, I walked all night. It was a cold winter, I was shivering and hungry. It was then that the idea of stationary music occurred to me, one that went beyond Bartók. Actually, the music I imagined, with its stationary acoustic scale, was not without precedent. You can find it in the prelude to Bartók's *The Wooden Prince*; in fact, it goes back even further in time, to the prelude to *The Rhinegold*. The latter may have influenced me subconsciously. I could not say, though, that I took my cue from Wagner for I never liked his music—rather, I hate and admire it at the same time.

BAV: Did Debussy and Ravel influence you at all?

GL: If you want to know about the music that was important to me as a child: I began to play the piano at fourteen. We had no instrument at home, I had to find one elsewhere so that I could practice; that's why, sadly, I am not a decent player. We did own a gramophone, however, and I listened to it all the time from the age of four or five. I was riveted by the *Feuerzauber*—I believe that is the piece we have to start out from.

You asked me about Debussy and Ravel. I would differentiate between the two. Debussy's importance for me has never changed, with the one reservation that he says everything twice over. He was a far greater composer than Ravel. I have also learned from Ravel, of course, and am impressed by the way he serves up the music: in *Bolero*, he is an incomparable culinary genius. The way he orchestrated that one-part music, the way he built it up, the accents he gave to its Spanish (pseudo-Spanish) melody, the subtle shifts of syncopation and triplets—those are marks of a very great master. However, I do not regard him as a composer of the first order. Debussy is one and so is, in his own peculiar way, Stravinsky.

BAV: Are the shifts and accents in your piano *Études* traceable back to *Bolero*?

GL: They have nothing to do with Ravel but derive from my great love for and interest in music from Machaut to Ciconia, including Dufay and later also Ockeghem. I did not hear Ockeghem in Budapest but knew him from Wüllner's Chorschule.[34] I played from his collection three- and four-part choruses on the piano in C—among them music by Ockeghem (if I re-

---

33 Endre Szervánszky (1911–77), Hungarian composer, professor of composition, and music critic.
34 Franz Wüllner (1832–1902), German composer, conductor, and professor. His *Chorübungen der Münchener Musikschule* was published in 1902.

member correctly, a movement each from a motet and a mass). I could play those quite well. I was a poor reader of orchestral scores but was good at choral scores because of my great fondness for polyphony. Later, when I was teaching harmony and subsequently counterpoint to choral conductors (I was of course not a professor but what was called "adjunktus," something like a senior lecturer), I did so in Palestrina style. At one time, my students included string players. I failed some of them at their exams which shows that I did take harmony very seriously. The Palestrina style was taken from books by Kodály and Jeppesen on the syllabus, whereas I knew little of earlier music. In playing, just for my own pleasure, the Ockeghem movements I mentioned earlier on, a whole new world opened up for me: I realized that there existed a different polyphony from Palestrina's.

My *Études* reflect not so much Ockeghem as the influence of an earlier era, the *Ars subtilior*. (The term is a recent coinage, it comes from the German musicologist Ursula Günther.)[35] I mean the music that has come down to us in the Chantilly Codex, works by forgotten composers, such as Soleg or Senleches. And, of course, Ciconia. I was most impressed by the rhythmic complexity of *Ars nova*, the possibilities inherent in its construction and notation, whereby any unit, whether *longa*, *brevis*, or *semibrevis*, was divisible by two or three. The triple division of note values, which was earlier regarded as perfect (for it corresponded to the Holy Trinity), was supplemented by the "imperfect" dual division. The possibility for a unit to be simultaneously divisible by three and two, with different sections that can be expanded so that they may also be divided by seven (for instance, twenty-one is divided by three times seven)—those crazy things fascinated me. I checked all that in great detail.

In other words, one influence was mensural notation, African music was another. During the course of the 1980s, I devoted more and more time to the music of Sub-Saharan Africa without ever visiting the region myself. I did hear a recording that induced me to look for other records and books; I also met researchers. All those chance events are for me of considerable significance.

BAV: I wonder what conclusion you would draw from the music of the past half a century. Would you agree with my theory whereby so much that started out—with great élan—as a revolution, eventually lost its impetus and ended up as evolution? Did the revolutionary zeal of some composers,

---

35 Ursula Günther (1927–2006) introduced the term *Ars subtilior* in the 1960s to replace the "mannerist style" that had until then been used in reference to late fourteenth-century music. In doing so, she wished to eschew the negative connotation of that term.

did Darmstadt dogmatism, which over the years lost much of its religious fervor, make sense in the long run?

GL: I believe that those caught up in revolutionary fervor (I am thinking of history rather than art) never ask themselves whether it makes sense. Did that question come up at the siege of the Bastille? Or at the time of Kerensky's revolution? (His was a genuine revolution, unlike [that of] Lenin, who arrested the social democratic government and expropriated the revolution in a coup d'état.) Nobody asked: Shall we do it? They just did it.

The arts are characterized by abrupt change. Remember what happened between Manet and Monet: there is a huge difference between the two. Monet's concept of the art of painting was wholly different. The next leap was Cézanne's followed by van Gogh's. What happened in van Gogh's case? In the 1850s, American men-of-war forcibly opened the gates of Japan. As from 1860, works of art were allowed to leave that once isolated country and reached the outside world. Hokusai's and Hiroshige's woodcuts and other chefs d'oeuvre from Japan completely transformed European art. That was the origin of the style known to the Austrians as *Jugendstil* and to the French as art nouveau. The change was fundamental. Something similar took place in Western Europe after World War II. In Budapest we learned of it from hearsay, far too late. Whether it all made sense is a rhetorical question.

BAV: I should have thought that Monet developed in the opposite direction: he became more and more revolutionary. His last paintings have nothing to do with landscape, they are wholly abstract. His pictures are made up of patches of color, similarly to Franz Marc's who eventually abandoned his horses, cats, and cows for the sake of abstraction. Their evolution ended up as a revolution. Monet in any case was a pioneer.

GL: Let me reply with a cynical remark: Monet did not turn into a revolutionary. He had a cataract and suffered agonies over his failing eyesight. Cézanne had no idea of perspective and turned that shortcoming into an admirable virtue. Really wonderful. Since you have mentioned my *Études*, allow me to be immodest: they are good piano pieces because I am a poor pianist. I had no other choice but to write virtuosic pieces that are beyond me technically. Others play them, impeccably. Very often, one creates something out of lacking a faculty. Often, but not always.

BAV: Let me return to the point I was trying to make: even though many of the pioneering composers lost some of their revolutionary fervor as the years went by, they have nevertheless produced remarkable music. Not all of them, of course.

GL: Some of them. Boulez, I believe, has remained a quite excellent composer. He is the only one of my generation I can vouch for without any hesitation. I can of course equally vouch for some other composers, but they are not part of this group. Such as Nancarrow or Claude Vivier, who died many years ago.[36] He was far younger than me. A composer I do not know personally but think very highly of is Galina Ustvolskaya, who lived through the years in St. Petersburg, Petrograd, Leningrad, and again St. Petersburg.[37] She is in her way a most interesting composer. Her music has something in common with [that of] Shostakovich, her teacher. What Ustvolskaya did in music was akin to Russian art of the 1920s: Malevich, Tatlin, and Rodchenko. It boils down to an extreme approach to constructivism that one can justifiably regard as progressive. It is not consciously constructive but appears to be so.

BAV: Has courage played any role in your composition? To single out just one example, was writing the Horn Trio an act of courage?

GL: I should not say I am cowardly in any way. Whether I am courageous, I do not know. These categories are out of place. Something else happened. As early as the 1960s, I began to realize that total chromaticism as apparent in *Apparitions* in the late 50s or *Atmosphères* in 1961, or between 1963 and 1965 in the *Requiem* or *Volumina* could not be carried on; I ran the risk of falling back upon clichés.

If one does the same thing too long, it may cease to be interesting. Yves Klein comes to mind.[38] He was *en vogue* in the late 50s; all his pictures had the same blue tint. To his misfortune—or fortune—he died suddenly of a heart attack.

I embarked on something new in the "Lacrimosa" movement of the *Requiem*. It is no longer chromatic music. It marks the beginning of revision—no revolution, no compromise, nothing like that.[39] I am aware of what my contemporaries of the older and younger generation are up to (with the passage of time, there is a growing number of composers who are

---

36 Conlon Nancarrow (1912–97), Mexican composer born in the United States. Claude Vivier (1948–83), Canadian composer.
37 Galina Ustvolskaya (1919–2006), Russian composer.
38 Yves Klein (1928–62), French painter.
39 Ligeti says "polgárosodás" in Hungarian, which means something like "becoming middle-class" or "bourgeois."

younger than I am). It does interest me and makes me consider, in my own one-sided way, what I ought to be doing.

My negative assessment of the entire postmodern trend is all too well known, but then I have also been described by some as postmodern. In a way they are right. Rudolf Frisius, for instance, has described the Horn Trio as wholly reactionary.[40] He says it sounds like Brahms. The truth of the matter is that the work is dedicated to Brahms, as stipulated by the commissioners, and it was premiered together with Brahms's Trio, but the piece has nothing to do with his; what it does have is a generous helping of Beethoven's influence.

Today I view the Horn Trio and the opera *Le Grand Macabre* as a big detour in my career. (The two harpsichord pieces I composed at the time do not count, they were marginal aphorisms and were only written as part of a debate with my pupils who were composing postmodern music as proof that I could also write that way).

Le Grand Macabre (1974–77) and the Horn Trio (early 1980s) led to an impasse. I then began something different with the Hölderlin choruses and choral pieces based on Sándor Weöres's *Magyar etüdök*—in a way, they mark a return to the constructivism of serial music.[41] This is especially true of the first etude, *Csipp-csepp*, which is a rigorously built constructivist piece. With that, I bade farewell to my postmodern phase. I then addressed myself to the piano *Études*. You can call them reactionary or progressive, depending on the angle [from which] you look at them.

BAV: You are no doubt aware of the curiosity with which your new compositions are scrutinized by your colleagues. They listen to your music exactly as you listen to theirs. Hence my question about courage: coming up with a daring, new idea is bound to send shock waves through the new music world. The other day, I read an interview with a young conductor. Hearing your Horn Trio had perplexed him: he felt as if he had gone to a favorite restaurant that had since his last visit, unbeknownst to him, been taken over by a new chef. Each new work of yours is tantamount to a declaration or proclamation; this cannot leave you indifferent.

GL: It is neither here nor there. I have no idea what reaction a new piece is going to evoke and am stunned by the pocket-Ligeti music I come across.

Talking of epigones: The Gaudeamus Foundation in Holland organizes annual composers' competitions. In the early 1960s, two works

---

40 Rudolf Frisius (b. 1941), German musicologist.
41 Sándor Weöres (1913–89), Hungarian poet. *Magyar etüdök* (Hungarian études) is a cycle of poems, some of which were set to music by Ligeti in 1983.

counted as pivotal: Boulez's *Le marteau sans maître* and Stockhausen's *Gruppen*. With Ernst Krenek and Stockhausen I was on the jury in 1961. We were greatly amused by the instruction written by an anonymous composer in his guitar piece: "with soft sticks." What on earth could he have meant? Later on, I chanced upon a manuscript copy of *Marteau*. It was difficult to decipher, for Boulez writes minuscule notes. In that edition, the guitar part was placed below the percussion instruments and the instruction "with soft sticks" had inadvertently found its way, probably from the xylorimba part, to that of the guitar. (Universal Edition later published a properly printed score.) Anyway, that was the explanation for the young composer's faux pas.

Beware of imitation—this is my message to those who take exception to my Horn Trio. Composition is not a question of courage or cowardice: you do your thing and spare no thought about the impression it may make. He who cares about it, is lost. He should go to Hollywood and write film music.

BAV: How do you find your way out of an impasse?

GL: I recently completed my seventheenth *Étude* of volume 3. I had planned it to be much longer: it is *presto* music, a canon in *stretto*, and I had imagined it to continue rolling on for some time. In the event, it stopped after six pages in fair copy. When I am composing, I hear the piece, it comes to life and I have no longer any influence on the large form. Initially, the form of the *Étude* had required a longer duration but it did not work. At a given moment I felt the piece was telling me that it was ready. I stopped and it turned out that that was all it had material for. That kind of composing is of course only valid within certain conventions. With Beethoven, the sonata form had a traditional structure, while Japanese court music, the *gagaku*, is based on an altogether different sense of time. The structure of African music is cyclical, repeating the same thing over and over again, with a great deal of variation. In my own rolling *Étude*, the same happens as in the last, *presto unisono* movement of Chopin's Sonata in B-flat Minor: it is very short and while it is great music, it strips the sonata of its balance, because it comes to a premature end. The movement consists of two sections: A and A variant, and it is one of the first pieces of atonal music in music history (although atonality only became relevant later, with historical hindsight). To get back to the seventeenth *Étude*: I have now realized that whereas the first four pages were properly composed, I wrote pages five and six the way a cogwheel runs itself: the piece stopped once it had run down.

BAV: What is the explanation for the emergence, in recent pieces, of Hungarian folk music? Your Violin Concerto could only have been written by a Hungarian composer.

GL: I wonder if it was any different in my "international" pieces, such as *Atmosphères* or *Apparitions*. I do not think so. Both show a strong link to Bartók.

I only composed twelve-tone music in the Schoenbergian sense in Budapest in 1956, because it was fashionable at the time. Such was the piano piece *Chromatic Phantasy*. I have not included it in my official list of compositions because it is not a good piece, even though a Swedish pianist has recorded it and plays it quite well. While in Hungary, I read René Leibowitz's book on dodecaphony. It had been smuggled into Hungary from Paris and I knew it was being widely read in the world. When I settled in Cologne, I realized that dodecaphony in the Schoenbergian—even in the Webernian—sense was obsolete.

To reply to your question: the Violin Concerto is openly linked to Hungarian folk music. I used at one time to work with folk music but I do not compose folklore pieces; instead, I use elements of it in an indirect manner. In the Violin Concerto, there suddenly crops up "The Mill That Grinds Sorrow." That well-known Transdanubian pentatonic melody emerged unexpectedly from a reservoir. I never looked for it, it was simply there in my consciousness.

Earlier, I had devoted considerable attention to Charles Ives whose collage technique made a strong impact on me—the total disorder in which he superposed "pictures" on top of one another. The fifth movement of the Violin Concerto is an odd, disjointed potpourri like that. I did not set out to make it that way, that's how it turned out. Perhaps I can nevertheless claim the concerto to be consistent, even though its second movement is "postmodern." In any case, I do not think it is more Hungarian than the pieces I composed in the 1960s. Because the last movement of Bartók's *Music* with its gradually emerging chromatic density lives on in me deep down and appears, indirectly, in *Atmosphères*.

BAV: I have been reading Berg's analysis of *Wozzeck* and have been struck by the calm, matter-of-fact manner in which he says of his own opera that it is a success, that it is a good piece. Are you capable of severing the umbilical cord of your compositions so that they can embark on a life of their own? Can you look at them objectively and dispassionately and say: yes, they are good pieces?

GL: It depends on the criteria I apply, also on the historical context. Let me give you an example from the distant past. I have a work called *Concert Românesc* (1951). It was never played in Hungary (although László Somogyi once sight-read it at a rehearsal) because Ferenc Szabó said it featured an adolescent, eccentric dissonance.[42] True, at one point there is an F♯ in a B-flat-major environment. By the way, the piece represented a compromise—I need not go into the political situation in 1950—because I tried to write a work that stood a chance of performance. Well, that is a composition that I can look at objectively today. I must admit that the first three movements are rather ordinary, but the last one is amazingly well or-chestrated. By the criteria of Darmstadt, of course, it is wholly without any interest, but if I examine it against the background of Rimsky-Korsakov, it is certainly a well-orchestrated piece of music.

On the advice of Ferenc Farkas, I studied Haydn symphonies in some depth and learned a great deal from them. Also, at the age of seventeen or eighteen, I played timpani in a semi-amateur orchestra at Cluj and learned a lot from that experience as well. We played symphonies by Haydn, Mozart, and Beethoven (the simpler ones). It helped me learn my trade as an orchestrator. That is why I can claim with some justification that the piece is well instrumented. It will be apparent once it is performed.

BAV: Whenever I try to pay you a compliment, I come up against polite refusal. It is a fact, however, that you are part of music history. The titles of your compositions are symbols. If one says *Lontano*, one immediately identifies it as a Ligeti piece, with an aura all its own. The same is true of *Melodien* and everything else you have composed. You have every reason to look back on the past half-century with some satisfaction. It is an idée fixe of mine that the passage of time is unstoppable; the question is what you make of the years given to you. You have really, really made the best of it. However self-critical you may be, I hope you do agree.

GL: Bálint, I am deeply unhappy with myself and this is no false modesty. It is a fact. I am ceaselessly looking for my idiom without ever finding it; I am always doing something new. The Horn Trio led nowhere; I imme-diately changed direction and wrote the first six piano *Études*, followed by the Piano Concerto, the Violin Concerto and new *Études*. Technically, I

---

42 László Somogyi (1907–88) was, until his defection in 1956, principal conductor of Hungarian Radio's Symphony Orchestra, which he had founded after World War II and professor of conduct-ing at the Academy of Music. The composer Ferenc Szabó (1902–69) was a dogmatic communist whose authority in Hungary was similar to that of Tikhon Khrennikov (1913–2007) in the Soviet Union.

believe, the *Nonsense Madrigals* are a success. Actually, I only accept the piano *Études* and the *Nonsense Madrigals*, the other works are a different story. However, I am still looking for means of expression; after all, there is no accepted norm today, there is no unified style in what is called serious music.

Let me cite two extreme examples: Arvo Pärt and Pierre Boulez. Both are well known, but do they have a common denominator? No, they do not. I am different from both of them, I do something wholly different. I have always changed my language and have indeed become a different person. I ought not to be saying this, it sounds like cheap self-advertisement, but I am a sincere person: Stravinsky did the same, yet remained himself. I hope that when on my seventy-fifth birthday I look back upon the past decades, perhaps I shall not be completely unhappy. After all, I have lost so much time in my life. First because of Hitler, then Stalin, and then I started a new life in the West as a refugee—all that was lost time. I had to make a living, do lots of senseless things, I could not compose as much as I would have wished, the way I would have wished. But I do what I can, as far as possible, and will go on doing my job. Now I would like to find a language which is really worth something. This is no false modesty, I am being honest.

And since we are talking on the eve of my birthday, let me finish this interview on a note free of any loftiness. In America, Bartók wrote a kind of testament: as long as streets in Budapest were named after Hitler and Mussolini, none should bear his name. Now there is a Béla Bartók Road in Budapest, and thank God there is no Hitler and Mussolini Square, nor is there a People's Army Street anymore. My wish is that nothing should be named after me. If it must be, then it should be called *Ligeti György tévút*.[43]

Vienna, 1998

---

43 The word "tévút" is difficult to render in English. I found a way around it when translating Ligeti's reference to his Horn Trio when he used the same word. The German equivalent is given, "tévút" being a mirror translation of "Irrweg." "Wrong Road" or "False Road" are poor approximations. "Tévút" is a road that goes in error in a particular direction.

KARLHEINZ
STOCKHAUSEN

1928−2007

I recorded two interviews with Karlheinz Stockhausen in Budapest, in October 1984: one for my three-questions book and one for Hungarian Television.[1] Both were included by the composer in volume 6 of his collections of writings, which goes to show, I believe, that he attributed some significance to them.[2]

In deciding on the main thrust of the television interview, I was bearing in mind the kind of viewers our conversation was likely to address. Rather than discuss questions of a musicological nature, I wanted to sketch a portrait of Stockhausen, knowing full well, of course, that it would come across anyway, thanks to his total dedication to his calling as a prophetic composer and his magnetic personality.

Even though I had expected him to come up with something uniquely original, his response to my first question exceeded all my expectations. With two older works of his being performed at Budapest's new music festival (HYMNEN and HARLEKIN), I asked him if he was still the same person as the Stockhausen who had written those compositions. I suppose the notion of identity with one's former self is something that occupies many people's minds. In the back of my own may have been a story by the Hungarian

1 The original version was titled *Three Questions—Eighty-Two Composers*, and was published in Hungarian in 1986 by Editio Musica Budapest. The English edition, revised and brought up to date, was published in 2011 by the University of Rochester Press (*Three Questions for Sixty-Five Composers*).

2 Karlheinz Stockhausen, *Texte zur Musik: 1977–1984; DuMont Dokumente* (Cologne: DuMont Buchverlag, 1989), 427–32.

writer Frigyes Karinthy (1887–1938): in "Encounter with a Young Man," he describes meeting his younger self who reproaches him for failing to live up to his ideals. Of course, in the case of a creative person like Stockhausen, the question concerns rather his ability to recapture the compositional processes that had produced his works written several years before.[3]

O

Karlheinz Stockhausen (KS): I can remember that Stockhausen. I know him as well as if I had last met him yesterday evening. As a matter of fact, I have a retentive memory that goes back to when I was two years old. What I remember is present in my mind down to the minutest detail, including smells. There are hiatuses between the exact memories saved in my brain, and those memories are all interchangeable, independent of time. They are all stored simultaneously, vertically, and successively—just like in a building. Depending on the kind of association that surfaces, a memory suddenly makes an appearance. The same is true of me, myself: I do not really know who I am. All I know is that whenever I remember a particular situation, I know the Stockhausen who is linked to it. For example, I know the Stockhausen of HYMNEN very well indeed, with many details of the time spent in the studio. I see myself as if from outside, sitting at the tape recorder. I possess the rather unusual faculty of looking at myself from behind. Can you see yourself from behind?

Bálint András Varga (BAV): No, no.

KS: Well, I can. I often see myself also from above. I can lie in bed with my eyes closed and see myself lying there and can spot, with total clarity, the mole on my face. I can look at my face in every detail.

BAV: It is somewhat like when you are dying and leaving your body you can look at yourself from outside. At least, that is what Raymond Moody describes in his book *Life After Life* (1975).

KS: I can look at myself from all sides; I can also walk right behind myself. When that happens, I am always a bit higher and can see what I look like from behind. Sometimes I even play [a game] with myself, in that I look at myself from different angles.

---

3   I am grateful to Suzanne Stephens of the Stockhausen Stiftung (Foundation), Kürten, Germany, for her revision of my English translation.

The same is true as far as events in my life are concerned: I can see myself in certain situations as I am working in the studio. How shall I put it? I can see my own hands pressing and turning buttons, or putting the tape on the machine, or removing it, placing the tape on a shelf in the archives, and so on. HYMNEN is of course linked to that. I see myself listening for months and months to the national anthems of 128 countries, listening to and checking them, or selecting an endless number of sound events from the sound archives of the radio, and so forth. In other words, I feel completely at home in the process of giving birth to HYMNEN.

Composing HARLEKIN is just as alive in me. But that is an altogether different world: a different country, an island, a particular cottage. Right now, at this instant, I can see it in front of me. A rocky shore with a small restaurant on it, and the timber house where I wrote most of HARLEKIN. I can see the oil that was poured on the floor to fight those horrid cockroaches, etc. All that has to do with HARLEKIN.

BAV: As a composer, however, you have left that world far behind.

KS: Traveling around in the past is like taking an occasional interest in one's own back. I do not believe that history has a direction. Nor does the history of a single person. Rather, all aspects of my work appear to me as a circle or a spiral but not along a straight line. I would never say "what I did ten years ago, I would not do again now"; or: "What I did thirty or thirty-five years ago, I would not do again." On the contrary, all aspects are for me valid possibilities, like stones in a mosaic. It is all more like a whirlpool around my consciousness and mixed in my consciousness, rather than strung on a chain. In this sense, when composing a detail of a new work, a few bars from a piece I composed twenty-three years before would emerge in my mind. I would then stop and jot down in the sketch "Remember PUNKTE!" Or: "Attention! Think of the treatment of percussion in KREUZSPIEL!" or something else along those lines. Things like that sometimes occur in my sketches to remind me of particular things I have found in my life before, because I want to use them and elaborate them further. I always have the feeling as if I had hit a number of billiard balls: they are rolling somewhere, to rebound to me, and I have to hit them again to bring about new constellations. All my life is a reservoir of possibilities that I can use at any time.

BAV: In commenting on the third region of HYMNEN, you refer to it as an experiment you conducted to find out whether well-trained musicians could make music the way you expected them to. How did it work out at the time, in 1971 in New York?

KS: Five rehearsals of two hours each. The outcome was rather an approximation. Owing to the fact that many musicians in the orchestra were skilled at faking, the listeners had the impression that the piece was meant to be the way it sounded.

BAV: How about now?

KS: Now it is far more accurate. I would never again accept an engagement with an insufficient number of rehearsals. Here in Hungary, I was given three eight-hour days of sectional rehearsals, and three days of tutti rehearsals—a first time ever. In the past, all I had were two days of sectional rehearsals, two days of tutti rehearsals in addition to the dress rehearsal and concert. Here we have had three days of sectional rehearsals, three days of tutti rehearsals, plus dress rehearsal and concert. And I needed every single minute, since I used all that time to work on details.

Alas, up till now, I have never got anywhere near the original concept of the work, which is that the musicians ought to know the tape so thoroughly as to be able to react to what they hear. Actually, whatever has been played for the past thirteen years has also been nothing but cheating. I cheat, too, together with the musicians. In other words: after so many years of futilely trying to acquaint the musicians with the tape, I have now written cue notes in the parts, with the events on the tape written in small notes. This morning, I was angered by two bassoonists who played a fragment far too early, before the corresponding passage had been heard on tape, simply because it was in the parts!

There has been an unsound development in performance practice, which forces musicians into a straitjacket, due to the limited number of rehearsals. As a result, I have made a virtue out of necessity and written cue notes of what is happening on the tape into the parts. The musicians improvise with the material that is *written*, even though they ought to be relying on their ears, just as in other pieces that I wrote between 1968 and 1970. In KURZWELLEN, SPIRAL, POLE, or EXPO, you react to music which you never heard before: you listen to the radio and elaborate it further.

The players, then, should be reacting to the tape, after having listened to it for so long and so often that they have absorbed it sufficiently to communicate with it, to transform the recorded musical material. In doing so, they ought to be able to rely on the art of improvisation, guided by certain symbols. But the goal is a kind of music which, given orchestral practice today, has no chance of materializing, unless there is a capable student orchestra with which one can study the piece for half a year, meeting twice a week. Each player could receive a cassette of HYMNEN and seek motivic material that appeals to him or her. This could then be elaborated further and in the process, the musicians can find their bearings—also in what their colleagues are doing. However, the cue notes have done away with the prospect of that ever happening.

Basically, no musician is interested anymore in what another musician sitting right next to him or her is doing. Instead, they are like soldiers: they sit in a row and do what they are told to do.

BAV: A frustrating situation for you . . .

KS: Yes. However, much of what I have done in my life has a futuristic element to it. Most of my work has to do with a musical situation that does not yet exist.

BAV: In one of your writings, you describe how the performances of your music in Osaka lost some of their intensity of concentration and radiation once you had left. I wonder whether as a musician, you feel rather lonely once in a while. A Christ figure betrayed by his disciples.

KS: That sounds far too dramatic. I admit, though, that during my life I have lost some friends, some beloved friends. They made music with me and at some point seemed to believe, for reasons I cannot fathom, that the only way they could get rid of me was to kick me in the backside. It appears as though there is sometimes no other solution but to hit me from behind. I do not wish to mention names. But there must be something in my personality that makes some musicians eventually feel claustrophobic in my presence: they need more space for themselves. Instead of leaving in peace (or, as I always put it, by means of considerate divorce), they make a crash landing. I do not like that at all.

Divorce is legitimate, it is feasible, and it can be the right thing to do, but it must be executed with empathy, charm, and humor. In other words: there is a correct way of ending a relationship before starting a new one. However, that presupposes a cultivation of the heart and mind—something you cannot expect automatically. Some manage it, others do not. It is a mystery and one should make no judgment about it.

It is true that I have lost some wonderful musicians. Only a month ago, a singer—with with whom I had had more than three hundred rehearsals and gave many concerts over six years—left me. He had told me a number of times: "With you I cannot earn enough money, I could be making a great deal more. Nor will I rehearse so much in the future. You make one rehearse far too much and it is always so arduous; you must understand that; you had better find someone else." I replied: "All right, but please do honor the engagements for which you have signed contracts. After all, I cannot make another three hundred rehearsals with a new singer within the next year, and I do not have another one anyway." But he said no. The offers he was receiving from the Met, from Bayreuth, and a number of other opera houses and orchestras were too alluring for him to refuse. He is already the third singer in my opera DONNERSTAG aus LICHT to have left in discord.

The conventional world has far more to offer than my music can. Actually, my music has little to offer apart from work and usually about one-tenth of the income that singers of traditional music can earn, once they have made names for themselves. Difficult.

BAV: Don't you see yourself as a pioneer of music history since World War II? As such, you may make it hard for others to keep pace.

KS: Yes, it seems so. Your question suggests that there is this prototype that is put forward again and again: this Stockhausen, born into a particular historical situation that brings with it a technological and aesthetic explosion. This composer is supposed to be playing a role—that of creating works, each of which is supposed to be a model, accepted by the others as such. That is also why he plays this part of a pioneer.

It is as if one was deployed in a war to fight on a perilous front—you are stuck there, you have no other choice. You simply go on.

It is true that I have an adventurous nature but I am also very pedantic. The combination of the artist and the scientist in me has perhaps produced a kind of composer that has been absent for a long time. I am to play this role and it is therefore difficult, apparently, to find like-minded companions, people who gladly come with me, even though it can be hard going.

BAV: May I finally ask you a difficult question: what is music's role in our lives?

KS: Music is the most sublime art to connect spirits through its oscillations, its sound oscillations. Music is the most insubstantial material, the purest material, which directly impregnates the soul and the spirit—which shapes our spirit.

I believe that mankind will eventually arrive at a state where everyone will be a musician. People will then communicate with one another by means of highly differentiated music in which we shall no longer be barking and howling (or perhaps just occasionally). Instead, for the most part we shall be communicating with one another as supremely differentiated singing and instrumental artists.

To be a musician is the ultimate that can be learned on this planet.

Budapest, 1984

CONDUCTORS

ERNEST BOUR

1913–2001

B y the time I interviewed Ernest Bour in Warsaw in 1978, I had seen him conduct often enough to have conceived unstinting admiration for his advocacy of new music and the authority with which he led world premieres at the head of his symphony orchestra of Südwestfunk, the South West German radio station in Baden-Baden.[1] He was a worthy successor to Hans Rosbaud who had died in 1962 but whose legend as a supreme interpreter of contemporary music was still very much alive.[2]

However, unlike the ascetic and monkish Rosbaud, Bour—a Frenchman with a remarkable mastery of the German language—exuded a genuine joie de vivre. He had a witty smile and was in the habit of starting his rehearsals with a joke to make sure his orchestra relaxed and would plunge into work in a good mood.

In my mind's eye, I can see Bour on the podium. His gestures were economical, rather like Boulez's. Very rarely, to make a point, he would take a step toward the orchestra or, just for a second, lean slightly forward. The overall impression was total control of the performance (he conducted invariably by heart) without the slightest emotional involvement. His interpretations

---

1 Here is a typical Bour program at the Donaueschingen Festival, on October 17, 1965: Alexander Goehr, *Pastorals*, op. 19, for orchestra (world premiere); Roman Vlad, *Ode super "Chrysea Phormix"* per chitarra e orchestra da camera. Soloist: Mario Gangi (world premiere); Luciano Berio, *Chemins (su Sequenza II)* per arpa principale e orchestra. Soloist: Francis Pierre (world premiere); Hans Otte, *Passages* for piano and orchestra. Soloist: Hans Otte (world premiere); and Enrique Raxach, *Syntagma* for orchestra (world premiere).

2 Hans Rosbaud (1895–1962), Austrian conductor, known as the first "radio conductor," was appointed to lead the newly founded Frankfurt Radio Orchestra in 1929 and the equally newly established Südwestfunk Orchestra in 1945. His other engagements included the Tonhalle Orchestra in Zurich.

were objective and sober, you might say dry, but then the music he presented required precisely that approach.

Oddly enough, I have kept absolutely no memory of our interview at the Warsaw Autumn Festival. Listening to the cassette after more than thirty years has not helped to revive any detail of our meeting, either. The recording has preserved his deep, pleasant voice and the power of his personality—the way he accented a word and modulated his voice was very much of a born raconteur.

I have looked at his discography. It includes Haydn, Beethoven, Brahms, Bruckner, and Debussy, but I suppose it is his renditions of new music that will keep his name alive. His best-known recording is surely that of György Ligeti's Atmosphères, *which inspired Stanley Kubrick to include it in his film* 2001: A Space Odyssey. *The list of Bour's recordings includes (apart from Stravinsky, the Second Viennese School, or Dallapiccola) composers who have since become salient figures in contemporary music such as Helmut Lachenmann or Wolfgang Rihm but also quite a few who have over the past decades faded into oblivion (Ivo Malec, Hans Otte, Jan van Vlijmen, Bengt Hambraeus, or Milko Kelemen).*

To begin with, I asked him what inspired his obviously unquenchable thirst for new developments in music.

o

Ernest Bour (EB): I have all my life taken a keen interest in whatever was new. I have never shied away from debating new ideas; indeed, I have always welcomed the chance of meeting people who thought otherwise and were ready to enter into a discussion. The decisive event in life was my meeting with Hermann Scherchen who exerted a profound influence on the path I was to embark on.[3]

I was living in Strasbourg and in those years—between 1933 and 1939—the city was the artistic and intellectual capital of Germany, with many great artists passing through at the start of their enforced emigration. Some stayed for a few days, others for several months or indeed years. Wladimir Vogel, for instance, lived there for a number years; Schoenberg made his way to Paris via Strasbourg.[4] Bartók also made a stopover.

Hermann Scherchen happened to be guest conducting in the city when Hitler came to power. On learning the news, he declared he would

---

3   Hermann Scherchen (1891–1966), German conductor of epochal significance for contemporary music.

4   Wladimir Vogel (1896–1984), Russian-born German-Swiss composer.

never again set foot in Germany. As far as I know, he was the first "Aryan" German artist to have severed contacts with his native country. He canceled all his concerts but kept his orchestra in Winterthur in Switzerland and traveled there for rehearsals and concerts from Strasbourg, where he settled for the duration of the war. That is how I became his pupil.

His method was quite extraordinary. He was of the view that the orchestra was the conductor's public when the two were meeting for the first time. In other words, it was the conductor's job to know the piece he was rehearsing as thoroughly as a pianist or violinist when playing in concert. He expected his pupils to be able to conduct a large repertoire without the benefit of a rehearsal, by heart, before a public, even when they were conducting for the first time. I am witness that none of his pupils ever failed to live up to it.

Also, he never stopped learning himself. It was actually a recurring phrase with him: "I learn with every rehearsal, I always learn something new." He was perfectly right, too.

Scherchen demanded that the conductor's every gesture should mirror the music in the most precise possible manner so that it would clearly transmit his intentions to the orchestra. To begin with, we studied from his famous manual.[5] Eight days in succession, twelve hours a day. We practiced all the different kinds of upbeat and fermatas, based on music examples. We then addressed ourselves to working on actual compositions, sometimes spending several hours on eight bars, until our movements were a faithful reflection of the score in every detail. Thanks to Scherchen's teaching, once we had absorbed those eight bars, we could come to terms with the rest of the piece by ourselves. Scherchen sat facing us for hours on end and reacted to our movements like an orchestra. He immediately spotted if anything was wrong with a pupil's inner image of a work or just a detail of it. For instance, he would say: "You did not hear the *pizzicato* in the basses!" He detected that in the would-be conductor's gestures.

He was also capable of mimicking orchestras of differing quality: he whistled or sang, responding to his pupils' gestures as a very good and willing ensemble, or a poor but willing orchestra, or a good but undisciplined one. He pointed out that outstanding orchestras could respond to tiny gestures and readily recognize the difference between *piano* and *forte*, whereas a poorer one would need clearer indications, that is, larger gestures.

Alas, I could not appear at the examination at the end of the course, for I had conducted once, just once, the student orchestra of the Strasbourg

---

5　Hermann Scherchen, *Lehrbuch des Dirigierens* (Leipzig, 1929).

Conservatoire. Scherchen only let those of his pupils do the exam who had never in their lives conducted. One of them, for instance, performed—without a rehearsal, by heart, before an audience—Berlioz's *Roman Carnival* without making a single mistake. It was a decent interpretation, too!

Thanks to Scherchen, my debut was also a success. True, I could not hear a thing in the first five minutes. Nothing! Then I told myself: "Enough of that! Don't be silly!" After that, everything went swimmingly.

Bálint András Varga (BAV): I have read some of Scherchen's letters and had the impression that he followed your career with fatherly concern. In January 1935, in Trieste, he wrote for instance: "Bour is doing wonderfully. At the beginning of February, he will be conducting a *Lohengrin* and a *Don Giovanni*." He was obviously delighted.

EB: Yes, ours was a father–son relationship. For some inexplicable reason, he had changed my name right at the beginning: "No, you are Henri," he said. From then on that's what he called me. We were very close. In Trieste, I was his assistant, we lived and worked together.

At the end of the course in Strasbourg, his pupils gave a series of concerts over a period of two weeks. One of them was my best friend and one of the most remarkable musicians I have ever met in my life: the cellist Vilmos Palotai. One of the programs featured Bartók's Piano Concerto no. 2, with the composer as soloist and Vilmos Palotai conducting.[6] Few people know about this, that's why I am telling you. The rehearsals had passed without a hitch, for Scherchen had prepared everything carefully. Bartók was very reserved—and very friendly. His playing was superb, incredibly hard-edged and clear, his touch almost chiseled. By the way, I own some letters from him: he immediately accepted our invitation to sit on the committee of our newly formed society for new music.

BAV: Did Scherchen's advocacy of new music have a bearing on the curriculum of the Strasbourg course?

EB: Yes, indeed. Scherchen had a catholic taste and he gave us an overview of all musical trends of any significance in the early 1930s, from Webern to Kurt Weill. During the course of the concert series following the end of the course, we put on two concerts a day with nothing but new music on their programs. Four or five of them included orchestral compositions, the

---

6   The concert took place on August 9, 1933, at the Strasbourg Conservatoire, before an invited audience of 100 people. In a letter, quoted in a book compiled by his son, Béla Bartók Jr., Bartók wrote that Palotai was a beginner, his conducting was nothing to write home about. Bartók Jr., *Chronicle of My Father's Life* (Budapest: Editio Musica Budapest, 1981), 331.

rest was chamber music. I, for one, played on a quartertone harmonium, together with Hába. I saw a great deal of the Czech composer in Strasbourg and we also met in Prague in the late 1960s.

BAV: You think highly of Scherchen as a teacher. How do you assess his work as a conductor? It seems to me that his recordings are rarely broadcast and his interpretations are slowly fading into oblivion.

EB: Well, yes . . . Let us try and be objective. Scherchen was an artist of genius who, much to my luck, was at the height of his powers when he had left Germany and settled first in Strasbourg, then at Winterthur. I owe him some of my most memorable musical experiences. I remember, for instance, a quite extraordinary Beethoven Third Symphony. True, I also owe him some highly questionable performances: he would time and again expound extreme views. For instance, he was rehearsing the third movement of Beethoven's Fifth Symphony when he declared: "It is impossible that double-basses in Beethoven's time were capable of playing in that tempo. Let's take it three times slower!" Next time, however, he reverted to the accepted tempo. Or the Bach, B-minor Suite. "This music," he pointed out had "played at the time of its composition the same role as jazz does today. Let's play it like dance music." Such ideas were not without interest, of course, for they made you think.

It should also be remembered that Scherchen was German to the core; what's more, he was every inch a Berliner. Perhaps, without realizing it, losing his native country had upset his inner balance.

BAV: Still on the 1930s: between 1934 and 1936, you organized new music concerts in Strasbourg.

EB: Yes, we put on five or six chamber concerts a year. For instance, we performed Bartók's sonatas for violin and piano (with myself at the keyboard), his string quartets (with the New Hungarian Quartet), Berg's *Lyric Suite*, and so forth. We called our society Groupe de Mai.

BAV: Why "May"?

EB: A professor at the Strasbourg Conservatoire had initiated a concert series along similar lines in the 1920s; it bore the same name. Ours was actually called Nouveau Groupe de Mai, to indicate that we were following up on his initiative.

BAV: You are credited with the French premiere of Bartók's opera, *Duke Bluebeard's Castle*.

EB: Yes, at the Strasbourg Opera House. It was sometime in the 1950s, I cannot recall the exact date.[7] *Wozzeck* reached us even later![8] I also conducted the first performance in France of Bartók's Concerto for Orchestra and that was his very first orchestral work ever to have been performed in Spain, in 1948 or 1949. It proved such a success that I was immediately engaged for the next season when I conducted the composition again.

BAV: You have been steeped in new music ever since your twenties, keeping abreast of its transformations, apparently never balking at revolutionary changes.

EB: That's right! That is precisely what makes music so fascinating: its development. I do my best to keep up to date with what is going on in the world, to track down what is new. I want to hear as much as possible, for I find that even so-called traditional music is changing, if we study it with our eyes and ears of today. Nothing stays immobile. Books and paintings also change, depending on who is interpreting them and what is going on in the world outside.

BAV: Composers have every reason to be grateful to you.

EB: I do my best to be of help.

BAV: Do you ever conduct pieces whose quality does not really convince you?

EB: Of course! However, while conducting, I am motivated by the conviction that the work I am about to premiere is the best there is. Later, if I happen to listen to a recording after a passage of four or five years, I may allow myself a subjective judgment.

BAV: You have worked together with numerous composers, Bartók for one. I suppose you also met Schoenberg in Strasbourg. How about Stravinsky?

EB: I made Schoenberg's acquaintance in Paris, at a reception given in his honor by Marya Freund, who had appeared in the French premiere of *Pierrot lunaire*.[9] It was actually a farewell party on the eve of the composer's

---

7   The French premiere took place on April 29, 1954, at the Opéra national du Rhin, Strasbourg, with Heinz Rehfuss as the Duke and Elsa Cavelti as Judith.

8   According to the Alban Berg Stiftung (Foundation), Vienna, the first radio production in France took place in 1950 under Jascha Horenstein and it was not until 1963 that *Wozzeck* was presented onstage. The conductor was Pierre Boulez (Opéra de Paris, November 29, 1963).

9   Marya Freund (1876–1966) Polish-born French singer. She created the part of Wood Dove in Schoenberg's *Gurrelieder* (1913) and was the soloist in the French and British premieres of *Pierrot lunaire*.

emigration to the United States. We only exchanged a few words; I remember he was rather downcast. He made the impression of an unhappy man.

As far as Stravinsky is concerned, we met in Baden-Baden, about a year after I had conducted *The Rake's Progress* in Strasbourg. That, too, was a French premiere.[10] Stravinsky could not attend, but Nadia Boulanger came from Paris to hear it. Based on her report, Stravinsky seemed to know every detail of the performance. At such and such a spot, the tempo had been too slow, at another the tenor had entered a bar too late. Boulanger had noted everything and gave Stravinsky a detailed account.

BAV: Determining the right tempo is one of the conductor's most difficult tasks.

EB: Yes, yes, it is an extremely thorny question. Scherchen was of the view (and he was right, too, in a certain kind of music) that every composition has only one possible tempo. Experience has sadly compelled me to leave that opinion out of account. After all, a composer like Stravinsky, who had a very clear idea of tempo, did not observe his own markings when conducting himself. He even said the tempo markings in the score were no longer valid. Similarly with Bartók: his metronome figures do not correspond to the duration he determined to the second.

BAV: As you have said, Scherchen did not practice what he preached either. In arriving at the right tempo, you obviously have to rely on your musical sensitivity.

EB: Yes, but it still remains an issue. Everyone has to find a convincing solution for themselves.

BAV: Have you found convincing solutions for yourself as far as programming in Baden-Baden is concerned?

EB: No, no. I was invited to Südwestfunk by Heinrich Strobel.[11] In his way, he was also a Scherchen-like personality. Unpredictable, stubborn—but in music, we were on the best of terms. I mostly agreed with his ideas about programs, so that I readily accepted his suggestions.

Strobel was a genius at *feeling* new music. He would peruse any score and sense whether the piece was of any interest. He was the one who

---

10 According to the Stravinsky authority Stephen Walsh, the premiere took place in April or May 1952, in Strasbourg.

11 Heinrich Strobel (1898–1970), German musicologist and critic. In December 1945, he was appointed head of the Music Department of the newly established Südwestfunk in Baden-Baden. In that capacity, he made the symphony orchestra one of the foremost ensembles of new music in Europe.

discovered the talent of Boulez, Stockhausen, Penderecki, Ligeti, Henze, and others and supported them to make their way. Those beautiful times are over. Strobel died, and, for sentimental reasons, I have more or less lost interest in the whole thing.[12]

Interestingly enough, I was present when Boulez first tried his hand at conducting. He is, no doubt, an excellent musician who feels music on the level of instinct as well. He first conducted a work other than his own in Strasbourg, in the early 1950s. I remember it was a symphony by Haydn. I attended his rehearsals. I attach a great deal of importance to phrasing, but Boulez's reaction to mistakes was like a wounded animal or a cat when you trample on its tail. He did not immediately realize what was wrong but mistakes like that caused him physical pain.

BAV: Is it true you are leaving Baden-Baden to teach at the Paris Conservatoire?

EB: It is. However, the two moves are not connected. As a result of a friendly "conspiracy," I was appointed professor at the Conservatoire last year and was supposed to take up my position on October 1. That did not work, of course, for in our profession, your time is booked three years ahead, with every day accounted for. During the first year, I was substituted [for] by one of my pupils. I do not have much time this season either: I have three weeks off in February; that is all. I wonder if I am going to be up to it in any case, for if you want to do this job properly, the time at your disposal is simply not enough.

I would have left Südwestfunk at the end of 1979 anyway, but I shall continue to conduct the chamber orchestra of NOS at Hilversum.[13] They are very nice and give me more opportunity to perform new pieces than in Baden-Baden. Eventually, I shall have to cut down on the number of concerts. . . .

BAV: How are you going to transmit what you learned from Scherchen, combining it with your own experience?

EB: Yes, that is the question. When I was young, I did have some pupils and was convinced that I was a capable teacher. I had a pupil who had never stood before an orchestra and I made him conduct the *Abduction* by heart.

---

12 I suppose with the death of Heinrich Strobel, Bour lost his closest partner in Baden-Baden—the person with whom he could discuss music, the man with whom he was on the same wavelength. The soul was gone from the Südwestfunk and Bour needed a change of environment, perhaps in the same way as one cannot go on living in the same apartment after a spouse's demise.

13 NOS is an acronym for Nederlandse Omroep Stichting, the Netherlands Radio Foundation.

The first act was so splendid that in the interval, I went up to the singers and asked them to make false entrances—one too early, another too late—to see how the young man would manage. The next act went off without a hitch but I do not think I would dare to do a thing like that today.

I have not done any teaching for many years. I am absolutely certain, however, that I shall be teaching the basic principles as far as movement, upbeat, fermata are concerned, in the spirit of Hermann Scherchen.

Warsaw, 1978

SIR NEVILLE
MARRINER

b. 1924

I f you are a regular listener to music broadcasts or recordings, you are
bound to have developed a sort of Pavlovian reflex: the NBC Symphony
Orchestra will call forth in your mind the name of Arturo Toscanini. You
will associate the Cleveland Orchestra with George Szell, and the Berlin
Philharmonic with Herbert von Karajan. In much the same way, the Academy
of St. Martin in the Fields is linked with the name of Neville Marriner—the
two are one, really. For years and years, I heard their recordings and became
an admirer, so that when I took up interviewing, pretty soon I was anxious to
talk to the conductor and find out about the ingredients of the unique chemistry that had produced this exclusive, élite group.

It took a long time to find a date and a city where our paths would cross.
Eventually, on March 2, 1978, I stood on the threshold of Sir Neville's London
home, rang the bell, and he let me in. We talked for about forty minutes. It
has stayed in my mind as an extremely pleasant conversation: for all his international success, the conductor was matter-of-fact about his achievement,
maintaining the sort of "emotional understatement" that he wishes to impart
to his performances with the Academy as well. An element of self-irony lent
the interview a welcome flavor of modesty, which is an endearing quality of
Britishness, I find. Listening to the cassette of our interview for the first time
in over thirty years, it was heartwarming to hear our laughs, particularly
toward the end, by which time it had really ceased to be an interview and we
seem to have forgotten about the presence of the microphone.

The Hungarian translation appeared in 1979 in my book Muzsikusportrék (Musicians' Portraits) and, soon enough, I was able to hand a printed

copy to Sir Neville, in Budapest's then best restaurant, the Gundel. Thirty-four years later, in 2012, he was able to actually read the original English text. He made very few corrections and added a postscript that brings our conversation up to date.

o

Sir Neville Marriner (NM): When we first started, we were really just a group of players, put together on a friendly basis. We virtually played for pleasure, for about the first year. We had no money anyway.

Bálint András Varga (BAV): When was that?

NM: 1957 or 1958, I suppose. I am really a bit hazy about when it started. It was Jack Churchill, our harpsichord player, who suggested that we give some concerts at the church St. Martin in the Fields, where he was director of music.[1] He said: "We have done all these rehearsals, we might as well give some concerts. Come and be our guests at the church."

And so we arranged six concerts, but we did not know how to advertise them. We did not want to call ourselves an orchestra, because we were so small, it would have been too pretentious. We did not want to be an ensemble either, for it alienates so many of the public if you call yourselves an ensemble. I do not know what it is, there is a snob element about it, as there is about chamber music, too. Chamber music is in itself, in English, an off-putting word. It already designates a particular sort of taste: there are those people who say we like orchestral concerts, there are those who say we like chamber-music concerts—they are quite different audiences.

Anyway, we fished around for a name which did not include orchestra, ensemble, or chamber music. I think it was Jack Churchill who said: "Around this part of London, in the seventeenth and eighteenth centuries, there were many academies of literature, science, art, and music. Why don't we call it an academy?" And really for the hell of it—we were not serious about it—we said we'd call it the Academy of St. Martin in the Fields. You could not have a clumsier title: it is long, it is impossible to get on to a poster, and we thought it was utterly unmemorable. But as we only intended to do half a dozen concerts, and then perhaps forget about it altogether, we thought it did not matter.

---

1   St. Martin in the Fields, in Trafalgar Square, London, was built between 1721 and 1726 on the site of a much older church, first mentioned in 1222. The architect was James Gibbs (1682–1754). William Hogarth and Joshua Reynolds are buried in St. Martin in the Fields.

I think it was at the third concert that the BBC came along and asked if they might broadcast it. And then, after about the fourth concert, a splendid woman called Louise Dyer, came along. She was an Australian sheep farmer who had, some years before, set up in Paris as a publisher under the name of L'Oiseau-Lyre.[2] One of the people she had sought advice from was Thurston Dart, the harpsichord player and musicologist.[3] Thurston Dart told her to come and listen to our orchestra. She then decided she wanted to make gramophone records as well as publish books. So she started the record company under the same name.

She had a very good eye for talent. For instance, Joan Sutherland made her first record with Louise Dyer and so did Janet Baker. We certainly made our first record with Louise. By the time we finished our series of six concerts, we were virtually launched as a going concern. It was a bit late to change the name then. We did make an attempt later on: we called ourselves the London Strings on the first tour we did in Europe because we thought no one would believe a title like the Academy. It was really a nonstarter. The record company immediately said: what is the point of making records under one name and touring under another? So we went back to the original name and we were stuck with it. Now of course it is a positive virtue—in those days, we always thought it was a great hazard.

BAV: Whose initiative was it in the first place for a group of players to get together and rehearse? What was your goal?

NM: I think it had an element of frustration. I remember I joined a string quartet when I was about twenty (I was a violin player). We used to have a book sent to us every year by the Incorporated Society of Musicians which gave a list of all the music societies in England and Wales that could support a string quartet for one concert.[4] There were something like 4,200 societies in England and Wales. This would be in about 1948, I suppose. I was in that string quartet for seven years. By the time I left, the number had dropped to about 300 addresses. The whole idea of provincial music had virtually died on its feet. No longer could they stimulate enough interest in provincial places to run music societies. And so the opportunities for

---

2 Louise Dyer (1884–1962) founded the Éditions de l'Oiseau-Lyre in 1932. In 2012, its eightieth anniversary year, the publisher ended its presence in Europe and reverted to its parent holding, the Lyrebird Press, at the University of Melbourne.

3 Thurston Dart (1921–71), British musicologist, conductor, and keyboard player. Many of his recordings were released on the L'Oiseau-Lyre label. His students included Michael Nyman, John Eliot Gardiner, and Christopher Hogwood.

4 The Incorporated Society of Musicians (ISM) is the United Kingdom's professional body of musicians, established in 1882.

young musicians to give their first concerts had diminished enormously. You suddenly were entirely dependent on the main towns of England and Wales in which to make your career. Since we could not sustain solo careers and could not survive as quartet players, for there was not enough work, many of us decided to go into symphony orchestras.

I joined the London Symphony Orchestra [LSO] at a time when they had just fired seventeen principal players. I was one of the replacements. Many of my colleagues were the same age and joined at the same time. The LSO was a very bad orchestra in those days and we were excited about trying to make a good orchestra out of it. For a couple of years, we worked very hard and then we began to win: suddenly the orchestra began to sound good. We discovered, however, that the responsibility of the principal viola or the principal second violin was not enough to fill your life if you were still ambitious musically. So we decided to form this group to play a completely different repertoire.

We had heard at that time the [group called] Virtuosi di Roma; I believe the Solisti di Zagreb was already playing. There was also the Stuttgart Chamber Orchestra—they were all that we knew about and whom we admired.[5] We thought we would form a group specializing in Italian Baroque music. But of course, after a time, we got tired of that repertoire and we decided we would like to include German, French, and English music of the same period. And then, as we started to make more gramophone records, it was suggested that perhaps we could widen our repertoire a little bit. We became very adventurous and played Mozart divertimenti as well as little bits of Haydn. Once we discovered that that was possible with the size orchestra we had, we then moved into the Mendelssohn string symphonies. We worked our way very quickly to the nineteenth century; of course, the nineteenth-century repertoire is pretty limited, and arrived at the twentieth century where the composers were writing for chamber orchestras much more again. We found that with a catholic repertoire like this, with something of every period, we had the best of almost every world.

Anyway, the orchestra had almost ceased then to be a toy, it was not any longer for pleasure, it had become quite serious, because there were quite a few gramophone records around. One of the great problems is: if you make your reputation on gramophone records, you will have to keep

---

5 The Virtuosi di Roma was founded in 1947 by the musicologist and conductor Renato Fasano (1902–79). The Croatian ensemble Solisti di Zagreb was established in 1953 by the Italian cellist and conductor Antonio Janigro (1918–89). The Stuttgarter Kammerorchester was formed by Karl Münchinger (1915–90) in 1945.

up the standard of your performance in concerts. So we found we had to work pretty hard.

Most of us stayed attached to other organizations throughout this period of our lives, [as did I] until I stopped playing the violin altogether.

BAV: When did you start conducting the orchestra?

NM: When we began to play more complex works, somebody was needed to conduct. The Academy hated it, they hate every conductor, they really dislike people waving a piece of wood under their noses, but they put up with it because it happens to be my orchestra anyway. They do not have much choice. In fact, I try to conduct as little as possible, only rhythmically complicated works, contemporary works particularly, and geographically works that are too big. In other words, if you play Beethoven's First Symphony, the distance between the front desk of the violins and the trumpets and the timpani is too great to be able to direct it from the concertmaster's seat. So somebody has to stand up and wave.

BAV: Did you study conducting?

NM: Yes, I did. While I was in the London Symphony Orchestra, Pierre Monteux was the principal conductor and he suggested that I [go] to study with him. So I went off to America and stayed with him. That was the beginning, that is when the rot set in.

BAV: You said a while ago that the London Symphony was a poor orchestra. That is really a reflection on Monteux as a conductor.

NM: At that time, Monteux was not the principal conductor. In fact, the LSO had no principal conductor when we joined. It was one of these messy arrangements where the orchestra was run by the players. I now believe that democracy only works to a certain extent with music. I think it is much better that there is one musical dictator for a large group of players like that, [someone] whom everybody can dislike rather than a group of members from the orchestra who form a committee and who proceed to tear themselves to pieces because they dislike each other or do not agree and consequently they tear the orchestra to pieces, too. So the mess in the LSO was in the late forties–early fifties when the committee virtually destroyed the orchestra by their disagreements. We all came in and proceeded to play our best and not meddle around with the politics of the orchestra too much.

The first principal conductor who really made a great impact was Kertész, and after Kertész Monteux. Perhaps it was the other way round,

I am not sure. Next in that position was André Previn.[6] Anyway, Kertész was largely responsible for the improvement of standards. We had very good guest conductors, too, people like George Szell, who used to come and tidy the orchestra up occasionally.[7] We also had Josef Krips who had a different attitude: he would always paper over the cracks, instead of demanding that the orchestra play better.[8] He managed to suppress the bad elements in the orchestra, so that he got a very smooth performance, even if the orchestra did not play any better at the end of his visit. George Szell was positive in this way. He demanded that the players either played better or they went. Those were the happy days when you could fire players for not being very good.

BAV: Even as a guest conductor?

NM: Even as a guest conductor, you could make it very well known that you had no intention of coming back again, unless certain things were done to improve the orchestra.

BAV: The more we talk, the more vistas open up. There are endless questions and I am groping in the dark. Our subject is the Academy of St. Martin in the Fields but obviously, it would be good to make a detour so that you can talk about Pierre Monteux as a teacher of conducting.

NM: Monteux took enormous trouble. When I crossed over to America for the very first time, I was pretty poor in those days. I was traveling with my wife and we flew a very complicated and cheap air route which took twenty hours to reach New York. Then we took a Greyhound bus and traveled overnight up to his place at Hancock in Maine. He was very kind and met us at the bus and took me straight to the rehearsal shed where the entire orchestra was assembled. It was made up of people like me: players from symphony orchestras from all over the world who wanted to conduct.

BAV: It was an orchestra of would-be conductors?

---

6 Pierre Monteux (1875–1964), French-born, later American conductor, who led the London Symphony Orchestra from 1961. István Kertész (1929–73), Hungarian conductor, was a pupil of Zoltán Kodály at the Budapest Academy of Music. He defected in 1956 and was appointed to head the London Symphony Orchestra in 1965. He stayed in that position until 1968. André Previn (b. 1930) was principal conductor between 1968 and 1979.

7 George Szell, born in Budapest in 1897 as György Széll, was a Hungarian-American conductor, pianist, and composer. He died in 1970.

8 Josef Krips (1902–74), Austrian conductor, was principal conductor of the London Symphony Orchestra between 1950 and 1954.

NM: That's right. The only reason why you were invited was that you also took your instrument with you. Each one had a turn to conduct. When we arrived, Monteux asked me: "Neville, now what will you conduct?" I had never conducted anything in my life, not even a bus or a train or anything. I preferred to play but Monteux insisted that I conduct. "You will conduct the [Mozart] G-Minor Symphony," he said. "We played it together about three weeks ago. You must know it!"

So very well, I conducted and he did not stop me, he never said a word. No, he did stop me and said: the Trio must be in one. That is the hardest thing to conduct, for there is nothing to do. It goes sort of One. One. One. So I was fairly pathetic. The next day I turned up, played a little and then he said: "Neville, come and conduct the G-Minor Symphony!" So I conducted it again. He was sitting in an armchair between the oboe and the flute, facing me. Again, nothing was said. I was totally depressed and went back to the little house he lent us. Then the telephone rang—it was Monteux. "Neville, you were much better today. But why do you stick out your behind when you want *pianissimo*?" That was the first lesson I ever had from him: why do I stick out my behind . . .

He always was immensely practical, he really envisaged the beat you are offering the orchestra to be in a tiny little square frame in front of your nose. He really did not like big gestures at all. He said that musicians do not need that sort of encouragement emotionally. They will deliver their own feelings about the music. You do not have to do it. What you have to do is the most important: you should remind them in plenty of time when to play, where to play, and how to play. By the physical manifestation of your beat you can indicate how they are going to play: short, legato, piano, forte. He certainly never talked about music in emotional terms at all. He would not philosophize. You know, particularly German conductors who emigrated to England and America, would philosophize for hours about blue tulips and things like that. Monteux was incapable of philosophizing in this way.

One evening, Monteux conducted us in Berlioz's *Romeo and Juliet*.[9] His wife was standing in the wings and she had tears in her eyes: "Pierre, it was so beautiful!"—it really was the most wonderful performance—and she asked: "Were you thinking of me while conducting?" "No," he said, "I was thinking of Eleanor Roosevelt." Probably the ugliest woman he could think of. He was really incapable of being sentimental about music.

---

9   *Roméo et Juliette*, a *symphonie dramatique* for chorus and orchestra, was premiered on November 24, 1839.

Whereas George Szell was probably the last of the son-of-a-bitch conductors who terrorized musicians. Do you know the story about the Toscanini funeral? When Toscanini died, so many musicians in America wanted to go to the funeral service that tickets had to be issued. Some members of the New York Philharmonic who could not get any decided to try and get in anyway. The organizers turned them away: "We are sorry, we can only let you in if you have tickets." They answered: "If you cannot give us tickets, will you please reserve some for George Szell's funeral?" Szell was infinitely disliked, whereas Toscanini, strangely enough, was liked, even though he used to fight with his orchestra. I enjoyed Szell's work, I liked the effect he had on an orchestra.

BAV: He was very cold, wasn't he.

NM: Yes, a very cold personality, but the way he could make an instrument play—I mean, Cleveland is still the best musical instrument in America, clinically.

BAV: Clinically? What do you mean?

NM: It means that every department is clear and clean. He got rid of all the bad players, he was still able to. He came into conflict with the unions eventually, but he was another person who, like me, thought that contracts are the death of an orchestra.

BAV: After that detour, let us return to the Academy. In order to play Baroque music properly, you have to master the style. It was probably not there when you started, but developed over the years. Still, you must have been good enough right at the beginning, otherwise you would not have attracted the attention of the BBC and Louise Dyer.

NM: In fact, we had a mixture of influences. My own personal influence was Thurston Dart. He was really the first major English musicologist who had any influence on performing style in this country. He happened to be a very close friend, someone with whom I played duos, and in fact had an ensemble, the Jacobean Ensemble, which has long since disappeared into the mists of time. He made it his life's study to work on the conventions of performing seventeenth- and eighteenth-century music.

A lot of this rubbed off on to me. A lot of the enthusiasm for this rubbed off on me, too, and so I was able to add something of the quality of style we wanted in the Academy. Then, there were two other players. One called Michael Bowie who is now teaching musicology at a remote university in Canada and another one called Simon Streatfield who had great convictions about style. Between us, we thrashed out what became the Academy style, with a sort of clarity of articulation, a slight understatement in emotional terms, and I think the general shape of the music that eventually we agreed upon. We had many, many long bitter months of haggling about what the style was, but eventually it crystallized to such an extent that even now, fifteen or twenty years afterward, I can still pick up a piece of newly printed music of a seventeenth-century composer and literally write in, by putting articulation, dynamics, various slurs and phrasings, with a pencil, in half an hour, and it will be the Academy performance. And it will not change because I know that our style is consistent and I know exactly how we would tackle each piece of music. So the Academy style crystallized quite early on, and it has changed only inasmuch as the personality of the ensemble has changed.

I mean, obviously, we changed the members of the orchestra fairly frequently. What happens is that you look for the best young talent in the country and introduce him into the orchestra; other people come along, they see these rather good players sitting at the back of the second violins and offer them a job as concertmaster in another orchestra somewhere. We are always sad to see them go, but we are delighted that the Academy has become a bit of a clearing house for players. But we can always invite them back again, and you sometimes have three or four concertmasters sitting in the orchestra and they still have the Academy style. The Academy does not offer a contract. I think that is the anathema of all artistic success, to offer someone a contract and security.

BAV: How can you organize a tour if the Academy is actually a pool of players from different orchestras, with schedules of their own?

NM: Ours are freelance players; many are not attached to any organization. Some of them still manage to make a career by being unattached. They play with us, they may play with the English Chamber Orchestra, they play with the London Symphony Orchestra or the Philharmonia occasionally; they have a string quartet that plays several times a month.

BAV: That means that they have to be musical chameleons, adapting to the style of whatever ensemble they happen to be sitting in.

NM: Well, actually, the English Chamber Orchestra is more chameleonic than the Academy, because they have different jockeys all the time. At least, we only have one conductor, you see. That's me or the concertmaster, Iona Brown, who takes the orchestra around.[10] But the style remains the same.

---

10 Iona Brown (1941–2004), British violinist and conductor.

BAV: Is there no danger of your crystallized style becoming fossilized?

NM: Boring? Absolutely, yes. In fact, I do not at all find it flattering if someone comes and tells me "I can always recognize the Academy style," because I do think it is in danger of becoming boring. What I am tending to do nowadays is to try and let the seventeenth century part of our repertoire slip away. I do not particularly want to repeat endlessly performances of Vivaldi, Corelli, Handel, Bach, because I sincerely believe that the new groups playing on old instruments are now beginning to take over that repertoire very satisfactorily. A few years ago, the sort of people that played original instruments were poor instrumentalists. You know, if you were a rotten pianist, you took up the harpsichord, if you were a bad cellist, you took up the gamba. It was a refuge for enthusiastic musicians who could not play their instruments very well. Now that has changed; there are many, many good players who have started to play these instruments really well and I think that for the next few years, that sort of repertoire should go to them.

I would like to turn the Academy into a Mannheim orchestra which starts with Haydn and Mozart and explores much more of the eighteenth- and nineteenth-century repertoire. This will be refreshing for us, too. But we are always asked to . . . we have just been asked to record the Bach Suites for the second time. You do not have a great change of mind, I do not think, in the few years between the two recordings. To put something down on record in the first place, you have to really believe in what you are doing and if you have these convictions, you do not change them too easily. Even in a period of five years. I think just to record them for another company is not very interesting. So we shall try and avoid that now and move into a different area of repertoire.

BAV: How do you conduct the ensemble when playing the first violin? How does it work?

NM: I have given it up, because my violin playing became so awful. You cannot conduct and play the violin, you fall between both stools. If the ensemble is small enough, it is like an enlarged string quartet; the concentration is considerably more aurally than visually. Looking back at performances—some of those I gave when I was playing were much better in ensemble and precision than they were when I was conducting. Even though I think my sort of conducting concentrates largely on being clear to the players, I do not try to stimulate them emotionally. For a small group of not more than nineteen or twenty players it is very possible to play with a concertmaster. After that they need a bit of assistance, usually.

BAV: You say you do not wish to stimulate the players emotionally; earlier on you said the style of the Academy was characterized by understatement. Why is that?

NM: I think it was a reaction against one or two groups who were also interested in our sort of music and I think we almost unanimously rejected the overemotional quality of their performance. For instance, the groups that are made up of virtuoso players tend to have wide vibrato, they tend to have individual characteristics in their playing which are very hard to suppress. I find this particularly with the American orchestra that I have. They are much more brilliant, much more extrovert[ed] than European players. They were all taught to be soloists, but a solo career is no longer available to them, because there are just not enough concert halls, so they join chamber orchestras. You suddenly get chamber orchestras of frustrated bravura players, with wide vibratos, playing Corelli and Vivaldi. So I spend my time in America suppressing this sound, to try and get a slightly cooler approach. I do not think I am entirely successful. I do not think if you transfer the Los Angeles Chamber Orchestra, for instance, into an Italian sixteenth-century villa or seventeenth-century castle, you would get any impression at all of that period. I would get an impression of a bunch of tourists taking over this place, to play some music. Whereas while the English players are cooler to begin with, their whole emotional temperature is a little lower, they are not trained over here to be bravura soloists, we do not have those sort of institutions. I think we try quite hard but we have no tradition here of Tchaikovsky-prize winners or big competition winners. We have a tradition of a large number of players who fit very comfortably into ensembles. They play intelligently but not uniquely. And so we get very good groupings. It is possible with people of this temperament and musical attitude to make very good ensembles and this I try to exploit with the Academy. You can have enormous quality from a group of players who are playing sympathetically with each other and not fighting each other as you find in other sorts of orchestras.

BAV: Teamwork is the byword . . .

NM: Absolutely! And they get a great deal of pleasure out of the end product of being a team.

BAV: I have read a review of your concert with the Tonhalle Orchestra in Zurich. It said you had changed the quality of the strings completely. You achieved a marvelous sound. How did you achieve a change of that dimension in a few rehearsals?

NM: First of all, if you were a string player yourself and you conduct, you are very fortunate because you have the vernacular of the string players' world at your fingertips. You know exactly what their problems are and you know how to solve them quickly. I think most conductors who are pianists or even wind players are at a considerable disadvantage because you have to spend so much of your time with the string section. Without having the right language to talk to them in is pretty difficult.

The Tonhalle in Zurich is a marvelous hall but it is impossible to rehearse in. It has the most flattering, the most beautiful acoustic. However, when the public comes in, the resonance of the hall goes down a bit and the imperfections will be revealed when it is too late. What I did was to try and take the orchestra to pieces, desk by desk, section by section, so they became more conscious of ensemble. The eighteen violins in the first violin section of the Tonhalle Orchestra can play anyhow, with no ensemble whatsoever, and it still sounds good in that hall. So what I did was to point this out. To begin with, they did not like the Elgar *Introduction and Allegro.*[11] They thought it was bombastic, jingoistic, nationalistic rubbish, but after two or three rehearsals they began to enjoy playing it. Because, first of all, it was together, it was in tune, it was logical the way it was bowed and phrased. They really began to lean into it like a well-tempered English orchestra playing its own music. The strings played enormously enthusiastically; the only difference I could see between when I started and when I finished with the orchestra was that they got that enthusiasm. I come back to my old hobbyhorse: this happens to all orchestras with contracts whether they play well or less well. Human nature being what it is, people take advantage of their rights under contract. I was delighted with the change in their style and also that, as you say, the press actually noticed it.

London, 1978

O

In July 2012 Sir Neville added the following postscript:
Now, after more than fifty years as the director of the Academy, I have become a phantom of their musical conscience. They need to maintain the youthful vitality, the very personal responsibility of independent musical collaboration that we achieved together during our years of progress. I conduct them when needed—fulfilling old relationships, state occasions,

---

11 Elgar's *Introduction and Allegro,* op. 47, was composed in 1905 for string quartet and string orchestra, for the newly formed London Symphony Orchestra.

charitable projects—and still with the same reservations that it isn't quite good enough yet, but there's still time!

Joshua Bell and Murray Perahia have the talent and judgement to keep the Academy alive.[12]

---

12 Joshua Bell (b. 1967), American violinist and music director of the Academy; Murray Perahia (b. 1947), American concert pianist is the principal guest conductor.

EUGENE ORMANDY

1899–1985

In 1973, I was seconded jointly by Editio Musica Budapest and Hungarian Radio to accompany the Budapest Symphony Orchestra on its tour of the United States. My job was to send back weekly reports, and to write a book. My tape recorder gave the trip its special purpose. It acted as a magnet, so to speak, or as a compass, drawing and directing me toward potential interviewees.

In Philadelphia, where the orchestra appeared at the Academy, it led me backstage toward an old man of short stature with a familiar if rather masklike, immobile face. Eugene Ormandy was quite obviously tense, in something of an emotional turmoil. He had not heard a Hungarian orchestra since the late 1930s and apparently could not resist the temptation to go to hear it. Undecided about what to do, how to behave, he had stipulated that he wished to remain incognito. He need not have worried, for nobody recognized him. That, in turn, disappointed and possibly hurt him. He was of course welcomed by the conductor, György Lehel, and as for me, I did not for a moment hesitate to ask for an interview. I was tremendously thrilled to see him in person, having heard his recordings all my life and seen his face on record covers. In fact, Ormandy was something of a legend for me (together with other great American conductors of Hungarian birth, such as Fritz Reiner, George Szell, Georg Solti, or Antal Doráti).

Ormandy's initial response was rather negative. No wonder: we were still in the middle of the cold war, and here was a Hungarian reporter wanting to record an interview with him. Surely he would ask tricky questions in an attempt to get answers that could be construed as political statements. He must have felt threatened and insecure and was on the point of saying no. Somehow, he ended up saying yes but made me promise to steer clear of *politics. We arranged for me to go next morning to the Barclay Hotel where he lived in an apartment on the ninth floor. We did not have much time, for the coaches that transported the orchestra all over the United States would not wait.*

An elderly lady opened the door. To the left of the entrance, I saw a spacious room furnished rather puritanically; it could have been the secretary's domain. I was invited to go straight on and reached an elegant if impersonal drawing room. It was all polished and shiny; two women looking like maids were busying themselves in a corner, talking in hushed voices. I was reminded of the manager's worried face the previous evening and his anguished request that I should leave the maestro in peace: I felt that these women were also in awe of the man they served.

When Ormandy entered, the atmosphere changed straight away. His tenseness had given way to amiability; his genuine hospitality put me at ease. Our exchange of words turned into an interview once I had switched on the recorder—the first interview in Hungarian he had given since the 1920s. Over half a century since his emigration, he still had a perfect command of his mother tongue, with just a trace of foreign inflection. He did not mix the two languages, only replacing a Hungarian word with its English equivalent on two occasions.

Eugene Ormandy struck me as a man of quick temper and passionate views. He could raise his voice in irritation when he sensed a slight in my attitude toward American orchestras ("Don't look down on them!") and let it grow mellow when he talked of his violins. "How can you say that?" he asked me at one point, totally incredulous at what he may have taken for my impertinence.

No wonder I could not really unwind. Frankly, I am not particularly proud of this interview—except for the fact that it took place at all. Rereading it for the first time since 1973, some of my questions make me wince. Their saving grace lies in the replies they inspired. Still, I cannot forgive myself for failing to ask Ormandy about the world premiere of Bartók's Third Piano Concerto that he had conducted on February 8, 1946, especially since I had interviewed the soloist, György Sándor, shortly before in Budapest.

In any case, I have decided to include the conversation in this book, because I hope that for all its failings, it provides a portrait sketch of Eugene Ormandy. He must have been having a good time, because in the end he was reluctant to let me go and even presented me with two LPs. One he signed as Eugene Ormandy and the other as Ormándy Jenő.

o

Eugene Ormandy (EO): I was twenty-eight or twenty-nine years old, working as a conductor for CBS in New York, when I had a call from Philadelphia: Toscanini had been taken ill; would I jump in for him to conduct a summer concert. I was not the only one to have been asked, but all the others had refused—they were simply afraid of the challenge. I was also cautioned against accepting. It would break my neck, Arthur Judson warned me. He was to become my manager later on (he is still a leading light in the profession).[1] Stokowski had just left on holiday and the man I would have to deputize for was none other than Toscanini. It would be suicidal to appear in his stead. I remained unimpressed: "Mr. Judson, I have nothing to lose but everything to win. I am going to accept."

I only had three concert programs on my repertoire. I offered all three—but they took a fourth one. There were two days to go before the concert, so I worked twenty-four hours a day to learn the pieces by heart. I took the seven o'clock train to Philadelphia, arrived at nine, and made my way straight to the Academy. (It is a mystery to me why it's called that: it has nothing to do with a music academy).

Apparently, the orchestra liked me because they invited me back for another week. At the same time, Henri Verbrugghen, the conductor of the Minneapolis Symphony Orchestra, was diagnosed with [a] brain tumor and had to give up conducting.[2] I was chosen to be his successor.

During my years in Minnesota, I often appeared in Philadelphia, and when Stokowski resigned, I was invited to succeed him. I nevertheless continued to conduct in Minneapolis as a guest.

By then, I only had one sonority in my ears: the Philadelphia sound. It had never existed anywhere before and does not exist anywhere else today. I had endeavored to obtain the same quality of sound from the Minneapolis Symphony Orchestra as well and I believe I succeeded: we made innumerable records between 1931 and 1936, and everyone said they could just about pass for the Philadelphia Orchestra.

The Philadelphia sound had been developed by Leopold Stokowski. I did not wish to alter it in any way. Today, of course, it bears traces of my own time with the orchestra: after all, I have been their music director for thirty-eight years. A long association like that is bound to make an impact.

---

1   Arthur Judson (1881–1975), American concert manager. Between 1915 and 1935, he was manager of the Philadelphia Orchestra, and between 1922 and 1956, he worked in the same capacity with the New York Philharmonic. His artists' management agency grew into Columbia Artists Management, Inc.

2   Henri Verbrugghen (1873–1934), Belgian violinist, conductor, and music pedagogue. In Brussels, he studied violin with Jenő Hubay. Verbrugghen was principal conductor of the Minneapolis Symphony Orchestra between 1922 and 1931.

In fact, I am the longest-serving American conductor ever. I have outdone even Frederick Stock, who was at the head of the Chicago Symphony for thirty-seven years.[3]

Bálint András Varga (BAV): What are the ingredients of the Philadelphia sound? I know that Stokowski experimented a great deal with the seating of the musicians.

EO: The seating only affects the sound up to about 20 percent. You must have the sound in your ears. My aural imagination was impregnated during my years at the Budapest Academy of Music where my teachers included Jenő Hubay, Béla Bartók, and Zoltán Kodály. Quartet playing was taught by David Popper.[4] My piano teacher may not be well-known outside Hungary: his name was Buttykay.[5]

I was very young at the time, about ten or eleven. I had been admitted to the Academy at five—needless to say, I was the youngest student.

Well then, I came to America with the sound I had heard and learned from Hubay. Over here I came under the influence of Stokowski and naturally also of Toscanini. I made a point of attending all his rehearsals and concerts when I was young. My first wife was harpist in his orchestra and through her I came in touch with the maestro. He grew fond of me—and he was my God. He still is. I merged what I learned from Stokowski and Toscanini with the heritage of Hubay—it was with that ideal of sound in my ears that I took over the leadership of the Philadelphia Orchestra.

BAV: The orchestra took a liking to you the very first time you conducted it. The "chemistry" of human relationships is difficult to analyze but perhaps part of it has been the working atmosphere at your rehearsals. You are no dictator but a primus inter pares, I suppose.

EO: We are all equal. We are friends, colleagues, spend a lot of time together, talk a great deal. In the rehearsal intervals many of the players come up and ask me if a particular passage could be done with a different bowing, whether any changes could be made. We discuss everything. I am no dictator: most musicians know as much as the conductor. Perhaps the conductor has a more thorough knowledge of the repertoire.

---

3   Frederick Stock (1872–1942), German conductor, led the Chicago Symphony between 1905 and 1942.
4   David Popper (1843–1913), Czech composer and cellist. Between 1886 and 1913, he was professor of cello and quartet at the Budapest Academy of Music.
5   Ákos Buttykay (1871–1935), Hungarian composer of operettas. Between 1907 and 1922, he taught piano at the Budapest Academy of Music.

It occurred to me just now that when I was conducting in Budapest in 1934 or 1935, the director of the music publisher Rózsavölgyi (I can remember his name: Bárczi) commented: "You have only been rehearsing with the orchestra for four days and already it sounds like the Philadelphia. Whoever may come after you, the sound will persist for two weeks—and then it will disappear."[6]

It is interesting that he should have noticed that sound. I could get the musicians to follow my instructions. Of course, the Budapest Philharmonic was a very good orchestra at the time and they really did *want* to play well. They did whatever I asked.

As a rule, if I notice that an orchestra is not cooperating, I say: "This makes no sense at all. I am leaving, good day to you." And I leave, too! Then of course they run after me and implore me to stay. I never quarrel. Either I get what I want or I don't. It's as simple as that.

BAV: Do you agree that each orchestra has a personality of its own?

EO: So they say . . .

BAV: You do not think so?

EO: Of course, they have their own personality but it can be changed. It is up to the conductor.

BAV: How can you change it in the course of a few rehearsals?

EO: It would take hours to explain in detail. Perhaps I could not even put it in words. You have to stand in front of the musicians and convince them that you *know* what you want.

BAV: What is it that takes precedence at rehearsals: verbal communication or gestures?

EO: It makes no difference whether the conductor talks a lot or not. I say very little. What counts is *what* you say with those few words.

BAV: Do you agree that your gestures give away your past as a violinist?

EO: There is something to that. I remember a concert in New York when I was sitting next to Olin Downes, the excellent music critic of the *New York Times*.[7] At one point he turned to me and asked: "This conductor was

---

6   Gusztáv Bárczi took over the music publisher Rózsavölgyi in 1908. His codirectors were Victor Alberti and Béla Ángyán.

7   Olin Downes (1886–1955), American music critic.

a pianist, wasn't he?" "I believe so," I replied. "I saw it immediately by the way he conducts." They say that my gestures are those of a former violinist.

BAV: Your past as an instrumentalist must be helpful in speaking the language of the string players of the orchestra. You can explain bowing to them and give them technical advice.

EO: The bowings are already in the parts. I have been in Philadelphia for thirty-eight years, I spent six years in Minneapolis, and I still do all the bowings of all the string instruments. That is what keeps me busy in the summer. Sometimes I get through sixty or seventy compositions in this way. When it comes to the rehearsal, I ask the musicians not to change anything. That's the way I want it. This is important, important, very important! George Szell also checked everything personally, even the wind parts! A conductor must know every instrument.

BAV: Do you ever feel nostalgia for the violin?

EO: No, I stopped playing a long time ago. I had two decent instruments, an Amati and a Balestrieri. I presented both to the orchestra, together with a Tourte-bow.[8] They are no use to me anymore: I have not touched a violin in thirty-five years.

BAV: Do you tour much with the orchestra?

EO: We tour a lot.

BAV: Also outside the United States?

EO: Yes, of course. We have just returned from China.

BAV: Why don't you take the orchestra to Hungary one day?

EO: It is up to my manager.

BAV: If you were invited, would you come?

EO: It does not depend on me, but on my manager.

BAV: As far as your program policy is concerned . . .

EO: Program policy? I do not know this word.

BAV: How do you determine the proportion of classical music, twentieth-century classics, and contemporary music?

---

8   Tommaso Balestrieri (1720–88 or 1790), Italian violin maker active in Cremona and Mantova. François Tourte (1747 or 1748–1835), French bow manufacturer, known as the "Stradivari of bows."

EO: When I came to Philadelphia in 1936, I was interviewed by a journalist. He asked me about the programs I wished to conduct, to meet every taste. I replied: you cannot satisfy everybody. Still, I shall attempt to do so. Each program will include a work everyone knows, one they do not know yet but must have heard about, and a new work as well. Ninety percent of the public are not musicians; this is something the conductor has to bear in mind. He should end each concert so that the public goes home whistling the main theme. I believe I have succeeded in achieving this: I am still here.

To my mind, a conductor is the musical chef of the city. He has to put together his programs—and also those of the guest conductors—to ensure that they can be digested by the public. The audience has to be served something great, from Bach and Buxtehude through the classical masters to the most recent music: it is important that they should also get to know that.

Conductors can rely on the orchestras, for they are first class. They have developed a great deal since the 1920s and 30s, although they were excellent then as well. At that time, however, they had difficulty playing a symphonic poem by Strauss, the *Heldenleben* or *Don Quixote*. Today those compositions feature on the repertoire of every orchestra all over the United States.

BAV: Does your budget allow for a necessary number of rehearsals?

EO: The top six orchestras in the United States give you four rehearsals of two and a half hours each. When I took up my position in Philadelphia, I had six three-hour rehearsals.

BAV: With less rehearsal time, you have to change your method, I suppose.

EO: It all depends on the conductor. One thing is for sure: an all-contemporary program is out of the question. A program like that poses too many technical difficulties; you do not have the time to master them all. I am sure you know Boulez: time and again, he has had to take a piece of his off the program one week before the concert, because of lack of sufficient rehearsal time.

BAV: The fact that orchestras do not play contemporary music regularly could also play a role.

EO: Not at all, not at all. In America, all the orchestras play modern music. They only need time to learn [the works]. Do not look down on American orchestras!

BAV: Of course not.

EO: Many Europeans do and that makes me very angry. The sound of our six best orchestras is absolutely unique in the world.

BAV: Everybody appreciates that. I am not expressing an opinion, just asking a question. It is just that so much attention is devoted to beautiful sound—having achieved that, what comes next?

EO: How can you say a thing like that? The sound is there as a matter of course, we never talk about it. You have to balance an orchestra!

Look, I am going to tell you a story. I was a young radio conductor. We were playing a classical program in a small studio, under difficult technical conditions. We only had two hours to rehearse; the concert was due to go on the air. "You must learn this, straight away!" I appealed to the violinists. "Let us play it slowly, then a bit faster, and finally in tempo." Nothing doing, I was still unhappy with the result. I lost my temper, I became angry. The first trombone player tried to calm me down by joking: "Maestro, never mind! We are going to play loud!"

In the end, it all went swimmingly. Alas I had got very worked up. I know it makes no sense for the conductor to lose his temper, but I do get nervous far too much. Less so with my own orchestra; mainly when I am guest-conducting. I used to guest-conduct until recently, but I have stopped now. After all, it can take a long time to teach a new piece. Look, I have eighteen first violins, sixteen second violins—let us just talk of them. Three-quarters of them take their parts home to practice. One-quarter does not—they are the ones who give me so much trouble.

BAV: It is like a school class. Some are bright, others are less so and often you have to adapt to the poor ones.

EO: Exactly. I believe a thing like that rarely happens in America, and even less in Philadelphia. As I have said, we are colleagues, we are friends. Incidentally, the last musician who played with Stokowski has just retired. Of the 106 musicians, each one is my man. However, when Stokowski comes to conduct us, the orchestra sounds exactly like forty years ago.[9]

BAV: That is due to the conductor's personality.

EO: That is his personality. Stokowski is a very great master.

BAV: He is also highly controversial.

EO: Yes, because he is no classical conductor. He has told me himself that he cannot conduct Haydn or Mozart.

---

9   At the time of our interview, Leopold Stokowski was still alive; he died in 1977.

BAV: And where are you most at home?

EO: Here, where we are sitting.

BAV: I mean, in music . . .

EO: Oh, in music? The question does not arise, I am at home in every style. I do not understand and do not feel the very latest music, ergo I do not conduct it. It makes no sense to conduct a work I do not regard as music. Others of course do.

I am sorry you [the Budapest orchestra] did not play yesterday the new Hungarian piece you have brought with you. What is the composer's name?

BAV: András Szőllősy. He was a pupil of Kodály and Petrassi.

EO: If he studied with Kodály, he must be excellent. Kodály and I became very good friends later on, and when he came to America with his first wife and many years later with his second wife, they were our guests at my summer house. We had a very good time. Kodály was no longer in good health, but after his arrival he went straight to his room, changed, and jumped right into the pool without saying a word. I was very worried and so was his wife because he was not supposed to swim. But he did not care.

BAV: What was your relationship with Bartók?

EO: We were friends, if I may use that word in connection with such a great master. I conducted the United States premiere of the *Divertimento* around 1940. I can still see him in my mind's eye, sitting in the first row of Carnegie Hall. After the performance, he came onstage and embraced me. He was satisfied.

BAV: You mentioned that you had studied with him in Budapest.

EO: Yes, rather indirectly. I was a pupil of Kodály and you had to be careful at that time . . . You needed to be tactful. Bartók never taught composition, it was Kodály's domain. At the age of eight, I joined the chamber music class of Leó Weiner. Hungarian music education was peerless in those years and I believe it still is. I never dreamed of becoming a conductor, but I had to learn conducting, orchestration, harmony—everything.

BAV: How did it come about that you have ended up as a conductor?

EO: By chance. I was a concertmaster in New York. Five minutes before the concert was due to begin, the conductor telephoned that he was feeling unwell. There was no one to take his place, so the manager asked me to step in as a matter of course. I mounted the podium, closed the score—one of the works on the program was Tchaikovsky's Fourth Symphony—and conducted the whole program by heart. I knew the pieces, for a concert-master must know everything, the entire repertoire, and all the parts of all the compositions. So do the soloists—pianists or violinists—so that they can check the balance of sound. Balance is the key to it all. Therein lies the secret of the Philadelphia Orchestra. Or rather, it is no secret, everyone with good ears is aware of it.

BAV: Finally: do you consider yourself a Hungarian conductor?

EO: I am American. I came to the United States in 1920, I was naturalized in 1927. I regard myself as an American of Hungarian birth. I am a citizen of the United States and I am proud of it. But I am also proud that I was born and educated in Hungary.

Philadelphia, 1973

HANS SWAROWSKY

1899–1975

egend has it that Hans Swarowsky was the illegitimate son of a Habsburg archduchess, who had gone to Budapest to deliver, in an attempt to avoid scandal back home. An attractive tabloid story, probably without a grain of truth. The fact is that Hans Swarowsky was born in the Hungarian capital.

That was where I met and interviewed him in 1974. He was conducting a concert and I attended one of his rehearsals. I can vividly recall him standing in front of the orchestra, an elderly, stocky gentleman in shirtsleeves, wearing braces, moving his right arm with mechanical regularity up and down, up and down. The music, whatever it may have been, sounded desperately dull.

Still, I was keen to talk to the man who was by then something of a legend, with Zubin Mehta and Claudio Abbado among his pupils. Also two young Hungarian conductors, the brothers Ádám and Iván Fischer.

Interviewing Swarowsky took some chutzpah (or lack of self-criticism), for my German was very poor indeed. What I did not realize at the time but am painfully aware of nearly forty years on, was my naiveté in holding my microphone to the mouth of a man, born in 1899, who had been an adult during the last war. It never occurred to me to question, at least in my mind, what it actually meant when he said he had left Switzerland to take up a position in Germany. It was a casual half sentence but it showed that he still felt there was nothing wrong with working in the Third Reich and admitting as much, through me, to listeners and readers of our conversation.

I wonder whether I would have asked for an interview in the first place, if I had known that Hans Swarowsky had been chief conductor of the Cracow Philharmonic Orchestra in what had been Nazi-occupied Poland and had conducted the world premiere of a work by Hans Pfitzner, dedicated to

Generalgouverneur *(Governor General) Hans Frank.*[1] *The dedicatee, known as the "Butcher of Poland," was sentenced to death and hanged in Nuremberg in 1946.*

If by any chance I had hinted at his role in Nazi Germany, he would probably have replied what he did in our interview in connection with Richard Strauss—that it had been an act of bravery to stay in Germany and to criticize (?) the regime from within.

Rereading my interview brought back the hazy memory of a brief meeting in Hungarian Radio with the German composer Werner Egk (1901–83). He was a friendly white-haired gentleman and I recorded a brief conversation with him in the studio, in blissful ignorance of his prominence in Nazi Germany. (Goebbels in his diary: "I am absolutely fascinated by his music and so is the Führer. He is a great discovery for us all.") It is another question, of course, why he was in Budapest in the first place and whose idea it had been for me to talk to him.

In any case, here is my interview with Hans Swarowsky, conducted in Budapest one year before his death.

o

Bálint András Varga (BAV): According to music encyclopedias, you were a pupil of Richard Strauss.

Hans Swarowsky (HS): I was not his pupil in the accepted sense of the word, but he took me under his wing, introducing me to the world of his music and improving my baton technique. We had met in Hamburg where I was conducting *Die Frau ohne Schatten* [The woman without a shadow]. He liked the performance, even thanked me before the curtain. Afterward, he said: "You did so well that I am going to tell you what I did *not* like. If I were not happy with your performance, I would not say a word."

He gave me advice, not only on that occasion but in the course of many more conversations. After the Anschluss, I settled in Switzerland. Strauss was living at the time in Baden near Zurich and we met regularly. I witnessed the gestation of his new compositions; we worked together on *Capriccio*, for instance.[2] I was sitting next to him when he was doing the instrumentation or making sketches. He let me fish from the wastepaper

---

1 Richard Strauss also composed a *Danklied* for Hans Frank for which he wrote the text as well (premiered on November 3, 1943).
2 The libretto of *Capriccio* was written jointly by Strauss and Clemens Krauss (1893–1954), with Swarowsky lending a hand.

basket the scraps of paper he had discarded, and to keep them. In this way, I have amassed quite a collection of his sketches.

Our relationship evolved into something of an intimate friendship which lasted for the rest of his life. When a contract bound me to Germany, we would also get together there pretty frequently. On the United States troops' occupation of Bavaria, I immediately made my way to his villa and arranged for two guards to be stationed in front of it, to make sure he would not be molested unnecessarily.

Strauss, you see, was misunderstood: people took it amiss that he had stayed in Germany. Of course, in those years people did not know what to make of their fellow citizens; those were difficult times. In Zurich I explained to Thomas Mann that in my view, it was the duty of the enemies of Nazism to stay in their native country, unless they had to flee for racial reasons, and to raise their critical voices at home. It was much simpler to fight against the Nazis from the outside. Strauss was misunderstood. Of course, all that is obsolete today, it is not worth talking about. I can, however, assert with conviction that Strauss never sided with the Nazis.

BAV: I have read a number of books in which the personality of Strauss is portrayed in some detail and have also learned about him from some of my interviewees. The British music critic Sir Neville Cardus, for instance, told me an anecdote to illustrate the composer's cynicism: on one occasion, when an English soprano desperately apologized for failing to do justice to her role in one of Strauss's operas, the composer comforted her by saying: "Never mind, the main thing is we had a full house."

HS: Yes. He could be ironic, but he was a highly cultured person of wide learning. He possessed a wonderful library and had actually read all his books. Drama literature was his prime concern, for he was anxious to master the science of dramaturgy. He said the most difficult thing in writing for the stage was to ensure that the characters entered and left the scene convincingly. He was also concerned about the dramaturgically correct placing of the characters onstage. *Rosenkavalier* works perfectly from that point of view, *Daphne* less so, for which Gregor's libretto was to blame.[3] The figures enter on one side and leave on the other, then come in again, with no apparent reason.

The whole issue was crystallized in *Capriccio*. It seeks to answer the question: what is more important, the words or the music? The opera ends

---

3   Joseph Gregor (1888–1960), Austrian theater scholar and writer. He wrote three opera librettos for Richard Strauss, *Friedenstag* (based on a story by Stefan Zweig), *Daphne*, and *Die Liebe der Danae* (after Hugo von Hofmannsthal).

without offering a solution. The libretto is reminiscent of the *Meistersinger*: it boils down to a theory of art in the guise of a plot. Strauss had the *Meistersinger* consciously in mind. Of course, there is a major difference between the two, for *Capriccio* is about the theater, whereas Wagner's opera is the theory of poetry set to music.

BAV: Did Strauss talk to you about his doubts regarding *Elektra*? Did he feel he had gone too far and would rather return to his style formed round the turn of the century?

HS: He did. He told me he could not understand what had got into his head when he composed *Salome* and *Elektra*. That's the way they turned out—he said. Later he balked at traversing the border of atonality. Schoenberg may have played a role there: he carried through what Strauss had broached and Strauss may well have been reluctant to have Schoenberg for company on that path. He declared that tonality had a host of unexploited possibilities still in store. He was true to his word, for he had so many ideas that gushed forth from his pen in a rich stream.

He possessed the admirable talent to notate his ideas straight into score. On many occasions, I would be sitting next to him in the Berliner Hof at Baden near Zurich, when he was writing his scores from top to bottom, without a rough copy, and without making a single correction.

BAV: Earlier, you talked of some sketches.

HS: He did write sketches, of course, but only to notate his themes. He did not need them for the orchestration. He used music paper manufactured in France and in view of the paper shortage, he orchestrated more economically to accommodate the music. He did that as masterfully as in his earlier compositions, only differently. I remember, for instance, that one of his works dispensed with a harp because there was no place for it on the paper.

BAV: According to Walter Legge, Elisabeth Schwarzkopf's husband, the founder of the Philharmonia Orchestra, Strauss was the greatest conductor of the century—and Legge knew everybody, including Toscanini.

HS: He was the most extraordinary conductor I have had occasion to meet. His gestures were tiny, to make the orchestra listen rather than look at him, for he believed that orchestral musicians were very well capable of playing their parts and listening to their colleagues at the same time. On another occasion, he said that a good conductor was superfluous from the second bar on. In other words, once he has determined the tempo and got the performance going. You need not take that too seriously, it was only by way of a bon mot.

As far as his operas were concerned, he was only concerned about the quality of productions in Vienna, Dresden, Berlin, and Munich. Other theaters did not interest him, as long as the royalties came in. He said they could not play his operas properly anyway. He was impressed if a small company invested a great deal of energy in preparing a work of his but maintained that for all their efforts, their production could never attain a high level, for they could not afford artists of the first rank. Only those four cities mattered to him, Dresden even more than the others. Dresden had to have the world premieres, otherwise his operas were bound to flop—on that point he was superstitious. He was proven right when the first performance of *Die ägyptische Helena* took place in Vienna and ended in a fiasco.[4] He said to me: "You see, here is the proof!"

Strauss was a real socialite. He never lacked money, for his operas earned him a lot, but not as much as he would have deserved. He asked me once to compute Wagner's income and compare it to the money others had made on his works. I started with Leichner, Wagner's barber in Munich, who alone made more money than his one-time customer. Leichner earned millions, especially after he was appointed court barber to the Emperor. And then there were the theaters, the orchestras, the singers, the managers.

BAV: You were a pupil and friend of Richard Strauss and subsequently studied with Arnold Schoenberg.

HS: I first saw Schoenberg in the Vienna Opera House when he was conducting *Gurrelieder*.[5] I admired the work no end and was enthusiastic about the composer's incredibly precise, secure conducting—in fact, his whole being. After the concert, I asked him to take me on as his pupil. He wanted to know why. I then named my professor at the Academy, notorious for his retrograde views on music. "Because he is my teacher right now!" Schoenberg laughed and said yes.

Studying with him was an unforgettable experience. He taught me, like the ancient Greeks, peripatetically; a single lesson was worth more than years at the Academy. I was really in awe of his wisdom.

---

4   Swarowsky erred here, for *Die ägyptische Helena* did receive its premiere in Dresden, on June 6, 1928. On the other hand, *Ariadne auf Naxos* was premiered in Stuttgart (1912) and *Die Frau ohne Schatten* in Vienna (1919).

5   The concert took place on June 13, 1920. Schoenberg conducted the Vienna Philharmonic, a huge chorus consisted of four Viennese choirs and soloists whose names are more or less forgotten today.

I was a regular visitor to the so-called Schönberg-Verein, that is, the "Society for Private Musical Performances," which represented Vienna's spiritual elite before Hitler's takeover. I heard renditions of contemporary music with the Kolisch Quartet, Eduard Steuermann, and other noted artists.[6] Orchestral works were played by us, students, in arrangements for piano duet. In this way, we could become acquainted with the structure of compositions that we could not perform in their original forms. The concerts of the Society were of course attended by Webern and Berg as well.

When Schoenberg left for Holland, my duties kept me in Vienna, so I became a pupil of Webern. His analyses were unique; their influence on my thinking has not waned to this day. Webern was incomparable also as a person. He came from the country and was full of warmth, a love of life and nature, a passion for art. It was an experience just to breathe the same air with him. The sincerity and depth of his emotions are mirrored in his works. Their brevity is made up for by their profundity. Like Schoenberg, he had also been influenced by Mahler. Mahler was fond of Webern—he felt a fatherly affection toward him. He could not fathom his idiom, but declared that the development of music was logically headed in that direction.

I participated in the preparation of many Webern premieres. I did the coaching, just like my friend, Hanns Eisler, with whom I also took lessons. He had joined Schoenberg and his circle earlier than me. I was impressed by his vitality both as a man and as a teacher. Next to Webern and Berg, Schoenberg's most important pupils were Eisler and Karl Rankl— Schoenberg himself thought highly of them.[7]

To get back to the Verein for a moment: the concerts were attended by many great musicians, such as Busoni, Ravel, and Bartók, whom I grew very fond of. Sadly, I never heard him play. Of the significant Hungarian artists of that period, I only heard concerts by Dohnányi and Hubay.[8]

BAV: Lovro von Matačić says conducting cannot be taught.[9] This is what he said: "I cannot teach how you *must* conduct; I can only tell you how you *must not* do it." Your activity at the Vienna Academy belies that statement.

HS: Matačić's opinion does not make sense. It is a witty paradox, nothing else. Music is the only art where even the dullest can make a career. Music,

---

6   Founded in 1921 by Rudolf Kolisch (1896–1978), the quartet was dissolved on his emigration to the United States in 1944. Eduard Steuermann (1892–1964), Austrian pianist and composer.

7   Karl Rankl (1898–1968), Austrian composer and conductor.

8   Jenő Hubay (1858–37), Hungarian violinist and composer. He was also an important teacher, with Joseph Szigeti, Stefi Geyer, Zoltán Székely, and Emil Telmányi among his pupils. Between 1919 and 1934, Hubay was director of the Budapest Academy of Music.

9   Lovro von Matačić (1899–1985), Croatian conductor and composer.

you see, has nothing to do with reality. Conducting—just as composition, for that matter—can be taught. It only requires intelligence.

We have indeed succeeded in setting up an excellent school in Vienna. Our basic principle is that the essence of a composition can only be learned from the composition itself. In other words, not from an interpretation or description of it. Only from the piece itself. Our motto is: do not look for *what* is in the score, but *why*. Of course, if we raise that question, we start out from the assumption that the composer himself was clear about the meaning of every single tone he had put in the score. Some composers, however famous they may be, were no masters. Tchaikovsky or Wagner, for instance, wrote highly effective music but could not account for every note, unlike Beethoven or Brahms. Brahms especially.

In any case, the "why" is the basis of our teaching; it helps us to get to know the compositions from inside. My pupils acquire a secure grounding in this way and it enables them to assess compositions. As a result, they need not experiment with tempos, they hit upon the correct one—for the tempo is the only aspect of music that the composer cannot indicate in the score. He may give a tempo marking but it has to be interpreted—and that is not easy. Records provide the clinching proof: the same work can be played in so many different tempos, even though, obviously, only one is correct, that which is closest to the composer's concept.

In addition to theory, we also provide technical training; I received the basis for that from Strauss. He meant to write a book on conducting, made innumerable notes, but never had time to actually formulate it. Eventually, he asked me to put it in writing, based on his instructions. We conducted long conversations on the subject, especially in Switzerland, and both of us were taking notes. My restless life is to blame that the book has not been written to date. I hope I shall manage one day. I cannot find the time because in my advanced age I have small children; the youngest one is two years old. I hope they will outlive me by many decades. In any case, they will still be going to school when I am no longer around. I must work hard to secure their future. That is why I cannot find the quiet necessary for writing a book.

BAV: As a pupil of Strauss, Schoenberg, and Webern you also studied composition; the principles underlying your teaching also presuppose some knowledge of composition.

HS: Ideally, a conductor should be superior to composers as far as technique is concerned. He has to know as much about composition as the composer does, without writing music himself. Ideally, too, the conductor should know as much about instruments as the players. He must also be capable of leading a large body of people, and especially of transmitting what he knows. Those who cannot teach conducting, cannot master compositions properly either—they will have to fall back upon improvising. Matačić is a conductor like that. We went to the same school, sat next to each other for eight years. He is a wholly different type of conductor from me; I analyze form down to the smallest detail.

I know Stravinsky's scathing diatribes against a number of conductors, including Furtwängler. I agree with them down to the ground. Stravinsky was a master who lived among us. He was incensed by the superficiality with which his works were performed, in violation of his wishes. After all, he took pains to indicate everything in the score very precisely, down to the metronome markings. If he later changed anything, it has to be regarded as a revision, the master's revision. No one else has the right to make alterations. He expected his compositions to be played exactly as he notated them, without "dressing" them up. He was a living example.

We know from Beethoven's biographies that whenever a work of his was played in his absence, his first question was: "What was the tempo like?" Nothing else interested him. Of course, such anecdotes have to be taken with a grain of salt, because a great deal was written about him after his death which may have sounded interesting but was not true.

Budapest, 1974

IVÁN AND ÁDÁM
FISCHER FISCHER

b. 1951 b. 1949

The preceding interview with Hans Swarowsky was published in my book
Muzsikusportrék *(Musicians' Portraits) by Editio Musica Budapest
(EMB) in 1979. I was in loose contact at the time with his Hungarian pupils,
the brothers Ádám and Iván Fischer; their father, the translator and conductor Sándor Fischer, had been my colleague in Hungarian Radio.*

*One day, the three of them came to my office at EMB and I recorded
a conversation with the younger Fischers, to draw a portrait of Swarowsky
from their perspective. They were relentlessly frank in their opinions (I can
still hear in my mind's ear their father's chuckle in the background). Also, they
were remarkably polite: they never interrupted one another. What could easily have been a debate were instead two separate interviews.*

*Nearly forty years have passed since, and both Ádám and Iván have es-
tablished themselves as conductors of international prestige—they have done
Swarowsky proud. Ádám, for instance, has founded the orchestra Österreich-
Ungarische Haydn Philharmonie and has given some exemplary performances of Haydn's symphonies. He has also appeared in Bayreuth and conducted much admired concert performances of Wagner operas in Budapest.*

*Iván established the Budapest Festival Orchestra in 1983 and has de-
veloped it into one of the top European ensembles. Miraculously enough, he
has succeeded in keeping it alive under the most adverse circumstances in a
politically and economically unstable country and has in addition carried
on an international career quite independently from his orchestra, restrict-
ing his conducting to five groups, including the Berlin Philharmonic and the
Concertgebouw.*

I thought it would be only decent to inform them of my intention to include our conversation in this book and ask them for their permission. Ádám agreed; Iván asked me to include his mail below.

o

April 30, 2012

Dear Bálint,

I can remember the text very well; also that I was never really happy with it. I feel we were too critical of Swarowsky (or rather, I was too critical; I cannot speak for Ádám).

I was unfair, for Swarowsky was a great man, a typical representative of the generation of "neue Sachlichkeit" [new objectivity]. We, his pupils, were perhaps irritated by his one-sidedness, but his tremendous knowledge, his talent, his devotion and his ability to spotlight the essence of the conductor's job are perfectly evident (and were evident at the time). What remains of his fanatical teaching is respect for the Composition. Also, the guiding principle that the conductor should seek to understand and perform the Work rather than be preoccupied with his own interpretation. Over the past decades, I have more and more identified with Swarowsky's principles and now accept that any interpretation is superfluous.

The role of the conductor could best be likened to Aaron's who transmitted Moses's ideas.

Greetings,

Iván

o

Iván Fischer

Iván Fischer (IF): If you wish to measure a conductor by the standards of Klemperer, Furtwängler, or Karajan—all of them magnetic personalities with a radiation all their own—then Hans Swarowsky was a very poor conductor. He had no radiation to speak of, he was not magnetic by any means; as conductors go, he was wholly mediocre. However, he never intended to be like Furtwängler or Karajan. His goal was to change conventions. From that point of view, his work was a milestone.

Around the turn of the century, conductors had a rather free approach to music; rehearsing was not their forte. Nikisch comes to mind as a good example. He was followed by Mahler who set great store by rehearsals, worked thoroughly, and had a galvanizing personality. Toscanini was the first one to keep strictly to the score; he did not tolerate a *rallentando* or *accelerando*, unless it was prescribed by the composer. He was succeeded by prima-donna conductors exemplified by Karajan and Bernstein: for their generation, the accent was not on the music but on who was wielding the baton.

That is what many Swarowsky students turned against. First and foremost Abbado and Mehta, who reinstated Toscanini's strict adherence to the score.

Swarowsky was also an enemy of the cult of conductors and did his best to debunk them. For instance, he averred that compositions were actually performed by the orchestra; conductors were no artists at all, their job was merely to beat time and make sure that the musicians ended the piece together. In his view, art was executed by orchestras.

Swarowsky was a dedicated advocate of German and Austrian music. He did not know much about composers preceding Bach or those active in the twentieth century. He defended Bach, Mozart, Haydn, Beethoven, Schubert, Bruckner, Brahms, and Mahler against any other kind of music as well as against a romantic approach. He strove for the authentic interpretation of the classics but lacked the talent to put it into practice. He had learned, for instance, that in classical music rhythm was freer than indicated in the score—but what that actually meant, which note was to be shorter or longer, was not quite clear to him. He would, for instance, ask a flautist at a rehearsal to read Philipp Emmanuel Bach's book, which will tell him that quarter notes were not to be played evenly.[1] "Please play it freely," he said. With nothing more tangible to go by, the flautist was just as much at a loss as to what he was actually supposed to do as before. In other words, that was about as far as Swarowsky could go. Do not play this way but some other way. Exactly how—finding that out would be the job of the next generation.

Bálint András Varga (BAV): Did he only tell you, his pupils, what you should *not* do?

IF: He was a negative teacher. Yes, I think that is the best way of putting it. He whittled away at our gestures that smacked of romanticism and

---

1 Carl Philipp Emanuel Bach, *Versuch über die wahre Art das Clavier zu spielen*, part 1 (Berlin, 1753); part 2 (Berlin, 1762).

tradition. If one of us took himself for a second Karajan, Swarowsky disabused him of it in no time. If we launched into an explanation that the famous chord of the *Egmont* overture came directly from the depths of Hell, Swarowsky stopped to remind us that Hell had nothing to do with it; it was D minor and G major. Then he made us sit down and listen to the orchestra playing without a conductor. And the orchestra played far better than with the young man flailing his arms on the podium.

On occasions like that, it began to dawn on us that the old ways of conducting were irrelevant. Our thinking underwent a transformation; we started to read books, do some research as to how music was actually to be played, what was missing from our approach, how we could make our interpretation better. He was not out to bring something about, but to kill off something in his pupils. If someone conducted a beautiful *rallentando* and Swarowsky did not like it, we had to listen to that passage in tempo, then again slowing down, and he proved that his concept was superior.

BAV: Did he teach you the basics, such as baton technique, what you have to do with your right hand and your left hand?

IF: Yes, he taught those things very well. He was highly intelligent and an excellent teacher. A glance at someone told him immediately whether he would make a good conductor. If he found a candidate without talent, he did not bother much about him and let him get on with it without interfering.

BAV: Was everybody admitted to the Academy?

IF: The entrance exam was not particularly stiff, many young people were admitted. What counted for Swarowsky was trumpeting his convictions and the more people he had in his class, the happier he was.

At the end of class, as we were streaming out of the room, we did our best to get close to him as he was descending the stairs, so as to hear what he was saying, to catch his remarks. That was perhaps my most important experience at the Academy, this fawning on him, which was done by everybody and which he enjoyed very much. He exploited it too.

As a personality, he was a mysterious and unpredictable blend of the humanist and the cynic. He advertised his views all his life with obsession—but he conducted a great many poor concerts and told us things like instead of trying to hypnotize the orchestra, we should count how much money we were making with each beat.

BAV: He must have taken that from Strauss.

IF: Possibly. He also boasted that he had been a close friend of the Webern family. The composer's daughter told me a different story: in the prewar years Swarowsky had been a regular visitor only because they cooked well and Swarowsky could have a free meal. Where the truth lies, I do not know. Swarowsky was no doubt cynical but he was also an idealist. Politically, he sympathized with the left, he even advocated communist ideals, but lived the life of a wealthy bourgeois.

He tolerated no contradiction, he was a real dictator. On one occasion, he was rehearsing in the Opera House and insisted that the orchestra take a faster tempo. The musicians protested that it was impossible to play any faster; the singers were also up in arms. No matter, he stuck to his opinion fanatically. Why—it is difficult to say now. Perhaps he was thinking to himself that the singers lacked a proper technique as did the musicians in the orchestra, that's why they could not play any faster—and faster they should have been playing. But he may also have been guided by idealism: the pureness and authenticity of the composition were to be guarded, a principle from which he would not budge in the face of whatever opposition. He was also cynical: he conducted the last movement of Beethoven's Fourth Symphony so fast that the bassoonist was often hard put to it to play his part properly. Swarowsky's reply was that in that case, the bassoon solo should be omitted, but the fast tempo would be adhered to.

BAV: Was he a good teacher?

IF: Very much so. He was a fantastic teacher. He was a sensational teacher. Even now, years later, I notice that I am wondering what he would be saying. He had boundless self-confidence. He made his pronouncements with so much self-assurance that he gave us a sense of security. Without having studied a particular work with him, I know how it would be conducted by Hans Swarowsky. Today I am aware of his limitations and have turned against eighty per cent of what he taught us. But the twenty per cent that remain continue to help me immeasurably.

o

Ádám Fischer

Ádám Fischer (AF): To my mind, what mattered was not so much *what* he taught us, for I did not necessarily agree with everything he said. He helped us to develop methodical thinking—that was what counted. I owe it to him that I know what is relative about musical interpretation; I have learned from him not to take over anything uncritically.

He eradicated a great deal of traditional mannerisms, *rallentandi*, changes of tempo that we revered as sacred because they were common currency among conductors. They are not in the score, he admonished us, keep away from them. That set us wondering as to why conductors would slow down there all the same—and as far as I am concerned, I do slow down despite Swarowsky's warning, but now I do so consciously, I know *why* I do that. I learned from Swarowsky what interpretation was on the one hand and composition on the other, and I do not mix up the two.

Swarowsky was such a great personality that you became a more valuable person just through spending two or three years in his company. It took us about a year to grasp what he was about. In the second year, we were well-equipped to follow his train of thought.

Bálint András Varga (BAV): What personal memories have you kept of his classes?

AF: I was conducting Brahms's Third Symphony and he stood right next to me, his arms folded, and watched me as if I was a peculiar sort of animal. I felt increasingly ill at ease and eventually stopped. Swarowsky patted me on the back and said: "You will make a lot of money one day. People love the sort of public show of lust that you put on in front of the orchestra. True, the musicians will not play any better for that, but that does not matter."

He used a stronger word than "lust" but I prefer not to quote him. His remarks were overheard by the class and also by the orchestra: Swarowsky was obviously out to humiliate me. As a rule, I take things like that very much to heart, they eat away at me for years, but in his case I did not mind. Perhaps because his self-irony was just as scathing—and because I knew he meant well.

BAV: The classes were attended by all the pupils and you took turns in conducting the orchestra?

AF: First of all, we discussed the piece on the third floor. We called those classes precisely that: "third floor," while "first floor" stood for orchestral practice. On the third floor, we discussed a work in theory, on the first floor we took turns performing it, perhaps not the same movement or just a section of it.

BAV: Who made up that unfortunate orchestra?

AF: It was called a "trade union orchestra," comprised of elderly musicians and students. Swarowsky did not let us rehearse: we would learn how to do that later on anyway, and the orchestra would not be any better as a result. He was right.

BAV: I have the impression that your education lacked some basic elements. Conductors have to know how to talk to musicians, how to mold their playing, suggest solutions, and so on.

AF: Those who wanted to learn things like that would do better to study elsewhere—that was his position. What he taught us could be learned from nobody else.

If you ask concert goers, 95 percent will tell you they have no idea what the conductor is gesticulating for: the musicians are only looking at their parts anyway. I would go further and say that even some conductors do not know what beating is for.

I usually liken the orchestra to a car that runs both ways: you either change gear by hand or switch to automatic drive. If the conductor changes gear skillfully, the car will run better than if it is left to fend for itself. Poor drivers, however, had better switch to automatic gear, in other words, let the orchestra take care of itself, for it works better that way. Many conductors are not aware that frequently there are no more than four or five tricky places in the score that need conducting, the rest can be left to the orchestra. Of course, there are those who prefer to change to automatic gear right from the start—and make a career that way. Those are the ones who will come a cropper in operas, because there you really do have to conduct. That was what Swarowsky taught us: the language of the baton. What to tell the flautist or the percussionist can be learned elsewhere.

BAV: Mehta, Abbado?

AF: They have taken over a lot from Swarowsky and sometimes when I hear them conduct, I have to laugh even today. Swarowsky, you see, had some fads. For instance, he said that you have to beat eight to the first bar of Schubert's Third Symphony; the fermata on it *naturally* means that it has to be held for seven beats. Or, this is *piano*, that is, *selbstverständlich* [naturally] *forte*, because *piano* means that its *effect* is *piano*, but it has to be played *forte*, in the upper register. There are many "fermatas" in music literature that Mehta or Abbado do exactly the same way, to four or eight beats—which does not matter, of course, because you can also hold it for ten beats, provided you have built up the necessary tension. For Mehta and Abbado that is a kind of "hommage à Swarowsky."

He had problems with tempi: he could not keep them. Therefore he taught us that before we begin a movement, we should imagine its fastest bar and adjust the rest to that. We are prone to begin too fast and when we get to that particular section, we have to slow down. As far as slow tempo was concerned, he suggested we should say a text in our minds—for instance, *Selbstverständlichkeit, Selbstverständlichkeit* which we cannot say any faster—that gives us the right tempo—tatatatata-tatatatata.

He hated Karl Böhm and Böhm hated him; we understood they had conceived their mutual antipathy during their student days. Here is a typical remark of Swarowsky: "At least I owe one thing to Böhm—he has helped me conduct the second movement of the *Pastoral* Symphony. All I need to say, like a prayer, is *"Böhm ist doch der Beste, Böhm ist doch der Beste"* [Böhm is after all the best one] and I have the tempo. Swarowsky suggested that we do likewise before starting with the movement.

His presence of mind was admirable, his reflexes were amazingly fast. Two examples: if he was tired, he made one faux pas after another at the rehearsals. On one occasion, right in the middle of a huge *forte*, the orchestra fell apart. He made them stop and asked: "Why was the double bassoon not playing?" Whereupon the bassoon player: "Herr Professor, I was playing all right!" "You missed your entry, why are you lying to me?" "Herr Professor, I did enter on time, only you did not hear me."

All of us were wondering what Swarowsky would do next. After all, he had been offended: a player alleged that he could not hear an entry. Swarowsky worked himself up into a tremendous rage, turned red in the face and shouted: "Do you think I can hear whether you are playing in a *forte* like that?! There are so many notes, I cannot hear them all. I looked at you and saw that you were not blowing into the mouthpiece!"

That incident occurred with the orchestra of the Academy. The other one was even more embarrassing, for it involved the Vienna Symphony Orchestra. They react immediately if the conductor makes a mistake. I think they were playing Mahler's Seventh Symphony. Swarowsky had lost his bearings, he kept on beating while feverishly turning the pages. The orchestra was playing until he gave someone a cue, whereupon the orchestra broke up and eventually stopped. "Why weren't you playing?" he pointed at one of the musicians at a desk in the back. The player did not even bother to reply. "I gave you a big cue like this and you did not enter. It's your fault that the whole orchestra has fallen apart. We have no time to wait for you!"

That was too much for the player. "Herr Professor, I had twenty more bars before my entry. But because you gave me a cue, I did enter and that's why the orchestra broke up."

The blood froze in our veins: what would Swarowsky do now? He reached in his pocket ever so slowly, produced his huge black-rimmed spectacles, looked up and asked: "Why, what is your instrument?" The man held up his horn. "Oh, I am sorry. I thought you played the trumpet. You have a sort of trumpeter's head." He had a wonderful sense of self-irony and could always save a situation with it.

BAV: I am sorry, it sounds as if he was a charlatan.

AF: Not at all! He knew what he knew and what he did not know. For instance, he had a poor memory and was afraid of conducting by heart. He taught us therefore that in addition to learning the score we should also make a mental note: here come eight bars *forte*, followed by eight bars *piano*. Then we could conduct it from memory. Of course, we did not take it literally, we translated it into his language. What he was actually out to inculcate in us was not to be afraid of conducting by heart and, importantly, to memorize the structure of the composition. If we know that eight bars are like this and eight bars like that, then we could concentrate on what was within those units.

His knowledge was immense. If I have not made it clear enough, it is because he was a great teacher thanks to what he did *not* know. One thing is certain: he was an outstanding representative of his generation. He was admirably well-read, he had a huge library. I also began to think highly of his human qualities when he was operated on in 1973. His will to live, his courage and stamina were unprecedented. When it was rumored that Swarowsky was dying, Josef Krips volunteered to write his obituary. However, Swarowsky was determined to recover—and he did. Half a year after his operation for [a] brain tumor, he conducted in the Opera House, flew to Japan and to Berlin. He never stopped working. And he read out the obituary at Josef Krips's funeral.

INSTRUMENTALISTS

ALFRED BRENDEL

b. 1931

I do not mind admitting to a character trait of mine that has not left me with advancing age: a laming shyness in the face of genuine greatness.

In the 1970s, when Alfred Brendel gave a number of solo recitals in Budapest, I did a radio interview and later on a television interview with him and he invited me to his hotel for lunch. I suppose he did not know anybody in the city and preferred my company to a lonely meal.

Making conversation with the great artist whose recordings of Schubert sonatas (a thick album of LPs) was the object of my boundless admiration proved extremely difficult. My solution to overcoming a temporarily paralyzed brain (I felt I was supposed to carry on a brilliant conversation and just could not think of anything to say) was to ask one silly question after another.

Initially, Brendel seemed quite willing to reply and told me of his background, which I seem to remember was a mixture of Czech, Austrian, Italian, and perhaps also of Croatian blood. In any case, all of a sudden, I became keenly aware of the moment he gave up on me. We reached the end of our lunch all right but I knew I had not qualified.

Sometime—weeks or months—later, we met in London. All I can recall is that I was waiting for the lift to take me downstairs (was it in a hotel? a restaurant?). When it did turn up, one of the people who got out was Alfred Brendel. He caught sight of me—and turned his head away. The intense humiliation I felt then is still very much with me. I knew he was right: I had nothing to offer—which made it that much worse.

The interview took place in Brendel's hotel room.[1] He had given me ten minutes, so that to gain time I spoke as fast as I possibly could. In the end, we

---

1 Varga, *Muzsikusportrék.*

*talked for well over half an hour and after I had switched off the tape recorder
and put on my coat, he was still talking. Standing at the door, ready to leave,
I turned on the machine again, to record his "encore." And Brendel carried on
when I was already in the corridor: "Tonight at the Academy," he said, "the
audience is going to hear some real pianos!"*

*That was true, but the concert started late. We did not know what
was happening: the hall was full, the lights were on but the door on the
right-hand side of the stage through which artists would enter just would
not open. We waited patiently but with growing uneasiness. Tension subsided when János Kovács, the artistic director of the concert organization
National Philharmonia, entered through a side door and took his accustomed place in row ten, I believe it was, next to his friend, the leading music
critic, György Kroó.*

Seconds later, Brendel appeared on stage and applause erupted.

*As I learned a few days later, he had refused to play because he was
unhappy with the piano. He had tested all the instruments the Academy had
to offer but none was up to the mark. János Kovács eventually succeeded
in convincing him that it would not be quite right to disappoint the audience waiting for him. The instrument Brendel had eventually settled on was
a Steinway B model, smaller than the grand piano we were used to seeing/
hearing at concerts. Of course, having just read his book* Musical Thoughts
and Afterthoughts, *which, published in 1976, was quite new at the time, the
care he took in selecting the piano on which he was willing to play and the
lengths to which he was ready to go in making sure that it would be in opti-
mal condition came as no surprise.*

*In my introduction to the Hungarian translation of the interview, I
commented on his eyes behind his thick glasses—the intelligent, smiling,
and ironical glance with which he looked at me—and also on his front
teeth, the two incisors that were unusually prominent and modified his
appearance, somewhat contradicting the intellectual, professorial impression he made. It was those teeth that helped me unwind and feel free to
ask my questions.*

*One more detail before proceeding to the actual conversation. During
the course of his recital, I was somewhat disturbed by the way he would tear
his hands off the keyboard, usually at the end of a movement but also after
a forte chord, as if it had burned the tips of his fingers. We had discussed the
extraneous aspects of piano playing in our interview that afternoon when he
demonstrated for me all the different variations of removing his hands from
the keys, using the table as a substitute. I thought he was joking or perhaps
making fun of the mannerisms of his colleagues—perhaps I even laughed. I*

*hope he did not mind: in the evening, I realized that he had actually shown
me his repertoire of gestures.*

o

Bálint András Varga (BAV): Your book *Musical Thoughts and Afterthoughts*
impresses your readers with your erudition. How have you succeeded in
keeping the spontaneity of your playing intact?

Alfred Brendel (AB): It presents no problem for me at all. The question
will only emerge for those who have read the book. They may indeed be
wondering how it is possible for someone who *thinks* so much about music, to also *feel* it. My attitude is different. I feel the music and in doing so,
I become aware of certain things. What comes to my mind, then, is the
outcome of a process rather than the input. In my view, this is the only
possible and valid approach to analyzing music. Artur Schnabel was of the
same conviction, incidentally.

BAV: Is it necessary do you think for an artist to have experienced in his
own life emotions expressed by the music so that he can fully perceive the
emotional range of a composition? Is he only able to render the infinite
sadness of the second movement of Schubert's Sonata in B-flat Major, if he
has been exposed to such sadness in his own life?

AB: It is necessary for the artist to possess, at least in a latent manner, the
capacity to experience such emotions. I should not say that he must have
experienced the full range of emotions mirrored by the music—that would
be well-nigh impossible. He must have the power of imagination that enables him to conjure up such emotions.

This is a mysterious thing. The Brontë sisters come to mind, those great
nineteenth-century British writers, who hardly ever left their father's par-
ish and only drew their experiences from books. They are nevertheless important writers whose work is marked by tremendous emotional charge.

I also think of an interview with a theater director that I read recently.
He says some of the best Shakespearean actors have no clear idea of what
they actually say onstage. And yet they can play their roles convincingly.
All that may sound odd but some people communicate the message of a
work like mediums.

Of course, I have no truck with that. I always seek to relive the emotions I felt when I first met with a work. I endeavor to experience them
again and again, and forget everything that I know about the composition.

Actually, it is not as difficult as it may appear. I then approach it anew and gain new experiences which may well lead to similar results as before—but the process itself is in any case fresh.

BAV: I am deeply affected by what you have just described because I am saddened by my inability to relive the tremendous thrill I had when I first heard the "Waldstein" Sonata on the radio or Bach's F-Minor Piano Concerto. Hearing them again, I find it impossible to recapture the same excitement.

AB: The performer is in a lucky position because he does not need to make do with listening to a recording a second time. He plays the piece himself. There may be neurotic artists who always perform a work in exactly the same way as when they had first "put it together." Like a computer—you press the button and hear exactly the same thing. I am different. I may be surprised by aspects of a composition even after having analyzed it down to its minute details. That is what makes a masterpiece: we always find something new in it.

BAV: You mentioned actors a while ago. Don't you think that performing musicians and actors have something in common? Both have to fill with life a text written by somebody else.

AB: Yes, there is a similarity. For me, musical compositions are often like so many characters. Each has its own merits and flaws, each has its circumscribed possibilities within which they can move—but they cannot transcend their boundaries. Those individual characteristics distinguish one work from another and for me, analyzing them, finding out what makes them unique is one of the most fascinating occupations. Merely to look for features they have in common would be too easy, too primitive.

BAV: Can you think of, say, Schubert's Sonata in B-flat Major as one personality? After all, the four movements are so different in character. Would it not be better to think of them as four distinct personalities or, perhaps, members of one family? I can more easily accept Liszt's B-Minor Sonata as one personality.

AB: The movements are, of course, different in character but always within a particular range. I see them in their balance. They either balance each other out—as in most Beethoven sonatas—or lead toward the culmination of the last movement, as in the late Beethoven sonatas or string quartets. The last movement can also be a kind of postscript, as in the case of the

Schubert sonata you mentioned. Obviously, it does not serve as a balance to the first movement, as it does in the A-Major Sonata.

BAV: Would it be anathema for you to think of music in concrete images? To stay with Schubert's Sonata in B-flat Major, have you thought of the trill in the left hand as distant thunder?[2]

AB: I very much think in those terms, if it helps to get nearer to the emotional world of a work. Much has been written of that trill, incidentally—for instance, that there is something upsetting, something frightening about it, or that it disrupts the cantilena. I do not agree. For me, the trill is the third dimension; it lends depth to the theme. It is part of the theme. The trill on the minor sixth is preceded by the major sixth in the middle voice of the fourth and fifth bars of the theme. The alternation of the two intervals plays a major role in the movement, in the entire composition, indeed in all three late sonatas. It is one of the motivic elements which unify the three works. Therefore, the trill for me is necessary; it has no disturbing effect whatsoever. On the contrary, it enhances the process of the music, although, when it first appears, it seems to be halting it. Without the trill, the theme would end. It is, in other words, the active element as against the relative passivity of the melody.

BAV: Instrumentalists never seem to comment on the sheer physical pleasure of playing, of mastering an instrument purely in a technical sense.

AB: Some people may derive pleasure from it—for me, it is wholly immaterial. I am glad if I succeed in playing something well technically, but never as an end in itself, only as a means of serving the music. It is impossible to consider technique by itself, separately from the music. I would not even know how to go about it because the two are so closely linked together.

BAV: Concentration is another subject one rarely hears about. Is the capacity of focusing for hours on end on practicing or playing on the concert stage the result of training or is it something one is born with?

AB: While practicing, concentration may be affected by the weather. If air pressure is low or is sinking, if the air has a high concentration of humidity, especially in late afternoon, I find concentration difficult. Physically, too, I cannot relax as much as would be necessary. If it is hard going, I prefer to stop. I never have such difficulties in the morning, even if I have been

---

2   Needless to say, it would never occur to me now, in 2011, to liken the trill to distant thunder. Back in 1978, I may have heard music more naively than I do today.

practicing for three hours without interruption. While giving a concert, I try not to think of such things at all.

BAV: In your book, you go into considerable detail about coping with the piano as a complicated piece of equipment so that it properly serves the purpose it was built for. What exactly do you mean by having a "voicing instrument?" Do you carry it around with you?

AB: This time I forgot to bring it with me, this is such a quick trip from London and back. The tool I use consists of a handle with one to three thin voicing needles, rather like the ones used for sowing. I apply them to the felt pads of the hammers. Even if the felt has hardened, it is prone to change. In fact, after each recital there are some notes on the piano which stand out too loud and these notes should be restored to the general level. The goal is for the keys from top to bottom to have the same dynamic intensity. The intensity should always be even; what comes out dynamically should be up to the player's fingers. Very often—as in this hall—one has the impression that the piano is playing the music and all the pianist can do is listen and despair. This is due to the lack of voicing.

Arturo Benedetti Michelangeli is one of the pianists who attach importance to this and while he does not do it himself, he has a technician he trusts who takes care of it for him. Paul Badura-Skoda and Jörg Demus have also learned voicing and apply it regularly out of despair because instruments are so rarely looked after properly. There is a shortage of reliable experts.

BAV: In your book, you point out the need for pianists to listen to their own playing so that they bear in mind what comes across to the audience. How can one make music in such a schizophrenic state of mind?

AB: Over the years, one becomes accustomed to that peculiar condition. One can actually do several—even contradictory—things at once. Before the concert, I usually go to the hall to try out the instrument.

BAV: The acoustics are of course different with no people in the stalls.

AB: That is true, but I do nevertheless go there to get a feel of the place, so as to at least have some idea of what to expect in the evening. If at all possible, I attend a concert the day before, to assess the acoustics from the audience's point of view. When it comes to my sitting onstage, I start by concentrating on the sound the piano is making. Of course, it may be misleading, for what I am hearing is different from what people can hear in the floor seats, in the gallery, close to or far from the podium, to the left or to the right. We cannot satisfy everybody but we must find some democratic solution.

BAV: If you have to worry so much about the piano and are often irritated by some members of the public (they cough, fidget about, and so on), why don't you draw the same conclusion as Glenn Gould and withdraw to the recording studio?[3]

AB: That solution would be all wrong. It is the idea of an extremely talented but sick person who refuses to face the realities of his profession. It is not my task to play for myself. Playing in concert halls cannot in any case be compared with making a recording. They do have something in common, but differ in many respects completely. The basic difference being that in the hall, there comes about an electric current: the artist's concentration is transmitted to the audience who amplify it and return it to the artist. That process often helps us in focusing our attention.

When I was young, I did not yet see that clearly enough. It took quite a few years before I realized that the presence of the audience had a beneficial effect. Earlier, I used to think it was a necessary evil. I still hold, however, that the public should not be regarded as the artist's judge: I have never sought to please the audience or the critics. I try to persuade the audience to listen to me. I serve first and foremost the composer, and [since] you have mentioned Glenn Gould: that is what I miss in his interpretations.

BAV: What makes you think that you have a key to the composers whose works you play? How do you know that you interpret their intentions correctly?

AB: I have never claimed to possess a key to every composer. I simply endeavor to understand their music to the best of my abilities. It is important that there should come about a synthesis between the composer and the performer's personality—the latter should, however, know that the composer has pride of place. Composers put many hints in their scores and performers should be able to pick them up.

BAV: This depends on the sensitivity of the performers' "antenna."

---

3   At the Budapest Academy of Music, Alfred Brendel could stand the incessant coughing of a lady
    no more and gestured for her to leave.

AB: Also on the era in which the artist lives, as well as many other things. I do not regard masterpieces as unalterable. They have a structure of their own, they have their framework, their individual organism. They are open to different interpretations—what you must not do is approach them through an a priori distorting mirror. That would be tantamount to taking revenge on the composer.

BAV: I have learned from your book that you keep a mirror next to your piano to check whether your facial expression and your gestures reflect the music faithfully enough. Do you still look into it?

AB: Yes, the mirror is still there but I rarely use it. Sometimes I want to see if my movements look silly, whether they could be more economical or more convincing. I frequently forget all about it.

BAV: Still on the stage behavior of the artist as a spectacle: A friend of mine recently played the "Hammerklavier" Sonata and impressed me no end. When he finished it, he rose from his stool with an obvious effort and left the podium slowly, with heavy steps. I sympathized with him: I thought he must have been exhausted by the intellectual and physical effort involved. I said as much in the artist's room whereupon he, much to my surprise, denied any exhaustion at all. He had just felt that after a piece like the "Hammerklavier" it would have been wrong to walk out buoyantly. The heavy steps had been part of the production. Do you fall back upon such acting at your own concerts?

AB: If I could jump up from my stool after the fugue of the "Hammerklavier" and walk out jauntily, I would no doubt do so (*laughs*). Psychologically, it would be preferable to stumbling from the stage. However, it is true that bringing a work to a close should be done properly. Starting and finishing it are equally important. In the case of a classical composition, starting it should contain in a nutshell the mood of the work. At the end, too, one has to find a suitable solution. Some performers (including conductors) finish everything in a stereotyped manner.

BAV: Are you thinking of physical movement?

AB: Yes, one's gestures, one's bearing when ending a piece. There are many solutions. We can tear a note off the instrument; we can raise our hands vertically; we can sit solemnly, with a straight back; we can pick up our hands sideways. It all depends on what the music has to say. It is beyond my abilities to put it all into practice satisfactorily, but I can at least picture it in my mind.

BAV: As for a straight back, Nikita Magaloff says it is the only correct way of sitting and he never changes it while playing.[4]

AB: I am younger than Magaloff. When I reach his age, I may also sit motionless at the piano.

BAV: Perhaps this is not a matter of Magaloff's age but that he represents a different generation.

AB: I think there have always been pianists who moved more while playing and there have been some who moved less. Cortot, for instance, belonged to the latter and in old age, he made an absolutely statuesque impression.[5] Only his hands and his wrists moved, with fingers outstretched. The sounds he won from the piano were magical. The physical appearance was odd. Have you seen Rudolf Serkin play?[6] He does move a lot! I think it is better for everybody concerned if the artist does not carry it to the extreme.

As far as facial expression is concerned, Liszt's must have been a faithful mirror of what was going on in the music. The same goes for Edwin Fischer.[7] He did not playact, he behaved in the most natural way and the changing expression on his face was a great help for the listeners to appreciate the music. Other artists, including Beethoven, did not move a single facial muscle.

That is where the interview ended. As described in the introduction, I switched off the tape recorder, put on my coat, and Brendel accompanied me to the door. All the while, we never stopped talking. Or rather, words came from him nonstop and I thought it would be best to turn on the machine again. Standing on the threshold, I held the microphone to his mouth and this is what I recorded:

AB: Piano pieces are often just reductions of the composers' vocal or orchestral ideas. Pianists are the only instrumentalists who can faithfully render a composition without having to reach a compromise with other musicians. That explains the unique richness of piano literature. In Bach's time, the instrument had a limited range. If you know the *Italian Concerto* or the

---

4   Nikita Magaloff (1912–92), Russian pianist. I recorded a most interesting interview with him in Budapest, only to realize afterward that the tape was blank: the machine had for some inexplicable reason failed to work.
5   Alfred Cortot (1877–1962), Franco-Swiss pianist.
6   Rudolf Serkin (1903–91), Austro-American pianist.
7   Edwin Fischer (1886–1960), Swiss pianist.

Fantasia in A Minor, you will have realized that the possibilities inherent in the music can be unfolded far better on today's instruments. The same is true of the Beethoven sonatas and even more so of the Schubert sonatas, which were written for the instruments of the future.

Budapest, 1978

YEHUDI MENUHIN

1916-99

I heard Yehudi Menuhin on two occasions: sometime in the 1960s, in Budapest, he played Bartók's Violin Concerto, and in the mid-1970s Frank Martin's Polyptyque. On both occasions, his music-making was a revelation.

I had heard Bartók's work a number of times with Hungarian violinists—Menuhin's rendition was altogether on a different plane. For the first time, the music soared naturally, it never occurred to me to be impressed by the soloist's achievement in playing a "modern" composition, as had previously been the case. Menuhin showed us that the concerto was firmly rooted in tradition, and it was a masterpiece of the order of Beethoven's or Brahms's.

Frank Martin's violin concerto, composed in 1973, one year before the composer's death, was dedicated to Menuhin. It was the first time I had heard a work by Martin and I was excited by its originality, its harmonic language colored by the Swiss composer's individual approach to dodecaphony. The experience was in the back of my mind when it became my responsibility to promote his music for Universal Edition some twenty years later.

Menuhin's greatness as an artist was for me never in doubt. His public utterances, however, eventually made me question his sincerity. It was all too good to be true. There was no cause on which he did not take a noble position, he was always on hand to support, to admonish, to speak up for and against.

He came once again to Budapest in October 1972 and I decided to meet him with the sole aim to find out what sort of a person he was. Never before and never since did I have to stand in line for an interview. With Menuhin available for the press, there were too many colleagues to claim his attention.

One of my questions was actually meant as a provocation: I wondered how he would react to my describing him as a latter-day Christ. Twelve years *later, I would provoke Stockhausen in the same way when I suggested he had been betrayed by his comrades-in-arms as Christ had been by his disciples.*

We had actually arranged the interview a few days earlier when I talked to him and his sister Hephzibah (1920–81) for Hungarian Television. I went up to him in the artists' room at the Academy of Music, looked into his eyes, and saw a strange face. He appeared to be older than in his photographs, but that was to be expected. The look in his eyes, however, was infinitely sad, bitter, and hostile.

When a few minutes later he appeared onstage for the interview, he was the Menuhin one knew. He was all smiles, friendliness, politeness, and gentleness. After the TV conversation—brother and sister were a delight to interview—I asked him for another chance to talk, and he agreed readily. When it came to my turn—I was the umpteenth reporter to hold a microphone to his mouth—Menuhin was patient and once again angelical in his gentleness. His was no doubt a highly complex personality.

O

Bálint András Varga (BAV): During World War II, you participated in the Brains Trust, a program of the BBC.[1] What is your relationship to the natural sciences?

Yehudi Menuhin (YM): Ever since my childhood, I have been interested in machines. I never studied mathematics, geometry, or trigonometry, but have a natural attraction to them. I have not had time to address myself to those disciplines in any depth, but ideas did occur to me once in a while. For instance, to do with airplanes.

During the course of an interview on Stuttgart Television, I talked about a design I had made as a child, which I actually sent to the Douglas Aircraft Company. It had no fuselage but consisted of a single wing which changed its flying angle depending on speed.

BAV: Where did you place the passengers and the engine?

YM: The engine would also have changed its place depending on speed and the direction of flying. The passengers would have been seated in the wing. The reporter of Stuttgart Television, himself an aircraft engineer, recently

---

1   My source of information regarding Menuhin's wartime participation was patently wrong: although the violinist did not correct me, he had actually taken part in a program after it had been transferred from BBC radio to television, September 4, 1955. With regard to the program itself, the British musicologist Arnold Whittall informs me that it covered "a wide range of cultural and artistic matters as well as politics etc."

sent me an American publication with details on current air-channel experiments in the United States. They were largely based on my idea, without of course their realizing it. They put the passengers and the engine in the section of the wing facing the direction of flight. However, the fuselage would have been kept. My design is superior precisely because it dispenses with that superfluous weight; it works with service load only.

Nevertheless, I was very pleased with that article, for it proved that my ideas of 1936–37 had become topical. Experts had at last recognized that flying would thus become more secure, for the aircraft could adapt to changing speed. This solution is also more economical, as borne out unequivocally by air-channel experiments. The designs only partially put into practice my ideas—in another thirty years, they may come around to them.

BAV: You as well as your sister have also devoted time to examining the therapeutic effect of music.

YM: Yes. I am interested in many things—I am simply curious. I try to understand things; I have an affinity to any human situation as well as all the different forms of expression. I am also thrilled by a whole range of music—such as Indian, African, and so on.

The significance of music therapy is on the increase. We are at the start of recognizing and exploiting it. Initially, they played all sorts of recordings for the sick—Schubert's *Ave Maria*, for example. Then they realized that the solution lay elsewhere. In our Western music, art music especially, moods alternate too swiftly. Folk tunes, dances, and improvisations, on the other hand, usually stay within one mood. The same is true of Indian music—a particular raga is marked by one particular atmosphere. One is played at sunset, another was composed to render the atmosphere of sunrise. Such music affects the sick more readily. Hippocrates knew that nothing helps the convalescent more than the sound of a shepherd's pipe.[2] But what can you hear of a shepherd's pipe in the middle of the Place de la Concorde? That is the curse of our civilization. I am not sure either whether a recording of a shepherd's pipe has the same effect as it did 2,500 years ago in Greece when the herdsman passed in front of your window. It was probably more effective.

To my mind, folk music ought to be subjected to thorough study, because Hungarian or, say, Spanish folk melodies might play an important role in music therapy.

---

2 Hippocrates (460 BC–370 AD), Greek physician and outstanding figure in the history of medicine.

BAV: Why are you interested in Indian philosophy?

YM: I like its unity: there is no division into heaven and hell, evil and good. It teaches that evil and good are a part of life; the god of creation is at the same time the god of destruction. Indian philosophy possesses a wholeness.

BAV: Does it have any relevance today?

YM: Very much so! After all, science now recognizes that we are permanently surrounded by a secret. We are all sentenced to eternal ignorance, but we can nevertheless acquire some knowledge. Material is energy, as demonstrated by Einstein. One day we shall surely realize that the same is true of life, and we are a part of Nature to a greater extent than we would ever have dreamed. To a certain degree, even a table has a soul. According to the faith of the Druids, trees are inhabited by spirits. I am convinced that every religion has a grain of truth. If we accepted the Druids' faith, we would fell fewer trees.

BAV: I have read many articles about you. Some seem to deify you, they depict you as a latter-day Christ figure who bears the suffering of mankind on his shoulders.

YM: I am certainly no modern Christ and I do not suffer—that much is absolutely certain. I have never laid claim to such things. It is true that I wish the world well, I pray and use any other means to help forestall the terrible catastrophe toward which the world is moving: the suicide of civilization. I sympathize with people. I talk a lot to young people, I maintain a little school, I endeavor to influence as many people as possible. I have no illusions. I do what little I can. Whether I shall succeed, I do not know. Whether my efforts actually bear fruit is not so important. We live our lives. I believe that man is to a great extent capable of deciding his fate. Perhaps we shall not be able to stop the planet—who knows—from exploding one day, or the universe from being annihilated. However, we do dispose of our own lives. We must create the opportunities and the means for that.

BAV: You have experienced crises in your life, and you have always come out on top. One crisis occurred, I believe, when you ceased to be a child prodigy and had to prove to the world that as an adult artist you were to be taken as seriously as a wunderkind. The past few years have not been without their difficulties either.

YM: I strive constantly to understand my means of expression and to master them. Luckily, I love music more than my career. If I made music only to show myself to the public, I would never have had the faith, the patience, and the perseverance to understand what playing the violin is about. I am grateful that I had to search and to seek because, in this way, I have become a better teacher. I have also learned a great deal through teaching: for instance, how to deliver something clearly and concisely.

When I was young, I could play well enough to ensure that my teachers never lost faith in me. I sensed the great compositions, and I played as I felt them. I was inspired by significant personalities, such as Enescu and by wonderful musicians such as my first teacher, Persinger.[3] No questions ever emerged until I started posing them.

My father liked to tell a story about a centipede. The centipede suddenly wondered: "Which foot shall I put forward first? And in what order should I then move one after the other?" From then onward, he could not walk any more. The same happened with me. Then came my first marriage and the war—all that tension affected me simultaneously.[4] Problems occur all at once, but gradually they are ironed out. Every day I knew, I felt that I was grasping a little bit more. And even though there remain things that need clarifying, perhaps I shall live long enough for them to be solved as well. Perhaps not. In any case, I try. I feel that, today, I understand music deeper and clearer than ever before.

BAV: My next remark may sound odd to you. I feel very strongly, whenever I attend the concert of a truly great artist, that appearing in public in a series of concerts, in one city after another, is unworthy of them. Of course, I cannot offer a solution, but for them to take a bow, to actually be part of a show, fills me with shame and unease.

YM: I may well have been something of a showman in my youth, but I was never wholly one. I was a musician. Today, I communicate with the audience, I talk to them about what is behind the music—and what is behind us, what it is that our existence and music have in common. Today, my concerts are on an altogether different plane.

But I do agree with you. Preparing for concerts is an extraordinary task. I must be convinced of every single tone—whether it is in place in my head, whether I can perform the work the way I imagined. All that fills me with a great deal of anxiety. It is also useful, for it places the artist before considerable challenges: self-discipline, a regimented life. One has to learn

---

3 George Enescu (1881–1955), Romanian composer, violinist, conductor, and teacher. His pupils included Arthur Grumiaux, Christian Ferras, and Yehudi Menuhin. Louis Persinger (1887–1966), American violinist, pianist, and conductor. In 1930, he succeeded Leopold Auer at the Juilliard School and taught violinists, among whom were Menuhin, Stern, and Ricci.
4 Menuhin divorced his first wife, Nola Nicholas, in 1947.

new pieces, one has to brush up old ones, and stand before the public at a predetermined time. I do not know how much longer I will do this, but it does give me much pleasure. And, of course, I also conduct.

BAV: I was going to ask you about that.

YM: I enjoy conducting very much. After all, I spent so many decades within the narrow bounds of the fingerboard, a few centimeters from my nose, where the smallest deviation counts and where precision must merge with intuition—no wonder I wanted to put myself to the test, to try out my faculties as a performer and as a human being in a much broader field. To begin with, I conducted chamber music, subsequently works by Beethoven, Schubert, and Berlioz—the *Symphonie fantastique*—and Bartók's Concerto for Orchestra.

I love working with a large ensemble of musicians, I love the human aspect of it. I succeeded in developing a pleasant relationship with musicians wherever I appeared: in London, Paris, New York, or Berlin. I should not think my conducting is up to my violin playing but I have now been doing it for fifteen years and it is going better and better. I do not conduct much, perhaps thirty or forty concerts a year and also make some recordings.

I started with a British chamber orchestra. Initially, it was called the Bath Festival Orchestra, then, after I left the festival, the Menuhin Festival Orchestra. Every single member is a wonderful chamber musician; they play in quartets and trios. They taught me how to conduct. It sufficed for me to tell them of my concept of the music, they understood straightaway and helped me if I asked them what was best for them, what the upbeat should be like and so on.

I have always been in favor of experimenting and do not mind if the result leaves something to be desired. I have no truck with Horowitz's standpoint: he refuses to learn new pieces lest the performance should not be up to the level of his ingrained repertoire. We must strive for perfection, but it is just human if we only manage 99 or 98 percent. The urge to achieve perfection can at one point turn into obsession and it tends to become an obstacle rather than an inspiration. We must give something to the public: that is what it is all about.

Budapest, 1972

ISAAC STERN

1920 – 2001

S eated in a stall of the Tonhalle in Zurich on March 8, 1977, I did something very reprehensible indeed: I secretly recorded the first half of a rehearsal, with Isaac Stern playing two short compositions by Mozart for violin and orchestra—the Adagio in E Major KV 261 and the Rondo in C Major KV 373. The Tonhalle Orchestra was conducted by John Pritchard.[1]

Thanks to that misdemeanor, I have now been able to listen yet again to the unique aural phenomenon that was Isaac Stern's violin playing. I closed my eyes, heard the introductory bars of the orchestra—and then, there appeared out of nowhere a bodiless sound illuminated by the halo of Stern's artistry. The sound floated, with ever so slight changes in color and dynamics. It had a sweetness shot through with melancholy, of the kind I had heard in my childhood on historic recordings of Bronisław Huberman and others.[2] I hope I may describe it as noble without appearing to be glib. I was not aware of any vibrato; that the sound was issuing from an instrument, that it was produced by a human being who, as I can still picture him, seemingly did nothing but move his bow up and down, up and down, was a veritable miracle. It was also a miracle what he did with that sound. It was but a means for him to transmit—to use a phrase by Stern himself—Mozart's message.

In my experience, Isaac Stern and Sándor Végh were the only musicians who really communicated the composition they were playing (in Végh's case,

---

1   Sir John Pritchard (1921–89), British conductor. The previous evening, he conducted Prokofiev's Violin Concerto no. 1, with Isaac Stern as soloist.
2   Bronisław Huberman (1882–1947), born in Poland to a Jewish family, lived most of his adult life in Vienna and—after the Anschluss—in Switzerland. He founded what is today the Israel Philharmonic Orchestra.

also conducting) to the audience.[3] *Their basic stance of interpreting a piece of music, that is, of translating the notes in the score into the composer's message was visible as well as audible. Strange as it may seem, I am reminded of gypsy violinists who come to your table, lean a little bit forward, look intensely into your eyes and talk to you through their violin. In certain moments, both Stern and Végh came to the edge of the stage and did just that, in an effort to establish direct contact with their listeners.*

(I must contradict myself: next to those two violinists, the Hungarian pianist György Cziffra was also one to talk, through his music-making as well as through metacommunicative means, to his listeners.[4] In his youth, he had made his living by playing the piano in bars where he transfixed the habitués by his breathtaking virtuosity. He was wont to look at them while playing, observing the effect he was making. At his concerts, too, he would turn his head toward the audience as if asking them: "Well, what do you say to this?" We were fascinated, also by the improvisatory character of his performance, especially of works by Franz Liszt.)

Interviews are portraits and self-portraits. I hope the conversation I recorded with Isaac Stern does give the reader a glimpse of his personality. The picture it gives of me as his interviewer is in my own admittedly very self-critical eyes not particularly flattering. I find my questions rather naive, those of a typical youthful music enthusiast. Their saving grace lies in the replies they elicited from the artist. His wisdom and his genuine modesty do come across. A simple question such as "how come you still enjoy making music after all these decades on the stage" called forth a moving statement on what it means to be a musician. That statement by itself justifies the interview's inclusion in this book.

One more comment on some of my questions: in those years, the late sixties and seventies, I would confront musicians with the views of their colleagues on a particular issue and ask them to comment—hence, the reference in the interview to the Hungarian pianist Andor Foldes as well as the violinists Henryk Szeryng and André Gertler.

Finally: I find much pleasure in remembering the honors that were to be bestowed on Isaac Stern after we met: the National Medal of Arts in 1991, the Presidential Medal of Freedom in 1992, and the Polar Music Prize in 2000, to mention just the last three. He thoroughly deserved them.

O

---

3   Sándor Végh (1912–97), Hungarian violinist and conductor.
4   György (Georges) Cziffra (1921–94), Hungarian pianist.

Bálint András Varga (BAV): Do you regard yourself as a representative of a particular school of violin playing?

Isaac Stern (IS): Not really, although what used to be called the old Russian school has been closer to my formation than any other. You see, my teacher, Naoum Blinder, was a pupil of Brodsky who premiered Tchaikovsky's Violin Concerto.[5] I began to study when I was eight and at the age of twelve I became Blinder's pupil in San Francisco. He was a very good teacher in the sense that he did not make me learn to play his way; he only kept me from doing wrong things and taught me to teach myself.

Now as for schools in the sense you are asking them (there was the French school, the German school, the Eastern European school, and so on), each implies a certain definite form, therefore a limitation.

To my mind, Debussy has to be played in a French style, Eastern European music in an Eastern European style. Bach, Beethoven, and Brahms not in a German style but in a melange, so that you can reflect the intellectual, national, and artistic impulses of the composers.

BAV: In other words, you have to study the composers' background.

IS: You have to study their background; you have to know in what context the composers lived: historically, socially, and so on. You can't just play notes. Notes don't mean anything. A machine can play notes better than a human being. But only a human being can make music.

By the way, you can hear very good music in the background (*somebody was practicing Bartók's Violin Concerto in the adjoining room, to play it for Stern after the interview*). I knew Bartók. We met in New York about a year before he died. I was very young; I played for him both *Rhapsodies* and the *Romanian Dances* and I discussed the problem of trying to play them in exactly the way he had written in the music.[6] "Oh, that was a mistake," he said. He had changed his mind a dozen times. I explained that there are certain things that I feel necessary in the music whether they are twenty seconds longer or twenty seconds shorter. "You could not be more right," he replied. I also broached the problem of the ending of the First Rhapsody. There are two versions but I liked neither: both bring the piece too abruptly to its conclusion. Bartók had difficulty finding a convincing ending to his pieces in other cases as well. "That's no problem! Let me just add a couple of chords," he said and he wrote them in my score.

---

5   Adolph Brodsky (1851–1929), born to a Jewish family in Russia, premiered Tchaikovsky's Violin
    Concerto in Vienna in 1881. The conductor was Hans Richter.
6   The Rhapsodies Nos. 1 and 2 for violin and piano were composed in 1928. The *Romanian Dances*
    is a suite of six short pieces for the piano, written in 1915. The arrangement for violin and piano
    was made by Zoltán Székely.

He was a lovely man. I sensed a natural warmth in him and was sad that he was living under such difficult circumstances. It is a terrible commentary that his great renown only came a few years after his death. Stravinsky did not suffer like that.

BAV: He had more of a business acumen.

IS: Very much so! I knew Stravinsky very well; he was also one of the most intelligent people I ever met.

BAV: Did you meet Prokofiev whose concerto you played yesterday?

IS: No, I did not. Both of his violin concertos are excellent pieces, although I prefer the first one: it is much more original.

BAV: It is full of humor.

IS: Full of sardonic humor! And very sophisticated in some ways, full of very warm romanticism at the same time. For me, some of his most powerful work was done in his Paris period. Prokofiev is primarily a master of color; he lacks Mozart's or Beethoven's depth.

Let me tell you quite frankly, and not because we are doing this interview: to my mind, Bartók's is the century's greatest violin concerto and in the sense of the great concerti progression, comes right after Brahms. It marks the highest point the violin has reached in the violin-and-orchestra literature so far in the twentieth century. His two sonatas are also wonderful, as are the string quartets.

This reminds me: Stefi Geyer, with whom Bartók had an early romance, was the wife of my manager in Switzerland. She mentioned to me on several occasions that she was guarding the manuscript of a work of his which could only be made public after her death. She wanted me to play it. That is also what happened. My impresario sent me word that the composition was at my disposal to perform: the early Violin Concerto. I premiered it here in Switzerland, at Winterthur, and I also played the first performance in the United States, conducted by Eugene Ormandy. We also made a record of it.[7]

BAV: It occurred to me at your concert yesterday: you have now been playing in public for forty-two years. Audibly and visibly, you are still enjoying it. How is this possible?

---

7   Isaac Stern probably had a memory lapse: Bartók's youthful violin concerto of 1907–8 was premiered by Hans-Heinz Schneeberger in Basel, on May 3, 1958. The Basel Chamber Orchestra was conducted by Paul Sacher.

IS: Why should I be playing onstage if I did not enjoy it? What right do I have? At least one person should enjoy it—that's me, even if nobody else does (*laughs*). You cannot be a musician and not love to make music. To be a concert performer, you need to be something of an extrovert, you have to be willing to show off. You must also dominate the audience; you must never go *to* the audience but bring the audience to you. It is an enormous difference psychologically. You must ask them to share your enthusiasm. For that, it is imperative that you should have enthusiasm yourself.

That is our only justification: that we are propelled, compelled by the music. Music is always alive, it is always changing. We cannot hope ever to be able to arrive at what might be called the finite performance. It is always possible to do better, it is always possible to find another way.

Music is a way of life, it is not a profession. That is the first thing. Music is what happens between the notes: we must always be searching for it, seeking it. We play in different halls, for different audiences and that is also something we must be sensitive to. Each performance is like a first performance, it is another one.

BAV: How do you feel about last night?

IS: (*Considers for quite a while; talks slowly and hesitantly*) It was on the whole pretty good. It was not completely the way I would like to have it. It was all right. The audience listened very well. The orchestra played well. Pritchard was a good colleague, we have played before.

But first of all: being a musician is a privilege. We must be thankful for being musicians.

You should also remember that the concert is not the end. It is a means to an end. To be a musician: that is what you work for and that work accompanies us all our lives. It is not enough to be instrumental players. We have to know the arts, history, many other things. It is not possible, for example, to play Mozart without knowing the quartets, the operas, the symphonies. You cannot just play the concerti by themselves, for they do not exist in a vacuum but are part of the totality of the man. You study, you learn, you read, you listen—about many things. That is what is called a lifetime in music. In the course of which you give concerts.

BAV: I heard your remark to the conductor that it was a good idea to program a Mozart symphony after the violin pieces. How do you plan your recitals, what are your guiding principles?

IS: Two large-scale compositions stand in the center, the other pieces play the role of preparing them. The two major works are usually sonatas, for one rarely plays concerti with piano accompaniment. You cannot base a recital on solo works either. One starts the concert with a work which takes the audience's attention: an early Beethoven sonata, or maybe a Handel or Bach for violin and harpsichord or a Brahms sonata (but not the one in D minor, or the second Bartók sonata: they are huge pieces which could finish the first half in a big way).

If there is a contemporary piece on the program that the public is not too familiar with, it is best to start the second half with it. By then, you will already have their attention from the first half, but they are not yet tired. They have had the refreshing moment of the intermission and they are ready to listen to more music. Then you finish up with something which is pleasant to listen to and end the concert happily in some way.

BAV: You are noted for your advocacy of rarely played or unknown compositions. What works have you discovered for the repertoire?

IS: I have not rediscovered anything; there is nothing very much new in the violin literature that has not been done before. True, there was a time when I programed Viotti's Violin Concerto no. 22, because I had in my ear the way it had been performed by Fritz Kreisler. The little pieces by Mozart that I played at yesterday's concert had also been largely ignored until I called attention to them. Now most of the young violinists play them.

I have premiered numerous new compositions, for instance, concertos by Leonard Bernstein and William Schuman. I was one of the first in the United States to play the violin concertos of Szymanowski, Hindemith, and Samuel Barber. I have recorded them all. Recently, I played the world premiere of a new American violin concerto: that of George Rochberg.[8] I have programmed it with twelve orchestras in the United States; next week sees the European premiere in Paris, to be followed by a concert in London. Soon it will appear in print and will be available for everyone. I have played it for about a year and a half. Right now, I am studying the concerto by Krzysztof Penderecki. The world premiere is scheduled to take place in Basel, if he finishes it on time. He still owes me the last six or eight pages, for he has not decided which way to end it.[9]

You know, it is not a question of rediscovery. What matters is to be always alive in music. That is why I have devoted so much of my time to chamber music. With Eugene Istomin and Leonard Rose, we have recorded

8   George Rochberg (1918–2005), American composer. His Violin Concerto was composed in 1974 for Isaac Stern.
9   Penderecki's Violin Concerto was premiered a few weeks after our interview, on April 27, 1977. The Basel Symphony Orchestra was conducted by Moshe Atzmon.

all the Beethoven and Brahms trios as well as both Schubert trios. The three of us have brought back the idea of trio playing as a valid public area for a solo artist combined with his fellow players. Playing trios has since become very popular.

BAV: Andor Foldes has mentioned that he no longer needs to practice on a regular basis, in the sense he did in his youth.[10] His muscles were still developing then, whereas nowadays it suffices for him to think about music, say, when shaving in the morning. Do you still practice in the accepted sense of the word?

IS: Very much so, since even those pieces which have long been on my repertoire have problems that need to be solved. As a matter of fact, as you grow older your muscles are not as pliable, and you have to work more to get them in shape. You learn more about how best to use your equipment. Obviously, one hour's work on any piece on my repertoire suffices to prepare it for a concert, for certain things are set in my fingers. At the same time, I am always studying or restudying something. I like to rework old repertoire which I have not played in a long time; that is why I keep changing my programs. I take compositions I have not performed for eight or ten years and think them over again. I am always working in one form or another.

BAV: Over the years, you will have developed an economical and effective method which helps you to concentrate on the essence.

IS: Of course, of course. No one knows your weaknesses as well as you do. The idea of being a valid artist is to recognize mercilessly and without any faking what your weaknesses are. Our virtues take care of themselves.

BAV: What happens if you are indisposed?

IS: I play all the same. You may feel indisposed ten minutes before you go onstage or three minutes after you have walked off, but not while you are onstage.

BAV: But, let us say, you have a splitting headache?

IS: It does not matter. I play anyway. I concentrate. The whole idea of performance is concentrating. You focus your intellectual and physical faculties, like a laser beam, on what you must do. It often helps to get rid of your headache.

---

10 Andor Foldes (1913–92), Hungarian pianist, was a pupil of Dohnányi at the Budapest Academy of Music.

BAV: I understand you have a wonderful collection of instruments.

IS: I have two Guarneris, two Bergonzis, a Guadagnini, two Vuillaumes, and some modern fiddles. Most of the violins are out on loan to younger players.

BAV: What instrument do you play on?

IS: Guarneri del Gesù. It used to belong to Ysaÿe. The other one ("Vicomte de Pannette") is misnamed "the Alard," even though that great French violinist played a Stradivari.[11] Those two Guarneris are my favorite instruments.

BAV: I would like to get back for a moment to the technical aspect of violin playing. In our interview, Henryk Szeryng admitted that for him it continues to be mysterious and unfathomable.[12] Is there a subconscious side to it, or do you act exclusively in a conscious manner?

IS: I am terribly conscious of the dangers, I am terribly conscious of the difficulties. That is the disadvantage of using one's brain while playing. I am often asked if I am still nervous. Of course I am nervous! As far as I am concerned, there are only two kinds of people who are not nervous: one is a child and the other is a fool. I am not one or the other.

BAV: While playing the violin, the strings are vibrating quite close to your head. According to André Gertler, this vibration affects violinists sooner or later.[13] They are, he says, often rather strange people . . . He also says that the way one holds the violin is unnatural for the human body. Do you agree?

IS: No. Maybe he knows strange people. I do not think that vibration near your head matters all that much. As far as posture is concerned, after a while it becomes quite natural, even if not to the same extent as the cello. However, the violin almost becomes a part of your body—another hand.

BAV: We have talked about this already: you have been concertizing for more than four decades, you are universally recognized as one of the greatest artists. You are overwhelmed by praise. You have been celebrated by audiences for nearly half a century. How have you managed to remain a

---

11 Eugène Ysaÿe (1858–1931), Belgian composer and violinist. Jean-Delphin Alard (1815–88), French composer and violinist.

12 Henryk Szeryng (1918–88), Polish-born Mexican violinist.

13 André (Endre) Gertler (1907–98), Hungarian violinist. As a young man, he appeared with Béla Bartók, a fact he was proud of all his life. He only regretted never to have made a recording with the great composer. Gertler was highly regarded as a teacher at the Conservatory in Brussels.

simple, accessible person, how can you live with your own, world-famous alter ego, how can you identify with the Isaac Stern?

IS: You must have a certain combination of arrogance and humility. You need to be arrogant to appear on the stage and say: look at me, look what I can do. Even though there is always somebody who can do it better—including yourself.

However, we must never forget that music is more important than the performer. It outlasts him by many hundreds of years. Artists come and go, some will perhaps be vaguely remembered. Most of them will be forgotten. But Bach, Mozart, Beethoven, Schubert, Brahms, Bartók are here to stay, forever. If you keep that in mind, you will not feel so self-important. Also, you must have a sense of humor. This is very very important, very useful. After all, once you start to believe what they say about you, God help you.

Zurich, 1977

TIBOR VARGA

1921–2003

"Are you related to Tibor Varga?" was a question invariably put to me on introducing myself wherever my travels as Editio Musica Budapest's promotion manager took me. The answer was no. I was aware who Tibor Varga was, although I had never heard him play the violin. His was a name one simply knew; I could vaguely recall his association with new music. He seemed to be a figure of the past, even though he was in his early fifties at the time, since he appeared to have given up the life of a traveling virtuoso. His presence was due to his past. Eventually news of the festival he had founded at Sion in Switzerland reached me and the programs revealed that he was conducting at least as much as he was playing the violin.

My curiosity was really awakened when Editio Musica Budapest published a selection of Schoenberg's correspondence, edited by Erwin Stein. Amid the many morose, angry, bitter letters, I came upon one exuding an altogether different mood. Writing just over two weeks before his death, Schoenberg was clearly gratified by the fact that a musician nearly half a century his junior—that is, representing the future—had done justice to his Violin Concerto in an exemplary manner; that his score had readily communicated itself to a young violinist.

When news of Tibor Varga's arrival in Budapest reached me, in 1980, I immediately rang him at his hotel to arrange an interview. I was received by a Pickwickian gentleman, friendly and talkative. Words gushed forth *presto giocoso, but they would form incomplete sentences or phrases that were obviously translated in his mind from German. The accent was perfect, but Varga stumbled on words, distorting or mutilating them. Who knows when he had last used his mother tongue.

I cannot remember, after over thirty years, whether I used the interview for a radio program. I have certainly never transcribed it from the cassette but have kept a clear memory of many details, especially of his mastering Berg's Violin Concerto within a week. This is the first time our conversation appears in print.

I began the interview by reading out Schoenberg's letter to its addressee nearly thirty years after it was written. An absolutely unique experience in my life as an interviewer. Here it is, in English translation, placed at my disposal by Therese Muxeneder of the Arnold Schönberg Center in Vienna.

o

Arnold Schoenberg
116 N. Rockingham Ave.
Los Angeles 49, California

June 27, 1951

Mr. Tibor Varga
32 Tavistock Square
London W.C.1.

Dear Mr. Varga,

My illness hitherto prevented my hearing your records of my violin concerto, also the fact that I had no suitable record-player. I once played it through on my very inadequate machine and even then received an amazing impression of your overpowering presentation of my music. But it is only now that I have heard it decently that I can fully and completely understand why everyone talks of you and your playing with such enthusiasm. It really sounds as if you had known the piece for 25 years, your rendering is so mature, so expressive, so beautifully shaped. I must say that I have never yet come across such a good performance without having myself helped with every detail. The fact that you discovered all this for yourself is not only evidence of your outstanding talent; it gratifies me, besides, in that it shows me how distinctly my music can speak to a true musician: he can know and understand me without explanations, simply through the medium of the written notes.

I am very grateful to you for this experience, and I wish I were younger in order to be able to provide you with more material of this kind. I shall in any case follow your performances with the closest of attention.

I hope I shall soon hear the performance of my Fantasia for Violin.

With very best wishes,
Arnold Schoenberg[1]

Tibor Varga (TV): This is an interesting story. In 1949, I was invited on an extensive tour of Germany, with some classical concertos as well as Bartók and Alban Berg on my programs. It was during that tour that I was approached with the idea of presenting the European premiere of Schoenberg's Violin Concerto, as part of the first postwar ISCM [International Society for Contemproary Music] festival, in 1951.

I must confess that the initial, admittedly fleeting, encounter with the score did not convince me. I did not have time to study it properly and kept putting off the definitive answer, in the hope that I would eventually be able to address myself to it in earnest. Three or four months went by until I received a telegram one day in my hotel in Stockholm: unless I committed myself by eight o'clock next morning, they would look for another soloist. I had the score with me and decided to study it during the night. At seven in the morning I sent a telegram that I would be ready to do the premiere.

Schoenberg was supposed to come and supervise the rehearsals but fell ill; sadly, I never met him. Neither did we keep in touch prior to the concert, so you can imagine my delight on receiving his letter. It was the finest recognition of my work and a support for the future—a reassurance that I was on the right track.

Bálint András Varga (BAV): Who conducted and which orchestra was playing?

TV: Hans Rosbaud conducted the Frankfurt Radio Orchestra. Rosbaud was a wonderful musician, we regularly concertized together in England, Germany, France, and Switzerland. After the premiere, I played the concerto in several European countries as well as in Australia.

BAV: Had you performed any music by Schoenberg before your encounter with the concerto?

TV: This is again a sad story, to do with the *Fantasia* that Schoenberg was hoping I might play. With his letter in hand, I asked for a score and was in due course sent a copy of the manuscript. I was living in London at the time. My friend, the composer Mátyás Seiber and I perused the music and

---

1   Arnold Schoenberg, *Letters*, selected and ed. Erwin Stein, trans. from German, Eithne Wilkins and Ernst Kaiser (New York: St. Martin's Press, 1965), 288–89.

were much impressed.[2] We rang the BBC straightaway and asked if there would be any interest in programming it. They agreed immediately and asked for alternative dates to choose from.

I shall never forget that day. I asked the BBC to time the concert so that it could be picked up by Schoenberg in Los Angeles. Within an hour, we were rung back at Seiber's apartment with the date and time of the broadcast, which made sure the composer could listen in on shortwave.

I said good-bye to Matyi Seiber and made my way to the nearest post office to cable Schoenberg. It was a typical rainy day in London. My wife prepared a cup of tea; we sat at the fireplace and turned on the radio to listen to the news. The last item announced the death of Arnold Schoenberg a few hours earlier. My telegram was en route to Los Angeles . . .

The *Fantasia* is a short but pithy work, highly concentrated, a remarkable piece of music. I have played it since many times.

BAV: I am glad my question was unclear, for the story about the *Fantasia* is fascinating. What I really meant was whether you had heard any music by Schoenberg before addressing yourself to the Violin Concerto.

TV: The concerto was my very first contact with his music. That was why it took me so long to make up my mind and why I needed a whole night to come to terms with the score. Since then, I have also played his string quartets and other compositions as well.

BAV: Will you describe that night in Stockholm in some detail? How did you find the key to the concerto?

TV: The key to any score is to try and find its basis, its core. You endeavor to trace it back to the central idea from where it starts out.

The difference between Schoenberg's music and the classical masters is far smaller than many people assume. The score reads very much like Bach or Mozart. Schoenberg's thinking was vertical as well as horizontal; in fact, he held that one ought to recognize a work by the cluster of all the pitches it contains.

I played the concerto with major conductors known for their antipathy toward modern music and succeeded in convincing many of them of the work's merits. The only one who would not budge was Joseph Keilberth.[3] He

---

2 Mátyás Seiber (1905–60), Hungarian composer. A pupil of Zoltán Kodály at the Budapest Academy of Music, he was influenced by Bartók and Schoenberg as well as by jazz. He taught at Morley College in London. György Ligeti dedicated his *Atmosphères* to the memory of Mátyás Seiber.

3 Joseph Keilberth (1908–68), German conductor.

did have a point, not just with regard to the Violin Concerto but any music by Schoenberg. In traditional composition, you see, music is made up of harmony, melody, and rhythm. If you look at works by Bach, Beethoven, and others, you will find that if any one of those elements is particularly intricate, the other two are more straightforward. Schoenberg, on the other hand, did not make such allowances: in his music, all three components can be equally demanding. That is why his work is difficult to digest for the general public with no professional background in music: their attention flags, they cannot concentrate on music of such density for too long. Webern helped his listeners by keeping the duration of his compositions short, whereas Schoenberg continued to observe classical forms.

BAV: Did Schoenberg know that you were going to premiere the Fantasia?

TV: I do not think so. In any case, there must be another letter as well, where he says that the actual world premiere of the piece will take place at his home, where he will be playing it with a friend of his who was ninety-one years old. The Russian violinist was born on the same day as Schoenberg and they wanted to play the Fantasia on their joint birthday.[4]

BAV: I understand you first played Berg's Violin Concerto as early as 1939.

TV: No, it was in 1946. Hungary had been liberated in 1945 and I applied for a passport as soon as it was possible, to play concerts in France and elsewhere. On one such trip I had to stop over in Vienna to obtain a visa. One day two gentlemen came to see me. They said the tenth anniversary of the world premiere of Berg's Violin Concerto in Lisbon was due in a week's time and they deplored the fact that the work had never been performed in Vienna.[5] Would I be interested in learning it within a week and playing it under Hermann Scherchen? I did not know the work and asked for a score. It was duly delivered to my hotel that same evening and within a week I played it by heart.

I tell my pupils about this, because my system of learning a new work has proved itself for me time and again. For three days, I did not touch the violin but learned the score by heart. For two days then I learned the violin part, never touching the instrument. I worked out the fingering to ensure that technically I would be up to the demands of the music. I only started

---

4   Tibor Varga's memory must have failed him, for the first performance of the *Fantasia* took place in Zurich, on September 11, 1949, with Francine Villers, violin, and Jacques Monod, piano. It was played two days later in Los Angeles by the dedicatee, Adolph Koldofsky, with Leonard Stein at the piano.

5   The first performance of Alban Berg's Violin Concerto took place in Barcelona, on April 16, 1936. The soloist was Louis Krasner.

practicing two days before the concert. The performance under Scherchen went very well and the concerto has been part of my repertoire ever since.[6]

BAV: It seems to me that Berg's Violin Concerto has become a staple concert item, whereas Schoenberg's does not seem to have quite made it by comparison.

TV: Yes. Few violinists performed it at the time; today, many of them take it in their stride. But it is true that Schoenberg's work has not achieved the popularity of Berg's. The only explanation I have is that Schoenberg's score is too dense. If Schoenberg were here with us, I would keep this to myself, lest I should hurt him. In studying his concerto, I prepared a reduction for two violins, with the orchestra condensed for one violin. That was the handiest solution I could think of, since I did not have a professional pianist to study it with and my wife was also a violinist. When it came to the first rehearsal with orchestra, I was rather disappointed. I found that even simple passages were scored in an unnecessarily complicated manner. Just imagine that of sixty-four sixty-fourths, a bassoonist is required to play a tone on the thirty-first and the thirty-seventh sixty-fourth.[7] His nerves will be frayed and he cannot concentrate on the actual music.[8]

I remember playing the Berg Violin Concerto with Hans Rosbaud. We had five rehearsals and played a very beautiful concert which was recorded by the radio. The artistic director of the concert series was Karl Amadeus Hartmann.[9] The three of us went to the studio to listen to the recording and we were all much taken with it. Hans Rosbaud turned to the composer and asked: "Mr. Hartmann, what was Mr. Varga's fee?"

Hartmann gave him the figure, whereupon Rosbaud asked: "Would you be willing to invite him next year to play the Berg concerto once again, for double the fee?"

"Yes, of course, it was very beautiful. But why double the fee?"

---

6   I wonder how many rehearsals took place, if Tibor Varga studied the work until the day of the concert. This is a question that I am afraid did not occur to me during the interview.

7   I do not know if Tibor Varga was referring to an actual passage of the Violin Concerto or simply wanted to give an idea of its unreasonably difficult scoring by citing an example *ad absurdum*.

8   Schoenberg's Violin Concerto was played in Vienna in February 2012, by Hilary Hahn and the RSO Wien Symphony Orchestra (the orchestra of Austrian Radio), conducted by Peter Eötvös. I have asked the first bassoonist, David Seidel, to comment on Tibor Varga's criticism. Here is his reply: "I can understand Tibor Varga's opinion and agree with him in that Schoenberg did not make it easy for the first bassoon. However, the part can be mastered with some concentrated study and it does not pose any unusual technical challenge. We play so much recent and new music that Schoenberg's works strike us as almost tonal and tuneful."

9   Karl Amadeus Hartmann (1905–63), German composer. He founded the concert series Musica Viva in Munich, dedicated to new music. The series is running to this day.

"Because next year I want to have ten rehearsals rather than five and then record the work again."

Conductors often delude themselves that ten rehearsals make for better results than five. (Rosbaud was eventually chased away by his orchestra for his excessive demands.) I do agree that a certain number of rehearsals is necessary—perhaps six or eight. It is then for the concert to put the orchestra at ease. I had the same experience with Fricsay who also favored far too many rehearsals.[10] I have often found that concerts with fewer rehearsals were more successful than those which were overrehearsed.

I refuse to go on tour with the same program and play a concerto thirty-two times in a row (four concerts are the maximum). However, I would not mind repeating Schoenberg's Violin Concerto five or six times in succession. I expect by the sixth performance, musicians in the orchestra would be able to relax and feel at home in the music. Sadly, more than two consecutive performances are not realistic the way musical life is organized. The soloist may of course play it again, but with another orchestra and possibly also with another conductor.

BAV: You were nineteen years old when Bartók emigrated to the United States. I could well imagine that you might have met him, perhaps at the Academy of Music.

TV: I turned pages for him at a concert. He had heard me play the violin and expressed a favorable opinion. I first heard him in concert when I was twelve and was fascinated no end.

A few years later he and his wife played in Győr.[11] At the reception following the concert I sat next to Bartók. I must have been fifteen at the time. He asked me about my plans, the music I was playing; we talked about the "Kreutzer" Sonata and other pieces. I found him open and warm, unlike conductors who could be afraid of him, especially when he turned up with his famed metronome . . . I saw that old-fashioned instrument at one of his rehearsals. It was like a meter you could pull out; the rate of the swinging depended on the length of the line hanging from the instrument. If asked what he thought of the performance, he would produce his metronome and say: well, this is what I say in the score . . . The same happened before the world premiere of the Concerto for Orchestra. Sitting in the empty hall, he called out to Koussevitzky to remind him of the tempi required in the score. The conductor preferred not to engage in a discussion within hear-

---

10 Ferenc Fricsay (1914–63), Hungarian conductor.
11 Győr (Raab for the Austrians) is a city in western Hungary. Tibor Varga was born there and so was the conductor Hans Richter (1843–1916), known to Hungarians as Richter János.

ing of the orchestra, suspended the rehearsal, and retired to his room with Bartók. When he returned to the rehearsal, he changed the tempi without any commentary.

BAV: How did Bartók strike you as a pianist?

TV: I loved his playing more than any other pianist's. I particularly admired his approach to Bach. His touch was exquisite, his tone was soft. A sovereign at the keyboard.

There was something else as well. More than many other composers, Bartók attached a great deal of significance to intervals, the distance between tones. For him, it was like climbing a mountain and descending to a valley for us normal people. For Bartók, intervals were a living reality. He could create incredible tension between two tones. A third one would open a wholly new dimension. His music possesses a depth that is missing in others, perhaps even great ones. Something similar is there in the *Große Fuge* and other late compositions by Beethoven.

The same approach to intervals characterized Bartók's playing of Bach. I can still recall what I felt when listening to his J. S. B. With other pianists, the music came from one direction: the stage. When Bartók was playing, one was *surrounded* by music. I could hear it behind me and below me as well; his pianissimo created a unique atmosphere. Those memories from my youth have stayed with me, indelibly.

I must tell you that this visit to Budapest has deeply moved me. I have heard so much music all over the world and played with great musicians. I understood and felt the way they made music. But I have never *lived* music as deeply as I did in Budapest when I was young.

Next to Bartók, I also owe a great deal to Leó Weiner. The two of them were peerless and I still live from what I learned at the Budapest Academy. I shall always be grateful for that as long as I live. If my help were ever needed, I should gladly do whatever necessary, to the best of my ability.

Budapest, 1980

SINGERS AND A RECORD PRODUCER

CATHY BERBERIAN

1 9 2 5 – 8 3

I first heard Cathy Berberian sing at the Warsaw Autumn Festival in 1974. I was bowled over, like everybody else in the hall: we had never heard and seen anybody like her on the concert stage. You had to see as well as hear her to fully appreciate the phenomenon that she was.

Cathy was born to sing in public. That was obvious the moment she entered the stage. I can no longer recall whether her hair was dyed white or very light blond—in any case, it provided a curly frame for her face, which was dominated by her large eyes enhanced by long false lashes and by her prominent nose with its Armenian curve. Her smile made you respond in kind, her speaking voice and her body language—where her hands spoke their own dialect—put you immediately at ease and held you captive. But what mattered most was that you sensed she was genuine.

When we met in her hotel, the hair and the eyelashes were in place; at close range they made a rather garish impression. Not to speak of her nails, their polish adorned with tiny music notes. Until the concert and the interview, the Cathy Berberian I had in mind was a rather plain and plump woman, with thick glasses camouflaging her eyes, and her dark, richly abundant hair worn in an unimaginative, rather prosaic hairdo. I had seen pictures of her in the company of her husband Luciano Berio, but also of Dallapiccola and John Cage. I could not really identify that woman with the singer who had performed the day before and who was now sitting right in front of me.

I believe the reason for this spectacular transformation can be deduced from our interview. Her stagey appearance was probably a bait to help make audiences swallow what she had to offer: new music written for her by some of the most significant composers of the second half of the twentieth century.

On my return to Budapest, I saw the artistic director of the state concert organization National Philharmonia and persuaded him to invite Cathy the following season. When the day of the concert arrived, I was delighted that the Great Hall of the Academy of Music was chock-full: apparently, her name had a pull I had not been aware of.

Something else I had not reckoned with: I was prevailed upon to translate for her onstage, a challenge exacerbated by the fact that the concert was broadcast live. It was something I had never dreamed of doing; in fact, I was and am the exact opposite of a stage personality. However, there was nothing to do but accept, and I found myself facing the hall, recognizing well-known faces (including that of the artistic director of the National Philharmonia), feeling rather dizzy—and suddenly realizing that Cathy was already talking, soon I would have to open my mouth and say something and I had not been listening.

I managed somehow, but was aware that I had misheard a date she had mentioned (the artistic director was shaking his head). It did not augur well for the rest of the evening. Curiously enough, one thing put me at ease: looking at Cathy from the side, I noticed that her lips were slightly trembling, even though her voice remained absolutely calm. So she was also nervous! That helped.

The concert was a great success. Cathy brought down the house: her musicality, her crystal-clear and supple voice, her sense of humor, and again, her genuineness. Afterward, I told her that her personality reminded me somewhat of Barbra Streisand. No, she said, she had a typically Armenian sense of humor.

I should also mention Bruno Canino, the excellent pianist, who in his quiet and subtle way contributed to the unique atmosphere of the evening and demonstrated his sense of humor in Cathy's piano piece Morsicat(h)y (1969).

Cathy was invited back three years later, with a program she called "From Monteverdi to the Beatles." The pianist was Harold Lester.[1] I have kept a cassette of the radio broadcast and listened to it again after thirty-four years.[2] "This is Bálint," she said by way of introduction and there was a ripple of laughter in the audience. "And he is going to translate for me," she continued. More laughter, as I asked: "Shall I translate that?" I was not nervous, thank God. In fact, I spent most of the concert sitting in a relaxed

---

1   Bruno Canino (b. 1935), Italian pianist and composer of piano pieces, Pianist and harpsichordist Harold Lester was Cathy Berberian's accompanist for about ten years.

2   I have not been able to track down the cassette of our interview. The text is my translation back into English from the Hungarian, which appeared in my 1979 *Muzsikusportrék*.

pose at the back of the stage, on a step of the podium reserved for choruses, in full view of the audience.

Cathy's pithy introductions to the music she was about to sing were an object lesson in enunciation and clarity. She started with Monteverdi, continued with an early song by Berio, composed in 1949, went on with Pergolesi followed by Debussy. And so she zigzagged her way in music history and styles throughout the evening, ending with the Beatles.

The principles underlying her choice of program were spelled out in Warsaw, in 1974.

Cathy Berberian (CB): It is quite simple: I love music and I am against the barriers some people put up between various styles. I am also against what is called tradition, for instance, when I am singing Monteverdi. Because, to my mind, it is but a style of performance developed by some singers in the past and taken up by others in the course of time, perhaps because they liked it. I want to create my own tradition—not that I think I am better than everybody else, but because each singer is an independent personality, each singer has a voice unique to them. When singing Monteverdi, therefore, I turn for guidance directly to the composer.

As for contemporary music, I am in an easy position: all the works on my repertoire were written for me by composers who know my strengths and my weaknesses. I also sing jazz—it is just as important as any other kind of music—and perform some Beatles songs in a Baroque style. People often come up to me after a concert and ask me why I call them Beatles numbers: they are lovely songs! I reply that the songs are indeed lovely, and they are certainly the songs of the British group; I did not change them except for their style.

Bálint András Varga (BAV): After that brief introduction, may I have a musical biography, please?

CB: Initially, I learned traditional, classical singing. I want to emphasize right away that all singers must be at home in the music of the past, even if they specialize in contemporary music. Everything I do today is based on what I learned early on. I mistrust young composers who claim to have sprung from John Cage's forehead. After all, Cage himself was a pupil of Arnold Schoenberg! He mastered the rules before transgressing them.

I employ a very large variety of vocal effects. I have been helped in this by the fact that during the course of my career I have sung folk music, jazz, and classical works; that is, highly diverging sound phenomena. I am convinced that most singers of new music will come in the future from the United States, because Americans are less inhibited than

Europeans. They do not regard it as beneath their dignity to perform jazz and folk music as well.

There is a psychological side to this: Europeans are far too formal. If you are serious inside, you can afford to act like a clown. That is what I do. I have no inferiority complex—or rather, I do, I also have my problems. I mean, I am not worried that the audience may not take me seriously. I know I am serious and so do they, for they know my career, my recordings. Worrying about what people might think of you is a sign of insecurity. It does not interest me what other people think, for I know what I can do. They can hear me in Monteverdi, they can hear me in my fin-de-siècle number (it is very funny), and also in Berio. In other words, they know that they must take me seriously.

BAV: How did you arrive at new music? Through Berio?

CB: Of course. We married in 1950. I had heard new music before, I believe, but I had not listened to it in any conscious way. Then, in 1952, we listened to *Wozzeck*. That was my first encounter with that opera. Luciano, my husband, was bowled over by the music, while I was saying to myself: "My God, this is simply awful!" Luciano listened to it again and again, and I admitted: "Well, it is not that bad after all, some bits are quite good." After a while, it was I who suggested: "Let us listen to *Wozzeck*!"

BAV: If it took you quite some time to grasp and actually enjoy Berg, what can you expect from average music-lovers, who . . .

CB: I do not condemn the public, but rather concert organizers who do nothing to ensure that audiences get to hear enough new music. Up to the beginning of the twentieth century, singers ignored so-called old music. They performed the music of their own time or of the immediately preceding period. Nobody played Bach in Mozart's time! That is why I have put together what I call my pioneering program. I take it to places that have had no experience of new music whatsoever. I begin with Monteverdi, continue with Debussy, followed by a subtle, soft Cage, then Stravinsky and Berio—the latter accompanied by tape.[3] After the intermission, I start with Berio's *Sequenza*, then two songs by Kurt Weill, and finally two Beatles numbers.[4] My accompanist plays a work by Berio, as well as my own piano

---

3 Berio composed *Thema (Omaggio a Joyce)* for mezzo-soprano and tape in 1958.

4 Of Luciano Berio's fourteen solo works with the title *Sequenza*, *Sequenza III* is the only one for voice. Written in 1966, it is dedicated "To Cathy." It was premiered by Berberian in that same year, in Bremen.

piece, but it is very short and also very funny. I end the program with my own *Stripsody*.[5]

Between each number, I talk to the audience. They could just as well read what I tell them in the printed program, but I much prefer to explain by the spoken word what it is that I do; I show them that I am a singer, a human being like anybody else, who understands why they find new music so difficult and who wants to help them. Even if not all of them can follow my words, they sense what I am getting at. And do you know which work goes down best? Apart from the funny numbers (they are always a great success), the *Sequenza* proves to be the most popular—the hardest piece of all. But I had built the program up to that culmination, difficult and easy numbers alternated with one another and by the time we arrived at the *Sequenza*, all prejudices had been demolished. Perhaps they do not understand it straightaway, but it talks to them.

To my mind, you cannot put together a program out of new music only, especially at subscription concerts. You must have something that gives the ears a rest. I myself cannot take more than forty minutes of new music either. In other words, after forty minutes, my ears get tired, I cannot grasp any more music.

BAV: What was Berio's role in the development of your vocal style?

CB: I am proud that many people call this kind of singing the Berberian style. After all, we all hope that something will survive us—something of immortality. The art of singers is transient, and recordings are not much help either. I am proud that this style started out from me. There were singers in the past, too, who exerted an influence on composers. Mozart, for instance, composed most of his arias for particular soloists. However, never before has there been any question of a performer changing the very technique of singing. That is why I am proud of my achievement.

It all started with Cage. He lived in Milan in 1958 and worked on an electronic piece. He spent much time in our house and joined us for our meals: in those days, he was poorly paid by Italian Radio. I happen to be a good cook. Cage heard me fool around in the kitchen (I am quite a clown in my private life as well; humor helps me get over the sad reality of everyday life. If you read a newspaper and do not shoot yourself, you should at least be able to laugh). Well, then, he heard me fool around and on one occasion he said to me: "Listen, how about my writing a piece for you? It would be fun, wouldn't it?" He composed his *Aria with Fontana Mix* (1958).

---

5 *Stripsody* was composed in 1966.

BAV: Fontana Mix?

CB: That is the tape. I performed it and it triggered quite a scandal. *Aria* uses ten different vocal styles: Marlene Dietrich, Marilyn Monroe, Chaliapin, and others. It is in five languages: Russian, Armenian, English, Italian, and French. It was quite daring at the time; today, of course, it no longer shocks anybody.

Bussotti heard the *Aria* and wrote his *Voix de femme* (1958–59). Luciano, too, realized that there was more to my singing than he had been aware of. That was when he composed *Circles* for me.[6]

BAV: How did you develop a vocal technique that did justice to Cage's piece? How did you prepare for the premiere of *Aria*?

CB: All I had to do was to master the rapid alternation of the many different vocal styles I had acquired. That is the hardest bit of it and that is the basis of my style. I have good reflexes, I can switch swiftly from one to the other. It is also important that I can fall back upon so many different types of voice. Initially, the switch was slower. Cage wanted one page to last not longer than a minute and I could not manage it under a minute and a half. Now I can do the whole piece in a matter of six minutes.

BAV: Let me go back to the very beginning. You said you could fall back on many different vocal styles, even before meeting Cage. How did you acquire the faculty of singing in different styles?

CB: Even as a child, I loved mimicking people. I heard the recordings of Lily Pons and sang with her the coloratura passages.[7] (*She demonstrates them.*) Then I imitated Shaliapin, because I liked the way he sang. (*She demonstrates that also.*)

Nobody told me I was not supposed to do that. A voice teacher would surely have forbidden it, for no voice is supposed to encompass everything from coloratura [soprano] all the way down to bass. Nobody warned me, so I went on mimicking whomever I wanted to and proved that singing teachers were in the wrong. Many singers are afraid that new music could ruin their voice. I have been at it for twenty years now, and my voice is none the worse for it. Callas never sang a note of new music—and she has retired from the stage.

---

6   Luciano Berio, *Circles* (1960), for soprano, harp and two percussionists, is a setting of three poems by E. E. Cummings (1894–1962).

7   Lily Pons (1898–1976), French-American operatic soprano and actress. As an opera singer, she specialized in the coloratura soprano repertoire.

BAV: Summing up then: you have developed your technique by imitating others, and Cage's piece was the first one to allow you to make use of it professionally.

CB: Cage is an extremely important musical catalyst—I suppose that is the best way of putting it. As for his piece, I am no longer fond of it; it has outlived itself. It was serious in its intention but not in its intrinsic value. It does have considerable historic significance, though, owing to the music it has inspired. Ligeti's *Nouvelles aventures* is based on my vocal technique. Stockhausen has also made use of it in his *Momente* and even in his *Stimmung*.[8]

BAV: Let us return to your musical autobiography. We have got as far as Cage, Bussotti, and Berio's *Circles* and *Sequenza*.

CB: *Circles* was composed in 1960, under the impact of Cage's *Aria*. Next came *Folk Songs*, with its eight different vocal styles. I sing in as many languages and each has an atmosphere of its own. As for the *Sequenza*: it was an epoch-making novelty, a revolution all by itself.

---

8   According to Louise Duchesneau, Ligeti's assistant between 1983 and 2005, the composer "did mention Cathy Berberian often, he loved her singing and her crazy personality. He also loved Berio's *Folk Songs*, which were written for her." In her mail reply to my question, Ms. Duchesneau also quotes the following paragraph from Richard Toop's *György Ligeti* (London: Phaidon Press, 1999), 95–96:

> As noted earlier, the basic ideas for *Aventures* date back to the period of *Artikulation*, and involve the creation of an imaginary language (shades of Kylwiria), according to what Ligeti now calls "a secret recipe" (one aspect of which involved associating particular vowel sounds with each note of the chromatic scale). Here the Cologne group's "Joyce evenings" had proved useful; even though Ligeti did not care much for the general ambience of Joyce's work, he found the writer's way of "treating language as raw material" instructive. Another contributing factor was a post-Cageian "emancipation of the voice," in which grunts, whispers and groans were just as welcome as conventionally sung notes. Once again, such ideas were in the air. In addition to Kagel's *Anagrama* (1955–8), Cage's *Aria* (1958) had made a big impact in Europe, especially when interpreted by Berio's wife Cathy Berberian. Berio himself had been inspired to write *Visage* (1961), a spectacular twenty-minute showpiece for female voice and tape in which the only "real" word used is "parole" (Italian for "word").

> Ms. Duchesneau continues: "Also, Harald Kaufmann wrote an article on *Aventures/Nouvelles Aventures*, which reflected absolutely Ligeti's ideas about the pieces (you can read the correspondence between the two in 'Harald Kaufmann—Von innen und außen'). Although Ligeti doesn't mention Cathy Berberian once, it would be very plausible that her vocal style was one of the influences which lead to both works." Finally, she draws the conclusion: "So I would go along with the idea that Berberian's vocal style was one of the inspirations for the vocal style of both *Aventures* and *Nouvelles Aventures*." With regard to Stockhausen, the noted German musicologist Rudolf Frisius, who has published books on the composer, cannot confirm that Cathy Berberian's vocal style influenced *Momente* or *Stimmung*, although Stockhausen may have heard a recording of *Sequenza III* with Cathy in Darmstadt in the 1960s.

BAV: What was your own role in that? Did Berio consult you? Did he ask you if particular ideas were feasible for the voice?

CB: Always.

BAV: Did you ever suggest a vocal effect?

CB: It occurred very rarely. With the exception of *Folk Songs*, new effects were always his invention and he would ask me to try them out.

BAV: For example?

CB: In 1963, when he was composing *Epifanie*, he needed a particular effect, the *nota battuta* that occurs in many of Monteverdi's compositions.[9] You know what I mean (*demonstrates it*). Well, that is *nota battuta*. I had never sung Monteverdi before because the Italians told me my voice was not suited to it. I believed them—in those years I was very obedient, I had little faith in myself. Luciano asked me to see if I could do it. He never told me it had anything to do with Monteverdi. "Try it!" he said. I did. "You sound like a lamb, you are bleating." I had another go at it. "Now you sound as if you were having a stomachache." I tried again. And suddenly there it was—I made it. Berio said: "That's it! Keep it!"

That was how I learned to sing *nota battuta*; it is not easy.

I also showed him an effect which he actually ended up using in *Epifanie*. I do not get it each time, for I do not know myself how I do it. It is an odd sort of hooting sound. I usually say it comes from the top of my head. I showed it to him, he liked it and put it in the piece.

When he was composing *Circles* in Massachusetts, we had a bird coming every afternoon and landing on our windowsill. (*She imitates the birdsong.*) We looked at each other, and it ended up in *Epifanie* as well. All in all, it is difficult to define how my influence on him worked. He heard me sing all the time and egged me on and on. And I did my best to go as far as my abilities let me.

BAV: It is like discovering a new instrument.

CB: Luciano is Italian and the voice is not only an integral part of Italian music, it is also part and parcel of Italian life. In Italy, people live on an operatic plane. Everything is on a heightened level. In the theater, a simple social comedy becomes transformed into a bloody tragedy. Nobody talks

---

9   The original version of *Epifanie* was composed in 1959–61 for orchestra and female voice. It was first revised in 1965 and then again in 1991–92. The new version bears the title *Epiphanies: Nota battuta* denotes the increasingly rapid repetition of a tone. Nowadays it is often called, in English, "trillo."

"normally." Instead of saying, "Will you please pass me the ashtray," they go (*she demonstrates it by repeating the words* fortissimo *and gesticulating*). For Italians, then, the voice is of central significance. Luciano, of course, loves opera—Verdi, Puccini. He also lectures on it. However, Monteverdi is closest to him.

BAV: And you, having inspired quite a range of composers, decided to try your hand at it yourself.

CB: You mean *Stripsody*? It all started out from the fact that I adore comic strips—you know, what I mean? Those series of comic drawings. Not that they are always funny. They can be very serious indeed. I know of philosophers who study them.

I once conceived of the idea of collecting the onomatopoeic noises that appear in the strips (*shows some*). I thought it would be fun to make a piece out of them. That is what I did: I collected those sounds and arranged them in a particular order. Originally, I thought I would pass on that "text" to a composer. First, however, I performed it for the Italian philosopher Umberto Eco.[10] When I finished, he said: "But you have the piece! Why should it be composed?" "Oh no!" I said. I could not believe it. "But of course!" he insisted. "It is the funniest thing I have ever heard!"

I polished it a little bit, memorized it, and linked it to physical gestures which are inseparable from the sounds. When they are playing cops-and-robbers, for instance, this is how they are holding their guns and this is what they do (*shows it*).

BAV: Is that your only piece?

CB: No. I have also written one for the piano and it has been published by Universal Edition. It is called *Morsicat(h)y*.

The pianist buys the music, finds a calling card in it, and sends it to me with a letter. For instance, he writes that he is a Hungarian pianist and would like to learn my piece. The piece has a code to go with it, linked to the letters of the alphabet. The pianist will compose the work based on my reply; he will play it with one hand.

It is all about a mosquito. One hand represents the insect, the other one the performer who tries to catch it as it whizzes about the keyboard. The end of the letter where I write "Sincerely, Cathy," is also the end of the piece. It lasts about a minute and a half, unless I happen to write a very long letter . . . The text is always different and so is the piece each time it is played.

---

10 Umberto Eco (b. 1932), Italian writer, philosopher, and semiologist.

BAV: How many letters have you written so far?

CB: Twenty or twenty-five. The funny thing about it is that it does work and comes off pretty well. The code is based, incidentally, on Morse code. *Tititi* are sixteenth notes, *ta* is an eighth.

I have made a start on another piece as well but have not finished it. I do not regard myself as a composer. My ideas are *trouvailles*. New music has two clowns: Kagel and me. Music must reflect our life and there is more to life than just serious things. People today do not realize that some of the compositions of the early Baroque and the Classics were musical jokes that made audiences laugh. We take it all seriously today—the humor is lost.

BAV: Just as Shakespeare's references to his contemporaries are lost on today's public as are most of his puns.

CB: That's right. Even his tragedies have their funny aspects. *Hamlet*, for instance. Let us not go into that right now. I also studied acting, and Peter Brook invited me to participate in the work of his research center for three weeks.[11] Acting is of help in singing as well, for it communicates the sense of the words more effectively.

BAV: In the program of the Warsaw Autumn Festival, you write that you want to rid your appearances of the rigid, ritual character of traditional solo recitals. I feel that the rigid ritual is acceptable if the music is valuable enough to keep one's attention. Failing that, you need to resort to all sorts of extraneous effects.

CB: You are wrong, and I am going to tell you why. Nowadays, especially in the West, recitals attract fewer and fewer people. Recitals are becoming obsolete. They will only survive if we modernize them. We are not carried in palanquins anymore but travel by jets. We still travel today, but the means are different. Recitals must address today's and tomorrow's audience. We can only accomplish that if we compete with the forms of entertainment that did not exist at the time the genre of recital emerged.

My performances are always attended by many young people: they know that I have them in mind. They come for the Beatles songs. But before they get them, they will receive some education. They do not realize I am educating them—I do not let them feel it. With all the means at my disposal I endeavor to make them like contemporary music, as well as the classics. Those of them who do not study at a conservatory hardly ever go

---

11 Peter Brook set up his Centre International de Recherche Théâtrale Paris (International Centre for Theatre Research, Paris) in 1971.

to concerts. If my recitals make them realize that Debussy and Stravinsky wrote beautiful music and so did Monteverdi, they may eventually become regular concertgoers. I am a missionary, a missionary of music.

This is no self-sacrifice—this is pure pleasure. I cannot stand the kind of singing that I usually call *lace-handkerchief style*. I do not think I could sing like that. Yes, perhaps I could. When, however, I enter the stage, I cannot control myself. I need my hands, my arms, my body. I would be desperate if I had to hold the music in my hands.

BAV: I think you are actually an actress who happens to have a voice.

CB: Interesting you should say that. I often say of myself that I am not a singer with a talent for acting, but an actress who can sing. Of course, whether I am a born actress . . .

BAV: But ever since we started talking, you have done nothing but act!

CB: You know, I do not have an easy profession. I perform little-known music, and all that plays an important role in my job. Many singers who may be better musicians than I am (more accurate and things like that) perform contemporary music with such dead seriousness that you do not feel they like it. They impart information to their audiences without making them feel that this music could become part of their lives.

That is why having a powerful personality is so important. It communicates music and makes the public accept it. People come up to me after a concert and say: "I did not understand it but I liked it!" And I reply: "If you liked it, you understood it." That is for me the greatest compliment. I cannot expect people to immediately understand it, as I did not immediately understand *Wozzeck*. All I want is for them to think to themselves: "Interesting. Perhaps there is more to contemporary music than I realized."

Warsaw, 1974

o

Cathy Berberian's heritage lives on. Many of the compositions inspired by her have become an integral part of the repertoire. Folk Songs is Berio's most popular work and this means that numerous singers have taken up the challenge of coming up with a viable interpretation—one that will always be measured against Cathy's. Circles, a major achievement of the musical avant-garde in the 1960s, likewise continues to be performed, with singers who brave Cathy's footsteps. Her recordings of both compositions serve as reference, as historic documents of Luciano Berio's intentions as realized by his wife and muse, Cathy Berberian.

Morsicat(h)y *is in print and, interestingly enough, a few copies are still purchased every year. With no one left to provide the code, the music is no doubt the object of scholarly study. I trust Cathy would be pleased.*

ELISABETH AND WALTER
SCHWARZKOPF LEGGE

1915–2006   1906–79

[**Bálint András Varga (BAV):**] Could I end with a more general question. In the third movement of *Sinfonia*, the first tenor cries out that music cannot stop war, cannot make the old younger, nor lower the price of bread. You refer to the same theme in one of your articles. I assume you mean by this that music has no practical use. Yet at the same time you are very much aware of the composer's responsibilities. Isn't there a contradiction here? After all, what is music for? You asked that question yourself in an episode of *C'è musica e musica*.

[**Luciano Berio (LB):**] Yes, but there is no answer. If we knew it, we would stop writing music. If we could give a logical, practical, rational answer, music would be like functional speech where "signifier" and "signified" are ready-made.

[**BAV:**] But I think there is an answer. I remember attending two of Elisabeth Schwarzkopf's Lieder recitals. On both occasions I felt as if the blood was circulating faster in my veins and for days afterward I felt a different person. I understood then that it was no empty phrase that music can make you better. And if music has that power, it does possess an important function.

[**LB:**] Well, maybe that shows that you are a sensitive person and that you are not indifferent to some of the emotions of music. But I don't believe that music can make anybody better. Better for what? The Nazi officers playing string quartets were no better than the people entering

the gas chambers next door; people absorbed in the music of Wagner and
Beethoven are no better than people enjoying a pop song.[1]

That extract from my book-length interview with Luciano Berio (conducted in January 1981 at his house in Radicondoli in Tuscany and originally published in Hungarian that same year by Editio Musica Budapest)
reflects my boundless admiration for Elisabeth Schwarzkopf. I had last heard
her not long before in Budapest and the powerful impact of her singing was
still very much with me as the reference to my blood circulation indicates.

I have included the composer's response in some detail to give an idea of
his sober approach to his art: he did not delude himself that music was suited
to making people better human beings. Perhaps he was right; I may have
used the word "better" too glibly, even naively, just because I had responded
so sensitively to Elisabeth Schwarzkopf's singing.

Of course, it was more than just her singing. She entered the stage of the
Budapest Academy of Music and the atmosphere of the ornate fin-de-siècle
hall was transformed. She had a regal air about her, with her flowing robe,
her slow, majestic gait, her blond head inclined slightly forward, with a faint
smile in her blue eyes and on her lips.

With her entered a world of which she was a supreme representative: the
world of German art song, the world of Schubert, Schumann, Brahms, Hugo
Wolf, Mahler, Pfitzner, Richard Strauss. Her bearing was also schooled on
her operatic roles, of course, such as her incomparable Marschallin in Der
Rosenkavalier. Surely there was something artificial about her stage presence
as well as her rendition, but I took delight in that artificiality, I succumbed to
it with relish, I reveled in the sounds her vocal chords brought forth as a result
of decades-long tireless training and rehearsal.

For Elisabeth Schwarzkopf was an indefatigable worker. In our first interview of any length, in Budapest in 1970 (I had done a brief one in 1967, in
her dressing room), she made it clear that she much preferred rehearsing and
recording to giving recitals. What she really enjoyed was experimenting with
various shades of interpretation. She needed unlimited time to approach a
song or just a particular passage of it from every imaginable angle. She would
repeat a work as many as twenty-five times in the studio before she was satisfied that it was ready for recording.

Schwarzkopf had no time for the spontaneity that the presence of an
audience might inspire. In fact, she wanted to forget about the audience, so

---

1   Luciano Berio, *Two Interviews with Rossana Dalmonte and Bálint András Varga* (New York:
Marion Boyars, 1985), 167–68.

much so that she arranged for spotlights directed at her eyes so that she could
not see the people she was singing for.

She had a congenial partner in her husband Walter Legge. The two of them
shared a concern for perfection and the soprano never hesitated to pay tribute
to Legge's role in making her the Elisabeth Schwarzkopf we knew and loved.

In fact, she had the air of a shy girl whenever she was addressing her hus-
band. I had ample time to observe them together, for they invited me to an
after-concert dinner at their hotel. It was a relaxed affair, the two of them remi-
niscing and conducting a dialogue; my role was restricted to holding the micro-
phone. The questions I did ask were not particularly bright, I am afraid; I was
too young and inexperienced, I suppose. I hope, nevertheless, that the atmo-
sphere of that evening has been retained to some extent in the transcript of our
conversation, even if you cannot see the two of them—Schwarzkopf showing no
sign of the strain of the recital, lively and talkative, Legge telling stories in his
U-English in the manner of a seasoned anecdotist.[2] And between them there
sat, quietly and self-effacingly, the excellent accompanist, Geoffrey Parsons.[3]

We did two interviews over dinner: I first talked to Schwarzkopf with
Legge commenting every now and again, then I talked to Walter Legge and it
was Schwarzkopf's turn to chip in.

My first question concerned Elisabeth Schwarzkopf's family—did she
grow up in an atmosphere conducive to her musical development?[4]

Elisabeth Schwarzkopf (ES): Like many other people, I played the piano and
sang as a child. I also had ear training and sang from hand signs. However,
my background was not really musical. My father taught classical Greek,
Latin, and history at a secondary school. He had had a beautiful voice as a
young man but his parents did not consider a musical career an option. My
mother had good ears and she was my most severe critic. She followed my
training closely and was the first one to warn me that I ought to change my
teacher. Indeed, I changed four times before I found the right one.

Bálint András Varga (BAV): Who was the right teacher?

ES: Maria Ivogün.[5] I understand she was of Hungarian birth. She lives
in Switzerland with her husband, the noted piano accompanist Michael

---

2 To follow Nancy Mitford's definition (U = upper class; non-U = lower class).
3 Geoffrey Parsons (1929–95), Australian pianist, a worthy successor to Gerald Moore. I remember
   his infinitely tactful, soft touch at the start of Schwarzkopf's last recital in Budapest, when the
   soprano was taking more time than in the past to warm up.
4 The recording of our interview has been lost; I have translated the text from Hungarian back into
   English.
5 Maria Ivogün (1891–1987), Hungarian soprano. Michael Raucheisen (1889–1984), German
   pianist and song accompanist. He also worked with Elisabeth Schwarzkopf.

Raucheisen. Ivogün was perhaps the greatest Zerbinetta. Well, she became my teacher and she made me sing coloratura songs, soubrette roles, and light music for a very long time.

BAV: According to music encyclopedias, you made your debut in *Parsifal* in 1938.

ES: Yes, that was thanks to my first audition ever, at the Deutsche Oper in Berlin. I forget what I was asked to sing; perhaps Sieglinde or something from Freischütz. In any case, they said they would take me on if I was ready to sing one of the Flower Maidens at one day's notice. I agreed, even though I did not know the part at all. I learned it overnight and sang it the next evening, with my eyes glued to the conductor.

I was duly engaged as a beginner, which was a two-year apprenticeship at the time. Those two years proved extremely valuable. I had to sing everything, even the tiniest parts, sometimes just two notes. However, I had to be ready to take over bigger roles any time. That is the right way to begin, even though one runs the risk of ruining the voice if one lands a big part too soon.

You asked me a while ago about my background and my music education. The truth is: my husband, Walter Legge, has been my prime influence. It is thanks to him that I began to sing Lieder and have never stopped singing them for the past thirty years now.

Walter Legge (WL): I heard her voice on the radio during World War II. When, after the war, I set about looking for the best artists in Europe to engage for my record company, Elisabeth was one of the first I cast my net out for. I asked some of my old friends what they made of her. Was she really as good as I thought? All of them replied that she was not my type. Then I knew that she was.

ES: Walter first heard me sing live in the house of a famous Viennese family who put on concerts in their home.[6] We did not actually meet, however, until some time later and he immediately offered me a contract. "But you have not even heard me sing!" I protested and insisted that he audition me. He assured me that he knew me well enough, but I did not give up and eventually had my way. Again, he offered me a contract—and that marked the beginning of real hard work. The first Lied we rehearsed was Hugo Wolf's *Wer rief Dich denn*. It lasts about a minute and we worked on it for three hours.

WL: I invited Karajan to the rehearsal to hear this girl who would not accept a contract unless she was auditioned. As Elisabeth told you just now, we

6   The concert took place in the house of Baron Otto Mayr (1887–1977).

worked on Wolf's Lied for three hours, but after an hour and a half Karajan got up and left. "I can't bear it any longer," he said, "this is pure sadism!"

ES: I was having a good time because I enjoy rehearsing. I had always loved it, but ever since my husband has looked after me, I work harder than ever before. Rehearsing is for both of us the utmost pleasure. That was, among other things, also the reason why I thought so highly of Josef Krips, founder of the noted Mozart ensemble in Vienna.[7] He would sit for hours at the piano and rehearse thoroughly with each singer in an effort to develop a unified Mozart style. It may have differed from what we did with Karajan later on, but the famous postwar Mozart style was linked to the name of Josef Krips. He rehearsed every day and all day, before and after performances—it was really wonderful.

WL: When Toscanini came to London one day to conduct the Philharmonia Orchestra, my wife and I met him at the airport. He did not even say "good morning" or "hello." Instead, he asked: "Brahms *Requiem*, first phrase. Can you do it in one breath? We have done it with Lehmann" (and he notated the first four bars of the soprano solo) "and she took breath at this point. Rethberg breathed here.[8] How would you do it in one breath?"

ES: Yes, we saw each other quite frequently and I would love to have appeared with him. He invited me to sing *Missa solemnis* in America, but obtaining a passport involved so much red tape that it did not happen. I shall always regret it.

BAV: And how about Brahms at the airport? Did you manage to sing it in one breath?

ES: I forget—I do not think so, but apparently it sounded as if I had managed. Perhaps I did, who knows? We ought to listen to the LP.

WL: On one occasion, my wife sang Bach's B-Minor Mass and Beethoven's *Missa solemnis* with Kathleen Ferrier, the great British alto.

ES: That was at the Scala in Milan and Karajan conducted.

WL: That's right. I was sitting next to Toscanini in a box. He suddenly took my arm and said: "These are the two most exquisite voices I have ever heard."

---

7   Josef Krips (1902–74), Austrian conductor.
8   Lilli Lehmann (1848–1929), German soprano. Elisabeth Rethberg (1894–1976), German-American soprano.

ES: Yes, those concerts with Toscanini in the box are unforgettable. Later, he conducted my husband's orchestra in London. Previously, he had heard it under Karajan and declared: "I am going to conduct the Philharmonia. I insist!" It came to pass and I must tell you frankly, I am prouder of that than of any of my own successes.

BAV: I suppose all singers who appear in Lieder recitals as well as in opera are asked in which genre they feel more at home.

ES: I have been very lucky because I have worked with the best conductors and directors, I have been given sufficient rehearsal time, so that each appearance onstage has been a wonderful experience. Still, I now feel that I prefer recitals because, together with the accompanist, we are solely responsible for the whole production. In opera, there are many external circumstances that can ruin one's performance. Poor lighting, for instance, or a too powerful orchestra, an unsuitable costume, wig, or makeup—all those can mar the evening.

At recitals, I am responsible for everything and will have practiced and rehearsed the music down to the smallest detail. Incidentally, Lieder recitals were reintroduced by my husband, after the war, at the Salzburg Festival. He felt Austria ought to commemorate the fiftieth anniversary of Hugo Wolf's death (in 1953); after all, the composer was Austrian. Wilhelm Furtwängler learned of these plans. We were performing Beethoven's Ninth Symphony somewhere in Italy. After the concert we had dinner together and he said: "Well, Miss Schwarzkopf, I hear you are singing Wolf Lieder in Salzburg. Have you got an accompanist yet?" "No, Dr. Furtwängler," I replied, "I haven't got one yet." "In that case, would you consider me?"

I was overjoyed, for Furtwängler was our God in those years. That he should be accompanying me—that was absolutely unheard of! The concert was broadcast by Austrian Radio and somebody recorded it on tape. For some mysterious reason, the original recording vanished and together with Furtwängler's widow I looked high and low for it for fifteen years. Eventually, we tracked it down in the summer of 1968 and it was subsequently released on a commercial disc.

BAV: Finally, what is your life like, now that . . .

ES: . . . no life. This is no life, no life. Life passes us by; our days consist of nothing but rehearsals and travel.

BAV: You have mentioned that you have a lovely garden in Geneva . . .

ES: Yes, but I see it for five minutes between two rehearsals. My husband plants wonderful flowers that will be in bloom while I am at home. And then we keep our fingers crossed that the weather, the rain, the sun will be kind to them. But of the two days I spend at home, five minutes are spared for the flowers, the rest is devoted to rehearsals, to unpacking and packing my suitcases.

O

In 1979, when the following interview was published in Hungary, I wrote an introduction in which I admitted to being of two minds about Walter Legge. I think I was put off by what I took to be his arrogance, his total conviction of his achievement, and I was particularly pained by his vicious remark about Otto Klemperer.

Now that I am older than he was at the time of our meeting, I can sense his disappointment and bitterness over his defeat in the debate with the British government that led to the disbanding of the Philharmonia Orchestra and Chorus—the apples of Legge's eye. I contacted the management of the Philharmonia (which had dropped "New" from its name in 1977) at the time and asked them to provide their view of the events but they declined.

In 1963, Legge had resigned from EMI and eventually left Britain to settle first in Switzerland, then in France. In 1967, he survived his first heart attack, which he attributed in later years to his all too abrupt farewell to his professional life. The man I met in Budapest may have been weakened physically, but he was full of ideas that he would dearly have liked to put into practice. He was frustrated because having cut his links with his company, nobody would engage him. The very standards that had made him a giant in the recording profession proved his undoing: employing him would have incurred expenses no label at the time seemed willing to shoulder.

I have used the word "giant" advisedly. The high standards he expected from soloists and orchestras exerted a lasting influence on music-making all over the world. He was far more than a pioneering record producer. In his capacity as director of artists and repertoire with EMI, he was credited with signing exclusive contracts with some of the greatest artists and then work-ing with them as their adviser, coach, and mentor in a joint effort to achieve unparalleled levels both artistically and technically.

That is in fact how he met his future wife, Elisabeth Schwarzkopf: he was looking for a young singer he could rely on to grow, under his guidance, into a major interpreter of the Lieder of Hugo Wolf—a composer he endeavored to reinstate among the great masters of Lied composition. At their very first meeting, Elisabeth Schwarzkopf demonstrated an eagerness to work that, coupled with the beauty of her voice, its instantly recognizable timbre, and her musicality, promised to make her the ideal artist to sign up for EMI.

Walter Legge discovered for the recording industry Herbert von Karajan, Wolfgang Sawallisch, Renata Scotto, and many other musicians. In his capacity as founder and proprietor of the Philharmonia Orchestra, he was in a position to invite (and thereby spotlight) musicians he had singled out as artists with whom he wished in due course to make records. He was shrewd enough to foresee that on Furtwängler's death, Karajan would be his logical successor as principal conductor of the Berlin Philharmonic. That meant losing him for the Philharmonia Orchestra. By inviting Klemperer, Legge ensured that the ensemble would continue to be headed by a great musician and also helped the conductor's return to international musical life after World War II.

He was obsessed with his profession and was prepared to go to any lengths to achieve the goals he had set himself. In September 1946, for instance, in war-torn Vienna, Legge surmounted superhuman logistic hurdles in an effort to organize a recording of Beethoven's Eighth Symphony with Karajan and the Vienna Philharmonic. The Soviet and American occupying forces had imposed a ban on the conductor pending his denazification. Legge persuaded them that the ban only applied to live concerts but did not extend to gramophone recordings. Karajan eventually signed a contract with EMI. His decision years later to defect to DGG (Deutsche Grammophon) was one reason why Legge resigned from the company.

Walter Legge's total dedication to what he considered his calling made him shut his eyes to Karajan's membership in the Nazi party (NSDAP)—not to speak of his wife's Nazi past, which was only exposed years after his death. If Legge shrugged off Karajan's membership in the NSDAP, others were very well aware of it. Raymond Leppard played the piano in the Philharmonia Orchestra on its tour of the United States, which made it possible for Karajan to conduct in that country at a time when his involvement in the Third Reich made him unwelcome in America as a guest conductor of local orchestras.

In 1977, I talked to Raymond Leppard in Manchester and he told me the following story (translated back into English from the Hungarian as published in my book in 1979):

> The Philharmonia Orchestra was playing very well for Karajan and there developed a sort of love–hate relationship between them. The concerts were well received, audiences were in rapture.
>
> The success encouraged Karajan's innate arrogance. For instance, he would call a rehearsal at 10 a.m. but in the end only go through a Mozart

Divertimento for thirty players, with the rest sitting there, doing nothing. Rather than apologize, he merely muttered something like "Never mind, it won't have hurt you."

The orchestra, of course, resented it. After all, the tour was exacting and the musicians were growing tired. Then, one day in Ann Arbor, Karajan grew very angry. I forget why; perhaps the orchestra had not been up to its usual standard. In any case, after the concert, Karajan left the stage and did not come back. The audience applauded for a while, then whistled, with the orchestra sitting there confused and embarrassed.

The musicians were incensed. At the last rehearsal before the end of the tour, in Boston, one of the players decided to speak up. It was Peter Gibb, who had fought in the war as a pilot. When Karajan turned up for the rehearsal, Gibb jumped to his feet and said: "Mr. Karajan, you must apologize to the orchestra." Dead silence—everyone was petrified. "Sit down," said Karajan. "Figure 52." "I will not sit down, Mr. Karajan. You owe the orchestra an apology." "Sit down, Mr. Gibb!" Karajan shouted at him. "I will not sit down!" Gibb shouted back. "I fought for five years against bastards like you and you have offended us in front of our American allies."

The whole orchestra applauded, then stood up and left the rehearsal. They were right; after all, Karajan had behaved with genuine Prussian arrogance.[9] *The concert took place but the orchestra and the conductor never again appeared together.*

In preparing for this book, I have read Elisabeth Schwarzkopf's tribute to her husband published by Faber and Faber three years after his death, in 1982: On and Off the Record: A Memoir of Walter Legge. *His death, though it did not come unannounced, had been a severe blow. To give some sort of sense to her life, the soprano went on giving masterclasses and addressed herself to editing this book. She also wrote introductions to the individual chapters and interspersed explanatory notes where necessary.*

The book for which Herbert von Karajan wrote the preface, gives the reader a rounded portrait of Walter Legge through his own writings and is also a testimony to the moving emotional and professional bond between him and his wife.

This is made plain on the very first page, with a quotation from act 3 of Die Meistersinger von Nürnberg, *in the original German as well as in (uncredited) English translation:*

But for your love's endeavor
What could I ever be?

---

9 Karajan was Austrian, but I suppose the adjective applied to him by Raymond Leppard did not refer to his background but to his conduct.

A childish girl forever,
Till you awakened me!
'Twas you who taught me
What is right,
'twas you who brought me
Mind's delight,
'twas you who bade,
'twas you who made
Me noble, free and true!
I blossomed forth through you!

A telling summary of the unique relationship between two artists dedicated and addicted to the art of music.

Schwarzkopf included in the book some fascinating extracts from Walter Legge's correspondence. They tell a great deal about his personality and the nature of his friendships and business contacts with some of the major figures of international musical life.

The following paragraph taken from a letter to Peter Heyworth who had written Klemperer's biography and also conducted a book-length conversation with the conductor, explains the reason for his reservations about the great man's approach to music:[10]

> I am working my way slowly through OK's Cosí. It is extraordinarily clear in texture, so painstakingly concerned with every note in every part that a good copyist could take the score down as dictation from the records, but the spirit of comedy and the humanity of what is for me Mozart's supreme masterpiece are drowned in Teutonic earnestness. No sun shines through in the laughs and heartaches and tenderness and jealousies are swamped under Schopenhauer.

The following lines from a letter addressed to the Israeli music critic Dr. Alfred Frankenstein reveal Legge's attitude to the accusations leveled against his wife and Herbert von Karajan:

> I think it is unfair for Israel that my wife's and Karajan's records are banned from your radio transmitters. They were about as Nazi as you or I are, and it seems grossly unjust to a generation too young to have heard either of them live that they should be deprived of the testament of two of the

---

10 Peter Heyworth (1921–91), American-born English music critic and biographer. His *Conversations with Klemperer* was published in 1973 by Orion Books; his *Otto Klemperer: His Life and Times*, 2 vols. (Cambridge: Press Syndicate of the University of Cambridge, 1983/1996); the second volume was completed by John Lucas.

greatest artists that Austria in the case of Karajan and Germany in the case of Schwarzkopf have produced.

The book ends with a selected list of records produced by Walter Legge. Space was not available to include all 3,500 of them. It starts in 1932 with Hugo Wolf's Prometheus *sung by the baritone Friedrich Schorr; the London Symphony Orchestra was conducted by Robert Heger. The last entry is dated 1979: Elisabeth Schwarzkopf and Geoffrey Parsons recorded a program of Lieder by Wolf, Loewe, Grieg, and Brahms. Legge and Schwarzkopf remained loyal to Hugo Wolf to the last.*

O

Walter Legge (WL): My father had been toying with the idea of purchasing a phonograph; he bought one on the day of my birth. He was a music buff and felt that the birth of his first son was as good an occasion as any to fulfill his old desire. The gramophone was regarded at the time as a silly toy and my mother could hardly believe her ears when my father announced: "I have bought the boy a present." "What present?" "A gramophone." "Well I never! Buying a gramophone for a one-day-old baby!" "He will grow to like it when he is older."

How right he was! I learned to read from record covers. By the time I was three and a half, I understood a few words of the German, Italian, and French inscriptions.

Elisabeth Schwarzkopf (ES): You knew most of the Italian opera arias at six, didn't you? You could sing them!

WL: I was four when my father began to teach me to read notes. He and I would play piano duets and because the lower part is more difficult, he wanted me to start with that. Later we swapped places.

I was not quite seven when I was first taken to see an opera. *Les Contes d'Hoffmann* was playing. From then on, I attended all the matinees (I could not go in the evenings: I was a schoolboy and had to swot for my classes) and in this way came to know the repertoire quite well. I also took piano lessons but did not like practicing; reading the notes was no problem. I much preferred to bury my head in scores. I first learned to analyze string quartets, later also orchestral compositions. I was astonished to realize that the records I was listening to had precious little to do with the scores. It was then that I decided: if one day I were to have a record company, I would make sure that the recordings would be true to the scores.

When I was nineteen, I was taken on by His Master's Voice on a six-month trial period. Three months later, I was told I was ill-qualified. What happened was this: The chairman's son had the same job as mine would be many years later: he was the artistic director. He invited me to the studio when the first act of *Die Walküre* was being recorded with the English conductor Albert Coates and three singers.[11] "Isn't that wonderful?" he turned to me. I did not beat about the bush:

> It's absolutely awful. It's money thrown out of the window. English orchestras cost exactly the same as those in Berlin. For the same money, you could have the orchestra of the Berlin Staatsoper or the Philharmonic, instead of this motley group of English musicians. For the same fee, you could have invited Wilhelm Furtwängler in Albert Coates's place. And you could have engaged Frieda Leider and Lauritz Melchior instead of the English singers.[12] With this cast, you will only be able to sell the record in England. If you had employed the greatest artists, the record would remain on the market for many years, all over the world.

I was kicked out after three months.

I was quite young when I made up my mind what I wanted to do in life. Forty years ago, I declared to Neville Cardus: I have three ambitions. I want to establish the best orchestra in Europe (that was to be the Philharmonia Orchestra); I will marry the world's most beautiful singer (here she is: Elisabeth Schwarzkopf), and I shall be director of a great opera house. In 1938–39 I was deputy director of Covent Garden but I realized that it was impossible in a theater to maintain as high an artistic standard as on records. I decided therefore that gramophone records would be my opera house.

ES: Your first great opera production was *The Magic Flute*, in Berlin. Beecham was conducting, if I remember correctly.

WL: In 1937, I asked Beecham to commit *The Magic Flute* to disc. That was my first ever recording of a full opera. I picked the singers, I rehearsed with them in Berlin, I put together the orchestra from among members of the Berlin Philharmonic as well as a chorus out of young professional singers. One of them was Elisabeth Schwarzkopf.

---

11 Albert Coates (1882–1953), English conductor and composer.

12 Frieda Leider (1888–1975), dramatic soprano, one of the most sought-after Wagner singers of her time. Lauritz Melchior (1890–1973), Danish heroic tenor, next to Max Lorenz, the leading Wagner tenor in the first half of the twentieth century.

ES: That's right! I was also there.

BAV: Until you appeared on the scene, then, the interpretation on records gave a false impression of the music. The same must have been true of concert performances.

WL: Orchestral playing did have rather a poor level. Genuinely great artists were of course conscientious: important Italian and German singers or somebody like Chaliapin.[13] Many conductors, however, lacked a sense of style, apart from exceptions such as Mahler and Toscanini.

ES: There were exceptions also among instrumentalists, such as Fritz Kreisler.[14]

WL: Kreisler had impeccable taste. However, the average was pretty poor.

BAV: The fact that concerts today are on a far higher level is due no doubt to the availability of great recordings. I suppose influences worked both ways.

WL: Precisely. Recordings set a particular standard and served as a yardstick. That is what I have worked for all my life: It was my goal to make records of a quality that would be an example for generations, a document to be studied by young singers, instrumentalists, and conductors. Conductors nowadays no longer spend years over a score; rather, they listen to whatever disc they have at their disposal, pick the best and produce their own synthesis.

BAV: Do you approve of that?

WL: It would be healthier if they took more time to study the scores. Basically, however, it is not reprehensible because if they are conscientious, they will not go below a certain standard. The same is true of critics. Most of them learn from records rather than from scores.

BAV: Do you think it is a result of your activity?

WL: To a large extent yes. Nowadays much of the repertoire is available on records. It follows that anyone can listen to more music in a year than in a previous generation in a lifetime.

I used to travel a lot when I was young but those who led a more stationary life had little opportunity to hear music. You cannot imagine the shock caused by the first visit of the Berlin Philharmonic to London after

---

13 Feodor Chaliapin (1873–1938), legendary Russian bass.
14 Fritz Kreisler (1875–1962), Austrian violinist and composer.

World War I! Never before had we heard anything like it. In England, the strings never played together and each orchestral musician used a bowing at his discretion. Practically each of them had their own A.

BAV: That is incredible. What could have been the reason? Perhaps the low level of music education?

WL: The orchestral culture that we now take for granted started with Mahler, Toscanini, and the super-brilliant Stokowski. There is no conductor who has not come under the influence of Toscanini's and Stokowski's recordings. They were a yardstick that no one could afford to ignore. Conductors learned from Stokowski what rich, lush string sound was like. As far as Toscanini was concerned, each of his recordings had the effect of a guillotine.

BAV: In the light of all that, it is logical for you to have set your mind on forming an orchestra capable of playing great music on the highest level. How did you establish the Philharmonia?

WL: I learned a great deal from Sir Thomas Beecham. He was the best British conductor at the time—nobody came anywhere near him either before or after. (Colin Davis appears to be promising, though.) When World War II broke out, Beecham settled in Australia. Foreign conductors were not available, except for Weingartner who had by then owned a Swiss passport.[15] He came over to London and conducted a few concerts. I also learned a lot from him. However, he died in 1942, and I was tied up with my job at His Master's Voice as well as the many concerts I was organizing for workers and soldiers.

I needed something to unwind. I formed a string quartet so that I could attain the level I was aspiring to, in the field of chamber music. For two years, I spent all my weekends with the four musicians. On Fridays we rehearsed from eight till midnight, on Saturdays and Sundays eleven to twelve hours. After two years, I told them: "I feel the time has come to go to a recording studio." That is what happened. I recorded the first "Rasumovsky" Quartet, Schubert's D-Minor Quartet (*Death and the Maiden*) and Mozart's *Hunt* quartet. The LP scored an immense success; it won a prize in the United States where it was hailed as peerless chamber-music playing. The ensemble was called Philharmonia Quartet. The name has since caught on; there are orchestras and smaller ensembles calling themselves Philharmonia all over the place. After the first disc, we took a step forward. Supplemented by a clarinetist, we recorded Mozart's Clarinet Quintet, then Beethoven's Trio for Clarinet, Piano, and Violin.

---

15 Felix von Weingartner (1863–1942), Austrian conductor and composer.

The war was coming to an end. Most young musicians were still serving in the army or the air force, many of them playing in wind ensembles. In preparing concerts for the army, I heard most of those groups and took note of the best players. "I am going to engage them once they have demobilized," I thought to myself. When I later recorded Elgar's First Symphony with Sir Adrian Boult, I took the first clarinetist of the BBC Symphony Orchestra aside: "I am going to set up a new orchestra. Would you like to join? I cannot give you the same pay as the BBC but I guarantee that soon I shall be able to get a lot of work for the ensemble." Thurston agreed readily.[16] Another member of the BBC Symphony Orchestra, Marie Wilson, followed suit.[17]

I recorded Purcell's opera, *Dido and Aeneas*, before the end of the war. I picked the members of the string orchestra. The conductor was Constant Lambert.[18] That was the first time I heard genuine string sonority comparable to great European orchestras. At the end of the war, I had the idea of mounting a concert. By that time, Beecham had returned to Britain and I went to see him. "Listen, I said. I have an orchestra. I have invested all my money in it. I want you to conduct our first concert."

Queens Hall had been bombed. I found an old Methodist church in its stead, Kingsway Hall, which had marvelous acoustics.

ES: Yes, we did all our recordings there.

WL: Its stage was small, but the hall seated 2,200 people. A great pity it is going to be demolished. Beecham and I agreed that he should conduct an all-Mozart program: two symphonies, a divertimento, and some German dances. The tickets were instantly sold out. We envisaged four rehearsals. All I forgot about was the fee. The concert brought the house down, the critics declared it was the first time they had heard a sound of comparable quality from an English orchestra—which was true.

After the concert, I invited Beecham for a drink.

"I forgot to ask you about your fee."

"My dear boy," he replied, "I am not going to take a penny for conducting an orchestra like that. But I would be grateful if you would treat me to a good cigar!"

I presented him with a whole box.

BAV: Why did you not conduct the orchestra yourself?

---

16 Frederick Thurston (1901–53), English clarinetist.

17 Marie Wilson was next to Paul Beard deputy leader (assistant concertmaster) of the orchestra. She had joined in 1930 and left in 1944, presumably the year when she was invited by Walter Legge to defect to the Philharmonia Orchestra.

18 Constant Lambert (1905–51), English composer and conductor.

WL: I had had a hard time with every single conductor, Beecham included, who had an orchestra of their own. They swore that whoever else was going to conduct it, would ruin it. Beecham, for instance, declared: "If that Furtwängler gets his hands on my orchestra, it will take me three weeks to make them play together again."

I am also convinced that no conductor or director should get to manage an opera house. In my view, therein lies the tragedy of German theaters: they are led by people who want to direct or conduct as well. The same is true of Karajan in Vienna or Solti at Covent Garden. Toscanini was not even artistic director of the Met—and yet, when the idea came up to invite Mahler for *Tristan*, he provoked an explosion in the United States that was only surpassed in power by nuclear experiments of later years.

Beecham and I fell out when he wanted to assume leadership of the Philharmonia. When he realized that he was not getting anywhere with me, he founded the Royal Philharmonic Orchestra [1946]. And, although we had been close friends, we severed all contact; we did not even talk to each other for five or six years. Then, to celebrate his eightieth birthday, a big dinner was organized in his honor. At one point he said: "There is one thing in English musical life I cannot understand. I have a friend who only imports foreign conductors, second-rate musicians—why, is beyond me. After all, we also have more than enough sixth-rate conductors."

BAV: You made it up with Beecham and no one ever interfered with the affairs of the Philharmonia Orchestra again.

WL: The Philharmonia Orchestra was indeed unique: I owned it, it was my property. In its first sixteen years, I did not receive any subsidy from the state and only accepted the offer of an Indian maharaja. He remitted 10,000 pounds in the first year, and 5,000 each in the subsequent two years.[19] He stipulated that the program be determined by a committee made up of musicians and critics. Those three years were miserable for me. All those so-called musicians and critics were out to put their favorite pieces on the

---

19 Jayachamaraja Wodeyar Bahadur (1919–74) was the last, twenty-fifth, Maharaja of Mysore. He was a connoisseur and patron of Western music, and possessed a large collection of recordings of this music. Bahadur had hoped to become a pianist but the unexpected deaths of his father and his uncle forced him to give up his plans and ascend the throne. His subsidy enabled the Philharmonia Orchestra to record works by Bahadur's protégé, the Russian composer Nikolai Medtner (1879–1951). It was also thanks to the Maharaja's financial assistance that Richard Strauss's last wish could be fulfilled a year after his death: the *Four Last Songs* was brought to London, with Kirsten Flagstad, soprano, and Wilhelm Furtwängler conducting the Philharmonia Orchestra.

program and their tastes were not exactly the best. They had no notion of what the public wanted to hear.

I am convinced that concert agents are duty-bound to satisfy and at the same time educate the public. That is only possible if we offer them the best music in the best interpretation. Radio stations are financed by the state or subscribers, they can afford to broadcast unpopular music that the public do not want to hear, or just a small proportion of it. A concert agent, however, wants to fill the hall. He need not make concessions to the audience's taste, he may offer them hard nuts, but must not foist all-contemporary programs on them.

Georg Solti wanted to conduct Bartók's Piano Concerto no. 2, with Géza Anda as soloist.[20] The concerto is not particularly popular in Britain, so we tried to make the program more attractive by starting with a Berlioz overture and ending with Dvořák's *New World Symphony*. The hall remained half-empty. If we had picked a piano concerto by Beethoven, it would surely have been full. I learned a lot from that flop.

ES: This is a problem that cannot be solved.

WL: In the last year, I was forced to accept a subsidy from the state. I had turned it down, for I did not need it: I could pay the orchestra from the income. I even earned a little on top of it, without making any concession to cheap taste. I said: I do not want the money, I wish to put on concerts my way. Whereupon it was brought home to me that if I did not take the money, I could not rent the hall. There was nothing for it but to give in and they had the right to interfere with my program policy. All that led to much controversy and debate and when government interference reached an intolerable degree, I gave up.

In a silly charitable gesture I had appointed Otto Klemperer to be chief conductor of the Philharmonia, for life. I did not expect him to live that long. Of course, at his age I could not expect him to keep a tight rein on the orchestra and demand immaculate playing.

There was another reason as well: the lack of talented young orchestral musicians. We had sixteen first-class violinists in the orchestra—and they were lured away by provincial ensembles, by offering concertmaster positions to third- and fourth-desk players. There was nothing I could do: it is natural for orchestral violinists to aspire to leadership. There was a time when no fewer than ten former members of the Philharmonia were concertmasters of English orchestras.

---

20 Géza Anda (1921–76), Hungarian pianist, a pupil of Ernő (Ernst von) Dohnányi.

In other words, I was the biggest employer of first-class musicians. At the same time, no music academy or university took the trouble of asking me for advice as to what orchestras needed and how education could be improved. If I had collected together the first double-bass players of all British orchestras, they would not have made a quarter as good a section as Karajan's orchestra in Berlin.

I turned to the British government with the request that I might employ foreign players so that I could maintain a high standard. The trade unions objected. If therefore I looked in vain for good musicians at home and was not allowed to invite any from abroad, quality was bound to suffer. I refused to link my name to an orchestra which was unable to keep the one-time standard of the Philharmonia.

BAV: Does this mean that the New Philharmonia Orchestra cannot be regarded as a successor to the Philharmonia?

WL: Certainly not. The New Philharmonia is led by the orchestral musicians themselves. They receive so much money from the state that they can do whatever they want. They can play like swine—they will get the money anyway.

BAV: Now that you have no orchestra and have stopped making records, one of your ambitions has remained intact: you are still married to the most beautiful singer.

ES: I would like him to write his memoirs!

WL: Yes, I ought to write them. But for that to happen, someone would need to present me with a sputnik and a first-class chef. My wife and I would live happily and comfortably, with no need to fear libel actions!

Budapest, 1970

A TEACHER

NADIA BOULANGER

1887–1979

I believe I first heard of Nadia Boulanger from Aaron Copland in Budapest in November 1969. In our interview, he remembered fondly the young woman he had studied with in 1921 at Fontainebleau; half a century on, she was still teaching in the very same rooms.

I met Nadia Boulanger in 1974. I had written her a letter asking for an appointment and she replied by return post. That would be a particularly busy week, she wrote, so all she had time for would be a short interview on March 12, at 6:45 in the evening.

I turned up punctually for our appointment but the maid who opened the door looked at me in surprise. "Mademoiselle is teaching," she said, "she is not expecting visitors." I showed her Boulanger's letter. She took it and disappeared behind a door. When she returned, she apologized and said there had been a misunderstanding. She asked for my telephone number and promised that I would be contacted.

Early next morning, the telephone rang in my hotel room. An age-old, deep voice said: "This is Nadia Boulanger calling."

It was embarrassing to hear her profuse apologies for having forgotten our meeting. Her eyesight was failing, she explained, and her secretary, who might have reminded her, was on leave. We arranged another time and after more apologies, the shaky old voice said good-bye.

First time around, however, there was to be no interview. "I only asked you to come," she said, "so that you could attend a lesson and gain a feel of the place."

She was right. Nadia Boulanger's apartment proved to be something of a museum. Not on account of the rather worn old furniture that filled the library and the spacious lounge (it was large enough to accommodate

two grand pianos, around which pupils were gathered) but rather owing
to the memorabilia of French spiritual life of the early twentieth century. Photographs on the walls were dedicated, with affectionate respect, by
Georges Rouault;[1] with thanks for inspiring enthusiasm and life force, by
Paul Valéry.[2] A drawing by Stravinsky, with a personal dedication to Nadia.
A photograph of Fauré, dedicated to Lili Boulanger.[3] More photos inscribed
for Lili by Debussy, Saint-Saëns, d'Indy, Paul Vidal.[4] And, of course, paintings—among them a Berthe Morisot.[5]

Some fifteen or twenty pupils were singing Bach when I arrived. Or
rather, they would have been singing, had Boulanger not stopped them at every other note. Now she would upbraid the shy young man at the piano whose
playing did not satisfy the aged teacher, now she would associate freely and
pronounce some general truths. For instance, when she had the impression
that the pianist was not dedicating his whole being to the music, she declared:
"Life is only worth living if we take a passionate interest in whatever we are
engaged in." The singing resumed, conducted energetically by Boulanger.
Later, she played the upper voice on the piano with her left hand, together
with the accompanist, to point to salient features of the music. And, just as
she was expecting it from her pupils, she was giving her utmost; her passion
for music-making was overpowering. She was guided by what she conceived
of as the music's essence and relentlessly weeded out everything that did not
wholly correspond to that idea.

After class, her pupils went up to Boulanger, ever so shyly and respect-
fully, exchanging a few words with her. She was then surrounded by elderly
ladies who enthusiastically commented on the lesson—Boulanger appeared
to be ignoring their effusion.

Presently she looked at me, her glasses magnifying the sharp look in her
large brown eyes. I assumed she had not recognized me; after all, her eyesight
was so poor. I was at a loss as to whether she was expecting me to talk to her
or she was about to say something. For a few seconds, we were staring into
one another's eyes, until I decided to introduce myself once again. She then
responded with disarming kindliness and self-irony and made a reference to
her bad eyes. We arranged another appointment and the interview took place
at last.

---

1   Georges Rouault (1871–1958), French painter.
2   Paul Valéry (1871–1945), French poet, philosopher, and essayist.
3   Gabriel Fauré (1845–1924), French composer, teacher of Nadia Boulanger. Lili Boulanger
    (1893–1918) was Nadia's sister, a talented composer, whom Nadia mourned and promoted all her
    life.
4   Paul Vidal (1863–1931), French composer, conductor, and music teacher.
5   Berthe Morisot (1841–95), French impressionist painter.

Of course, it was anything but an interview in the proper sense of the word. I held the microphone close to her lips and let her say whatever came to her mind. My instincts told me that questions would be unnecessary; all Nadia Boulanger needed was a hint suitable to trigger off a train of thought. As to the nature of the hint, I endeavored for it to encourage her to sum up, to draw conclusions, and to recall her contacts with great musicians—anybody, in fact, she had had during the course of her long life occasion to meet. Eventually, I decided to leave it all to her. Whatever she wanted to say would be of interest.

By way of introduction, I cited a recollection of Elliott Carter's that I had found in his conversations with Allen Edwards:[6] *Boulanger had explained not only the reason for a particular arrangement of tones in the score but also pointed to alternative possibilities—what the composer might have done instead. Hence my first question.*

Bálint András Varga (BAV): What, in your view, is composing?

Nadia Boulanger (NB): Carter attributes to me something that I do not deserve. I do not know what composing—this mysterious and wonderful activity—is. The most important things are unknowable.

Recently, I bought a book by André Malraux.[7] I had long wanted to read it. Now at last I have it but have not yet had time to read it. The blurb says, among other things: "A reply to questions to which there can be no answer." I wonder whether this sentence comes from Malraux; in any case, I believe that composing is a reply to questions to which there can be no answer.

I visited a school one day. Twelve- or fifteen-year-old boys were sitting in their rows. I told them: "If I knew what it is that interests you, I would try and give you a reply." I shall never forget what happened after that, even though it goes back some forty years. A little boy stood up and asked: "Do you mean that if I ask you a question, you will answer it?" "I did not promise that," I said. "I shall try to reply. Ask your question." The little boy pondered for quite a while and then said: "Can you explain the difference between a very good piece of music and a masterpiece?" That was the most beautiful question anyone had ever asked me. Still, I could not reply, for even though I knew the answer, I did not know it. There is much else I do not know. What is imagination? I know and yet I do not know. Or

---

6   Allen Edwards, *Flawed Words and Stubborn Sounds: A Conversation with Elliott Carter* (Chicago: Norton, 1972).

7   André Malraux (1901–76), French writer and politician.

personality? What constitutes it? Even weaker works by great composers bear the stamp of their personality. But where does it come from?

For me, mathematics is a closed book, but one of my pupils is at home in it. He says some calculations can be taken to a certain point but you cannot go any further. For thousands of years, mathematicians have addressed those problems but none of them has found a solution. I believe the moment a composition has become an individual, unique creation, something has been born for which we live, in which we believe but which we cannot define. Can you explain why of all people Leonardo, Dante, and Shakespeare created masterpieces? No. And yet, you can immediately identify them as works of geniuses. I do not even try to find an explanation. This is to a certain extent a question of faith. Really important things in life are in the long run inexplicable.

Actually, it does not make much sense to attempt to explain too many things. I read an interesting article in this morning's paper. We talk so much about sexual life—it says—we analyze it, describe it in detail to such an extent as to extinguish people's appetite for it. I think if we incessantly attempt to explain beauty, it stops being the extraordinary mystery it is. On the other hand, there does exist something that you can analyze. However, is analysis the only explanation for the result? I should not think so. I might put it like this: if the means are unsuitable, we cannot reach the highest peaks. That could be true.

BAV: It was those means that you have been teaching these past decades.

NB: I do not know. I have been teaching for seventy years this year, ever since graduating from the Conservatoire. There is something that astounds me, for which I can find no explanation: young people come to me, some stay for months, or perhaps one or two years. I am old and know I shall not see them again. Why then do they interest me so passionately? I suffer and do not know why and what from. I cannot change anything. But if they did not interest me so much, teaching would be torture.

I had the enormous luck to have attended the classes of Fauré. We had already acquired some academic training by the time we became his pupils. In those days, it only consisted in the grammar of music, its orthography, writing exercises—the rudiments.

I have often been asked—I have in fact asked it myself ever since 1902–4: what lay behind the tremendous influence Fauré exerted on us? Did he have a system, did he have a method? Did he force anything on us? What did he actually say? I remember, sometimes he remained silent and we thought he was not paying us any attention. One day, however, he made a remark which did not seem to have anything to do with the matter in hand but through that remark he induced us to consider the problem again. He did not issue any instructions; neither did he express an opinion: he respected us. He tried to persuade us to reassess our views.

The most important feature of Fauré's teaching was his respect for the opinions of others. That is precisely how he made such a deep impression on us. My parents maintained a friendship with him over many years and I always thought highly of him. Nevertheless, we could never persuade him to talk about his music. In his friendly way, he would get around it and turn the conversation in a different direction. It was no artificial modesty, much rather self-protection. He did not want us to interfere in his private world.

BAV: Summing up: in order for the individual to develop freely, he needs thorough classical training.

NB: We were lucky in that we received a thorough elementary technical education early on: solfeggio, sight-reading, ear-training—all of which is beyond the reach of so many children nowadays. We only acquire it at twenty-five or twenty-eight when it is too late: we ought to have begun at five. After all, it would be absurd if we only started to learn reading at twenty-five. If one has a lively imagination but has not got the necessary background, one can end up in a dangerous situation. I may be wrong; in any case I do believe that if we do not know a language, we cannot express ourselves in it.

My mother was Russian but my command of the language is restricted to some forty or fifty words. I cannot even put together a sentence out of them. I just can't. I only know individual words and am glad I know them because I love the Russian language. However, I cannot speak it. My command of German is slightly better. I know, for instance, that verbs have to be placed at the end of sentences and I blindly observe that rule. As far as French is concerned, I lack Latin and Greek culture, consequently, I have no firm ground under my foot in my mother tongue. I use it a lot, consequently I can speak it fluently but have no clear picture of it in my mind.

As for music: I am what I am. Not much. I know that whatever I may have composed was useless. Still, I am at home in music, because I have been living in it ever since I was five and have been trained to move in it freely. Perhaps not very brightly and with no great success, but we could write a fugue within the given time and improvise on the organ according to the rules.

There is a great deal that needs to be taught. Style, for instance, which is based on the adherence to certain conventions. He who accepts them and can apply them freely, will realize that conventions can be filled with life. Those who have analyzed a great many compositions will know, sooner or later, that the fundamental structure of music did not change much between Bach and Ravel. This has changed since, but small wonder: after all, it was different in the Renaissance and, as far as we know, in ancient Greek music as well. There have always been, however, fundamental rules.

BAV: I understand you analyze classical masterpieces with your pupils. I wonder if you also encourage them to compose pieces which you then subject to analysis?

NB: I do not think analysis is particularly useful, but of course neither does it cause any harm. We might make a comment which for the young composer throws a new light on a particular aspect. It would, however, be rather childish, I think, for me to point to a note and say: you should change this. The need for change should be a realization on the part of the pupil.

My pupils and I make an agreement. I attempt to reply to their questions but failing questions I never reply. It would be dangerous, I think.

One has to teach a purely conventional, fundamental system. It has to be mastered, for he who does not know figures, cannot count. I am also convinced that we should help people to find faith. Everybody believes in something—of this I am sure, even if they deny it. Unconsciously, they do not tell the truth. We were all born and we shall also die sooner or later. Our bodies carry a fantastic secret: intelligence, brain, which will eventually conquer everything. Birth ... when did existence begin? Where did the first human being come from? Who knows? In trying to find an answer, we are like children who take their dolls apart to see what is inside. The doll is gone but there is no answer. Unavoidably, we come up against a secret.

BAV: I have attended one of your classes and gained the impression that beyond teaching music you also teach life. Perhaps somewhat like classical Greek philosophers did.

NB: How could we teach anyone without having a human contact with them? You will have seen a little boy in class. He is merely twelve years old, but his reactions are extremely interesting. He saw a film on Stravinsky last Tuesday. The day after, he told me: "How lucky I am! I spent two hours with Stravinsky and now we are spending two more with Bach." He is just twelve! His words show that he is already a personality. Teaching him without interfering with his development is no easy task.

It occurred to me this morning that we grow trees and flowers in the garden which are supposed to make a combined impression. If you look at them one by one, they lack any individuality. Then, there are also some which stand by themselves in the garden, there is no plant quite like them. We have to respect the growth of a unique plant, the possibly unorthodox way of its development. It may well have a surprise in store for us.

Stravinsky's mother was no musician. I used to know this kind and charming old lady. I am sure she wondered once in a while what an unusual boy she had brought into the world. Even if she may not have said as much, I presume she was nonplussed by *Sacre du printemps* when she first heard it. Incidentally, it was no surprise for me that an outstanding musician like Casals rejected new music. He was a great man and a great artist; we had to accept that he drew a line beyond which he would not go. Up to that point, however, he served music conscientiously, with admirable faith. It goes without saying that some contemporary compositions can be rather poor, but some are masterpieces. It has never been otherwise. Even with a genius like Bach, I would not dare to claim that all 210 of his cantatas are on the same high level. They are all very well done, of course, for Bach was a master of his trade.

Perhaps you know Valéry's dialogue with an architect.[8] The architect goes for a walk in the city with his friend and says to him: "Have you noticed that many of the houses here are mute? Some talk—and a very few of them sing."

As I mentioned to you early on in our conversation: the nearer I get to the end of my road, the more I am aware of the influence Fauré exerted on me in his quiet way. Because he was modest and had respect for us. He never talked about himself. And he observed us without our noticing it. I remember how astonished I was that he should have remembered one of my exercises ten years on. My dear master! How could I ever thank him for the attention he paid me? Attention, after all, is a sign of esteem.

We live our lives next to one another without actually taking note of one another, without listening to one another. We read without grasping what our eyes see. And we utter again and again the terrible words: "I am afraid I have no time." I myself say them, day after day. I give lessons and each has to last sixty minutes. Why sixty? Ten would do sometimes, at others even three hours do not suffice. Organizing our lives that way is absolutely impossible—we cannot even exist like that.

BAV: Casals drew a line in music, you have said. How about you?

---

8   Paul Valéry, *Eupalinos ou l'architecte* (1923).

NB: I believe I have not stopped. Of course, an outsider is better placed to see that. I do, in any case, make choices. I am sure you remember a wonderful remark of Valéry [that] an artist has to be judged by what he rejects. That is, where he says no to something.

Rejection is perhaps a silly gesture—but then again, we might be justified to do so. I try to be honest and steer clear of blind prejudices. You can only open yourself to the world if you are no longer very young. You can then come to like something which is alien to your personal taste but you recognize beauty in it. If a work of art carries truth within itself, in other words, if it is authentic, it is immaterial whether it appeals to our taste.

We have been talking of Stravinsky. I knew him quite well. His human greatness evoked respect. He was not without frailties, of course, but they were of no significance—after all, he was no saint in the conventional sense of the word. He was genuine, true to himself and to others. He was not devoid of prejudices, but his actions were sincere. In accepting a new system of composition, he was not out to please others. He took an interest in it. And he was able to concentrate with all his energy—on anything, in fact, whatever engaged his attention—for instance on the arrangement of chairs in his room.

One day, he kindly agreed to give a class to my students. One of them was rather weak and the composition he had produced was even weaker. I asked him not to show it to Stravinsky, even if he asked for it. He should say he had brought nothing. My pupil, however, insisted on showing his piece. "If Stravinsky were to express the wish to take a look at it, I shall do so," he said, "I deserve criticism."

I was apprehensive about what was going to happen. Stravinsky took the music in his hand, and addressed the pupils as if they were his own children (of whom he happened to be very fond). And he told the young man that his piece was totally worthless in a way as to make him feel positively happy. Perhaps he decided there and then never to compose again, but he was filled with inner peace.

Stravinsky and I spent a great deal of time together in California. I was actually staying at his house in Hollywood. It was intriguing to observe how he pretended to be pleased about having become American. At the same time, he continued to speak Russian, quoted from the Bible in Russian, ate Russian food, adorned his rooms with icons. He was profoundly Russian—and yet, he made believe that he was happy about his U.S. citizenship, his American environment.

BAV: Wherever I happen to be in the world, I meet your pupils. Do they keep in touch with you?

NB: Hardly a month goes by without an exchange of news with Copland. Others, too, write to me. Last year, one of them invited me for lunch with two of my assistants. At the table, he asked me: "Do you know why it was so important for me to see you again?" "No," I replied, "but I rather think we are celebrating some sort of an anniversary." "Fifty years ago today," he said, "you gave me my first lesson." He still comes to see me once a year.

BAV: Do they send you their compositions?

NB: Sometimes. There must be a limit; after all, we only have one life!

Now, however, you must go. I do not know when I can see you again. I am going to be terribly busy in the next several weeks.

o

I had hesitated to put my last question, for Boulanger was palpably becoming restless. Her request for me to leave was made in a voice that commanded obedience. Reluctantly and rather too slowly, I gathered my things and in doing so, I attempted to get her to talk. It was then, one or two minutes before I left, that she mentioned she had met Bartók. I would have looked expectantly into her eyes if I had not known that she was practically blind.

I took my leave and on arriving home, immediately wrote a letter to Nadia Boulanger to thank her for the interview and to ask her to put to paper anything she wished to say about Bartók.

She replied in hand, in irregular letters. This is what I managed to decipher:

> *It was infinitely moving for me to meet the man who carried his genius as a responsibility. Over the years, we met a number of times; on two or three occasions, we lunched together at my mother's house. His death was a great tragedy. I was not in New York at the time and did not learn of his passing until sometime later.*
>
> *We used to talk a lot about him with my dear, excellent friend, László Lajtha.[9] We would evoke memories of the past, the penetrating conversations we had conducted. What a noble soul Bartók had, what [a] splendid mind! For us who loved and admired him, he is very much alive.*
>
> *I shall never forget the profound impression his personality made on me, but I lack the ability to convey it in words. Fragility and strength, reserve and generosity were combined in him. Every word he uttered was*

---

9 László Lajtha (1892–1963), Hungarian composer. His music, published in France, was closer in spirit to French culture than to that of most of his colleagues in Hungary.

expressive. His extraordinary dignity saved him from any back-slapping familiarity. His simplicity was more than what the word conveys.

I also remember meeting Zoltán Kodály. First at the BBC in London, then in Paris where he visited me, finally at a school in Budapest where he gave so many young children an inestimable key to understanding music.

Please do what you can with these notes, hastily jotted down. I have so many obligations to keep in mind that I find I cannot create order in the past, even though for me it never ceases to be the present as well. With apologies and many good wishes, Nadia Boulanger.

At the bottom of the page, in a different handwriting (possibly the secretary's) I found the following postscript:

I hope sooner or later you will be able to do something for the music of my little sister. If you should not be familiar with it, I shall be happy to send you some scores. You will then surely understand why I admire the music of that fragile, so young girl who carried within her such dramatic power and who had such great prospects opening up for her.

Paris, 1974

MUSIC ADMINISTRATORS

SIR WILLIAM GLOCK

1 9 0 8 – 2 0 0 0

W illiam Glock was one of the doers, the accomplishers. Also, one of those who sought to improve the world he had inherited, to make it better for others: in his case, for composers and their public. During his years with the BBC, between 1959 and 1972, he succeeded in bringing about enduring changes in British musical life, opening its doors and windows for the music of the twentieth century. The dimensions of his achievement are indicated by the fact that those years have come to be known as the Glock Era.[1]

We met in 1976, after William had retired from the BBC. I was aware of his stature in British musical life and was suitably impressed when he offered to come to my dingy little hotel for our interview. For him, it appeared to be the most natural thing in the world. It was a rainy day in London, but he turned up on time, even slightly early, for, as he explained, he needed to change before going to the opening of the National Theater.

William Glock was one of the most unassuming and most lovable of the great men I have had occasion to meet. He inspired respect and, as the years went by, sympathy.

Perhaps it was in the year of our interview, perhaps somewhat later, that he introduced me to his second wife, the lovely and charming Anne, whose beautiful head was crowned by abundant white hair. We had arranged to meet in a café, principally to see Oriel, William's daughter from his first marriage, who was staying briefly in London on a visit from Brazil where she had settled. I felt rather out of place; I still cannot quite understand why William wanted me to be there.

---

1   Leo Black, *BBC Music in the Glock Era and After: A Memoir* (London: Plumbago Books, 2010).

In any case, it was a sad occasion: the young woman was visibly in poor health, having been infected in Brazil by some virus that in those days could not be cured. She died a few years later, in 1980, and William never ceased to mourn her. But in that café, their conversation struck me curiously as one between two strangers; it had none of the intimacy I would have expected between father and child.

When Editio Musica Budapest was organizing an international composers' competition, my boss asked me to think of an illustrious personality he could invite to sit on the jury. I immediately thought of William, and László Sarlós was delighted. Thanks to that idea, William and Anne spent several days in Budapest and I got to know them a bit better. I remember asking how I might address them. He said simply: William! And that was that. No question of Lady Glock either—just Anne.

What one ought to have reckoned with: the former director of Dartington Summer School and subsequently the controller of music at the BBC took his responsibility extremely seriously. His fellow jury members had long made up their minds, William was still poring over the scores. A degree of irritation was the result.

We continued to keep in touch by exchanging letters. He always wrote his by hand, the margins characteristically describing an inward curve, the words always legible and tidy. When in 1984 it came to marking William's tenth anniversary as artistic director of the Bath Festival (a festival best known to the musical world from the years when it was directed by Yehudi Menuhin, 1959–68), it was a matter of course for me to attend. The more so, since for all his success, some people had decided ten years were enough and it was time for him to go.

William had no intention of leaving and it pained me to watch his face as he was being celebrated—for celebrated he was—much against his will. Some concerts were given in his honor. One included the world premiere of Boulez's Dérive *and of a piano duet by György Kurtág, performed by the composer and his wife Márta.[2] They had rehearsed conscientiously, of course, and asked me to listen to the last rehearsal prior to the concert. I was supposed to*

---

2   *Dérive* carries the dedication "pour William Glock, 8 juin 1984, Bath." I seem to remember hearing its first performance on that day, even though the official world premiere did not take place until January 31, 1985, in London, with Oliver Knussen conducting the London Sinfonietta. However, I must believe William Glock, who says in his *Notes in Advance: An Autobiography in Music* (Oxford: Oxford University Press, 1991), 174–75, that Boulez was late in delivering the score and the piece was not played at the farewell concert. Kurtág arranged a choral work for four hands and called the piece *Responsorium.* It is also dedicated to Glock and was published by Editio Musica Budapest in Book 8 of *Játékok* in 2010.

comment, which I did, dutifully, and the Kurtágs carried out my suggestions as if I had had any authority to make them.

One evening, William appeared as a pianist, together with a string quartet. I wish I had retained any memory of his music-making. I can see him vividly, sitting at the piano on the left-hand side of the stage and the quartet at the other end of the grand piano but my brain has no sound to associate with it. My only explanation is a psychological one: I was so anxious for him to succeed—I almost had stage fright on his behalf—that I did not register the music.

I remember a visit to William's house in the country. Anne was in the hospital and he seemed desperately lonely and worried. Still, he had the energy to cook a meal for me and as we took our seats at the dinner table, William described her illness. "It does not mean she has to die, does it?" he asked me. She survived.

Royal Festival Hall, London. Postconcert reception. William and Anne were sitting side by side, both of them looking very old and very frail. Nobody seemed to be noticing their presence, until John Drummond, a successor of William as controller, made a short speech, welcoming the Glocks and commending William's significance in British musical life. William was obviously embarrassed, looking straight ahead, his face slightly red (but then he did have a ruddy complexion). Anne was leaning sideways, against William, her eyes cast down.

That was the last time I saw them. Anne died in 1995, and William followed her, aged ninety-two, in 2000. John Drummond, a generation younger, born in 1934, died far too young, in 2006.

Back to that small room in the King's Hotel, off Hyde Park, in London in 1976. With no Internet, it had been difficult to glean details of William's biography by way of preparing for our interview. I found out that he had been a pupil of Artur Schnabel, so we started from that.

William Glock (WG): I became Schnabel's pupil when I was twenty-two. I had started playing the piano at five. Then I was sent to a private school, and continued my studies in Cambridge. I obtained my degree in history.

Bálint András Varga (BAV): In British public schools, it is supposed to be difficult to hold your own if you are drawn to the arts rather than to sports.

WG: I was fond of cricket.

BAV: That may have been a saving grace.

WG: Perhaps. In any case, I can well remember my Latin master who suffered from a bad case of asthma that may have aggravated his cantankerous bent. He did not at all take kindly to the fact when, at the age of sixteen, I was allowed to devote more time to music than to classical Latin authors. I played the piano and the organ. That is how I was granted an organ scholarship in Cambridge.

BAV: You said just now that you had studied history.

WG: I studied history and music. I received an organ scholarship, which meant I was regularly playing at services, and also conducted the chorus at Caius College. I spent four years at university, between 1926 and 1930.

BAV: Did you meet any interesting people there?

BAV: Edward Dent was my professor. He was well known in musical circles in Europe: he was president of the International Society for Contemporary Music since its foundation in 1922.[3] He suited the requirements of that position ideally, for he spoke most European languages, even Hungarian, I think. He was on friendly terms with everybody, he understood their needs and helped them whenever he could. His day seems to have consisted of forty-eight hours: twenty-four he devoted to his own work, and as many to his colleagues, musicians, who turned to him. Dent was not only a major scholar but also a great man, enterprising and with a wide horizon.

I was also fond of Boris Ord who taught at King's College.[4] He had recently returned from Germany, knowing all the latest music he had heard on the Continent. He and I performed Stravinsky's Concerto for Piano and Wind Instruments, in an arrangement for two pianos.[5] That was in 1927.

I had many friends who were far more knowledgeable than I. One of them, for instance—his name was Robert Collet—knew Bartók's Second String Quartet by heart! In those years, it counted as a remarkable achievement.

In Cambridge, there were numerous opportunities for us to listen to music. On a foggy Sunday morning in the autumn of 1930, a friend knocked on my door and said: "Schnabel is playing in Oxford this afternoon, why don't you come?" It took us six hours to reach Oxford in that weather, but we made it. He played Schubert's posthumous A-Major Sonata and Beethoven's Opus 111, among other things. I made up my mind there and then to go to Berlin and study with him. That's what happened.

---

3 Edward Dent (1876–1957), noted writer on music, was president of the ISCM between 1922 and 1938.
4 Boris Ord (1897–1961), British organist, composer, and choirmaster of King's College, Cambridge.
5 The Concerto for Piano and Wind Instruments was composed in 1923–24.

BAV: Can you remember what it was that made such a deep impression on you?

WG: Primarily, I suppose, the tremendous intensity of his playing. That the scales, the accompaniment and figurations sounded with a clarity I had never even dreamed of, and also that every single strand of the music lived a life of its own. That was in part due to his extraordinary capacity of concentration. He sat motionless at the piano. That was, of course, nothing out of the ordinary: I remember Rachmaninov who sat at the keyboard as if he had swallowed a sword. In any case, that electrifying experience during a foggy Sunday afternoon many decades ago, changed my life.

BAV: What was Schnabel like as a teacher?

WG: Very patient. And he never forgot anything. Usually, we played him a big work; on one occasion, I showed him the *Diabelli Variations*. He listened to it and afterward he could remember every single detail [of my playing]. He was kind but extremely strict. Sometimes, we would practice a bar or a phrase for half an hour until he was satisfied with it.

BAV: Did he concentrate on piano technique or questions of music?

WG: He only addressed himself to technical problems if something was going badly or was not working at all. He would then make suggestions. Otherwise he did not waste time on purely technical matters. We learned most from listening to his playing. The same with Cortot. I once asked Vlado Perlemuter, the French pianist, what he had learned from Cortot.[6] "I listened to his playing," he replied.

BAV: I do not expect, though, that you attempted to play the piano exactly like Schnabel.

WG: Of course not. That was the great risk. Many ended by absorbing his style without matching the level of his playing. Primarily, we learned from Schnabel principles, the philosophy of musical interpretation.

Interestingly enough, he was against teaching the same work twice. He did not want us to show him a work again that we had studied at the previous lesson. In his view, we did not study that particular piece, but music, in general. Sometimes, the lessons lasted a very long time, four hours even. Afterward, I felt I had so much to digest that I did not return for two weeks.

Of course, I was also allowed to attend the lessons of my fellow-students. I would arrive in the Wielandstrasse 14 after lunch and leave at 11

---

6   Alfred Cortot's (1877–1962) pupils also included Dinu Lipatti and Clara Haskil.

p.m. Schnabel was indefatigable. In this way, I came to know an immense repertoire. It goes without saying that I also had to play in front of my fellow pupils—a daunting audience.

BAV: Those classes remind me somewhat of the way Liszt taught.

WG: I think Busoni and others also taught along those lines. In a certain sense they were quite a challenge because some of my friends played far better than me. I do not mean that the students were not also allies but it was certainly more of an ordeal to play for them than for an average audience. Schnabel was in a way the most generous of them. However, no weakness ever escaped his attention.

BAV: Did he make any suggestions as to how you should practice?

WG: In Cambridge, most of my time had been taken up by the organ, the chorus, and history. I also gave in a rather lighthearted way dozens of piano recitals. Now I know that I had failed to prepare properly. I had never got round to studying the piano properly.

When Schnabel auditioned me before accepting me among his pupils (I remember I played some Bach in Busoni's arrangement, a piece by Mozart and an excerpt from Schubert's posthumous Sonata in A Major) he said I was musical but added that I needed much more discipline. "You will have to learn to play *rubato* in time," he said. Not that he always succeeded himself . . . But I knew what he meant. He suggested that I take a few lessons from one of his pupils, Richard Laugs. I followed his advice but did not gain much from it.

An interesting thing happened after that. A friend of mine came to Berlin and one day I visited him in his hotel. I played for him Beethoven's Sonata, op. 110. Presently a lady entered the room. In her youth, she had studied with d'Albert and Teresa Carreño.[7] She said: "You know, you are very musical but you do not play the piano well enough. I am going to teach you every day." "I am sorry," I said, "I cannot afford it." "You will pay as much as you can," she replied.

I was staying at the time in Potsdam, with the family of a general. I traveled every day to Berlin to work with the lady. That was technical exercise indeed. For eight months, I never returned to Schnabel and when I played for him again, he was very happy with me. I had indeed made great progress and from then on, I benefited more from his classes, for I was better suited to realize his suggestions.

---

7   Teresa Carreño (1853–1917), Venezuelan pianist and composer.

BAV: Your technique had been developed by a musical grandchild of Liszt.

WG: You mean through d'Albert? Yes. In a way, I was taught by a great-grandchild of Beethoven and Czerny. There is also another music-gene-ological connection; one need not attach too much significance to it, of course. When I went up to Cambridge, there lived in the town a famous organist, "Daddy" Mann, the organist of King's College.[8] He auditioned me and as a result I was granted a scholarship. Well, his teacher had been taught by Handel! Is that not incredible? Handel must have been very old and his pupil not more than ten years old.

BAV: What was Berlin like in the 1930s?

WG: Very exciting indeed. It was not unusual for me to hear Furtwängler on Sunday and Monday (the dress rehearsal and the concert itself), Weingartner on Tuesday, Toscanini on Wednesday, Bruno Walter on Thurdsay, Leo Blech at the opera on Friday, and so on.

BAV: Klemperer conducted in the Kroll Oper in those years.

WG: Klemperer introduced many new pieces in the Kroll Oper. I heard a number of important premieres under his baton. In Berlin of the thirties, there was music all the time. Above all opera. Do not forget: there were three opera houses!

BAV: Politically, though, the situation was growing ever more precarious.

WG: I was innocent in politics. Perhaps I still am. But I had many Jewish friends, so it was impossible not to be aware of what was going on in the country.

BAV: How long did you live in Berlin?

WG: For three years, between 1930 and 1933. I left four months after Hitler came to power. Schnabel left at the same time: he moved to Como. I followed him there that summer and I think I stayed till August. Classes started at eight in the morning and finished at lunch: it was too hot to continue.

BAV: The next information I have of your life is that you were appointed music director of the BBC. But what happened before?

WG: I returned to Britain in 1933 and found employment as a music critic.

---

8 Arthur Henry "Daddy" Mann (1850–1929), organist at King's College for forty-two years (1876–1927). During his tenure, he raised the standard of choral singing, turning the choir into one of the best in the country.

BAV: I find it odd that having spent so many years with Schnabel and invested so much energy in playing the piano, you became a critic rather than embarking on a soloist's career.

WG: I do not think I was meant to be a soloist. Neither did I feel like it. I went to Schnabel because his was the most exciting music-making I had ever come across. I learned more about music from him than from anybody else. Dent was, of course, also excellent, and so was Boris Ord, but Schnabel gave me more than anyone else, especially with regard to Beethoven. To a certain extent, his Schubert was even more instructive but of course everything he played and taught was marked by the same masterful unity of line and form. His Schubert playing married lyrical expression to a rhythmic drive and discipline that lent it all a new kind of vitality.

Well then, I returned to England and did appear in concerts from time to time, mostly in Mozart piano concertos. During the years I spent in Germany, however, a London periodical had asked me to report on musical life in Berlin. My articles appeared with some regularity and soon on my return home, I was approached first by the *Daily Telegraph* where I worked briefly, and then by the *Observer*, where I stayed for eleven years.

BAV: For three years in Berlin, you heard some of the greatest conductors. How did London musical life compare, what impression did British orchestras and conductors make on you?

WG: There was one outstanding orchestra in London: that of the BBC. It was regularly conducted by Toscanini in the thirties. He actually said that if there was one orchestra with which he would gladly tour the world, it was the BBC Symphony. Beecham was also in his prime: he conducted the London Philharmonic Orchestra. And of course many chamber concerts were organized and the world's best soloists appeared in London.

BAV: I expect Dohnányi and Bartók were among them.

WG: I only heard Dohnányi from records. No, I am wrong, I am sorry. I did hear him live, once, perhaps immediately after the war. Very impressive. I also admire Bartók, but I never met him in person. The only significant composer of the century I did know quite well was Stravinsky.

BAV: I hope you will talk about him in some detail. But first of all, I would like to find out about your work as a critic. It was your job as a very young man to review concerts of conductors you admired. Did you have the courage to find fault with their interpretations at all?

WG: I was twenty-five or twenty-six years old when the *Observer* employed me. Indeed, far too young to be a critic. I think I was prejudiced in that I condemned any interpretation that deviated considerably from Schnabel's. I see now that at thirty-five you are more likely to accept a range of different views than when you are ten years younger. Now, at sixty-eight, even more. I do see that fault.

However, youth also has its advantages: enthusiasm, intensity. My boss was an extraordinary man: Fox Strangways.[9] He was fifty years older than I was and while it is easy to argue with people who are twenty-five years older, fifty years do make a difference. We agreed on most things. However, he was addicted to argument. One day he lost his patience: "Damn you, I cannot make you angry!" Whereupon I replied: "You should try harder!"

He was a marvelous man, with one reservation: he knew exactly which concert would be of interest and kept it for himself. I had to cover the dull ones. Most of the time, he would be writing about Toscanini, not I.

However, I did get to Salzburg. I believe it was in 1936 when Toscanini performed *Falstaff* and *Fidelio* and also conducted Verdi's *Requiem*. I remember I criticized *Fidelio*, something which made quite a stir back home, but my senior, Fox Strangways, defended me: "Well done, wonderful!" he said. I forget what I may have written, it cannot have been all that important. In any case, this answers your question if I had the courage to criticize the greatest conductors. I really was not taken with *Fidelio*.

BAV: Shall we now talk about your friendship with Stravinsky? How did you get to know him?

WG: I think by accident. Perhaps not entirely. In 1954, I became chairman of the British Section of the International Society for Contemporary Music. For a number of years, we mounted fourteen to fifteen concerts per season and in the autumn of 1956, I invited Stravinsky and Craft. It led to the first British performances of *Canticum sacrum* and of the *Chorale Variations on "Vom Himmel hoch."*[10] The venue was the church St. Martin in the Fields in Trafalgar Square, and Stravinsky was in attendance. He had recovered from a heart attack shortly before; he took my arm and asked me for the bathroom. That was the beginning of our acquaintance. We became friends and he often

---

9 Arthur Henry Fox Strangways (1859–1948), music critic of the London *Times* (1911–25) and the *Observer* (1925–39).

10 Stravinsky, *Canticum sacrum ad Honorem Sancti Marci Nominis* (1955) for chorus and orchestra. *Chorale Variations on Bach's "Vom Himmel hoch,"* arranged for chorus and orchestra (1956).

came to conduct the BBC Symphony Orchestra during my tenure as music director of the radio.[11]

BAV: Those who knew Stravinsky usually described him as a controversial, complex personality, full of attractive and not so attractive traits.

WG: Do not forget that I first met him in 1956 when he was seventy-four years old. If he had been younger, I am sure I would have been alarmed by him.

To tell you the truth, I did meet him once, much earlier, in 1934 or 1935, in a train, traveling from Bournemouth to London. I had been there to hear Stravinsky perform the *Capriccio* and to review it.[12] As chance would have it, we boarded the same carriage. Young as I was, I took a seat next to him, introduced myself and posed him a silly question: "What are you writing these days?" "A concerto for two pianos," he replied.[13] I then asked him an even sillier question: "And what is it going to be like?" I shall never forget his answer: "It will be like the 'Hammerklavier' Sonata, but much more concentrated."

So I had met Stravinsky once before, but twenty-two years had to pass before seeing him again. From then on, we often spent some time together. I frequently entertained him for lunch in the company of Boulez and others. He also visited me in my house and in 1957 he spent three weeks at the Dartington Summer School which I directed. It was a great experience; we performed many of his compositions.

BAV: Did Stravinsky interfere a great deal with the performances of his works?

WG: No, because he trusted Craft. He himself conducted his own pieces completely differently, of course. He did not interfere with the rehearsals but he was always sitting there, listening attentively, keeping an eye on everything. He was present with his whole being.

Sometimes, he could be sharp. One evening we were having a guitar concert at Dartington and at the end, after an encore, he turned to me and

---

11 I have asked the Stravinsky expert Stephen Walsh to put a figure behind the rather vague word "often." Here is his reply: "As far as I can establish he conducted the BBC SO only once before the war, in *Persephone* in 1934 (it's sometimes hard to identify the orchestra from reviews, but I think this is right). After the war he conducted them four times in the years between 1958 and 1961 (including the UK premiere of *Agon* in December 1958, a concert of *Oedipus Rex* and a studio recording of *Oedipus Rex* and the Symphony in C in 1959, and *Persephone* again in the autumn of 1961). I think that's all. These postwar performances were, of course, under Glock's aegis. Whether you call that 'often' or not, I suppose, is a matter of taste."

12 *Capriccio* for piano and orchestra was composed between 1926 and 1929.

13 The Concerto for Two Pianos was composed in 1935.

asked: "Who wrote that?" "Villa-Lobos, I think," I replied.[14] "Whenever I hear a poor piece of music, it invariably turns out to have been composed by Villa-Lobos!"

BAV: What was Stravinsky like in day-to-day contact?

WG: He was above all friendly, warm, and extraordinarily spontaneous. For instance, when I was handing him a glass of good wine, he said: "Silence! Let us drink it in silence!" He enjoyed everything spontaneously and also physically.

BAV: Did he ever discuss with you his conviction that music does not express anything?

WG: In conducting, he did not create the impression as though he was guided by that idea.

BAV: Did it never come up in conversation?

WG: We talked of many things, also about conducting. A great pity I cannot remember so much that I ought to. After a BBC concert, a friend and I invited him for lunch and it was then that he remarked that he thought it unthinkable for anyone to sit down to conduct. A conductor also had to act the role, his gestures might resemble those of a dancer. That, I think, was an interesting comment.

BAV: In other words, Stravinsky was in favor of a choreographic style of conducting.

WG: Yes, I think you can put it like that. His own movements, on the other hand, were simple—they had a dramatic simplicity. I remember, years later, BBC Television broadcast a performance of *The Firebird* conducted by Stravinsky, with the Philharmonia Orchestra.[15] It was an unforgettable experience; a pity the camera did not show him at the end. His eyes mesmerized everybody. He had an incredible alertness at the age of eighty-one. Yes, we did talk of a great many things but never about the idea that music does not express anything. Perhaps he had changed his mind by that time.

BAV: Now we have arrived at the time when you acted as music director of the BBC. During the course of those thirteen years, between 1959 and 1972, contemporary music was given far more prominence than ever before. What were your guiding principles?

---

14 Heitor Villa-Lobos (1887–1959), Brazilian composer and conductor.
15 *The Firebird* (1910), ballet, choreographed by Michel Fokine.

WG: To put it simply: it was my goal to meet the public's needs. More importantly, I endeavored to create new needs, to plan more boldly. Let us go back a few years to make the picture clearer.

In 1948, I was asked to direct a summer music school. Initially it worked at Bryanston in Dorset; five years later, it moved to Dartington where it has stayed ever since. In those years, the programs of the BBC were rather conservative, whereas at Bryanston and then at Dartington, the concerts ranged from Perotinus to Berio and Boulez, that is, from medieval music to the avant-garde of our times. The teachers included composers such as Berio, Maderna, Nono, Elliott Carter, Lutosławski, and many others, also some of the most outstanding instrumentalists and singers (Enescu, Szigeti, Elisabeth Schumann, Dietrich Fischer-Dieskau, and so on).

Those two principles—that is, a boldly varied repertoire and high-level performances—guided me also when I joined the BBC in 1959. I could also say that at the BBC I attempted to further develop the goals and principles of my work at Bryanston and Dartington on a far larger scale.

As I have mentioned, the music programs of the BBC were rather gray and uninteresting when I took over leadership of the department. In the first era of broadcasting, Edward Clark had been music director. He organized some memorable concerts in the 1930s. Sir Adrian Boult, the first permanent conductor of the BBC Symphony Orchestra, was also a very enterprising musician. The situation, however, had completely changed by 1959. Schoenberg's works were hardly ever on the air, Webern was never broadcast, and even Berg extremely rarely.

I started a chamber music series I called "Thursday Invitation Concerts." They were capricious in their programming, in the number of various ensembles appearing on each occasion, in the invigorating succession of the greatest compositions and in the way the old and the new complemented one another, or, if we were lucky, contrasted with one another in an instructive fashion. In 1960, for instance, at the very first concert, *Le marteau sans maître* (1953–55) was placed between two Mozart string quintets. It may well have been an odd idea . . . I remember other programs as well: Beethoven's Septet and Schoenberg's *Serenade*, or *Pierrot lunaire* and the *Goldberg Variations*. We also performed all major recent works (as far as you can make a reliable judgment on something like that), together with old music, beginning once again with Perotinus and Machaut.

The Invitation Concerts immediately caught the imagination of the critics and the public, as if they had all been longing for this to happen. One practical outcome of the series has been (and this still fills me with pleasure today) that a number of excellent ensembles sprang up, several of which continue to be part of our musical life. Those ensembles were formed under the impact of the Invitation Concerts, influenced by the program policy represented by those concerts.

BAV: As far as I know it was your idea to appoint Boulez to be principal conductor of the BBC Symphony Orchestra. Many people thought at the time that it was a daring choice, for Boulez had not yet convinced everyone that he was a significant conductor.

WG: I had by then known Boulez for a long time. In 1951, he wrote the article "Schoenberg Is Dead" for the journal the *Score* of which I was the editor at the time.[16] The article met with a rather stormy reception and I lost one or two friends for a few years because of it. Boulez was regularly informing me of the concerts of the *Domaine musical*, of his own compositions and other activities.[17] In 1956, as chairman of the British section of the ISCM, I invited him with the *Domaine musical* for a concert in London. We met quite frequently, in London and in Paris.

In 1963, Boulez and I were sitting in the Savoy Hotel with a small piece of paper in front of us. It had the titles of eighteen or twenty works which Boulez wished to conduct in the coming season. During the course of our conversation, a few more titles were added which I had suggested. The concerts with the BBC Symphony Orchestra in 1964 scored an immense success. Then, in the spring of 1965, the ensemble toured the United States, with some unforgettable concerts conducted by Boulez at Carnegie Hall. The success was repeated in Moscow and Leningrad, early in 1967. On those occasions as well as at the Proms in 1965 the orchestra was accorded a reception which only matched that of Toscanini.

It required then no "daring" for me to invite Boulez to become the orchestra's principal conductor, after Colin Davis had taken over Covent Garden in 1967.

Needless to say, I had first had to obtain the agreement of my bosses. Having succeeded, I immediately flew to Holland where Boulez was conducting at the time. We walked seven miles on the seashore near Scheveningen on a very windy day, and by the end I was so exhausted that I had sore muscles for two weeks afterward. Boulez was not tired at all, but I could hardly walk. I told him: "I could not have asked you before but now

---

16 William Glock founded the music journal *The Score* in 1949, and served as its editor until 1961.
17 Boulez launched the concert series *Domaine musical* in the 1953/54 season; it ran until 1973. Boulez himself conducted the concerts until 1966/67, when they were taken over by Gilbert Amy (b. 1936).

I do: would you be prepared to become chief conductor of the BBC?" He said yes—that is how it happened.

BAV: The concerts in the Round House were also your initiative, I expect.

WG: Yes, with Boulez. We had long been looking for a venue in London until we found a place suitable for orchestras to play eighteenth-century and new music. We wished to take the orchestra out of the studio and out of the Festival Hall. Not that we had anything against either, but it was our goal to find a venue which would lend itself to new kinds of concert where a new kind of audience would follow us. The Round House held some 800 or 1,000 people and it had a pleasant, informal atmosphere. I think it was the right choice, even if not everyone was happy with it. The other place was St. John's Church at Smith Square near the Houses of Parliament where Boulez conducted new music, Haydn masses, and works like that. St John's is just the right place for that purpose.

BAV: In other words, Boulez proved an ideal partner for you to realize the ideas you had conceived for Bryanston and Dartington.

WG: Yes, but he added to them his own personality. I am a sort of trial and error man, whereas Boulez is a planner and creator.

BAV: As music director of the BBC it was also your responsibility to devise the programs of the Proms, one of the largest festivals in the world. What method did you follow in planning it?

WG: Each September, just before the end of the previous season, I put two huge sheets of paper in front of me, with sufficient room for the programs of fifty-five concerts. I started with a blank page and usually with a blank head as well. Gradually, both were filled. To begin with, I tried to decide the programs of the twelve major events. I was mostly looking for compositions which included a chorus and ended up, more often than not, with operas. I realized, you see, that the average orchestral repertoire was not rich enough to yield fresh, substantial, and varied programs. You soon used up the usual run of pieces. Apart from the Mozart symphonies—and of course, there are not so many of those really . . .

BAV: But you also have the Haydn symphonies!

WG: There are many of those, that is true. It is just that they do not happen to attract the public. You have to protect the Haydn symphonies as you have to protect Schoenberg. It is scandalous but true. Anyhow, we still put them in.

One of my first decisions which broke with the orchestra-centered tradition of the Proms was to invite the Glyndebourne Opera. Then Covent Garden contacted me: why not us? Naturally, why not? The next step was the engagement of the English Chamber Orchestra and other chamber orchestras. I could be assured that the music literature of the eighteenth century would be perfomed in authentic interpretations. The new groups that I have mentioned already . . .

BAV: Could you please name some that were formed in those years?

WG: The Vesuvius Ensemble, the Pierrot Players (today's Fires of London), a little later the Nash [Ensemble]. There were many. The Melos [Ensemble] started earlier but it was, I think, inspired to play more new music because of our policy.

We expanded the repertoire in both directions: enriching the range of new music and going back to the eighteenth and seventeenth centuries, the Renaissance, the Middle Ages. It was a sort of sleepwalking act in a way. You had to watch what the others were doing, the other orchestras, and bring the best of that into the Proms. Then you had to sense what was needed, a little bit ahead of the public.

It was, of course, not just I. The beginning of interest in Mahler here was started by the BBC and that was before I came on the scene. All the symphonies were played twice over, in very fine performances, in 1958. Very little Mahler was done before that.

BAV: The prominence you gave to new music on the radio and concert programs must have inspired composers as well. What was your relationship with British composers and what new works were written for the BBC?

WG: Before I joined the BBC, the radio had commissioned very few new works. The tenth anniversary of the Third Programme in 1956 was an exception: several composers were asked for new works. As from 1960, we commissioned ten new pieces annually. Four were premiered at the Proms, one at the Cheltenham Festival where the BBC took part, one or two at the Festival Hall, and the rest within the framework of the Invitation Concerts.

I am sure you know Stravinsky's remark that symphonies were bought the way governments bought up surplus corn. In other words: we commissioned works nobody wanted and which invariably turned out to be poor. To my mind, the best solution was that when I heard that someone was writing a new work, I took a look at it and at the end I may have decided: all right, we are going to buy that. The best commissions included Peter Maxwell Davies's *Worldes Blis* (1969) for orchestra, a splendid work;

Scenes and Arias (1962; rev., 1966) for soloists and orchestra by Nicholas Maw; *Scenes from Comus* (1965) for soloists and orchestra by Hugh Wood; and one of Tippett's finest works, *The Vision of St Augustine* (1963–65) for baritone, chorus, and orchestra, that was premiered at the Festival Hall.

BAV: I now want to ask you something completely different. Is it true that you are descended from Gluck?

WG: Oh, I do not think so. My father carried out some research to find out what is behind it, but he never succeeded in obtaining absolute certainty. It is a fact that one of my ancestors was a conductor at the Berlin Opera House in the 1780s and he is said to have been related in some way to Gluck. But it is far from certain. His son fought under Blücher at Waterloo and his descendants eventually settled in Ireland. I am a quarter Irish, a quarter Bohemian, and a quarter German, perhaps.

BAV: And finally a few words about the four years since you retired. I understand you are more active than ever.

WG: I dabble in many things. I am music director of the Bath Festival and chairman of the London Orchestral Concert Board. It is my goal to persuade orchestras to play more new music and, in general, to offer more interesting programs to the public. That particular activity I have just started. I teach at the Royal Northern College of Music in Manchester. That is also an exciting occupation. As pianist, I recently recorded twelve Haydn sonatas for a new label, Nimbus. I also edit a series of books for Eulenburg. One of the upcoming volumes will be a symposium on Boulez—the first important collection of studies on his music ever.[18] There is a book in the making on Elliott Carter and on Sir Michael Tippett—the latter is already with the printers.[19] There is a lot to do. And there is also some weeding to do in my garden!

London, 1976

---

18 William Glock, ed., *Pierre Boulez: A Symposium* (London: Ernst Eulenburg, 1986). The book includes William Glock's contribution under the title "With Boulez at the BBC."

19 David Schiff, *The Music of Elliott Carter* (Ithaca, NY: Cornell University Press, 1983), actually preceded the book on Tippett. Ian Kemp, *Tippett, the Composer and His Music* (London: Eulenburg Books, 1984). The Boulez symposium was longest in gestation, as Glock admitted in his introduction to *Pierre Boulez: A Symposium*.

WOLFGANG
STRESEMANN

1904–98

D r. *Wolfgang Stresemann was intendant of the Berlin Philharmonic Orchestra from 1959 until 1978 and again between 1984 and 1986. In all those years, Herbert von Karajan was principal conductor.*[1]

He was the son of Gustav Stresemann, one of Germany's major politicians between the two world wars who was decorated for his services as foreign minister and chancellor with the Nobel Peace Prize (1926). Who knows what turn European history would have taken if he had not died in 1929. Could he have hindered Hitler's rise to power?

Gustav Stresemann married a Jewish woman; his son Wolfgang emigrated with his mother to the United States in 1939. A lawyer by profession, Stresemann had also studied music and appeared as a conductor in Berlin in the 1920s. In the United States, he was principal conductor of the Toledo Symphony Orchestra between 1949 and 1955, and acted as assistant to Bruno Walter. He also tried his hand at composition, with symphonies among his works.

In addition, Stresemann was a regular contributor to the New Yorker Staats-Zeitung und Herold, *a German-language newspaper for which he was music critic between 1945 and 1949. He wrote hundreds of articles for émigrés from Germany—not only critiques and the season's previews but also essays on general musical subjects, such as the placing of instrumental groups in a symphony orchestra, illustrated by several examples.*[2]

---

1 Herbert von Karajan was appointed in 1955 and retired in 1989.
2 Wolfgang Stresemann's estate has been acquired by the Music Archives of the Berlin Academy of Arts. It has been presented in a booklet edited by the archives' leader, Dr. Werner Grünzweig

Wolfgang Stresemann returned to Germany in 1956, to take up his posi-
tion as intendant of the Radio-Symphonie-Orchester Berlin. In 1959, he was
invited to take over the Berlin Philharmonic Orchestra.

I remember sitting in his office in the Berlin Philharmonie designed by
Hans Scharoun.[3] *When I looked out of the window, I saw, disconcertingly*
nearby, the Berlin Wall and in the no-man's-land directly behind it, an East
German guard with his rifle, standing on the plateau of his watchtower.

Wolfgang Stresemann was stern and reserved. Try as I might to interest
him in the music of Hungarian composers, he was not impressed. He erected
a wall between us. I happen to know the year of my visit, for I remember
telling him about the music of Sándor Balassa (born 1935). "How old is he?"
Stresemann asked. "He is thirty-five." "If a composer has not made his name
by the age of thirty-five, he never will."

My visit was a flop. Seven years later, however, in 1977, we met again
in Budapest where he was on the jury of Hungarian Television's Second
International Conductors' Competition. Stresemann proved an ideal inter-
viewee. I was fascinated not only by what he said but also by his voice: it was
hushed as if he were telling me secrets, but also passionate. He clearly identi-
fied himself with the orchestra he represented and the iconic conductor who
was his boss.

In 1977, the Berlin Philharmonic was ninety-six years old and Herbert
von Karajan was only its fourth principal conductor, his predecessors being
Hans von Bülow, Arthur Nikisch, and Wilhelm Furtwängler.

o

Wolfgang Stresemann (WS): Yes indeed, the orchestra has been lucky
enough throughout its history to find principal conductors who suited it
best. It is important that the ensemble should attract top musicians for its
members but it is just as imperative that they should be led by a significant
musical personality of supreme authority. He guarantees the orchestra's
unmistakable identity.

When the Berlin Philharmonic Orchestra was founded in 1882, it was
governed by the musicians themselves. They also took artistic decisions,
including the choice of conductor. Their autonomy is valid to this day. That
is why those hoping to join the Philharmonic are auditioned by the entire

---

(*Wolfgang Stresemann: Archive zur Musik des 20; Jahrhunderts* [Berlin: Wolke, 2004]). I have taken
the information on Stresemann's journalistic activities from his introduction.

3   Hans Scharoun (1893–1972), German architect. He designed among others the Philharmonie in
Berlin (built between 1956 and 1963).

orchestra. The majority vote carries the day. Karajan has the right of veto: he may decide that a candidate is not suited for making music with the ensemble. He has, however, not used it to date.[4]

Admission is followed by a test year. When it is over, a two-thirds majority decides on the candidate's fate. Karajan's veto is valid also at this stage. Even a favorable decision, however, does not allow musicians to rest on their laurels: the orchestra may find that any particular member no longer meets its standards.

The musicians elect their principal conductor and their intendant; the latter has a committee of two to work with.

Self-government makes for a sense of responsibility shared by all the players: each of them contributes to the achievement of the ensemble as if it was a question of their personal success, beyond the prestige of the Philharmonic. This is particularly true of guest appearances. It goes without saying that the orchestra cannot always give its very best but it is thanks to self-government that it plays above a certain level even if a guest conductor may not be quite up to the mark. The orchestra is proud of its achievement and observes its own performances with unflagging self-criticism.

On the one hand, then, there is a conductor of genius and on the other, a democratic orchestra-republic which submits itself to the conductor of its own free will. Karajan, for his part, recognizes the right of self-determination and cooperates with the orchestra.

Bálint András Varga (BAV): Let us talk about the repertoire of the Berlin Philharmonic. I understand it was Arthur Nikisch who initiated the orchestra into the idioms of Beethoven, Brahms, and Bruckner.[5]

WS: As far as Beethoven and Brahms are concerned, most of the job had been done by Bülow. It was Nikisch, however, who introduced Bruckner to the orchestra.[6] Initially, Bülow was a supporter of Wagner; later, understandably enough (his wife, Cosima Liszt, had left him to live with Richard Wagner), he distanced himself from the composer and gradually moved closer to Brahms. It was Bülow who established the Berlin Philharmonic's

---

4   Karajan did veto the appointment of Dr. Otto Tomek (1928–2013) to succeed Stresemann upon the latter's retirement. Although supported by the orchestra and the Berlin Senate, Tomek's friendship with Krzysztof Penderecki and his frequent visits to the Warsaw Autumn made him suspect in the conductor's eyes, who said he wanted no communist as intendant. In hindsight, Tomek was grateful for Karajan's rejection, for he realized that he would have had a very hard time indeed, crushed between the millstones of conductor and orchestra, as was Dr. Peter Girth who was appointed in his stead.

5   Arthur Nikisch (1855–1922), Hungarian conductor.

6   Hans von Bülow (1830–94), German conductor and pianist.

Brahms tradition. Beyond advocating the music of Bruckner, Nikisch's taste was catholic enough to program symphonies by Mahler.

BAV: I believe his personality was diametrically opposed to Bülow's.

WS: Bülow was anything but tolerant; his correspondence tells us about his passionate likes and dislikes. He was an intellectual conductor and pianist who took an active part in the internecine warfare of musical life, the intensity of which is difficult to fathom today.

BAV: Interestingly enough, the name of Mozart never seems to come up in connection with Bülow or Nikisch.

WS: Mozart was played quite regularly. But, you know, at the time of Strauss, Mahler, and Bruckner with their powerful, surging streams of music, Mozart was regarded as too light, too rococo. One thing is certain: Bülow conducted *Don Giovanni* in Hamburg on several occasions, and the very first concert he ever conducted with the Berlin Philharmonic featured a Mozart symphony. The event was quite a sensation, for it continued with Haydn and ended with the "Eroica." The program was thought to be too demanding, too unorthodox: toward the end of the nineteenth century, the public was used to being served a fare of many shorter pieces, interspersed with solos. Bülow made some allowances at his second concert which he began with an overture, followed by an aria, but he also performed a Brahms symphony. It is in any case true that Mozart had a low profile on his repertoire, as indeed also on Nikisch's.

BAV: How could Bülow's dictatorial leanings be reconciled with the democracy of the orchestra-republic?

WS: It looked like this: Bülow was taken under contract, with the orchestra's approval, by the concert agency Hermann Wolff. Initially, the ensemble had sixty or seventy members who had eked out a precarious existence: they were chronically short of money. To tide them over their financial difficulties, a range of associations was formed, such as the Society of the Friends of the Philharmonic. The Music Academy also joined the ranks of those dedicated to helping the orchestra. Still, they needed a decisive force, a personality of the calibre of Bülow.

He was engaged at the time in Meiningen, where he led the court orchestra, and in Hamburg where he directed the Opera House. He was soon released from his duties in Meiningen (we need not go into the reasons) and it was at that point that Hermann Wolff, the first great impresario, who had Bülow on his roster, persuaded him to take on the representative concerts of the Berlin Philharmonic Orchestra, in addition to his position in Hamburg. The musicians knew very well that if they were to develop further, they needed Bülow. They were overjoyed that the conductor had agreed and submitted themselves quite consciously to his artistic will.

In his first letter to Wolff, Bülow made it clear that he would leave the orchestra the moment he found they were not following his instructions. He demanded four rehearsals which counted as unusual in those years: orchestras usually made do with half a rehearsal. The cooperation between Bülow and the Philharmonic proved highly successful, thanks to the musicians' determination to better themselves.

BAV: Sadly, Bülow did not live to see the advent of gramophone records. Is it at all possible to reconstruct the way he conducted?

WS: It is difficult. I think I could best liken him to a conductor who is no longer with us but we still remember him vividly: George Szell.[7] Both of them strove for a clear line and laid perhaps less stress on expression. Unlike Szell, however, Bülow was an eccentric. He would conduct a work at far too slow a tempo, and another time far too fast. He was, however, the first one to make sure that the orchestra actually played the notes in the score. He did not tolerate the scandalous laissez faire that was the order of the day in Berlin and surely elsewhere.

Initially Bülow's job was no doubt to teach the musicians to play together. I can well imagine that *espressivo* had to take second place. We must not forget, however, that Bülow was also an absolutely outstanding pianist and will have sensed the big line in every composition. We know that his piano playing was not devoid of expression, it was never hard.

BAV: How about Nikisch? You have said that artistically, he differed from Bülow a great deal. So did his personality, I suppose.

WS: Nikisch was a real gentleman: refined, friendly, and kind. Unlike the hard, awkward and rough Bülow, he was softer, full of charm. When it came to making music, however, he knew exactly what he wanted. He radiated a well-nigh hypnotic power which compelled musicians to play better than they were actually capable of. When asked how he did it, Nikisch said he did not know. "I stand in front of the orchestra and they play beautifully." These are irrational things which cannot be explained in a logical manner.

BAV: I believe you have seen him conduct.

---

7   Born in Budapest as György Széll in 1897, George Szell made a spectacular career in the United States, especially as principal conductor of the Cleveland Orchestra. He died in Cleveland in 1970.

WS: My mother took me to one of his concerts when I was a child. It would be wrong to make a judgment on the strength of that one encounter; I was too young and inexperienced in any case to draw conclusions about his style based on just one performance.

BAV: Perhaps you can recall the audience's reaction.

WS: The audience was always in rapture with Nikisch. People, you know, idolize great personalities, because they have a need to celebrate a hero. A strong personality at the height of his career always convinces the public; it forms its judgment on the basis of the overall quality of a performance and not its particular details. The so-called expert, the *mélomane*, develops an idea of his own about a composition and that makes him intolerant toward any other approach—that renders him dangerous. There were Walter fans, Furtwängler fans, and Toscanini fans. Someone I knew actually claimed he could listen to the *Meistersinger* only with Toscanini. That is prejudice carried to the extreme. This is in any case something we have to bear in mind in talking about success.

Nikisch was in his time *the* great conductor. In his last years, however, the press began to show signs of satiety. I can remember that myself. He was criticized for conducting Tchaikovsky yet again and also for the *grand-seigneur* character of his leading the orchestra. The young Furtwängler had appeared on the scene: he was giving concerts with the Staatskapelle. And although the public did not pose the question, the press did: wasn't it time for a change? The twenty-five years Nikisch had spent at the head of the Philharmonic was, after all, a long time. Perhaps it will strike you as too hard or unjust what I am going to say; I do not mean it like that: Nikisch was lucky to have died when he did, at the apex of his career.

BAV: Furtwängler was, I suppose, the first major conductor with whom you had personal contact.

WS: Yes, yes, but our contact was not close by any means. I felt at the time—perhaps mistakenly—that Furtwängler and the other great conductors were giants a mere mortal like me was not worthy of approaching. I was of course present at practically all his concerts—each was a memorable experience. I also met him in person and once in a while talked to him briefly, for instance, after World War II when we met in Zurich.

BAV: I have read that when he was conducting, the concert hall was transformed into a sanctuary: he seemed to be communicating the message of higher powers with which he stood in direct contact. He created the impression as if he were conducting in a trance.

WS: That is precisely what it felt like. It was as if the process of creation had been repeated in him while conducting. "Sanctuary" is the right expression: Furtwängler radiated a kind of holiness. He abandoned himself wholly to music, each and every bar, every note from the first to the last one. And he seemed to be receiving those tones directly from the composer. He transformed interpretation into a devout act and the bourgeoisie who attended his concerts, followed him in a fitting spiritual state of mind.

All that has to be seen in perspective, however. Furtwängler was the highly respected leader of the Berlin Philharmonic, but he only conducted eight to ten concerts per season; some he repeated. In those golden years of musical life in Berlin, the 1920s, Bruno Walter appeared six times a season, Klemperer four times, and other great figures also handed each other the torch.

BAV: The noted photograph occurs to me, with Klemperer, Furtwängler, Toscanini, Bruno Walter, and Erich Kleiber standing next to one another. They would all share the seasons in Berlin.

WS: Yes, they are all together in that picture. Kleiber conducted primarily in the opera house. Of the five, I knew Walter really well: we became close friends in the United States.

BAV: For Bruno Walter, music was also a moral force.

WS: That's right. On one occasion, he gave a remarkable talk on that subject. In his view, it was the artists' responsibility to reveal the ethical and moral power of music: that is what interpretation was to focus on. It follows that his forte were the slow movements. Furtwängler was similar. This does not mean, of course, that Walter was devoid of temperament. It is in any case easier (though by no means simple) to bring off fast movements than, let us say, a Beethoven *Adagio* in the Fourth Symphony or the Ninth.

In talking of conductors, there are those who achieve first-class performances in second-class music and of course those who are second-class interpreters of first-class music. Bruno Walter and Wilhelm Furtwängler were first-class interpreters of first-class music. The more significant, the more profound a composition he was conducting, the higher Bruno Walter's art soared.

I am simplifying, I am afraid, but in the framework of a conversation like this, one has no other choice. Whereas Furtwängler was a heroic conductor, Walter was a lyrical one. He was so carried away by the lyricism inherent in a composition, that he simply could not maintain the tempo. He slowed down. He was aware of that danger and it took him decades to get over it. In those years, of course, changes of tempo were nothing extraordinary, in fact they were a matter of conscious decision. Furtwängler, for instance, felt that a particular theme required a slower tempo than other passages in the same movement. Nowadays we call that style postromantic.

Walter conducted a great deal of Mozart in his Berlin years; he even did all-Mozart programs, something which was extremely unusual in those years.

He was consumed in music. He could transmit its experience with such coercive power, he carried his listeners away to such an extent that—to use Stefan Zweig's beautiful phrase—there were moments when he seemed to vanish to be replaced by the composer.

BAV: I feel that someone like Bruno Walter must have had a hard time coming to terms with daily life.

WS: He went through many difficulties. He was too sensitive; he took too much to his heart. He suffered immensely because of the Nazis. Many tragedies occurred also in his family. His daughter wanted to divorce her husband to marry Ezio Pinza.[8] During the course of a row, she was shot by her husband who then killed himself. Terrible.

Walter, however, was stronger than one would have assumed. He lived to be eighty-five and went on recording until the very end. When I last visited him three months before his death, he was still planning to make an LP of *Fidelio*.

Toward the end of his life, he was wise and philosophical enough to cut down on his concerts. When, however, he did make an appearance in Carnegie Hall, everyone rose to their feet. He enjoyed unprecedented respect and esteem, especially in the United States. When he was conducting, we felt that he *believed* in the Schubert or Mahler he was performing, or indeed in Bruckner of whom he was a marvelous interpreter. He was something of an apostle: the apostle of creators.

Then there is an altogether different personality, like Toscanini. Stefan Zweig commented that in his greatest moments, the listener forgot about music and only saw Toscanini. The same applies to Karajan, I should think. All attention is concentrated on him so that the composer, the music, are pushed into the background. Many people go to his concerts just to see him and to hear the orchestra.

---

8   Ezio Pinza (1892–1957), Italian bass. In 1942, he sang in Bruno Walter's recording of *Don Giovanni*.

BAV: I would like to ask you about Karajan later on. First, however, I wonder if Walter ever told you anything about Mahler.

WS: Yes, he did say one thing or another. For instance, he told me a little story that might be of interest. Mahler, as you know, was a hard nut for many people in his lifetime. His symphonies are all expressions of his inner conflict, his tragic personality. He was not a happy man. Practically each of his symphonies is a self-portrait. Most musicians are at a loss as to how to approach those immense compositions. When someone asked Mahler how to find the key to his music, he gave a wonderful reply: read Dostoevsky. Mahler today is enjoying a worldwide renaissance, for there is hardly any other music with such a staggering effect. In his music, Mahler mourns the fate of mankind. Bruno Walter told me about this on one of our walks together.[9]

Interestingly enough, it was not until quite recently that Karajan found the key to Mahler. He has had the *Song of the Earth* on his repertoire for many years; eventually he got as far as the Fifth Symphony. But he had to become sixty-nine years old to try and tackle the infinitely affecting, tragic Sixth. It took him two years to prepare for it.

It is surprising and moving that for all their tragic character, Mahler's symphonies end on a hopeful note: the First Symphony, the "Titan," the Second, the "Resurrection," the wonderful *Adagio* of the Third, the Fourth in which he sings, like a small child, of the beauty of heaven, and the Fifth, which has a positively merry ending. And then the Sixth which, according to Walter, says at the end: *non placet*.[10] Three blows are felled—eventually he omitted the last one—as if mankind had suffered a heart attack. Three times he tries to rise to his feet and each time Fate strikes him down. Death triumphs. Everything has come to an end. Karajan has only now felt able to conduct this infinitely moving music.

BAV: It has become something of a tradition for Hungarian Television to broadcast Beethoven's Ninth Symphony on New Year's Eve, with Herbert

---

9 The booklet *Wolfgang Stresemann: Archive zur Musik des 20; Jahrhunderts* includes extracts from the correspondence between Bruno Walter and Wolfgang Stresemann. In his letter of December 5, 1957, written in Palm Springs, Walter warns: "Now to reply to your question regarding Fischer-Dieskau. I invited for my first performance of *Das Lied von der Erde* (the world premiere) the *great artist* Friedrich Weidemann, since Mahler allows a choice between an alto and a baritone. *Never again*, I told myself at the time and have since always taken an alto for the part (Cahier, Torborg, Onegin, Ferrier, etc.). Please tell Fischer-Dieskau, whom I hold in high esteem, that two male voices do the work no good. Mahler never heard *Das Lied von der Erde*. It is my firm conviction, supported by experience, that he himself would have realized his mistake in giving the three Lieder to a baritone."

10 "It does not please" (Latin).

von Karajan conducting the Berlin Philharmonic Orchestra. The first time I watched it from beginning to end but the second time I just could not bring myself to it. I could not bear looking at Karajan's closed eyes, his head bent, brow knitted. I could not watch the choreography of his gestures. The underlying ideology is also alien to me. Karajan told the Hungarian conductor György Lehel that television was for men and women in the street and conductors were supposed to act as ordinary people expected them to.[11]

WS: Let me make it clear: Karajan does not put on a show even if he may appear to do so. The latest films on him have been shot live and they are far better than the one you saw. I happen to know that the music was recorded first and the picture afterward. That method is, luckily, no longer used.

It is still a moot question whether television is suited for music broadcasts. One thing is sure, however: it has laws of its own. Those of the concert hall do not apply. In Japan, concert broadcasts are viewed by 20 to 30 million people. It is a question of taste how the conductor behaves on the podium. However: if he behaves as he does in the concert hall, people will switch off their sets. As long as the screen is rather small and sound quality is not ideal either, there is no other way but to resort to theatrical means in an attempt to attract the viewers' attention. You will have seen people in the audience who watch the pianist or the conductor with binoculars. This is terrible but we have to accept it. Furtwängler went to recording studios against the grain, for he missed the audience. Kreisler would not play on the radio, for the same reason. "I need the public!" he said. The inspiration provided by audiences is inestimable.

Privately, Karajan is reserved and prefers to spend his time with his family or a few friends. He hates masses of people and only goes to parties if he thinks it is his duty or if his wife and children want to go and ask him to appear for ten minutes.

Already as a young man, Karajan kept people at a distance. He told his biographer that he had always had difficulty making contact. He can be polite, kind, and charming but perhaps he lacks warmth in lasting relationships. Do not forget: innumerable people hope to meet him or want something from him, no wonder he needs a shield to protect himself.

One thing is certain: he has never ceased to be loyal to those who helped him at the start of his career when he was unknown. There, there is a genuine bond of friendship.

---

11 György Lehel (1926–89), Hungarian conductor. Stresemann actually said that Karajan wanted to be seen on television as the Lieschen Müller expected conductors to behave—in other words, as naive, rather silly average women.

Also, he is helpful. If members of the orchestra or even their acquaintances turn to him for support, he never says no. At the same time, many people find him cold, even arrogant. That is not true. He is extremely impulsive, has immense willpower and takes decisions within seconds. His father is said to have taken ages before coming to a decision—a memory that has affected the development of Karajan's character.

He takes a warm interest in young people and is always at the disposal of fledgling conductors who need his advice or help. He has offered, for instance, to teach courses in Japan, the United States, and Leningrad, free of charge. On one occasion, he said he wanted to spare them the difficulties he had experienced.

For Karajan did go through some hard times. He was a brilliant pianist when Ulm offered him his first position as a conductor. It was a small orchestra of forty musicians and Karajan had a monthly salary of 80 marks. He spent five years there (1929–34) and learned the entire repertoire. And now comes a tragic—but also wonderful—turn of events: he was sacked. The intendant told him: "I have to kick you out, for you are far too good for this place. If I do not force you to look for something better, you will get stuck here and never make a career." Karajan was without a job for months, his applications were turned down all along the line.

Finally, much to his luck, the position of first conductor in Aachen became vacant. He saw the intendant and veritably hypnotized him to take him on. Peter Raabe, the general music director who was seventy at the time, said: "If the young man proves himself, let him be my successor." Eventually, Karajan became general music director in Aachen.[12]

On one occasion, he appeared in Berlin with the local chorus and made a favorable impression. He was duly invited to conduct the Philharmonic and also an opera performance. His success was overwhelming. He came to prominence through Berlin. Everyone recognized in him the man of the future. Furtwängler was of course not really happy about this and it was not until some twenty years later that Karajan was appointed principal conductor of the Berlin Philharmonic Orchestra. It is in any case interesting that Salzburg-born Karajan should have come into his own in Berlin.

BAV: Let us now talk about your responsibilities as intendant.

WS: I am head of the administration, in charge of the budget that the Berlin Senate places at our disposal. It is quite a sizable sum but we must not overspend. Money is becoming increasingly short, so my job is not

---

12 Peter Raabe (1872–1945), German conductor, musicologist, and Nazi cultural politician. A member of the NSDAP, he succeeded Richard Strauss as president of the *Reichsmusikkammer*.

exactly easy. In relation to the orchestra, I represent the employer, and I represent the orchestra in relation to other institutions.

My brief includes drawing up the season's programs. That is one of my most important responsibilities. Karajan's contract is for six double concerts; luckily, he conducts slightly more. Of the thirty-two subscription concerts, however, which we give in four different series, he leads only four or five. For the rest, I have to find guests. It is my job to invite them, as well as of course the soloists and choruses. The same applies to contemporary music. Of the five evenings, Karajan takes over one, four are conducted by guests. I have to be up to date in the repertoire and have to know the artists, what makes them tick. On top of all that, I am also intendant of the Berlin Philharmonie—our new headquarters; I am in charge of maintenance and so on.

BAV: Isn't that rather an oversize responsibility?

WS: Not at all! I also prepare and oversee the orchestra's guest appearances. A great deal depends on Karajan: if he does not wish to conduct in a particular city because he is not happy with the hall, we do not play there.

BAV: Clearly, you are aware of his musical preferences as well.

WS: He decides what he wishes to conduct but he frequently discusses his programs with me. Beethoven, Brahms, and Bruckner are featured each season.

Concerts are by definition similar to museums: masterpieces of past centuries must be kept alive; they have to be presented to young audiences, in exemplary interpretations. In the past, orchestras only played contemporary music. Today, our programs must comprise compositions from Bach and even earlier masters right up to the present.

BAV: And there we have arrived at contemporary music. I know from Ligeti that Karajan has programmed one of his pieces.

WS: His attitude to new music is marked by caution. He is no champion of the avant-garde by any means, nor would it be honest: at close to seventy, he could not be expected to be one. If, however, a score interests him, like Ligeti's *Atmosphères*, he conducts it to perfection. He has also performed Penderecki, Berio, and Nono. And, you must not forget that he has made peerless recordings of the Second Viennese School. I do not think any recording surpasses his of Schoenberg's Variations for Orchestra, op. 31. The secret of its success is the fact that he seated the musicians differently for each variation. He says he can only listen to the piece on this disc.

Budapest, 1977

O

The interview ended at this point: Stresemann looked at his watch and took a hasty leave to meet his next appointment. Still, I must not complain, for he gave me plenty of time. When I next saw Dr. Wolfgang Stresemann, in Berlin in the bookshop of the Konzerthaus on the Gendarmenmarkt, he was an old man of over ninety, rather shrunken in size, but his face wore the same expression of worried preoccupation as if he were still carrying on his shoulders the well-being of the Berlin Philharmonic Orchestra.

SNIPPETS

CLAUDIO ABBADO

b. 1933

I interviewed the conductor in Budapest in 1968. He was thirty-five, I was twenty-seven. We were both happy-go-lucky young men and chatted rather than did a serious interview. I mean it was certainly serious in its intent but the way Abbado talked to me, munching on an apple and speaking with his mouth full, was totally relaxed. We were to meet many more times over the years and I became his "official" interviewer: whenever he appeared in Budapest, I would turn up in his hotel room with my microphone.

The subject of his nearsightedness—which he shared with Arturo Toscanini—also came up.

o

Claudio Abbado (CA): I played and conducted a Bach piano concerto in Milan with Toscanini in the audience. After the concert, we talked for a long time. I am, as you know, nearsighted and he explained that it was more important for the orchestra to see the conductor's eyes, than for the conductor to see the orchestra. And if you conduct by heart, it is better anyway not to wear glasses.

Bálint András Varga (BAV): Do you always conduct without a score?

CA: Always. If I were to use a score, it would mean that I have not learned the piece properly. I want to know compositions thoroughly, in all their details. Often, I study a work for several years, such as *Wozzeck* or *Tristan*.

But to get back to my memories of great masters: Toscanini once expressed the view that Furtwängler's tempi in Beethoven's Ninth Symphony

were too slow. I had also heard the Ninth with Furtwängler and it had impressed me no end; I felt that his tempi were perfect.

I can understand Toscanini, of course, for he was a wonderful conductor, the best of them all.

Furtwängler was aware of Toscanini's comment and this is how he reacted to it: "I am German," he said, "I understand Beethoven better and
am also more familiar with the tradition of Beethoven's interpretation. His
allegretti are fundamentally different from those of Italian composers." He
was right, too.

When I said that Toscanini was the best conductor, I meant his personality, his ability to transfer his will to the orchestra. Under his baton, ensembles were always playing admirably together. The tension engendered
by Furtwängler's music-making, however, his culminations, gave me more.
His performances were not perfect, the orchestra was not always together,
but it did not matter. Musically, it was always wonderful.

As far as Bruno Walter is concerned, I loved his Mozart and Schubert
interpretations most of all. They lacked, however, the tension (*Spannung* in
German expresses it better) I admired so much in Furtwängler.

SIR NEVILLE CARDUS

1888–1975

At the time we met in London in 1970, Sir Neville Cardus was the British music critic personified. At eighty-two, his reviews were still appearing regularly in the Guardian, a daily paper to which he had contributed articles since 1916. Sir Neville, however, was also noted for his writings on cricket. In both capacities, music critic and cricket critic, he had spent the years between 1939 and 1947 in Australia, writing for the Sydney Morning Herald.

When I turned up for our interview, he was standing at the entrance to the building where he had an apartment in the basement. With legs wide apart, his paunch pushed forward and his ears protruding, he was like a young boy and was amazingly old at the same time.

o

Neville Cardus (NC): I am convinced that critics are also artists. When I go to a concert, I record the aesthetic reactions evoked in me by the music. I write about music as my sensations dictate it and leave the public out of account. Of course, it is also our responsibility to report whether the performance was good or not. I would call it the news aspect of the review. If I do not like a particular detail of a conductor's performance, I do not criticize him for, say, choosing the wrong tempo in the first movement. I expect him to know more of tempi than I do. If he took a faster one this time, he must have had a reason for doing so, so I try to understand his concept.

I do not dream of telling Yehudi Menuhin how to play the violin. When he was seventeen, Menuhin could play better than anyone else. His tone was so beautiful that whatever he may have been playing, whether Bach or Bruch, all sounded exactly the same. Therefore, he had to rid himself of his own perfect tone. He went through a critical period five or six years ago; he attempted to find his way behind the sensuous beauty of music (as Mahler said, music is not only in the notes). As a result, his intonation turned uneven. A young critic actually wrote that Menuhin's intonation was insecure and poor. It never occurred to him that the mature master was playing that way because he was looking for something. My own attitude has always been to try and grasp what it is that the composer—and the performer—want to say.

My colleagues usually take the score to the concert, with their eyes glued to it throughout the performance. To my mind, you cannot concentrate on the music and read the score at the same time. Those are two different activities. The critic must have absorbed the score before going to the concert and must listen to the music with artistic devotion. Listening to music is like the Holy Communion: you take the body, the flesh, you taste the composer's blood. The best reviews are also a work of art. I would like to live to be a hundred—I might then be able to write a really good one. I always strive to make the public understand whether the composition had been done justice to at the concert so that we actually came in touch with the composer.

To get back for a moment to scores: on one occasion, Elgar reproached a young conductor for the tempo he had taken. "But Mr. Elgar, I was following your metronome marking!" "Oh," replied Elgar, "I have since changed my opinion. I expect each of my works to be re-created whenever they are performed; no concert should be a routine performance."

Routine must be avoided by everybody—whether an artist, a critic, a gardener, or a bookbinder. The artist who has fallen victim to routine is lost.

o

I knew Elgar, though we were never close. He was the prototype of the English country gentleman. He was best at home walking along a path in the country, with his dogs jumping about at his feet.

He was a highly complex character, extroverted and introverted at the same time. I last saw him when he was very old. I remember his tall figure and his white hair as he was conducting *The Dream of Gerontius* at Hereford Cathedral.[1] Previously, a friend of mine had arranged with him for us to meet after the concert and have a drink. The performance was

---

1 Elgar's oratorio was premiered in 1900.

so gripping that I feared he would not want to see anybody. My friend persuaded me to keep the appointment and we made our way to the club. We found Elgar in the smoking room, with a newspaper in his hand. "Do come in!" he cried, "Let us have a glass of champagne. I have just placed a bet on a good horse."

That also goes to show what a great man he was. Only the minor ones lock themselves up in an ivory tower.

I also met Richard Strauss a number of times. In Salzburg in 1934 or 1935, he was sitting in the hall listening to a performance of *Die Frau ohne Schatten*. The music proved difficult for the audience at the time; today, people are gradually accepting it and realize that it is one of Strauss's finest compositions. At the end of the performance, he was clapping like a schoolboy. I mustered my courage, went up to him and told him how much I admired this opera. He looked at me and said: "This is my masterpiece."

Later on, we also had occasion to talk longer. "I have heard you conduct *Elektra*," I told him, "and in 1924 I was there when you conducted *Die Frau ohne Schatten* in Vienna. But why don't you ever conduct *Der Rosenkavalier*?" "Oh, it is too difficult!"he replied.

AARON COPLAND

1 9 0 0 – 1 9 9 0

I forget what took me to Leeds in October 1976, but I expect it had something to do with the promotion of Hungarian music. It may have been
some sort of a festival, for Aaron Copland was also there, to hear a performance of his Nonet for three violins, three violas, and three cellos (1960). It
goes without saying I had my tape recorder with me. I scribbled the date of
our interview on the cassette: October 18. Four days later, I used the other
track to record an interview with Witold Lutosławski in Amsterdam (also
included in Snippets).

Copland and I had first met in Budapest in 1969. Two years later, I
was asked by Editio Musica Budapest to translate his book The New Music
into Hungarian.[1] Copland was invited in time for its publication; he also
conducted a concert which included Roy Harris's Third Symphony and his
own Clarinet Concerto. That was in 1973; in the same year, we also met in
New York.

In 1976, then, it was a question of resuming our conversations left off
three years before; in the meantime, we had exchanged quite a few letters.

My questions did not immediately strike a chord, even though I had expected Aaron to launch with relish into the subject of the authenticity of interpretation. The performance in Leeds of his Nonet came in handy from that
point of view. However, he turned out to be the sort of composer who was
relaxed about the way his scores were performed.

o

---

1   Aaron inscribed my copy with the dedication "For Balint Varga who has made my career in
    Budapest, from a grateful author." The original edition was Aaron Copland, The New Music
    1900–1960, rev. ed. (New York: Norton Library, 1969).

Bálint András Varga (BAV): Do you find that your notation is clear enough so that it conveys exactly what you mean to the performer?

Aaron Copland (AC): Well, that is too much to say. Our musical notation is not that exact, so that it would be amazing if every performance reflected exactly what you meant. But there are some that come much closer than others. I think musical performers have to add something of their own understanding and reading of the work. It is impossible to get into a composer's mind and know precisely what he meant by a phrase, a tune and rhythm. One has to depend on the musical feeling of the person who is performing your music.

Composers have to be, I think, a little free in their own minds as to how their own music should go. If they are very precise and only one way of playing it seems right to them, they are into trouble, because it is very hard to get. I should like to be more free, more easygoing in relation to a performance and try to see it reflected in somebody else's musical mind. Sometimes you get a person who reads a work of yours in a way you had not thought of yourself and you say, "Gee, why did I not think of that? It is even better than what I thought." The opposite, unfortunately, also happens.

BAV: The last time we met you said you had stopped composing. The piano piece you had written for the Van Cliburn Competition was your last work. Are you adamant that you will never compose again?

AC: Oh no, I never said that. It would be very nice to go on just as if nothing happened. But if you have had the opportunity to express yourself over a period of half a century like I have, it would be very remarkable to go on churning the stuff out. Delightful, even. But I am not going to feel guilty about not composing. I may start tomorrow, I do not know.

To be in the mood to compose is a very special thing and either you are in the mood or you are not. If you are not, it is no use trying to force it.

ANTAL DORÁTI

1906 – 88

A ntal Doráti was a regular visitor to Budapest. We first met in 1968, I believe, and from then on kept in touch either in the company of my microphone or through letters. He was a prolific letter writer, always by hand rather than typewriter.

Interviewing Doráti was thrilling, for he enjoyed controversy and never shied away from acerbic remarks. His voice was rather high and hoarse, and the manner of his speaking made it sound rather as if he were irritated. His voice did not match his appearance, which, as the years went by, reminded me more and more of Beethoven.

When his autobiography, Notes of Seven Decades, appeared in Hungarian, it was quite a challenge for me to interview him in public. We drove to Szeged, a university town in southeast Hungary (Doráti's wife, the pianist Ilse von Alpenheim, as well as my boss, László Sarlós, were traveling with us) and made our way to the Ferenc Móra Museum, the venue of the celebration of the book's publication. I was stunned by the masses of people who filled the hall, all anxious to meet the conductor. We had not discussed the questions I was going to put him, so he was just as unprepared for them as I was for his answers. I needed to be on my mettle to match the speed with which his original ideas were gushing forth.

In the interview we did after his concert in Budapest in 1970, I asked him to what extent a conductor can change aspects of interpretation on the spur of the moment. Clearly, it was less easy to bring off than for a soloist. Doráti said he found the idea of changing his interpretation at short notice unimaginable, for he had developed it carefully over the years.

Antal Doráti (AD): Minor changes are of course possible. They are even necessary, and for a good conductor and a good orchestra they ought to be no problem. Yesterday, I conducted here in Budapest Bartók's Concerto for Orchestra, and although we had rehearsed well and the actual concert revealed nothing new, I realized many nuances which had been missing from the rehearsals: they occurred to me under the impact of the fact that the Concerto had been preceded by the *Cantata Profana*. I had never performed those two works one after another. The *Cantata* had created an atmosphere which in a way threw a new light on the Concerto. The changes came wholly unexpectedly but I had no difficulty carrying them out. Of course, it was not a question of doubling the tempo or things like that, but there were certainly palpable nuances.

Bálint András Varga (BAV): To change the subject: I understand you encouraged Menuhin to commission Bartók to write the Solo Sonata. What is the authentic story?

AD: I took Menuhin to see Bartók. This is what happened: Menuhin visited me in my house in the United States and I showed him the manuscript of the Violin Concerto. "Look at this," I told him. "Here is a very interesting new violin concerto, you ought to learn it." He happened to have his instrument with him, and we played through the score right away. I did not know the orchestral part, and he did not know the violin solo, so it sounded rather odd and we laughed a great deal. We were of course laughing at ourselves, not at the music. The music gripped us immediately. (I had never heard the concerto before, I only knew it from the score.) Then Menuhin seriously got down to learning it and proceeded to program it. We appeared with the piece on several occasions and released three records of it.

I suggested that Menuhin meet Bartók and it fell to me to introduce them to each other. Bartók was very friendly and their acquaintance grew into a friendship.

I think it was my idea to ask Bartók if he would write a solo sonata for Menuhin. Ten minutes later Menuhin telephoned him and Bartók agreed. I was there when the two of them read through the score. It was still in manuscript. Menuhin played some chords and asked Bartók if some changes would be possible here and there. Bartók considered it a long time and then decided: "No, let us leave it as it is." Later on, he agreed to make some slight changes in other places—a note in a chord, things like that, to better fit Menuhin's fingers.

BAV: You have mentioned that you saw the Concerto for Orchestra when the ink was still wet, so to speak. Can you remember if Bartók commented on the work in any way?

AD: Interestingly enough, he as well as his publisher expressed the view that it would make a good ballet. I actually persuaded a ballet ensemble to buy an option from Bartók, and so he was paid a small sum of money. It was a bit of help in his precarious financial situation.

I played the Concerto for Orchestra on the piano in 1944 so that the members of the ballet ensemble could listen to it as much as they needed to; my playing was recorded privately. Koussevitzky got wind of it: he was to conduct the world premiere in December of that year. He asked for the record to help him learn the score. He then actually conducted it the way I had played the music on the piano.

GÉZA FRID

1904–89

I met the Hungarian-born Dutch pianist and composer (a pupil of Bartók and Kodály) in Amsterdam. For once, I did not have a tape recorder with me. I happen to remember, however, a story Frid told me that I want to preserve for posterity, in case it has not come down through other channels.

Frid related a night-long conversation with Ravel in Amsterdam's Vondelpark. Ravel was an insomniac, Frid explained, and the two of them walked all night, with Ravel describing the way he imagined the ideal performance of his Bolero. It would be conducted by a robot, which would increase in size with each repetition of the theme. By the end, the robot would have grown to giant proportions—only to collapse at the end.

I could not find a suitable spot for this anecdote in the memoirs, until I realized that if anything, this was a snippet, relating a brief encounter with an émigré Hungarian musician who appeared to be enjoying the chance to speak his native language.

SYLVIA GOLDSTEIN

1919–2002

The music publisher Boosey and Hawkes represented Editio Musica Budapest in the United States as well as in several European countries, so their New York office was my base on the few occasions I flew overseas to promote our composers. My opposite number was David Huntley, but I also met the corporate vice president, Sylvia Goldstein. On realizing that she had been with the firm since 1940, I asked her if she had met Bartók. Her reply in the affirmative led logically to the question of whether she would be willing to give me an interview. That was in May 1984.

Listening to the recording today, I am appalled by the poor sound quality. I have had to rewind the cassette time and time again; even so, I could not make out every word. My colleague at Universal Edition, Jonathan Irons, came to the rescue: but for him, only a fraction of the interview would have made it to this book.

The year in which Sylvia Goldstein was employed as secretary to Hans Heinsheimer, 1940, was also the year of Bartók's emigration to the United States.[1]

O

Sylvia Goldstein (SG): At that time, we also had an artists' bureau, run by Andrew Schulhof (before his emigration, he had been connected with the Berlin Philharmonic). He signed up Bartók and his wife as artists, whereas Heinsheimer took him under contract as a composer.[2]

---

1 For details of Hans Heinsheimer's life, please see part 2, chapter 13 on Universal Edition.
2 Andrew Schulhof was born Andor Schulhof in Hungary. Initially, he signed Bartók and his wife for concerts between April 1, 1939, and August 31, 1940. Bartók was bitterly disappointed by

Before actually meeting him, I remember seeing in the office Bartók's photographs and publicity which were part of a campaign to improve his image with the American public. He ought to have counted as a well-known personality, performer, and creative talent from Europe but he did not have that effect.

Bálint András Varga (BAV): Was Boosey and Hawkes aware of his stature?

SG: With two Europeans running the company (Heinsheimer was Austrian, Ralph Hawkes was an Englishman), we were very, very aware of him. In fact, I seem to remember—but I cannot be held to this—that the Sixth String Quartet was Ralph Hawkes's idea: he thought so highly of the first five.[3] The first work we had anything to do with was *Mikrokosmos*.

Bartók was already a sick man; it was not until later that I—or the world—realized that he had leukemia. At one time they thought he had tuberculosis or a lung problem. He was frequently ill and feverish. As a result, he had an inner glow to his face. He seemed to have a halo, an aura around him. With his beautiful face and with this glow it was almost unreal to look at him.

BAV: Do you remember the first time you saw him?

SG: Not really. I can remember him coming to the office: a small man with a very beautiful blond wife. Ditta was lovely at that time. She was very reserved; also, she could not speak English. Bartók had mastered the language, so he did most of the talking.

BAV: What sort of an impression did he make on you?

SG: He was a very honest, a very direct person. He lived by the letter of the law, expected you to follow the letter of the law and any compromise was out of the question. It was very difficult to aid him financially, because he would not accept charity. He did not want to feel that he had not earned his keep. For instance, he would not accept any advance on the commission from Koussevitzky until he had delivered the score. Today, anybody

---

Schulhof's performance as his impresario and reproached him for failing to deliver on his promises, so that his income was far lower than Schulhof had made him believe.

3 The truth about the quartet is revealed by Ralph Hawkes himself: "My last meeting with Bartók was in December, 1944, just before I left for England. At this time, I had commissioned and arranged to pay him for a Seventh String Quartet which he had expressed a desire to write. I vividly recall this meeting over dinner at the Gotham Hotel during which we discussed an article he had written for "Tempo" on the pronunciation and spelling of names in music. He was a great authority on language and had profound knowledge of the subject as applied to music." The quotation is taken from Ralph Hawkes's contribution to the Bartók issue of *Tempo*, no. 13 (Autumn 1949), which appeared under the title *Béla Bartók: A Recollection by His Publisher*.

would want thousands and thousands of dollars as an advance. He refused to take anything until he could deliver because maybe he would be too sick to complete the score.[4]

A Hungarian friend of his wanted to give him money but could not do it. He had a small record company, so offered him a false royalty statement, and asked me to send Bartók a check for one hundred dollars. Bartók sent it back: "You have forgotten to take your commission," he wrote. That is what I meant when I said he lived by the letter of the law. So we had to take our commission to get him the money and he said: "I don't understand. Why is it that this little Hungarian record company can sell my records when RCA can't?"

We would get mail from him on a postcard—they were two-cent postcards at that time. He had an incredibly delicate handwriting, and could get more on the postcard than you can get on a two-page letter. He would detail his complaints and everything else.

BAV: What sort of complaints?

SG: I remember he and Heinsheimer had an argument about the spelling of the word "symphony"—whether it had y's or i's; whether it should be the anglicized spelling or the European spelling—that sort of thing.

We would send him salami and balogna which he liked because he went to places like North Carolina and Saranac Lake where he did not have the kind of food that he was used to.

I remember taking packages to him at a little hotel which no longer exists, over in an area where the Lincoln Center is today. At that time, they were living in a very small room and he came to the door to take the package. I distinctly remember him in woolly slippers. But he came, not Ditta.

Ernő Balogh told me that when he went to visit Bartók and Peter [his son] was also there, Peter would act like the father saying, "It is all right, father, I will take care of it."[5] In many cases, Peter was acting like the adult. Balogh had many, many stories of this type, where Peter assumed a kind of authority to shield his father.

Getting back to *Mikrokosmos*: I remember how difficult it was to sell. Schulhof went out across the country and pleaded with teachers to just put

---

4   László Vikárius, director of the Budapest Bartók Archives, referred me to copies of correspondence he had received from Peter Bartók. They reveal that the composer accepted Koussevitzky's conditions whereby he received half of the commission fee ($500) on signing the contract, and the rest on delivering the score. Sylvia Goldstein may have remembered Bartók's conduct in connection with another commission, according to Vikárius.

5   Ernő Balogh (1897–1989), Hungarian pianist, composer, editor, and teacher. He enrolled in the Budapest Academy of Music at the age of seven, where his professors included Bartók and Kodály. Balogh settled in the United States in 1924.

it on their pianos. At that time, with the level of teaching, people could not understand how you could teach piano music with such a complex, developed book. People were teaching at a very different level. It took many years until teachers accepted it. Of course, today *Mikrokosmos* is part of the standard repertoire. But it was very difficult to get it launched.

BAV: Did you take part in promoting Bartók?

SG: No, I was very young, just a secretary. Later on, I worked in the rental department for Heinsheimer. It was not until later that I went through law school, and at that point Bartók was no longer with us.

o

I have asked the foremost Hungarian Bartók scholar, Professor László Somfai, to identify the Hungarian friend who recorded some of Bartók's works to help him financially. Here is Professor Somfai's reply:

It was Donald H. Gabor ("Don Gabor"), the owner of the Continental Record Company. In his small studio, in October 1942, he had Bartók record the following works:

    Petite Suite
    Bagatalles no. 2 and Three Rondos no. 2
    Improvisations nos. 1–2, 6–8
    Nine Little Piano Pieces no. 9
    Three Hungarian Folk-tunes

And, playing duets with Ditta:

    Seven Pieces from Mikrokosmos for two pianos nos. 2, 5–6

They were released in 1942 (also on LP, around 1949). The recordings have naturally been included in Hungaroton's centennial edition, as well as on its CD version. I cannot remember all the details of the story, but it seems to me that Don Gabor, in an effort to help Bartók, generously paid him more royalties on sales than the number of discs actually sold.

The fact that a recording of extracts from For Children *was also planned in February 1943, can be documented from the unpublished correspondence between Bartók and Boosey and Hawkes.*

Just a few facts on Don Gabor: he was born in Budapest in 1912 and was able to reach the United States before the outbreak of World War II, in 1938. He died in 1980. His parents had refused to leave: they were fond of their native country and could not believe that their lives, as Jews, were in danger. As were more than 500,000 Hungarian Jews, they, too, were murdered by the Nazis.

Bartók's recordings released by Don Gabor's Continental Records have been made available on CD by Hungaroton (Bartók at the Piano HCD 12326-31, on disc number 12331).

RALPH KIRKPATRICK

1911 – 84

I was familiar with Ralph Kirkpatrick's name from the music programs of Hungarian Radio. His recordings were broadcast about as frequently as those of Wanda Landowska, Zuzana Růžičková, and George Malcolm.[1] In those years—the late sixties and early seventies—I was addicted to the harpsichord and dreamed of buying an instrument so that I could play it at home.

I was particularly taken with his renditions of Domenico Scarlatti's sonatas, without knowing at the time that Kirkpatrick had written the composer's biography and published a critical edition of his complete works. Kirkpatrick was Scarlatti's Köchel, so to speak: his numbering system has long been universally accepted as authoritative.

Before flying on holiday to Dubrovnik in 1973, I found out that the summer festival was featuring Ralph Kirkpatrick on its program. I took my tape recorder with me and on arrival contacted the artist at his hotel, the Excelsior. Lying just outside the massive medieval walls of that city of marble streets, ancient monasteries, and narrow alleys, the Excelsior was the most elegant place you could stay at.

All I can remember of our meeting is his friendliness, his ready smile, and the fluent and easy manner of his talk. Our interview appeared in my book of interviews in 1979—I am translating extracts from it back into English.

In asking Ralph Kirkpatrick about Wanda Landowska, I soon realized that his reaction was similar to that of cellists if you asked them about Pablo

---

1 Wanda Landowska (1879–1959), significant Polish-born harpsichordist and pianist of Jewish origin. In 1925, she founded at Saint-Leu-la-Forêt her school École de Musique Ancienne, where she was to teach Ralph Kirkpatrick. Zuzana Růžičková (b. 1927), Czech harpsichordist. George Malcolm (1917–97), English harpsichordist, organist, and conductor. Together with Růžičková, he was a frequent visitor to Budapest. His pupils included the pianist András Schiff.

Casals: admiration was mixed with irritation. A younger generation sought a path of their own and did not wish to be reminded of distinguished ancestors. Kirkpatrick had worked with Landowska in Paris for nine months.

o

Ralph Kirkpatrick (RK): This is a complicated thing. I knew right from the start that I wanted to proceed in a different direction from hers. I disliked the instruments she used, for I preferred eighteenth-century harpsichords. During the months we spent together, our contact grew highly complex. I did not take to her as a person, but I was aware that I could learn a lot from her, even though I knew that I would need to completely transform everything I had absorbed.

Bálint András Varga (BAV): In Hungary, we regard Landowska as the artist who early on in the twentieth century established the harpsichord as a concert instrument in its own right. For us, she is a symbol of harpsichord playing.

RK: That is what she was. In the twentieth century, she was the first to raise the performance of old music to the same level that is expected from the interpretation of nineteenth-and twentieth-century music. My generation owes to her the recognition that harpsichord playing needs to be measured by the same yardstick as the accomplishment of pianists.

BAV: What was it in her artistic concept that you disagreed with?

RK: That is too complicated a question. I have always endeavored to avoid this subject. I shall write about it some day.

BAV: May I put it then this way: are you a purist?

RK: I was one when I was younger. Now I am an impurist.

BAV: Could you elaborate?

RK: The pureness of art can be conceived within very narrow limits. In that sense, I am no longer a purist. After all, any art is an infinite, limitless series of choices. Historicism is merely a means to help us interpret the art of the past; it must not raise barriers. I respect the striving for authenticity, but I am also aware that it is impossible to arrive at the whole truth about certain composers and certain styles—only a fraction of the truth. We have ample information about eighteenth-century French music. We know far more about Couperin than about Frescobaldi. The fragments we do know fail to reveal the whole picture, just as shards brought to light at excavations cannot give us a complete idea of a civilization.

BAV: In playing Couperin, do you endeavor, as far as possible, to observe rules of performance that were valid in his lifetime?

RK: I would rather put it this way: I provide today's translation of rules that were valid at that time. We know those rules very well: the grammar and syntax of harpsichord playing were laid down in a precisely circumscribed manner. The rules must be conscientiously observed especially in the case of Couperin, for his notation happens to be extremely precise. Practically everything has its aim and sense. Of course, observing the rules does not lead by itself to interpretation.

BAV: You must be a scholar and an artist at the same time.

RK: That is right. In my first years in Europe, I perfected my instrumental technique and also became acquainted with the entire keyboard literature prior to 1800. I spent months at the National Library in Paris and the British Museum in London, and prepared a bibliography. I studied not only compositions but also all available published material regarding performance practice. I can assert that I know all the material to do with performance styles of both the harpsichord and chamber music. That was the goal I had set myself.

BAV: You have mentioned that you came in touch with the harpsichord through the works of Johann Sebastian Bach. What is the situation regarding the performance style of his compositions? He is perhaps the most disputed composer from this point of view.

RK: Bach is indeed a special case: he did not by any means respect the peculiarities of the instrument as did the French or Scarlatti or English virginal composers. Bach confuses you because, when he set his mind to it, he was as perfect a master of keyboard sonority as, in the cantatas, of instrumental sonority. Sometimes, he also wrote works that sound good when sung (*laughs*). Largely, however, he wholly ignored the special features of the harpsichord—he was simply indifferent to them.

BAV: Did Bach wish to transcend the limitations of keyboard instruments?

RK: That is precisely the case. But we might also think in terms of impatience and indifference with regard to the material itself, the physical sound, something which is difficult to understand, precisely because in some of his works he demonstrated such a high degree of sensitivity to them.

Now I no longer differentiate between objective and subjective performance, because all music that makes any sense is rooted in man. Rhythm, which not only exists on paper, has to do with movement. Either with the movement of our body or with what we see around us. I wonder what kind of music would emerge in a state of weightlessness. The artist, if he is to communicate, must transform everything into concrete physical sensations. Otherwise, it is all just abstraction.

BAV: Music *is* abstraction, isn't it?

RK: No. Music is a vision of the abstract that becomes comprehensible with the help of the resources of the human body. In other words, we hear music not just with our ears—we hear it with our whole being.

WITOLD
LUTOSŁAWSKI

1 9 1 3 − 9 4

W ith the upcoming centenary of Witold Lutosławski's birth, I want to pay tribute to this wonderful composer and wonderful human being by including an extract from our interview done prior to the world premiere of his Mi-parti in Amsterdam, on October 22, 1976. I have not heard the work since, but I can remember how impressed I was at the time by the sheer beauty of this music.

It was written for the Concertgebouw Orchestra, an ensemble the composer admired for the musicianship of its soloists, especially of the clarinets, the horns, the oboes, and the bassoons, and tailored the work so that it would give those instrumentalists a chance to display their qualities to best advantage. He also commented on the sound produced by the strings, providing an ideal background for the wind soloists.

In the interview, I told him of the impression the work had made on me (we talked after the dress rehearsal). I thought it was a piece of classical music, with no ambition to be "modern."

o

Witold Lutosławski (WL): Maybe. I do not mind if you consider it is not modern. You know, when one develops and reaches maturity, one aspires to a sort of synthesis. One is not terribly preoccupied with the question of whether the music is modern or not. What interests me is to say what I have to say. Nothing else.

Bálint András Varga (BAV): Before our interview, you remarked that it was a very personal piece for you and that you were feeling rather lonely among composers today. Would you elaborate?

WL: I am feeling lonely because I see that music is developing in different directions. What I have been working on especially in recent years is the organization of pitch, with the aim of creating a variety of beautiful harmonies. Variety—that is, sharp contrasts. I believe this composition represents the result of many years of efforts.

BAV: When did you work on *Mi-parti*?

WL: I started work at the end of 1975, after completing *Les espaces du sommeil*, and finished it in June.[1] In other words, it took me six months to write. In fact, it had been in the back of my mind for quite a long time, but all my sketches had found their way to the wastepaper basket. I started it anew.

BAV: I think there are aleatoric passages in it.

WL: Not many. There is an aleatoric part at the beginning and there is a longer section after the first allegro. The second time the same material returns, it becomes more organized. As you have seen, I conduct it very slowly, just indicating the beginnings of short sections. Then the third time this kind of music occurs, it is conducted, in the same tempo as the intervention of brasses which establishes the allegro tempo.

BAV: There was one thing that rather nonplussed me [*here I imitated the motif*]. What is it supposed to signify?

WL: Oh. It is there to disturb. It is a surrealistic, irrational element in the piece. As you will remember, we have talked about this aspect of my music. In the Second Symphony, for instance, a trombone appears toward the end of the first movement; it turns up, to use a French phrase, *mal à propos*. That is, as if from a different world. Something similar happens in one of the preludes in *Preludes and Fugue*, the one with the two cellos.[2] There appears a sort of march out of the blue. Those surrealistic moments are very essential features of my music. If that moment in *Mi-parti* disturbs you, that is precisely what I was aiming for.

---

1 *Les espaces du sommeil* was composed in 1975 for Dietrich Fischer-Dieskau, to a poem by Robert Desnos (1900–1945).

2 *Preludes and Fugue* for solo strings (1972). The work was commissioned by Mario di Bonaventura (b. 1924); I attended the world premiere at the Styrian Autumn Festival in Graz on October 12, 1972. It was after that concert that I proposed to the composer the idea of our doing a book-length interview. It materialized amazingly fast: in March 1973.

VLADO PERLEMUTER

1904 – 2002

The French pianist—born to a Jewish family in Kowno, Lithuania—played Ravel, Debussy, and Chopin in Budapest in 1968 and 1970. He readily granted me an interview, even though he must have known that I would be asking him about his friend and mentor, Maurice Ravel. If he was tired of having to talk yet again about the composer, he gave no outward sign of it.

I remember his china-blue eyes, the curiously swarthy tan of his skin, the incredibly straight parting in his snow-white hair, and his amazingly high voice. As I translated this interview, I realized I could not recall his piano playing. A brief listen to his recordings provided the explanation. My musical background had not prepared me for the very special idiom of Ravel and Debussy. Their world was foreign to me. Now I cannot but marvel at Perlemuter's artistry. In playing Ravel, he transformed the sound of the piano: he erected an edifice made of crystal and glass, transparent, glittering, cold, devoid of any trace of sentimentality. When he played Chopin, the instrument sang under his fingers. His *ritartandi and* rallentandi, *the carefully placed accents were revelatory in lending the melodies an absolutely unique suppleness; he seemed to be stroking the music. Where virtuosity was called for, it was mastered with bravura. Vlado Perlemuter was a great artist, a great musician.*

o

Vlado Perlemuter (VP): I was nineteen or twenty years old when I met Ravel. He was simple and rather reserved; he did not like to talk about himself. He was very interested in the students of the Conservatoire who in their final year were studying his compositions. His name was already well known, though not as much as today.

I practiced all his piano pieces with Ravel as my tutor and two years after our first meeting, I played them all at two recitals.

Through Ravel, I developed an interest in French music. Cortot used to play a great deal of Debussy, Fauré, and Franck (if I may count him as French) but not so much by Ravel. It was natural for me to be attracted to French music. Apparently, I had a flair for it, too—as a matter of fact, it was Cortot who suggested that I address myself to it in some depth.

Works by Ravel, such as *Pavane* or *Gaspard de la nuit* were quite popular, but they were not yet part of the repertoire, so that I did not have an easy time of it to get them programmed. However, *Miroirs*, *Valses nobles et sentimentales*, and other compositions were wholly unknown, especially some of the works that make up *Miroirs*.[1] *Alborada del gracioso* did crop up on some programs, but the others were never played. Today, young pianists perform most of Ravel's compositions but oddly enough, some of the *Miroirs* pieces are not among them.

I also want to tell you that Ravel himself was rather fed up with *Pavane*. When I announced that I was about to play it somewhere, he cried "*Comment? Vous jouez ça?*" He had a highly developed critical sense and did not spare himself either. If not directly, than through the way he reacted to my playing the *Pavane*.

Bálint András Varga (BAV): What did he think of the Sonatine you are playing tonight?

VP: He liked it. Like other composers, he was fond of his neglected works. Incidentally, the Sonatine was his only piece that I heard played by him. In my own interpretation, I do not wish to imitate him, for he had long ceased to practice and was a very poor player. I have, however, tried to follow his instructions as far as tempo, accents, and pedaling are concerned. I have written a little book on Ravel's piano works in which I have summed up everything he told me about them.[2]

---

1 *Miroirs* is made up of the following five pieces: *Noctuelles, Oiseaux tristes, Une barque sur l'océan, Alborada del gracioso,* and *La vallée des cloches.*

2 Vlado Perlemuter with Hélène Jourdan-Morhange, *Ravel d'après Ravel* (Lausanne: Editions du Cervin, 1953). The book is made up of transcriptions of radio conversations with Vlado Perlemuter.

ARTHUR RUBINSTEIN

1 8 8 7 – 1 9 8 2

I n my own private mythology, the date of my conversation with Arthur
Rubinstein—October 19, 1966—has a particular significance, in that it
marks the beginning of my career as an interviewer. I was not yet twenty-five
at the time, so my impression of his recital in Budapest has to be taken with a
grain of salt. For me, his playing was gray, devoid of any expression. I saw an
old man toiling away at the keyboard; the sounds he produced simply failed
to come across as music. I am sure I am being unjust, but that is what I felt
at the time.[1]

In the artist's room, I saw at close range that he was made up for the
stage: his eyebrows were drawn in black pencil, his hair appeared to have
been curled artificially. The interview itself, though brief, was of course fascinating. Rubinstein exuded the air of Parisian salons of the past, where
witty conversation was spiced with bons mots. We talked in English with
Rubinstein mixing in some German and French expressions, when he was
lost for the right word.

O

Arthur Rubinstein (AR): Ravel and I were good friends. Debussy I did not
know. I was introduced to him, he reached me his hand without so much
as looking at me. I was very young. I did not interest him. As far as their

---

1 Rubinstein played the following program: Schubert, Sonata in B-flat Major, op. posth.; Schumann,
Carnaval, op. 9; Debussy, *Hommage à Rameau, Ondine*; Ravel, *Forlane*; Chopin, Ballade in G
Minor, Two Études, Polonaise in A-sharp Major. Two days earlier, he appeared in an orchestral
concert where, with János Ferencsik conducting, he played Chopin's Piano Concerto in E Minor,
op. 11, and Brahms's Piano Concerto in B-flat Major, op. 83. I did not hear that concert.

music is concerned, I tell you frankly: you cannot learn anything from composers. They have no idea how their works are to be performed and change their opinions faster than artists do. Beethoven played a movement of one of his sonatas in a slow tempo one day, and three times as fast a few days later. We know this from Czerny. He never played anything again the same way. That is why I could not learn much from Ravel—from his works, however, I did learn a great deal, because they talk to me. That is what I try to communicate to the audience.[2]

---

2   In the first volume of his autobiography, *My Young Years* (New York: Knopf, 1973), Rubinstein
     makes no mention of that brief personal encounter with Debussy. He does relate, however,
     the first time he heard Debussy's music: Ravel and he played the string quartet on the piano.
     Rubinstein wrote that this wonderful music was a revelation. In later years, he would play a great
     deal of Debussy at his recitals. A concert of his at the Théâtre des Champs Elysées was attended
     by the composer's widow. The pianist proudly recalls her comment: "Il a joué *Ondine* mieux que
     personne" (He played *Ondine* better than anyone).

GYÖRGY SÁNDOR

1912–2005

The Hungarian pianist György Sándor was a pupil of Béla Bartók at the Budapest Academy of Music. They grew close after the composer's emigration to the United States, where Sándor himself had settled in 1939.

Beyond recording an interview with him in 1971 in Budapest, we spent some time together privately. He struck me as a man of the world of the old school: he wore his wavy hair rather long combed back; he was always impeccably dressed, with a silk necktie and a matching kerchief in his breast-pocket. He was a superb causeur; I could listen to his anecdotes for hours.

Sándor was also a serious musician. I attended his course at the International Bartók Seminar in Budapest and was fascinated by his analysis of From the Island of Bali from Mikrokosmos. He illuminated its details with the exactitude of an X-ray and also gave his students an idea of the process of creation. Individual tones and chords were lifted out of their context, examined from different angles, and then replaced in the fabric of the music.

György Sándor premiered Bartók's Piano Concerto no. 3 on February 8, 1946, in Philadelphia, with Eugene Ormandy conducting. That alone secures him a place in music history. He also recorded all the piano works of Bartók, Kodály, and Prokofiev; all three releases were highly regarded.

I asked him if Bartók talked to him about his compositions.

o

György Sándor (GS): No. Perhaps just once, shortly before he died. We got together frequently in New York, especially in the last two years of his life. When I returned from a tour of South America in the summer of 1945, I spent the last weeks with him, even in the hospital. Some ten days before he died, he gave me the score of the Concerto for Orchestra and asked me to look through the second proofs, for he was afraid he would not make the publishing deadline. On that occasion, he made some very interesting remarks regarding the piece. I took the galley proofs with me, looked through them, corrected some notes and put them in the post. By the time I had finished and visited him in his ward, he was very unwell and died the next day.

Bálint András Varga (BAV): Did Bartók say anything about the idea that the Concerto for Orchestra would lend itself to choreography?

GS: No, he did not, but he may very well have thought so. With Bartók, as with all other great composers, the instrumental realization of a work is never definitive. He took it for granted that a piece could be transcribed for a different instrument or a solo work could be arranged for an ensemble.

Nowadays, we live in pseudo-scientific times. The idea that arrangements are anathema is gaining ground all over the place, also in the United States, for they are supposed to go against the wish of the composer. Every composer from Bach onward has arranged his works for different instruments! Bach's greatest compositions were not meant for any particular instrument. The *Musikalisches Opfer* or the *Kunst der Fuge must* be instrumented, for Bach did not specify the performers.[1] Bach himself arranged movements of his solo violin sonatas for keyboard instruments or orchestra.

Arrangements, then, are perfectly permissible. Bartók himself did some, and many more ought to be transcribed. Almost each of his piano pieces. Practically the whole of *Mikrokosmos* could be arranged; he himself transcribed some for two pianos, while Tibor Serly prepared versions for string instruments and piano.[2] They sound much better than the originals.

BAV: Did Bartók hear Serly's versions?

GS: He did. I was present at a celebration of his birthday when Ditta and a string quartet performed them. Bartók's eyes were bright with pleasure.[3] They did sound better than on a piano, because he used so few notes, he worked so economically that richer colors enhance the effect of the music.

---

1   This opinion, once widely held, is no longer accepted by Bach scholars, who have demonstrated that the open-score format of these contrapuntal works was probably intended for performance on a keyboard instrument such as the harpsichord or organ.
2   Tibor Serly (1901–78), Hungarian violist, violinist, and composer. He prepared a performing version of Bartók's incomplete Viola Concerto.
3   Ditta Pásztory (1903–82) was Bartók's second wife.

BAV: Did you understand Bartók's music at the time?

GS: No. I studied the Sonata with him for months, and then performed it in public for a long time without actually having an idea of what I was playing. It was so alien, so different from what I was used to playing, that I simply could not grasp and could not feel it. I learned his works by heart— and still, they did not come naturally. The public may take forty, fifty, sixty years to grow up to the music of a composer and as my example demonstrates, an artist may also take years, even though he lives steeped in music. Eventually, of course, he will love it as much as any other music.

I was lucky enough to record all of Bartók's works for the piano. Previously, I used to think, like many other people, that Bartók wrote a few wonderful pieces, several very interesting ones, and then some weaker works as well. One is prone to generalize, but after a while one realizes that one was wrong, especially in the case of a genius. A genius possesses a sharp critical sense and discards whatever he deems not up to the mark. When I recorded his works and learned each composition thoroughly, it became clear to me that he has no weak pieces. The weak ones were all written prior to his Opus 1. They are now being unearthed and programmed, even though Bartók himself suppressed them.

WALTER SUSSKIND

1 9 1 3 – 8 o

W alter Susskind may be largely forgotten today, but he was a well-respected conductor, with positions as music director of the Scottish Orchestra, the Victoria Symphony Orchestra in Melbourne, the Toronto Symphony Orchestra, the St. Louis Symphony, and, toward the end of his life, he was principal guest conductor in Cincinnati. Born in Prague, he fled on March 13, 1939, two days before the German invasion, and made his way to Britain, becoming a naturalized British citizen after the war.

I failed to write a date on the cassette of our interview; it took place in Budapest sometime in the 1970s. The reason why I wanted to talk to Walter Susskind was the fact that he had made the very first gramophone records of Bartók's Cantata Profana, Duke Bluebeard's Castle (with Endre Koréh and Ilse Hollweg as soloists) and The Wooden Prince. How did it come about? I wanted to know.

o

Walter Susskind (WS): Those records were made for Peter Bartók, the composer's son, who is, as you know, a recording engineer. At that time, in the 1950s, he lived in New York and many people who knew him also knew me. They suggested me as a possible conductor for those pieces. I was living mostly in London and he telephoned me there to ask if I was interested. I was indeed, and for many years, those records were the only ones on the market.

Bálint András Varga (BAV): Had you heard those three Bartók works before, live, conducted by others?

WS: Those three I had never heard before. You must not forget that it was around 1955, and not much Bartók was played then. He was more of a connoisseurs' composer—now he is a household name like Stravinsky. I had heard very little Bartók; I had played, as a pianist, the piano sonata and some other works. I did know all six string quartets and considered them to be very important. As you see, I was no newcomer to Bartók's world.

BAV: It cannot have been easy for the orchestral musicians or the chorus in the *Cantata Profana* to come to terms with Bartók's idiom.

WS: Fortunately, the chorus was that of the BBC, which is constituted of professional singers. As for the orchestra, it was put together for the occasion; they called themselves the English National Orchestra. I had the finest players, including soloists—it was the best orchestra I had ever conducted, apart from the Berlin Philharmonic. The tenor was Richard Lewis—the second Peter Grimes, incidentally. The baritone was Marko Rothmüller, a Yugoslav singer.

BAV: One reason why you were suggested to Peter Bartók could have been the fact that you had established yourself as a record conductor with some of the greatest soloists, such as Solomon and Jascha Heifetz.

WS: The first world-famous soloist I recorded with was Solomon. I was quite young, shortly after the war. Strangely enough, we played no Beethoven or Brahms, but Liszt's *Hungarian Fantasy*. The disc was heard by Artur Schnabel, an admirer of Solomon, and he asked me to record with him. That is how all those records came about: my name spread by word of mouth, so to speak. I recorded the Tchaikovsky Violin Concerto with Jascha Heifetz and Rachmaninov's *Paganini Rhapsody* (the same work I am conducting here) with Arthur Rubinstein. I also worked with Dennis Brain, Leon Goossens, and Ginette Neveu (she only made two recordings before her untimely death: the Brahms with Issay Dobrowen and the Sibelius with me). I have been lucky enough to have continued to release recordings with some of the greatest soloists and greatest orchestras ever since.

JOSEPH SZIGETI

1892–1973

I n the Introduction to his autobiography My First 79 Years, *Isaac Stern lists Joseph Szigeti among violinists who were of "immense importance" for him.*[1] *He adds: "He was one of the most profound musicians I have ever known, and a very good friend." Describing Szigeti's rendition in the mid-forties of Brahms's G-Major Sonata for violin and piano (with Nikita Magaloff), Stern says: "It was one of the most ennobling performances I have ever heard. Nobody in the hall breathed. You were not listening to a performance of someone standing on the stage at Carnegie Hall; you were surrounded by a golden aura of music."*

By the time I met Szigeti in Budapest in September 1968, he had long since stopped playing the violin. He looked older than his seventy-six years. The skin of his face and hands was like parchment; his voice was weak and unsteady. He seemed to find it difficult to produce words, with long pauses between sentences. During the interview, he never looked at me but somewhere in the distance. Asking him questions was like an act of cruelty, so I kept the interview short—far shorter than I would have wished.

Szigeti had agreed to be a patron of the International Music Competition in Budapest (the other patron, Pablo Casals, had canceled his visit). The competition included one for string quartets. Prior to meeting Szigeti, I had talked to a member of the jury, the British violinist and quartet player Sidney Griller.[2] *I started the interview, reporting Griller's enthusiastic account of a concert of Szigeti's he had attended in 1932 and of his recording of Brahms's Violin Concerto released in 1928. (The interview was to be broadcast on*

---

1   Isaac Stern, written with Chaim Potok, *My First 79 Years* (Cambridge, MA: Da Capo Press, 1999), 4–5.

2   The string quartet named after Sidney Griller was founded in 1931 and existed for thirty years.

*shortwave, in English, so we were both speaking in a language that was for-
eign to us, rather than in Hungarian. The cassette's fate shared that of many
others of my recordings: it was lost.)*

o

Joseph Szigeti (JS): I am fully aware of the transient nature of our art.
The fact that Sidney Griller still has such a vivid memory of my 1928 recording of the Brahms Violin Concerto, conducted by my friend Hamilton
Harty, means more to me than if someone were recalling my concert cycle
of Beethoven sonatas in Washington in 1944.[3] My records as well as my
contacts with composers are for me of prime importance.

You ask me about my achievement and naturally, I must think of my
records. I am happy that major labels are now aware of the historic value
of old recordings. The greatest pleasure of the past months was for me the
release by EMI in London of two discs from 1937, where I played Brahms's
D-Minor Sonata with Egon Petri and Bach's Double Concerto with Carl
Flesch, that great violinist who has more or less been forgotten today.

I am convinced of the significance of preserving continuity, so that we
can assess our own achievement as well as those who come after us. All that
is an unbroken line—a development which is not devoid of detours and
returns to past concepts, past styles. Continuity is of increasing importance
because I find that the young generation tends to steer clear of the thorny
path of trial and error, and prefers the shortest and easiest way.

Let us take the fifteen Mozart sonatas that were recently released in the
United States. They mean more to me than any other recordings that I have
made of well-known compositions. I feel that I have done my duty by masterpieces which have yet to come into their own. I am grateful and happy
that I was able to record all those superb sonatas in one group.

o

Bartók was a stupendous artist with a style all his own. It is an immeasur-
able loss that he should not have left behind more Liszt and Beethoven
recordings, or those of his own compositions. We have to be grateful that
his interpretation of chamber music has come down to us—that our joint
recital in the Washington Library of Congress in April 1940 was recorded.

---

3   Sir Herbert Hamilton Harty (1879–1941), Irish composer, conductor, and piano accompanist,
    best known today for his reorchestrations of works by Handel.

It was only thanks to the fact that every event in the library, whether conferences, speeches, or concerts, was routinely recorded. Twenty years after his death, it was released commercially, so that we can hear his convincing and moving rendition of the "Kreutzer" Sonata, we can hear his interpretation of the Debussy Sonata or indeed of his own Second Sonata.

In 1928, Bartók and I recorded his *Romanian Dances* and some Hungarian folk songs in my own arrangement. I shall never understand how it was possible for a record company, with Béla Bartók sitting in their studio, not to insist that he should also record his own piano works. It is a lesson for us to appreciate, to recognize historic moments for what they are.

PART TWO

A MEMOIR

INTRODUCTION

We are all contemporaries and heirs. Also, ancestors. Born into the present, we bore our way into the future and let the minutes fall away to become the past. As we try to establish a niche for ourselves, we come into contact with people who arrived before us. We grow older together for a time; gradually they depart and we find ourselves in the midst of younger generations.

In a memoir, you remember your own past and the men and women who formed it. You shed a shaft of light into the darkness, which deepens with the passage of time, and illuminate those figures, yourself among them, and situations you acted out in concert and in conflict. A memoir is stocktaking. You take stock of the way you made use of the time given to you; you know most of it is up and look back at your actions, as before a tribunal chaired by yourself. The real protagonist of any memoir is Time. It is the one given that is shared by us all. It is our common enemy: it eats away at our cells, transforms us, and kills us.

As a child, I used to imagine that by some miracle, I could make time go backward so that my mother would grow younger instead of older. Her health was fragile, she was always in pain of some sort, and I wanted to make her healthy and young.

On November 3, 1961, at 10:30 in the morning, I sat at a university seminar in Budapest and looked at my watch. As the minute hand passed on, I told myself: I shall never again be twenty.

It was around that time that I read a story about an old man who swapped bodies with a youth. It is now but a vague memory but what I have retained of it is the revulsion with which the young man looked at the wizened old body he had moved into. I could never accept that one day I, too, should grow old.

Death has never been far from my thoughts. Sitting in a concert hall, I would see all those heads around me, with hairs of varying colors, lengths, and quantities covering them, turn into skulls. We are all skeletons, carrying a perishable body. The awareness of the transience of our existence is common to us all. A memoir is one possible manifestation of that awareness.

CHAPTER 1

ANCESTORS

The earliest date that can be established in my family's history is 1492: together with some two hundred thousand Sephardic Jews, they were expelled by Ferdinand and Isabella from Spain.[1] Their trace was then lost for centuries. They must have wandered eastward, for they first emerged again in the eighteenth century at Dunaszerdahely in northwest Hungary.[2] All I know is that an ancestor of my father's was a rabbi in that small town.

My first forebear on my father's side to be known by name is my great-grandfather Farkas (Wolf) Weisz, who lived in Székesfehérvár, a major city southwest of the Hungarian capital, Pest-Buda. (In 1873, the twin cities on the Danube were united to form Budapest.)[3] Farkas Weisz was a member of the tailors' guild in the first half of the nineteenth century. His charter has been preserved in our family archive. Actually, all my ancestors were Jewish craftsmen who lived in the Hungarian half of the Austro-Hungarian Empire. For some reason, they did not wish to improve their lot by moving to the imperial capital, Vienna.

Just as a point of interest: another Hungarian Jew of the lower middle class, the shoe vendor Samuel Schönberg, born in 1838 at Szécsény, in

---

1 Sepharad is Hebrew for Spain. Having won the Granada War in 1492, which ended Arab rule in Andalusia, Ferdinand and Isabella, the "Catholic Monarchs," proceeded to expel Jews and Moors in the very same year. The year 1492 also saw the discovery of North America by Cristoforo Colombo (Christopher Columbus).
2 The peace treaty of Trianon following World War I assigned it to Slovakia. It is now called Dunajska Stredá.
3 The fiftieth anniversary in 1923 was marked by the world premiere of three compositions commissioned for the occasion: Dohnányi's *Festive Overture*, Kodály's *Psalmus hungaricus*, and Bartók's *Dance Suite*.

Nógrád County in Northern Hungary, decided to move to Vienna at one point—a decision which was to have a major impact on twentieth century music history: if he had been happy with his prospects in the small town of his birth and found a wife in the local Jewish community, his son Arnold would never have been born.

The move to Vienna, however, had no bearing on his citizenship or indeed on that of Arnold Schoenberg, who kept a Hungarian passport until late in life. As a matter of fact, based on his citizenship, Schoenberg could well be regarded as a Hungarian composer.

To return to my family history: Farkas Weisz's son, the jeweler Henrik Izrael Weisz, born in 1846, chose the Hungarian capital in which to spend his life. Pest and Buda were inhabited at the time by a largely German-speaking population; Henrik apparently spoke Hungarian with an accent. My father Pál (1900–1975) Hungarianized his surname as a teenager, with permission granted by the Royal Hungarian Minister of the Interior.[4] Henrik Weisz's wife, Cecilia Berg, came from Northern Hungary, the industrial city of Miskolc where her father, Jónás Berg, was a hatmaker.

My maternal great-grandfather, Sia (pronounced Sheea) Nasser, was born in Gálszécs (now Sečovce in Slovakia). Like Henrik Weisz, he was a jeweler and set up business in an outlying district of Budapest, then a self-standing community. His sons, including my grandfather József Lipót (Joshua Leb) Nasser, followed in his footsteps. József was a talented draughtsman and designed the jewels he sold; eventually, he established a small factory in the inner city, with twenty-odd employees. There was an international demand for his designs, with orders coming in years after his early death in the 1910s.

József Nasser was a handsome and talented man, with close-cropped hair and a small moustache turned upward. He was a passionate photographer—I still own some of his pictures, mostly landscapes, taken in the last decade of the nineteenth century or in the first years of the twentieth. He was also a figure skater, a cyclist—and a shy, taciturn man. His shyness was inherited by his three children and has been handed on to me through my mother, Piroska Nasser (1904–66).

I have great admiration and affection for József and am sad to have never met him. His last name has intrigued me. Why did my mother's family have an Arab surname? My parents told me that we were either of Arab

---

4   Weisz, the Hungarian spelling of Weiß, is German and Yiddish for "white." "Sz" is also a way of spelling "ß" in German. Many Jewish surnames are derived from colors, such as Schwarz (black), Grün (green), Gelb (yellow), Braun (brown), and Blau (blue).

Ancestors 271

descent on my mother's side or our ancestors had lived in an Arab environment. Nasser has two meanings: "help" as well as "victory."

When Gamal Abdel Nasser became president of Egypt in 1954 (I was a schoolboy at the time), I wrote him a letter to say we were probably related. I never had an answer, of course, and have since learned that Nasser is a rather common surname in the Arab world. For a time, I used to look it up in the telephone directories of the cities I visited on my travels. In the majority of cases I found Arab first names to go with it. Once in a while, a Nasser would be European and I was tempted to ring their number, but never did.

At the age of fourteen or fifteen, I enrolled as a visiting student at the University of Budapest to study Arabic. My professor was the noted orientalist Gyula Germanus, a delightful old gentleman given to entertaining us with anecdotes.[5] We learned little from him apart from the Arabic characters and the conjugation of some verbs, such as فَعَلَ, transliterated into English as *fa'ala* meaning "to do."

My maternal grandmother, Hilda Ürményi, was a great beauty with abundant brown hair worn in a knot at the back of her head. When released, it reached down well below her waist. She was born in Nagyszentmiklós in the early 1880s—I fancy she might have passed in the street Béla Bartók, a native of the same place (now Sânnicolau Mare in Romania). Left a widow with three small children, she took to wearing black, a color she stuck to even after her second marriage to the interior decorator Pál Jermy. According to a cousin who remembers her well, she exuded an air of the most profound depression. The atmosphere in her home was as black as her clothes. By the age of sixty she was an old woman, with snow-white hair, a wrinkled face, and a tired, lifeless look in her eyes. She died of cancer during the war and her body was pushed on a cart by her daughters all the way to the cemetery.

Pál Jermy needed an energetic young man to help him in the firm. In 1931 or 1932 he found my father. Pál Varga was good-looking with black wavy hair and the figure of a sportsman: he was an excellent fencer and water-polo player. Today we would describe him as "macho," Mark Twain would have called him a "manly man," a phrase I have found in the writer's autobiography.

Indeed, my father was manly, strong in mind and body. Once after attending the funeral of an old friend of his where he had been asked to deliver the oration, which he did by addressing the dead man as if he were

---

5   Gyula Germanus (1884–1979) converted to Islam and traveled on a pilgrimage to Mekka, thus acquiring the right to call himself a hadji. There is a square in Budapest named after him.

still alive, he said to me on our way out of the cemetery: "A man is not afraid of death." The simplicity and finality of that remark has impressed itself on me, for life.

My masculine father was not an ideal match for the bluestocking that my mother was. Theirs was not a happy marriage. If my mother had not died of a heart attack in 1966, they would have divorced, after a life shared for thirty-four years.

Before the war, my parents rented an apartment in a small villa located in a quiet street on Gellért Hill in Buda and walked downhill and across Elisabeth Bridge to reach my grandmother's place, which also housed our firm. My grandmother was widowed a second time in the mid-1930s, and the running of the company was taken over by my parents. It continued to thrive until anti-Jewish legislation and the takeover by the Hungarian fascist Arrow Cross Party made work impossible. Eventually, my father was sent to a forced-labor camp. My mother was confined with us children to the ghetto.

My father was lucky enough to have a humane commander who employed him in the camp's bureau. He even permitted my father to visit his family in Budapest and detailed two armed guards, ostensibly to keep watch, but in actual fact to protect him. On arriving in front of the building where we were put up, my father found the entrance locked. Quick to fly off the handle, my father lost his nerve knocking and pounding on the gate, rattling the handle to no avail. He did not consciously register the frightened look on the faces of his guards. Suddenly, he heard a loud voice: "What do you think you are doing there?" It was an Arrow Cross man. My father took a quick look at him and shouted back, "Are you a father?" The man, taken aback, replied, "Yes, I am." Whereupon my father bawled at the man, "In that case, you must help me. I want to see my family."

As he told me this story, my father's face mirrored the emotions he had gone through at the time. The Arrow Cross man did help him, and the family reunion did take place. There was just one problem: small as I was, I was clearly frightened of this strange man who wanted me to sit on his lap. I fought and resisted until, in desperation, he gave me a good spanking. I then cried and let him love me.

My father was an intelligent, well-read man who coedited a quarterly magazine in the 1930s titled *Keresztmetszet* (Cross-section). It had a small circulation and I am sure was not lucrative in a financial sense. However, it provided a forum for some of the brightest young writers, poets, and graphic artists who were to become major figures in Hungarian cultural life in later decades. I have found a short story written by my father in one of the issues; my mother was a regular contributor of book reviews.

My father had studied at an academy for commerce; my mother was excluded from higher education under the *numerus clausus* introduced in 1920 by the right-wing regime of Admiral Horthy, governor of the kingless Kingdom of Hungary (by which time my father was about to complete his studies). It may well have been the first legislation of a fascist nature in Europe. My mother attended lectures on philosophy and art history but never obtained a university degree.

My parents spoke German, my mother also read books in English and French. Both were passionately interested in the arts and bought some paintings by contemporary Hungarian artists. They enjoyed traveling, especially to Italy, with Florence a place my mother continued to hanker after until the end of her life.

My parents could have led a life in harmony, had it not been for my father's old-fashioned attitude to women: after all, he had been brought up in the spirit of the nineteenth century. My mother was too clever for him, too intelligent, unwilling to play a subordinate role. Also, my father came from the lower-middle class and had less exacting expectations of a standard of living that my mother—of the middle-middle or upper-middle class—took for granted. She may have been something of a snob, which I suppose I have inherited to a certain extent.

They were loving parents who set great store by the education of their children (my brother Péter was born in 1936—I shall have rather a lot to say about him later on). They also set a good example by spending much of their free time reading. They took us to exhibitions, concerts, and the theater and we walked in the Buda Hills on weekends.

Still, our home was fraught with tension. My brother and I could not but take sides—he remaining closer to our father, me supporting my mother who appeared to me to be the weaker of the two. Who knows, my brother's two divorces could have had their roots in his childhood experiences. As for me, until I met my wife as late as my thirty-fifth year, I excluded the possibility of marrying: I simply did not believe in the institution.

CHAPTER 2

ON BEING JEWISH

Q uestions with vague answers.

The fact that my Jewish background is mentioned on the very first page of chapter 1 is the result of decades of coming to terms with my origins, a process still in progress.

My parents were born in the Mosaic faith but were brought up in secular families. My father mentioned once that as a child he had heartily hated religious education at school. It was a casual remark, quickly passed over. In 1937, my parents and my one-year-old brother converted to Calvinism in the expectation that anti-Jewish legislation, which was making everyday life increasingly suffocating, would not apply to them. I was baptized a Calvinist at birth; however improbable it may sound, I seem to remember being lowered into the font by Bishop László Ravasz, a man of tremendous authority at the time, and looking up at his receding face above me.

Our Christian faith notwithstanding, we were sent to the ghetto, and, as mentioned earlier, my father was taken to a labor camp. For the world outside, we counted as Jews.

My memories of the ghetto are hazy. At the age of three, I found it fun to share our apartment with many other people. One night my mother picked me up from my crib, wrapped me in a blanket, and took me to the air-raid shelter amid sirens shrieking like mad. I was too drowsy and too young to be aware of any danger. In the shelter, I remember my mother sitting on a chair in the middle of a room, silently suffering from a stomachache (something that would accompany her all her life). I also remember unconcernedly walking out of the house, taking my cousin with me, to explore the neighborhood I suppose. We were picked up by a policeman on a bicycle and while my cousin was crying for fear (she was four months my junior), I enjoyed our ride tremendously. My aunt was anxiously waiting for us at the gate: she was not supposed to leave the building to look for us. I was not told off, nor did I receive a spanking, as far as I can remember.

Another scene is waiting to be conjured up: I am standing in the street just outside our house—it must have been right after the war—and watching a cart being pulled by two men, with a skin-and-bones woman, weakly smiling, sitting on it. "She has come back," I heard someone say. "Coming back" was a phrase I was to hear many times in the months ahead. It never occurred to me to ask where from, I suppose I knew instinctively.

I spent my childhood with survivors of the holocaust. I took it for granted that everyone around me was Jewish. A friend of my father's had married a Christian lady (we never used words like *goy*) and somehow I was aware of her being different. Perhaps I attributed to her characteristics to make her different; perhaps she lacked the warmth, the homeliness that turned Jewish families into cozy nests.

It was natural to be Jewish, it was something I never questioned. But what did it actually mean, being Jewish? What *does* it mean, being Jewish? I have no rational answer. I know nothing about the Jewish religion. I have made many attempts to grasp at least the rudiments of it— my mind has consistently rejected the information. Neither am I familiar with Jewish tradition. We never lighted candles, never observed any religious holidays, did not eat Jewish food (except for *sholet*, once in a while, for my father loved it). Am I Jewish in the eyes of devout Jews? I do not know. Perhaps not.

In what way, then, am I Jewish? As I grow older, I tend to think that I belong to a people who left its home in the Middle East in the first century AD and has miraculously retained its identity over two millennia. (Miraculously? Possibly thanks to keeping the very faith I have turned my back on.) Being Jewish is being descended from that people. But being Jewish is also, perhaps, carrying in my brain a melody, an inflection of the way my aunt, my father's elder sister, said "unberufen!" (the English equivalent could be "well I never!"). I could not notate it, for you cannot notate the quality of a voice. There is such a thing as a Jewish voice. There is also, for that matter, a Jewish smile.

Being Jewish means responding to a throng of people filling the ground floor of the Hakoah Club in Sydney: I had never met any of them but instantly felt at home. I was surrounded by relatives—uncles, aunts, and cousins. I belonged. I had been taken to the club by my brother so that I could hear Hassidic singers from Israel. Musically, the concert was a disappointment: they sang what sounded like pop music, to Hebrew texts from the Bible. But at the start the audience stood up and everyone sang the *Hatikvah*, the Israeli national anthem. The effect on me was overpowering. I realized that there was a country I could call home, one I could always go to if I needed shelter, a country founded and inhabited by Jews like me. The *Hatikvah* gave me strength, it filled a void I had until then not been aware of.

Being Jewish means chancing upon Barbra Streisand on YouTube and being profoundly moved by her singing that melody to a hall packed to capacity, singing it as a prayer, as if she were the mouthpiece of the Jewish nation.

Being Jewish means entering the sixth form of my primary school in Budapest—I was eleven—and being confronted by the rest of the class facing me in a corner, as if they had been waiting for me. The moment I turned up, they shouted in chorus: "Go back to Arabia!" Why Arabia, I do not know. But I saw instantly what they meant. That experience has put a stamp on me for life.

My snobbishness was to blame. The boy sitting next to me had observed that our names (his meant barber, mine cobbler) indicated that our ancestors had been craftsmen. No, I replied, my father's original name had been Weisz. Ostracizing me, poking fun at me, beating me up was the logical result of my faux pas. Decades later, when I happened to meet my classmate, the "barber," at a bus stop in Budapest, he confessed that he, too, had Jewish blood . . .

Being Jewish means that you are particularly vulnerable to a letdown like that, because it has been perpetrated by a fellow Jew. Failings of relatives hurt doubly.

It may appear idealistic but I do feel that Jews ought to be particularly careful not to cause offense. If just one of us goes astray, it casts a negative light on us all.

Being Jewish means that you are identified by non-Jews with all those—geniuses and villains—who have over the past centuries risen to prominence. It is a question of prejudice, bias, culture, the presence or absence of fairness that decides which aspect of the composite picture of what Jews have created of themselves is given precedence over the other. Whether you think of the Jew with a book in his hand on Titus's triumphal arch in Rome celebrating the conquest of Jerusalem in 70 AD—Jews as the People of the Book—and the chain of associations takes in Maimonides, Spinoza, Moses Mendelssohn, or Freud. Or you think of Judas Maccabeus, the revolutionary leader, and you group him with Marx, Trotsky, Rosa

Luxemburg, and genuine villains like Lazar Moyseievich Kaganovich or Mátyás Rákosi. Franz Kafka or the Merchant of Venice? Lorenzo da Ponte or Rothschild? Chagall and Einstein or Julius and Ethel Rosenberg? Teddy Kollek or Archbishop Lustiger of Paris? Peter Falk of Columbo fame or Mark Zuckerberg? All the great Jewish musicians I cannot even begin to list. The mosaic is formed by them all, along with millions of men and women in the street: doctors, advocates, teachers, merchants, and archi-tects—the Diaspora.

To return to a personal plane: being Jewish means you have to fight your own struggle to come to terms with your heritage. Jewish self-hatred, "*heraus mit uns*," is a common phenomenon. There was a time, in my teens, when I suppressed and even denied it. It was with a shudder that I brought myself to tell my daughters they had a Jewish father. One of them took the revelation with equanimity, the other one cried: she was afraid of what might happen to her. Even today, I divulge my background only to people whom I regard as intelligent enough to accept it for what it is.

In 2011, the noted Hungarian writer György Konrád (born 1933) pub-lished a collection of essays under the title *On Jews*. There he says that if you are a Jew, you cannot for a moment dissociate yourself from it, it is something you think about every single day. He is right.

CHAPTER 3

GROWING UP
IN POSTWAR
SOCIALIST HUNGARY

M y brother is sitting at our newly acquired, small upright piano and is going through the motions of practicing. He would have been eleven at the time, which makes me six and the year 1947.

Our family had survived the war like other Jews in Budapest whose deportation to concentration camps had been stopped by Admiral Horthy under pressure from the Allied Powers. The ghetto was liberated by the Soviet army in February 1945 and we moved to my grandmother's apartment in the city center, near the Danube. Miraculously enough, the house remained intact, even the chandelier was in place, with its apple-shaped lampshades covered in cobwebs and dust. Only the broken window panes indicated anything amiss. Much to our luck, no one had taken possession of the place, and we were free to move in.

I remember standing in the middle of a room, taking it all in—my first conscious glimpse of the apartment that I would leave only in 1980, with both of my parents dead, my brother an Australian citizen since 1957 and my wife expecting our twin daughters. I can also faintly recall the presence of my father, recently released from the forced-labor camp.

Before the war, the apartment had also housed my grandmother's interior decorating company, with my father as junior partner. It occupied just one of four rooms, with rolls of upholstery fabric on rods one above the other rather like wall bars. There was also a counter that folded up in the wall. At least that is the way the room looked after the war, my parents having decided they would try to revive the firm. After all, it had enjoyed a good reputation: it was not just a shop, for my parents also offered advice to their customers as to how they could best furnish their homes. I remember wood samples in different colors, so that one could judge whether a particular material matched the furniture it was meant for.

Indeed, the company of "Pál Jermy's Successors" was an elegant affair, with Archduke Albrecht, Count Károlyi, and popular actresses like Gizi Bajor and Anna Tőkés among the clientèle. The materials, imported from Western Europe ("velour damien" is one I can recall), were of exquisite quality and taste—something my parents succeeded in maintaining in the first postwar years when the country's political system was still in the balance.

The first couple of years seemed to justify my parents' bold decision: the old customers returned, new ones joined them, and the firm made good money. (Anna Tőkés returned after the war. As I was looking up at her, she stroked my face and said in her deep voice: "What a nice little boy!" After she had left, I asked my parents: "Why was she so sad?" "She is a tragic actress," they replied.[1] More than half a century on, I can remember that exchange, with me wondering just what "tragic actress" was supposed to mean.)

My father furnished our flat and actually designed some of the furniture so that the apartment became something like a showcase for the firm: that was the way the material we imported could be used to best advantage.

I never questioned my parents' taste and have been influenced by it all my life. In fact, I now live with the same furniture in Vienna that my father designed and had made in the late 1940s. I am especially fond of darkish warm colors—of the velvet covering the armchairs and beds as well as of the Persian carpets on the floor and hanging on the wall. I have no time for ornate Jugendstil or what I conceive of as impersonal and cold Bauhaus design. I also love antique silver and pewter tankards, or the large Chinese bronze incense burner my father brought home one day. I use silver cutlery as a matter of course and surround myself with beautiful objects of daily use, such as a silver sugar dredger from the eighteenth century. I am averse to anything mass-produced.

I am sure I would be a patron of the arts if only I had the financial means. While living in Budapest, I bought paintings, drawings, and

---

1 The deep resonance of Anna Tőkés's (1903–66) voice matched her statuesque appearance and stood her in good stead in roles like Regan and Goneril (*King Lear*), *Mary Stuart* (Schiller), or Alkmene (Kleist's *Amphytrion*).

sculpture by contemporary Hungarian artists on installment; in Vienna, I acquired some lithographs by the wonderful Austrian sculptor and graphic artist Alfred Hrdlicka (1928–2009). Lately, I have bought some pictures by psychiatric patients of the hospital at Maria Gugging to the north of Vienna.

o

Whether my brother was asked if he wanted to play the piano, I do not know. It was delivered to our place one day and my brother's practicing and composing little pieces was my first encounter with live music. Frankly, though, it was not the works he played but rather their colorful covers that evoked in me the desire to take piano lessons as well.

My first teacher was a kindly elderly lady whose very kindness, her artificial sweetness of manner filled me with unease. It positively made me cringe. She was married to a much younger man and I instinctively felt something odd in their relationship, as if she were desperately clinging on to him. He appeared to be cringing as well. The only piece I remember her teaching me was Schumann's *Am Kamin*, which was far too difficult both musically and technically for a seven-year-old boy. I think I was downright drilled to play it, with one or two notes left out and some tricky fingering to fit the size of my hands. I performed the work at the end-of-year examination for which my teacher had hired the recital hall of the Academy of Music. I must have played it like an automaton but it went off without a hitch and I was treated to ice cream by a relative afterward. It cost two forints, a huge sum to me at the time. I was probably as impressed by the price of the ice cream as by its taste.

I continued my studies at the Municipal Music School, a state-run organization that employed piano teachers far more professional than the elderly lady. Music was taken very seriously indeed, both the practice and the theory of it. That is precisely what proved to be my problem. I was happy enough to practice and loved the music I was given to play (what a thrill it was to be assigned a piece by Handel with a passage in thirty-second notes! It was a challenge that made my blood circulate faster and I felt terribly proud having mastered it), but I was lost when it came to solfège. Each lesson was a frustrating experience. I was quite good at looking at a melody (mostly a folk song), determining the *do*, and then solmizating it. What gave me a headache most of all was notating a melody played on the piano by our teacher. Neither did I enjoy the innumerable and, to my mind, dull singing exercises of Kodály's we were force-fed, as I then felt. I derived more and more pleasure from playing Bach, Handel, Mozart, or Beethoven—but if I were to carry on, I was also supposed to attend those horrid solfège classes that made me feel like an idiot.

Choral singing in class, on the other hand, could be a thrilling experience. One day, still in primary school, I found that my voice was leaving my throat in a considerably lower register than my classmates' voices. Our teacher, Emil Ádám, immediately responded by signaling me that I should carry on. After all these decades, I can still vividly remember the sheer physical excitement produced by my baritone joining the soprano of the rest of the class. I turned all hot, with my prominent ears no doubt glowing red.

The reason my parents had agreed for me to follow in my brother's footsteps was the manner in which I had responded to music as soon as I was old enough to stand up: I danced. It was probably something à la Isadora Duncan and it irritated my brother no end, with all those ohs and ahs from my adult audience, whether at home or in the lobby of a hotel where we happened to be staying. I can in any case recall the pleasure I derived from expressing my emotions through movement. No wonder my parents took me to the ballet school of the State Opera House. The first time, I was bored by the overly simple exercises we were given: going around in a circle, ankles staying on the floor, toes raised. The second time, a teacher got hold of my ankle and raised it so that it touched the top of my head. It was agonizingly painful and I fled as soon as my foot touched the floor again—never to return.

In those days before television entered private homes (stifling any communal activity such as conversation), my parents, my brother and I would regularly assemble in our lounge to listen to long-playing records (LPs). That is how I came to know a great deal of piano music and the names of artists such as Edwin Fischer or Wilhelm Backhaus; also violin concertos (Beethoven's two *Romances* among them—all too rarely programmed to this day) played by Georg Kulenkampff or Joseph Szigeti; opera overtures and arias (Flotow's *Martha* was a favorite, also because of its attractive label in gold). I could never have enough of Amelita Galli-Curci's coloratura soprano with its breathtaking virtuosity tinged with melancholy and vulnerability and was deeply touched by *Kol Nidre* as sung by Dezső Ernster.[2]

---

2   Amelita Galli-Curci (1882–1963), celebrated Italian coloratura soprano. The Hungarian bass Dezső Ernster (1898–1981) made it to the Metropolitan Opera in 1946 via the Bergen-Belsen concentration camp. I heard him as Sarastro in Mozart's *Die Zauberflöte* at the Budapest Opera House and caught my last glimpse of him as he was driving his huge American cabriolet across Chain Bridge over the Danube, his white mane picturesquely waving in the wind.

Contemporary music was apparently beyond the pale for my parents, although we did possess an LP of Bartók's opera *Duke Bluebeard's Castle* with the noted Hungarian bass Mihály Székely and the soprano Klára Palánkay, János Ferencsik conducting.[3] On the whole, however, Bartók was deemed "ugly," "too modern"—music to be switched off whenever it was on the air.

Frankly, I do not think I understood most of what I heard during those sessions. I loved the mighty chords introducing Tchaikovsky's Piano Concerto in B-flat Minor and reveled in the C-major splendor of Bartók's opera when the Duke sings "Lásd, ez az én birodalmam" (Look, this is my realm) and also following Judit's shy and frightened "Szép és nagy a te országod" (How beautiful and vast your empire is).

Once the B-flat Minor Concerto really got started, however, I lost my bearings. I could not fathom what was going on. I may have picked up a melody here and there, the emotional energy of the music may have made some sort of an impact, but on the whole I was out of my depth. "Understanding" music would be a major preoccupation in the decades I was to spend promoting contemporary composers. More of that later.

What those listening sessions may have taught me was, first of all, the very activity of sitting down in order to concentrate on music to the exclusion of anything else. Perhaps my parents discussed the pieces just heard, perhaps not. But while listening, we did nothing else. I remember changing the needle once in a while, I remember also turning sides (and even today, I know where exactly in particular compositions the music stopped so that one of us had to get up to turn the record over). Beyond *listening*, just spending time *together* and the closeness achieved by *sharing* an experience have made a lasting impact. Once again, the source of my enthusiasm for promotion lay in the desire to share with others something I felt strongly about. Sharing—not just music but books, a beautiful landscape, or even a joke in which Hungarians take particular delight, whether political, bawdy, or indeed Jewish (with Cohen and Grün two of the staple characters).

We were also regular concertgoers. Our heroes were the conductor János Ferencsik, the pianist Annie Fischer, and the violinist Ede Zathurecky, to name just a few. Why my parents never uttered the name of Otto Klemperer who was appointed music director of the State Opera

---

3   Like Ernster, Mihály Székely (1901–63) was a Hungarian bass of Jewish birth. He survived World War II thanks to a Catholic priest who gave him shelter. Legend has it that Bartók adapted Bluebeard's part to Székely's voice—its range and unique silky timbre. Bartók's opera was to remain his most successful role throughout his career, which also took him to the Metropolitan Opera (1947–50 mainly in Wagner operas) and Glyndebourne (1957–61 in Mozart's operas).

House in 1947, why they stayed away from his performances, I cannot fathom. Unless, of course, my memory fails me. Klemperer, who remained until 1950, raised the level of productions to unprecedented heights—unprecedented, that is, but for the three years his one-time mentor, Gustav Mahler, had directed the house (1888–91).

I do remember our family having two subscriptions later on and my brother and I were sometimes allowed to see a production just by ourselves. On one occasion, I found *Don Pasquale* with the wonderful Oszkár Maleczky (1894–1972) in the title role so irresistibly funny that my brother had to repeatedly warn me not to laugh so loud.

By the time my brother and I were sitting in row six of the theater, enjoying Donizetti's music in that jewelry box of a building, which unlike the Vienna Opera House, had been spared bombardment in World War II, my parents had had to give up their business to forestall nationalization. The years between 1945 and the adoption of the Soviet-style constitution of the Hungarian People's Republic in 1949 had been marked by a systematic elimination of all political parties but the Hungarian Communist Party, which, under the name the Hungarian Workers' Party, swallowed what had remained of the Social Democrats and the Independent Smallholders' Party.

The Iron Curtain diagnosed and foreseen by Winston Churchill in his Fulton speech of March 5, 1946, had descended along the borders of the so-called socialist countries. If you were lucky and possessed the necessary funds, you could still get through the frontier to Austria as late as 1948. Friends of my parents, a middle-aged couple, risked it and were caught by border guards. Once released from prison, they made another attempt and slipped through. Their goal was Britain. Entry visas were issued to them on condition that they accepted employment with a rich old lady, he as valet and she as maid. Eventually, he could sell his patent and became co-owner of a factory. Their adventure had a happy ending.

My father, on the other hand, had to start life anew. At the age of fifty-one, he had to learn bookkeeping in a small Budapest theater where he had managed to get a job through friends. To begin with, what he accomplished during the day had to be undone and redone in the evenings. To top up his small salary, my mother accepted menial jobs such as hemming handkerchiefs. Economizing and selling off whatever had been saved of their valuables became the order of the day.[4]

---

4   If you wonder how we could afford a subscription in the Opera House even though we were living from hand to mouth, the answer lies in one of the few positive features of the socialist system: culture was accessible for all. The Cheap Library series, for instance, which comprised masterpieces

Meanwhile, at school, each morning started with us shouting "A dol-gozó népért és hazáért, Rákosival előre!" (For the working people and our fatherland, forward with Rákosi!)[5] We rattled it off, without thinking about it.

To canvass for its policy, the party and government sent around "népnevelők" (people's educators) to private homes. No doubt they were also supposed to write reports on the homes they visited. They always came in pairs. One evening, the bell rang and there in the corridor stood our educators. The reason I am telling you about them is this: I was eleven or twelve years old at the time and had trained myself (or rather, the world in which I was living had trained me) to become an adroit dissembler. I fetched, to impress our visitors, volumes from our library: works by Stalin. For of course, they were on our shelves, meant perhaps for occasions like this. Dissembling, saying one thing publicly and another thing at home, mistrusting everybody but the closest relatives and friends (it turned out after 1989 that even your best friends could very well have spied on you)— that was what informed our lives.

Political upheavals notwithstanding, I continued to take piano les-sons. While I did not exactly relish practicing, I loved music and gobbled up quantities of it. It was tremendously exciting, for example, when my teacher decided I was mature enough to study Haydn's Piano Concerto in D Major, Hob. XVIII:11. I ran to a music shop as fast as I could and ran on home to sight-read it. At that stage in my development, I could not yet appreciate the music's originality, especially of the second movement. Obviously, I was not yet mature enough, after all . . . Technically, though, it was within my reach. But no matter, I was insatiable and terribly impatient.

Also, I was very shy. Gone were the days when I happily "danced" for my captive audiences. I had to be literally pushed onto the stage and my only hope was not to make a mistake or have a memory lapse. Whether I was making music was less of a concern.

---

of world literature, cost the price of a loaf of bread per copy. Theaters employed "organizers" whose job it was to visit factories and sell subscriptions to workers for next to nothing. My piano lessons, too, were more or less gratuitous.

5   Mátyás Rákosi (1892–1971) established a dictatorship of terror in Hungary. An ardent follower of Stalin, he slavishly imitated his idol, introducing a cult of personality. I can still remember the rhythmic clapping that greeted whatever he had to say at party congresses; also, his portraits adorning all public institutions and, on a May Day parade, we schoolboys walking past the dais underneath Stalin's giant monument where he was standing, waving to us (we were also told when to wave). His reign was also marked by rigged trials, executions, the rustication of class enemies, the relentless persecution of wealthy peasants (kuláks), the enforced collectivization of agricul-ture, an all-powerful secret service (ÁVH) along the lines of the East German Stasi and Romanian Securitate.

I loved playing for myself, for my parents or relatives and once in a while I thought I was playing quite beautifully. More than half a century on, I can still recall a Sunday afternoon when Schubert's *Impromptu* in C Minor, D 899, suddenly flowed from under my fingers as never before and never after—as if I had been seized by the music's spirit.

Clearly, I was not destined to become a professional pianist. I did more and more sight-reading at the expense of practicing and actually won a prize at a competition where I was presented with a volume of Haydn's piano trios. Soon enough, I got two friends to play them through. My very last appearance in a concert was with the trio in G Major, I believe, with a *Rondo all'ongarese* for a finale. I was so nervous that I took an impossibly fast tempo, so that the others could hardly keep up. It was then that I decided once and for all: playing in public made no sense whatsoever.

On finishing secondary school (passing the Hungarian equivalent of the Austrian *Matura* and German *Abitur*), the question arose as to what I should do with myself. Having decided that music performance was not to be my profession, my parents and I opted for languages. I knew I would not want to teach, but the natural sciences or law were out of the question. A degree from the arts faculty of Budapest University would open up many avenues, we reasoned.

In those years, the late fifties, you had to sit for a pretty stiff entrance examination. If you had the right background, that is, if your parents were workers or peasants, you stood a good chance of admission. If, however, you were, like me, "other," that is, neither of those two, you started with a handicap. My application was turned down. There was nothing for it but to make sure next time I would rate as a worker, so I found employment in a small factory producing building material. You had to stick to it for nine months to qualify and I left the place nine months to the day.

The underlying idea of the powers that be was to ensure that young people hailing from "other" families would become acquainted with genuine workers, live their lives, and share their experiences. I got up at a quarter to five in the morning, started work at six, knocked off at four and spent those ten hours (Saturdays were free) carrying sacks, grinding asbestos (not exactly good for your health but we were given milk by way of protection), and things like that. I lost eighteen kilos (almost forty pounds) in the process and, indeed, learned a lot about what workers were like.

It was of course an alien world. Our boss was a heavy drinker who did not spend much time with us but appointed a deputy to rule over our group (we were about eight). When our boss learned that I had something to do with music, he burst into song, bloodshot light blue eyes bulging, red face turning purple. The sound he made was so atrocious that I could not help laughing. A desperate look in his eyes made me realize that he meant it seriously. Luckily, he did not take offense.

My colleagues included peasants and what were called "déclassé elements." One of the latter regaled me with stories of spiritualist séances and brought me books with blood-curdling pictures of mediums in trance, some whitish stuff emanating from their mouths.

I grew fond of a middle-aged man who spoke an attractive dialect and had a no less attractive sense of humor. He made me laugh a lot, perhaps unintentionally, with his racy style—I am finding it difficult to properly characterize him. He was like a peasant lad of the sort I had only read about in fairy tales—the one who always wins in the end. Eventually, my colleagues warned me that he had been in prison for theft, and that I should make sure to shut my locker properly. It was a bitter disappointment.

One day my colleagues went out for a drink, leaving me behind. Why not try to do the work of our group all by myself? I was by then familiar with the production process and set about it forthwith. By the time they returned—in high spirits—all was in sacks, with me standing next to them with a no doubt self-satisfied look on my face. Naive as I was, I had expected praise. Instead, one of the older men (with eyes no less bloodshot and bulging than my boss's) flew into such fury that he raised a spade to hit me; he was angry because I demonstrated that a single person was perfectly capable of accomplishing what a team of workers was doing. Luckily, he was grabbed on both sides by his companions who were less inebriated. It was a scene that has burned itself in my brain.

One thing I learned in those nine months was that workers were not by definition adherents of the Party. In fact, just one of them had joined up—a semi-moron, with a sheepish smile, unsteady eyes, and a stooping posture. I cannot remember his ever having said a word.

CHAPTER 4

MARGIT

I have given this chapter a name for a title. Margit used to watch me many times as I was typing away at my radio programs or whatever I happened to be busy with, marveling at my ability to transfer something from my head straight onto a sheet of paper, without copying it from somewhere. She leaned back comfortably in the green velvet armchair that for so many years had been my mother's preserve, with Margit standing in front of her. The idea that she, too, might take a seat, did not occur to any of us, probably least of all to her.

Margit was our maid, our cook, our cleaning lady, and our nurse. She had been engaged by my mother around 1935, at an employment agency in Budapest. Margit, twenty-five at the time and newly arrived from her native village of Zsigárd, was sitting at the agency along with other peasant girls, waiting to be picked by a lady of the middle class and taken by her to the apartment that was to become her home and workplace—for some months or, if her masters were satisfied, for years. In the event, Margit outlived my parents and remained part of my life, though no longer in our or my employment, until her own death in 1979.

Before the war, no middle-class family did without at least one maid; my grandmother had two: one to cook for her, the other to clean the rooms. Maids were a feature of the social system and were staple characters in novels and plays of the time—such as in Ferenc (Franz) Molnár's "suburban legend" *Liliom* (1909). They were usually pictured as young, innocent, naive, lost in the big city, at the mercy of the whims of their mistresses, and exposed to the sexual advances of their masters, or their masters' sons. The story often took a tragic turn. The maid would become pregnant, be banished forthwith, and have to return home in shame. A new maid would be found in no time.

Alternatively, a maid would meet a young man (she had a day off to meet friends—whether once a week or once a month, I cannot remember), fall in love, and start a family of her own. In Molnár's play, both Juli and Mari find their men and henceforth serve them rather than their masters' families.

I do not know what Margit may have looked like in 1935; she was probably homely rather than pretty. She had to leave us during the war (you did not take your maid with you to the ghetto), but she returned sometime after 1945 and took up service with my parents, until political events forced them to give up their business. I have described those years in an earlier chapter. Margit had to find a job elsewhere, and pretty soon she landed one with the post office as cleaning lady. She worked there until her retirement.

I cannot put a year to Margit's reemergence in our lives. It was probably in 1946 or 1947. By then, we had moved into my grandmother's apartment in the inner city. On entering, you faced a cubicle separated from the anteroom by a glass-and-timber wall with a door. That tiny little room, with no window, was Margit's domain. Her workplace, the kitchen, was right next to it. It was furnished very simply, like a nun's cell. I remember a bed, a white cupboard, a table, a chair. I also remember a smell. It had neither negative nor positive qualities; it was simply Margit's smell, which she took with her to the very first apartment in her life she had all to herself, one floor above our own—and with her death, the smell vanished once and for all.

The cubicle was a considerable advance on our prewar apartment in the Buda hills: that apartment was smaller and had no separate room for the maid, so a part of the kitchen was given over to her, separated by a curtain. (I was just over two years old when we had to leave that apartment and have retained no memory of it at all. My brother has told me about Margit's accomodation in our kitchen.)

At mealtime, we rang for her and she brought in the dishes, with a timid smile on her face. My father was quick to criticize her cooking, and her smile signified that she knew what she was in for. However, if a remark was indeed dropped, she would be quick to snap back and defend herself. Ringing for Margit when we were ready for the next dish, observing the way my mother talked to her at mealtime or indeed at any other time, gave me a glimpse of prewar class society. Especially my mother would treat her with some condescension and restrict any exchange strictly to her tasks, such as shopping, the next day's menu, or details of the cleaning she had to do. After that, Margit was supposed to leave the room and retire to the kitchen. I think Margit respected and feared my mother whereas my father she treated with respect tinged with friendly banter. Perhaps she could not take him quite seriously, or sensed less of a class barrier than with my mother.

Once, just once, I saw Margit kiss my mother's hand. I have no notion what the occasion might have been. In any case, Margit's face bore her timid smile, while my mother's showed that she was finding the ceremony extremely embarrassing. (She also hated it when gentlemen kissed her hand.) Still, the two of them went through with it, for they knew it was part of the roles life had traditionally assigned them.

Margit addressed my parents as Madame and Sir, later Mr. Varga (the German *gnädige Frau* and *gnädiger Herr* are much closer to the Hungarian exquivalent); she called my brother and me by our first names and used the familiar second-person singular.

We were in a way her children. She never married, although she confessed that she had met a man she loved: Uncle Géza. She was extremely reticent about him, answered my questions in curt sentences, but she did reveal that the reason for their breakup had been one of religion: Margit was a Calvinist and Uncle Géza was Roman Catholic. It followed that a match was simply not possible. What amazed me was her apparent indifference: no shade of emotion was detectable in her voice. My inquisitive questions revealed that Uncle Géza was also employed by the post office and the two of them would occasionally run into each other. He had found another wife and that was that.

For me, Margit inhabited a no-man's-land. She was, of course, an adult but clearly she was subordinate to my parents. In a way, she was also subordinate to my brother and me, and with the cruelty typical of children, we would get a great kick out of teasing her. For instance, we rang for her and she dutifully appeared each time, only to find that we were just joking. My brother and I called her *boszi*, short for *boszorkány*, that is, witch. That was our way of taking revenge for her scolding us when we left our stuff lying around or whatever. Margit was to that extent part of the adult world: she had the right, or laid claim to the right, to call us to order.

But she loved us dearly. I was terrified of my father who was something of a believer in corporal punishment and on one occasion, when I feared he was about to spank me, I fled to the kitchen and hid behind Margit's broad back. She bravely defended me ("Don't you touch that poor child!"), and my father relented.

No one could tuck me in the way Margit did. With her hands smelling of onions and garlic, her rough skin rubbing against my face, she arranged my bed cover so that I felt snug, protected, and loved. I enjoyed being ill for her tucking.

Covered up to my chin so that she could open the windows, I would watch her clean the rooms. She removed the carpets, slipped one foot into the strap of a floor brush that she had waxed beforehand, and danced through the rooms, with her hands folded on her back. Much later, probably after my mother had taken over the cleaning from Margit, we bought an electric contraption with three round brushes.

While cleaning, she hummed or sang some tunes. They were probably not genuine folk songs; I am afraid I cannot define what they may have been. I remember some sad ballads about tragic love affairs, but after sixty years or so, the memory is extremely vague. The fact of her singing has remained and also the atmosphere of the kitchen where she received one or two friends from her village. They talked quietly and knitted or did some embroidering, and I enjoyed sitting there and listening.

Margit spent her holidays at Zsigárd with her relatives (her elder sister's daughter and her family) and brought back what in the British Isles is sometimes called black pudding (blood sausage) and white pudding (liver sausage.) My father loved them. I much preferred her niece's poppy-seed strudel, of which I would gobble up large quantities.

Spoiled and self-centered as I was, it never occurred to me that Margit had not ever seen or bathed in what Hungarians like to describe as "the Hungarian sea." Balaton is the largest lake in Central Europe with popular resorts all around its shores. Once I had a car (I bought a Fiat Cinquecento in 1969), I would drive there for the day, to swim and bask in the sun. One day, Margit reproached me for never taking her with me, so with a guilty conscience I invited her. She put on her black bathing costume and settled on the grass looking like an old hen with its feathers loosely stretched out. Her happy smile only exacerbated my guilt. But she never went near the water.

When my mother went on what turned out to be her final stay in the hospital, Margit visited her regularly. On some days, my mother reckoned she would recover and return home, on others she expected to die. On such a day, she made Margit promise that she would look after me, which Margit did, as long as I remained a bachelor. Cooking and cleaning for me gave purpose to her life. Sometimes, in the evening, she would come down from her apartment and sit in my mother's armchair, watching me write or looking nowhere in particular. When she was ready to retire for the night, she would ask me if I wanted her to make my bed. The sounds of her moving about in the neighboring room gave me a similar feeling of being loved and protected as being tucked in by her had once done.

All was well and went its usual way until I met my wife. Margit, along with my stepmother, had never ceased to urge me to marry. They returned to the subject day after day. Rather like a Protestant pastor, Margit preached that God had ordained that man should take a wife, start a family, and produce children. I readily accepted that eternal verity but pointed out that I had not yet found the woman I was ready to take.

One day—on September 14, 1976—I did find her. I had refused to believe that such a thing was possible: I saw her and from then on floated on air. I *knew* she was the one. Four months to the day, on January 14, 1977, Kati became my wife.

Margit soon realized that she would have to relinquish her primacy in my household. Neither could she visit me anymore as she pleased: I was no longer alone. Kati wanted a washing machine, she wanted to replace my thirty-odd-year-old refrigerator with a new one, and she introduced other changes as well. I did not interfere, and Margit was not consulted.

One day she upset Kati by bringing it home to her that she was a penniless girl with no dowry; she needed to prove she was worthy of me. That village mentality upset me, too, and I had a word with Margit. The conversation took place in her apartment right above our kitchen. Kati heard every word. I had landed in a situation fraught with tension. It was extremely delicate, for I did not want to hurt Margit's feelings, nor did I want Kati to have any doubt at all as to my allegiance.

Finally, Margit stopped her visits altogether and I went up to see her whenever I could. Our conversations, which never failed to touch on my marriage, were often witnessed silently by my wife downstairs. Things came to a head when Margit learned we were looking for a larger apartment, complete with a nursery. Our twins would only be born two years later but we knew it was advisable to leave plenty of time to find a place that suited us. I shall never forget Margit's voice and the expression on her face as she asked: "Is this not good enough for you?" My heart ached, for I knew what our possible departure would mean to her. Still, life had to go on and there was nothing I could do.

Fate spared Margit the ordeal of having to watch us move out and live on in the house, which, without me, would have seemed desperately empty to her. Early in 1979, she was diagnosed with cancer and she died in May of that year. My wife had helped her find a good hospital and she also informed her relatives at Zsigárd.

We arrived somewhat late for the funeral, the guests were on their way home, but Margit's niece and her family nevertheless welcomed us into their house.

A few years ago, Kati and I drove to Zsigárd to visit Margit's grave. We had to ask an elderly woman tending a grave near the entrance to point it out to us. She hesitated for a while, then her eyes lit up: the Szuh family grave was in the Calvinist section of the cemetery—we were in the Catholic one.

Standing at Margit's grave, I rang my brother in Sydney, so that he would also be present. And now the least I can do is to devote this chapter to our maid/cook/cleaning lady/ nurse, Margit Szuh, who shared the life of the Varga family, with interruptions, between 1935 and 1979.

CHAPTER 5

TAPESPONDENCE

F our years after the Hungarian Revolution and two years following the execution of its leader, Imre Nagy (1896–1958), I enrolled in Budapest University in September 1960, to study English and Russian. There ensued five rather uneventful years ending with my graduation in June 1965.

Of course, the nine months in the factory had taught me to appreciate the luxury of having nothing to do but prepare for my classes and diligently take notes at lectures on Chaucer, Gower, or Turgenev. It was just the ideological subjects that gave me a headache: dialectical materialism, political economy and the rest with their claim of exclusivity and infallibility were hard to swallow.

However, the atmosphere in Hungary was relaxing, I felt I could breathe more freely and looked optimistically to the future.

What I did not realize until much later was that the single most decisive event in my life had actually taken place in 1961 with the purchase of a tape recorder. It was an unwieldy monster and the tapes on sale were of shoddy quality with the magnetic layer likely to flake off.

My brother, on learning of my new acquisition, paid for my membership in what was called the Australian Tapesponding Association. "Tapespondence"—the exchange of recorded messages in place of letters—may or may not have been a long-lived hobby on an international scale but it has changed my life. My name and address appeared on the membership list and since I was the only one from behind the Iron Curtain, soon a steady trickle of small-sized reels arrived from all over the world. It was tremendously exciting to listen to those messages in all the various accents of the English-speaking countries and it was also, of course, a thrilling challenge to reply to them.

I received a Grundig microphone as a present and recorded my own typed messages, for of course I found ad-libbing heavy going. Sending off my tapes, hoping they would arrive safe and sound, proved to be a bureaucratic hurdle race: I had to have them checked by an institution established for the purpose, which then sealed the parcel and provided a certificate.

One of my tapespondents was a Scottish baronet, Sir Mark Dalrymple, of Newhailes, Musselburgh, Midlothian. I was impressed by his impeccable accent, his soft-spoken voice and quick, unexpected bursts of laughter as indeed by the stately home he called his own near Edinburgh where I visited him in 1964. Today it is a carefully restored seventeenth-century building, refurbished in the eighteenth, with an impressively rich library of national fame. In those days, however, Newhailes was in a rather poor state of repair. Mark showed me the library, casually mentioned that it represented an important collection, and quickly took me upstairs. The curtains were drawn and in the half-light I only had time to note the dust as well as the outlines of furniture under gray covers.

Mark and his wife Antonia, an earl's daughter, lived in a tiny flat on the top floor (they could not afford to heat the house) and served me a modest meal. Afterward, Mark drove me to the Firth of Forth to treat me to a sight that never ceased to fascinate him: the departure and arrival of ferries with cars rolling on and off them. We spent rather a longer time there than I would have wished; Mark's childish pleasure did not rub off on me. Still, it was an encounter I have not forgotten: it afforded me a glimpse of an altogether different kind of existence. A few years later, about to set out on a trip, Mark heaved a suitcase into the trunk of his car, collapsed, and died of a heart attack.

Another tapespondent, Andy Underhill, was an American music-lover who collected, and shared with me, little-known composers—little-known, that is, to me. Listening to symphonies by the eighteenth-century English composer William Boyce (1711–79) conducted by the versatile German American musician Karl Haas (1913–2005), was a welcome discovery. The same went for the Bohemian Franz Krommer (František Vincenc Kramář, 1759–1831) and some of his masses, which impressed me at the time.

More important, Andy Underhill owned a small record company specializing in American folk music. The songs were embedded in evocative background sound effects and linked by narration through husky-voiced actors impersonating rough, life-hardened characters. One of Andy's releases was called *Yankee Whaling Songs*. It featured a group of merry sailors who, amid the screeching of seagulls and the creaking of tackle, sang some stirring tunes—all very attractive and infectious.

"Why don't you try to sell this to the radio?" my mother suggested. That question, that idea, started the ball rolling.

To make a long story short: my first-ever radio program, based on Andy Underhill's *Yankee Whaling Songs*, was broadcast in 1963. Some more in a similar vein were to follow and, needless to say, I boasted about them to my fellow students. It was only natural, then, for the English Department to suggest my name to the English Section of Hungarian Radio, which was looking for a student they could offer what was called a "social scholarship." It was considerably higher than other grants and also went with a job after graduation. An ideal solution for me.

This is the place for a confession.

During the long summer holidays, to practice my English and make some money, I did some interpreting for trade union delegations. More often than not, it proved to be an exercise in attuning my ears to a wide range of accents—from the cultured modulations of Will Owen, MP for Morpeth, through George Fraser, trade union secretary from Glasgow as well as delegations from Ghana, Zanzibar, and other African countries right up to a young man from Iceland who represented his trade union at an international conference in Budapest. I ended up writing his address for him.

Thanks to that activity, I happened to be sitting in the lobby of the Grand Hotel on Margaret Island in Budapest when I saw a short old gentleman with a cane, slowly making his way to the armchair nearest to the entrance. I recognized him immediately: it was Igor Stravinsky.[1] Someone gave me a sheet of white paper so that I could ask for his autograph. Stravinsky did not even look at me let alone say a word—but he did write his name on the paper that I was holding for him, supported by a book. I watched mesmerized as he slowly drew a large I and a large S followed by the rest in the German spelling of his name, with a "w" for a "v." I had it framed and it has adorned my wall ever since.

My graduation present from my brother was a check for £25, quite a decent sum in 1965. It was certainly sufficient for me to apply for an exit visa, for I decided to spend it on a trip to Austria and Italy.[2] However,

---

1 Stravinsky conducted a concert of his music in Budapest in 1963.
2 The forint not being convertible, the economy suffered from a chronic shortage of hard currency. If you wanted to travel to the West, you had to apply to the National Savings Bank for an allowance of fifty dollars before approaching the Ministry of the Interior. You were entitled to fifty dollars once every three years. In possession of the bank's authorization, you stood a good chance of being granted an exit visa, which consisted of what we called a "window" in our passport. You were then free to leave the country but once you returned, you had to start from scratch if you wished to leave again. If, however, you owned an account in hard currency (sent to you by

the passport failed to arrive in the mail. A letter from the Ministry of the Interior came in its stead, summoning me to a conversation with a Comrade Dunai.

Comrade Dunai took rather long to come to the point. He had been informed that I was going to work during the summer as an interpreter at the International Course of Hungarian Language and Culture at Debrecen in Eastern Hungary. The ministry would grant me permission to leave the country provided I agreed to help the authorities. There was reason to suppose that spies would infiltrate the course; it was our job to stop them from inflicting damage to the country. Would I be willing to report on anything that struck me as being suspect?

I certainly did not like the idea of anyone wishing to cause damage and readily agreed to cooperate. We arranged for me to go to a café on the outskirts of the town at regular intervals where a young man would be waiting for me. I also had to promise never to give any sign of recognition if I were to bump into him anywhere else at any other time. "That is what we call conspiracy," Comrade Dunai explained.

My passport turned up a few days later in my mailbox and I duly took a train to Debrecen. In attendance were several young Britons of both sexes who had for some obscure reason taken into their heads to study the Magyar language and culture. They were blissfully unaware of the presence of a spy in the person of a twenty-four-year-old friendly native keen to study *their* language.

Nothing remotely suspect caught my attention during the four-week course and consequently, I had to disappoint the young man who must have gotten up in Budapest at the crack of dawn to make our appointment in the early morning. There was nothing to report and, after he posed some unnecessary questions for form's sake, we parted company. (I did meet him again a few years later, at the headquarters of the Hungarian Journalists' Association. After the briefest of eye contact, we looked past each other.)

I was an innocuous one-off informer. In making me earn my passport, Comrade Dunai assured me that there were numerous ordinary citizens in the country who were working for the Ministry of the Interior out of an inner patriotic conviction. I did not really need his assurance; one was aware of a network of informers, in some cases readily identifiable among one's colleagues or acquaintances. They supplied reports to what was called the III/III Department of Internal Security.

---

relatives in the West), you could skip the application to the bank and were usually allowed to leave, provided you left your family behind. Married couples were likely to defect—families with children even more so.

It was not until after the collapse in 1989 of the socialist camp, also known as the Warsaw Treaty Countries, that the exposure of one-time spies turned into a highly effective means of blackmail in the Hungarian body politic. Although many documents in the III/III Department had been destroyed, a sufficient number survived to denounce whoever was in your way.

You are now free to visit the archives and ask to inspect your own files if you wish to find out who spied on you or indeed on a member of your family. That is precisely what the writer Péter Esterházy (born 1950) did. Having written a sizable book on the history of his family, which he named after the composition *Harmonia caelestis* by one of his illustrious forebears, Prince Pál Esterházy (1635–1713), he decided to examine his father's files. To his absolute horror and mortification, he discovered that his father, the book's dedicatee, had also been an informer. He now understood why he had been allowed to study mathematics at university—after all, aristocrats in postwar Hungary were personae non gratae, they were excluded from institutions of higher education. He understood, too, why he had been allowed to travel to Austria to visit his relatives, such as Countess Monika Esterházy, a sister of his father's and a former inmate of the women's prison at Kistarcsa in Hungary. Whether Mátyás Esterházy had readily complied with the demand that he spy on his fellow aristocrats so that he could help his children or whether he had agreed under duress, I do not know.

Under the greatest secrecy, only known to his publisher and a handful of other confidants, Esterházy sat down to write a sequel to *Harmonia caelestis*, which he titled *Javított kiadás* (Revised Edition, 2002). In it, he reveals the exact content of Mátyás Esterházy's files and, in a possibly unique chapter in world literature, he curses his father, hurling an avalanche of desperate abuse and invective at him in an unprecedentedly poignant attempt at self-purification. *Harmonia caelestis* and *Javított kiadás* are, for me, the epitaphs of a social system in its dying agony.[3]

---

3 *Harmonia caelestis* is available in English under the title *Celestial Harmonies*, translated by Judith Sollosy (London: Flamingo, 2004).

CHAPTER 6

BIRTH AND DEMISE OF A (COUNTER)REVOLUTION

A Boy's-Eye View

I cannot undertake to write an objective and exhaustive report on what we used to call, euphemistically, the "regrettable October events." The Hungarian uprising that began on October 23, 1956, and was put down by Soviet troops on November 4 has been analyzed in a variety of ways, each according to the analyst's political affiliation. There may not be any one canon acceptable to all. What I can offer is my own personal experience.

On October 23, I went to school as usual and found the gate locked. Just one of my classmates turned up. The janitor heard us trying to get in, opened the door, and told us to go home. He could not tell us when teaching would start again.

What began as a peaceful demonstration—I saw a huge crowd slowly marching along one of Budapest's main thoroughfares and was struck by their happy faces—turned within days into an armed confrontation, with the lynching of members of the hated secret police (ÁVH—State Defense Authority). I remember the same thoroughfare about a week later with graves lining the pavement. When I stepped out onto our balcony and looked down, I saw wounded Russian soldiers in armored vehicles parked outside our house, with bloodstained dressing on their heads. Sporadic shooting was heard in the distance.

Neighbors of my parents' generation who had experienced the war as adults (it had only ended eleven years before) were wondering if they should go to the cellar, while I, on the contrary, was pounding away at the piano all day long.

My parents were not alarmed. My brother, however, got hold of a pistol somewhere and drove about (or was driven?—I no longer remember) in an ambulance. I think he was having a good time and it never entered his head that he might be hit by a stray bullet. My father tried to convince him to come to reason. There was an incredible scene in our corridor-like anteroom: my brother was standing at one end, with a pistol in his hand, and my father rushing in his direction with my aunt hanging on to him from behind. My father's anger, anxiety, and frustration lent him tremendous strength and as he was moving at great speed toward my brother, my aunt appeared to be flying in the air after him, her hands grabbing his clothes.

Soon, the question of defecting came up. My father was fifty-six, my mother four years younger—they decided they were too old to flee to the West and start life anew. They agreed, however, that it was best for my brother to leave: he had not been admitted to university and was bound to be called up, which would mean two or three years of his life squandered.

On December 8, 1956, my brother, his girlfriend, and two other young women who also wanted to leave but did not dare to go by themselves, set out in the early hours of dawn. My parents and I softly opened the shutters and watched the four figures walk toward the street corner and disappear at the far end. We next saw my brother eight years later, in 1964.

When school reopened eventually, we looked round to see if any of our classmates were missing. I think they were all there, but almost all of them had relatives who had made it over the frontier. Russian was no longer compulsory; our Russian mistress now taught us German, a language she had more or less forgotten. Soon enough, however, Russian was back on our curriculum and our beloved head teacher came to our class to say good-bye.

He had been introduced to us sometime early in 1956 by our Latin master who said Mr Antall was going to teach us history. He looked young but was an adult, consequently, on the far side of the abyss that separates the world of adolescents from that of grown-ups. He was in fact merely nine years our senior. Soon enough, we grew very fond of him. We loved his sense of humor, tinged with irony, we were impressed by his neckties (unusual in their quality and the size of the knot) and we loved the way he taught us, usually with some asides to amuse or educate us. He suggested for instance that socialism was doomed to failure because it was based on idealized human qualities. Capitalism, on the other hand, owed its success to the fact that it was based on negative, consequently real, human traits. His opinion of women will no doubt incense feminists: in his view, women were unsuitable to fill any responsible position (such as in politics) because for one-third of their lives they were not accountable for their actions: while menstruating, during menopause, and as young mothers. At a suggestible age you are bound to remember statements (warnings) like that.

Gradually it transpired that Antall's father had been a government minister in the first coalition government after the war (his name was in the telephone directory, with "minister emeritus" standing next to it) and that our teacher had been brought up in an atmosphere steeped in politics. He, too, wanted to become a politician. No wonder, then, that he was elected a member of the school's "revolutionary council" (all factories, enterprises, and institutions in the country had one)—something that was held against him after the defeat of the revolution. This is how it came to his farewell speech, which he delivered while walking about in the classroom. His face showed no emotion. We were sitting on our benches petrified, and when, at a suitable point in his speech, he had reached the door and stepped outside, we continued to sit silently, not knowing what to say or what to do. Many of us had tears in our eyes.

József Antall was to become Hungary's first prime minister after the collapse of the socialist system. A bust of him adorns a small square in Buda and whenever I walk past it (which does not happen often) I stop to look at him. It is not a good likeness.

József Antall lived opposite our house with his parents and his wife. We would wave to each other when I was standing on our balcony and he appeared in his window. He visited us a number of times, especially after he had been dismissed from school and was out of a job. My father, by then financial director of a major Budapest theater, offered him employment as an "organizer." (As mentioned earlier, it was the organizers' job to sell theater tickets and subscriptions by going out to potential buyers rather than waiting for them to go to the box office.) Antall nodded briefly, smiled, and accepted the offer. Also, he told my father about his farewell speech in class. To my absolute amazement, I learned that every single detail of his speech—including looking out of the window—had been a studied performance. I was nonplussed and shocked.

He never forgot my father's gesture at a difficult time in his life and decades later asked me to drive him to the cemetery where he bowed his head at my father's grave.

As Hungary's first democratically elected prime minister (in 1990), he was not, to my mind, much of a success: he seemed to want to follow in the footsteps of his predecessors in that office between the two world wars. He also did not have much time to accomplish what he imagined to be the right thing for the country: he was diagnosed with cancer and died in 1993, at the age of sixty-one. He did not want to live a long life, he had said in a statement, but rather to have an active one. To that extent, he was a success.

In 2003, my brother visited us in Vienna. It was a kind of farewell to the city, to the country that had received him and 200,000 other Hungarians with open arms, at a time when Austria herself was rather poor, having just shaken herself free from the Soviet occupying forces. I wondered if my brother could remember where he had actually crossed the frontier on December 8 1956. He could not: it had been during the night, he could see nothing. We decided to visit instead the bridge at Andau—a timber structure over a narrow canal, which still marks the border between Hungary and Austria. It had been the scene of an exodus of refugees in the last months and weeks of 1956. That spot as well as the Hungarian Revolution had been immortalized in James Michener's nonfiction book of 1957, *The Bridge at Andau.*

My brother, my wife, and I drove from Vienna to the province of Burgenland (the easternmost Austrian province), as far as the beginning of a narrow causeway leading toward the bridge. The start of the road is marked by a poignant monument to the refugees of forty-seven years before. I was deeply moved, for I had not expected it and saw it, as my brother was standing in front of the stone sculpture, as a monument erected in my brother's honor. Then we walked along the causeway, with carved wooden sculptures on either side, each showing two refugees in dramatic situations—one too exhausted to walk on, the other helping him to stand up. Far too pathetic to be taken seriously, but since we were by ourselves in the total stillness, the atmosphere of the place—the road, the sculptures, the bridge and the canal in the distance, with a look-out tower next to them— was rather uncanny.

We walked onto the bridge, the middle of which is marked by a small gate: the frontier. Passing it had changed the lives of thousands of Hungarians.

It occurred to me yet again that history was in a way a purveyor of suitable spots for sightseers. The greater the tragedy at the time it happened, the more people flock there to shudder. In comparison with battlegrounds where thousands of soldiers had lost their lives, or concentration camps or, indeed, Ground Zero, the bridge at Andau is insignificant. For the three of us, however, shuddering was a natural reaction, for we had all lived through the Hungarian Revolution, its memory was still vivid, and one of us, my brother, had actually escaped in the dark across the frontier. Nearly half a century later, he met his own monument in stone.

CHAPTER 7

BROADCASTING 1

After an absence of several decades, in May 2011, I visited the wing of Budapest's Broadcasting House, which used to be occupied by the Foreign Broadcasts Department. Not a soul was around. The door to what had been the secretariat of the English Section was locked. Another door, behind which hid the cubicle where I used to type away at my scripts, also refused entry. I felt like a ghost from the past.

When I turned up for work on September 1, 1965, the Foreign Broadcasts Department represented an important branch of Hungarian Radio: it housed a number of "Sections" whose job it was to convince listeners the world over that the socialist system, as realized in the Hungarian People's Republic, was working in an exemplary fashion, proving the superiority of communism-in-the-making over capitalism.

Programs were put on the air in English, German, Italian, Greek, Spanish, and also in Hungarian (it went by the name "Our Native Land"). There was a Central Editorial Board, which provided the sections with daily political commentaries and some other texts to be translated and broadcast by them all. The rest was left to their discretion but was no doubt thrashed out at sessions of section leaders under the chairmanship of the head of the department.

The radio journalists were partly émigré party members, partly Hungarians who were supposed to have a perfect command of the language they broadcast in. The Greek Section was a rather complicated outfit in that it brought together under the same umbrella representatives of opposing factions of the Communist Party. Every now and again, they were still fighting over texts as they descended the stairs on their way to the studio. (Programs were always prerecorded and broadcast on shortwave, with several repeats.)

I hardly knew the head of the department. He had his office on the top floor with two rather plain ladies (that is, female comrades) guarding entrance to his bureau. My boss thought very highly of him, which automatically meant that I, too, held him in high regard. It was therefore all the more shocking to learn one day that András Tardos had shot himself in the head in a forest near Budapest.

Underneath him in rank and floor sat in state an absolutely formidable old lady, Anna Péter. She was small, had a wizened face under tousled snow-white hair, her voice was hoarse and her tiny eyes looked at you with suspicion and mistrust. Anna Péter had Hungarian roots but came from the United States—a committed communist fighting a lifelong battle for the cause.

On my first day in the Section, I was escorted to her office to be bellowed at (Anna Péter had a frighteningly loud voice), vetted, put in my place, and eventually allowed to start work three floors below.

Charlie, Len, Ronnie, Jules, Pali, Judy, and all the others—most of them dead now, some in retirement—for six years were my colleagues. I looked up to them in utter deference, anxious to improve my English, to learn to write programs, to read them in Studio 17 without my tongue stumbling over words (which it initially did with exasperating regularity), and to get on with everybody.

In the first months, I was rather intimidated and also discouraged. Intimidated because I became part of a community that spoke English as a matter of course whereas I, although best of my group at university, discovered that my degree was totally useless. Charlie Coutts, the head of the English Section, then in his early forties (that is, an old man in my eyes), was a Scotsman from Aberdeen with an accent I had a hard time deciphering. Also, he appeared to be rather gruff and demanding and I felt not up to it. I was discouraged and disappointed because, to begin with, my job consisted in filling out QSL cards, the least inspiring assignment you can think of. It was brought home to me that our broadcasts were picked up by radio amateurs ("hams") who sent us reception reports. Our QSL cards, which acknowledged the correctness of their data (wavelength, time, program content), were returned to their addresses, to be pinned on their walls. Filling in the empty spaces of the printed cards bored me to tears. It was at least as dull to translate and record "wave-propagation forecasts," which no doubt provided welcome help for hams, but was tedious to distraction.

I remember, too, the very first text, issued by the Central Editorial Board, I was supposed to translate into English. What were all my studies of Maria Edgeworth, Elisabeth Gaskell, John Gower, or James Joyce for, what use was the effort to make sense of *The Lay of Igor's Campaign* if I had to look up every other word in the dictionary—even the title: Water Economy.[1] What was I doing in the section when I was feeling so out of place anyway, hopeless in the studio, attending section meetings where Charlie would address us as "Comrades" and where matters were discussed, rather heatedly, which were totally beyond me? Meetings where I sensed tensions, personal ambitions, manifestations of relationships developed over years of working together—with me, a neutral and foreign body? Would it occur to anyone to ask me point-blank, out of the blue: "Are you actually a communist?" If so, should I dissemble or just be me, hoping to get by somehow, without attracting too much attention?

As the months went by, I gradually found my bearings. Above all, I learned not to fear, but on the contrary, to admire Charlie. He came from a working-class background and what I first interpreted as gruffness was just his way of communicating. But he was a delightful person to work with and to work for, a man of sharp intellect, a wonderful journalist who mastered the ins and outs of the profession and whose corrections and advice one could follow with conviction and gratitude. He was a deep-feeling, helpful, and honest man who readily admitted to his personal weaknesses. His fondness for women, for instance. Whether his wife, Erzsi, was aware of his escapades, we never found out. He had a great sense of humor, larding his stories with a generous helping of f_ _ _ing. Charlie's Hungarian was quite fluent if colored by his strong Scots accent and not quite impeccable grammar. It served him well when he was invited to comment on soccer matches—his great hobby—on the home service. He would arrive in the section, whistling or singing a Scots folk song and our rooms were immediately filled with life. Charlie was my first boss (not counting the failed tenor with the bulging eyes) and I am grateful to Fate for those six years under his leadership.

He was rather contemptuous of our other British colleague, Len Scott, who broadcast under the pseudonym of László Pintér (a precaution that I am sure failed to mislead the British authorities. Incidentally, because of his Scots accent, a Hungarian name was out of the question for Charlie. He opted for Jock Taylor). Len was also a member of the British Communist

---

1   *The Lay of Igor's Campaign* (Slovo o polku Igoreve), an anonymous twelfth century poem in Old East Slavic, which served as the basis for Borodin's opera *Prince Igor*.

Party but perhaps not a distinguished one. Charlie described him, with an ironical smile, as "a loyal comrade."

Unlike Charlie, Len's Hungarian was absolutely hopeless. In my eagerness to learn new words, I would look up words I heard him say—and fail to find them in the English–Hungarian dictionary. No wonder: what sounded like "botchernot" was his way of pronouncing "bocsánat" ("sorry" in Hungarian). I was also mystified by "hooaye" only to find out from him that he had meant to say "hülye" (idiot).

Although he was dismissed by Charlie, I am also very grateful to Len. Not only did he correct my English texts for years, he also helped me with my accent and intonation. "Don't drop your voice at the end of a sentence, it sounds as if you were dejected," was one of his injunctions.

I was keen to enrich my vocabulary and spent hours every day reading the *Guardian*, copying into dozens of books words, phrases, and entire paragraphs, memorizing them and looking them up again and again. I only read English literature at home, spoke English most of the time during the day, recorded texts in English—and found a few years later that I could not be used for programs in Hungarian, for I had a foreign accent. During the six years in the section I came nearest to living in an English-speaking country.

I also want to call forth from the realm of shadows Rosemarie—Ronnie—Prockl (Rose Pataki for listeners), a Hungarian American whose tragedy in life was her near-blindness. Her phenomenal memory stood her in good stead, for she could not read texts. Her handicap turned her into a bitter, indeed vicious, person who hated to be at the mercy of whoever was around to help her. Gyula (Jules) Gulyás, another American of Hungarian parentage, was a former student at the Budapest Academy of Music who for some reason did not make it as a professional musician. Now and then I would catch him writing scores. He had a Pickwickian stature, bald with large pores on his face and bulbous nose. As Charlie disclosed on his last visit to Vienna around 2002, Jules had been hopelessly in love with Ronnie who would ruthlessly reject his advances. I never noticed anything of all that.

As my command of the language improved, Charlie would give me challenging assignments. He asked me, for instance, to write a program marking Poetry Day (April 11, the birthday of Attila József, 1905–37).[2] On another occasion, he sent me to visit castles around the country and do a

---

2 Regarded in Hungary as a major twentieth-century poet, Attila József created an oeuvre varied
   enough to be misused by successive political regimes to their particular purposes. In socialist
   Hungary, he was the epitome of the working-class revolutionary poet, with his love poetry and

program about them. I enjoyed the luxury of a chauffeur-driven car and was allowed to take my then girlfriend with me. In those years, between 1965 and 1971, my ambition in life was to please Charlie. I was the happiest man on earth when he said "Good job, Bálint." Even today, more than forty years later, I can hear his voice as he said it.

My responsibilities included the translation and recording of news. Eventually, I reached the stage where I could look at the Hungarian original and type the English translation as if I were copying it. For the first—and last—time in my life, I was confident of my capabilities. I was proud to hear Len read my texts, which he no longer needed to correct. I had come into my own.

To get back to my fear of being exposed as a bourgeois reactionary (reactionary bourgeois?), one day, I overheard Charlie say to someone: "You cannot by any stretch of the imagination describe Bálint as a communist." It was a tremendous relief. So he knew . . .

He adapted surprisingly well to the changing times. The collapse of socialism did not drive him back to his native country; he stayed on in Budapest and continued to work for the section but died before the entire Foreign Broadcasts Department was dissolved. On a visit to Vienna around 2002, he said quite openly that in his programs, he had not striven to portray Hungary as it was—rather, he presented the country as he hoped it would one day be, a sort of ideal Hungary, which has yet to be born.

---

expressions of his schizophrenia, which eventually led to his death (he threw himself in front of a train) conveniently suppressed.

CHAPTER 8

BROADCASTING 2

harlie was of course well aware that music was my primary interest. It was thanks to his help, for instance, that on one of my visits to London I was received by some of the leading figures of the folk music revival in Britain in the 1950s and 1960s. I recorded a long interview with Ewan MacColl and his wife Peggy Seeger (and I heard them perform at a club). I also met A. L. Lloyd and Tom Paley.[1] They all gave me records to take home and, as a natural sequel to the program on the *Yankee Whaling Songs*, I introduced those singers to Hungarian listeners. Charlie and I even collaborated on the script of a dialogue in Hungarian, a sort of mock interview in which he talked about his favorite Scottish folk songs. It was broadcast in due course: probably the first and last radio program in Hungarian by a Scots journalist.

Charlie also let me meet and interview classical artists who guest-performed in Budapest. The conversations were broadcast in English (and even émigré Hungarians, such as Andor Foldes, István Kertész, or Antal Doráti humored me, only Géza Anda could not be bothered) and soon enough I approached the home service in an effort to sell them my loot.

That is how my "career" on Hungarian Radio took off. Soon enough, I was on the air once a week, on Saturday afternoons, as part of a regular feature that included concert reviews and reports. I was given four minutes

---

1 Ewan MacColl (1915–89), British author, poet, actor, folksinger, and record producer. Daughter of Ruth Crawford Seeger and half-sister of Pete Seeger, the American folksinger Peggy Seeger was born in 1935. She was married to Ewan MacColl. A. L. Lloyd (1908–82), British folksinger and folksong collector, author of important books on folk music. Tom Paley (b. 1928), American-born folksinger, fiddler, guitarist, and banjo player.

at the most, and until my departure from Hungary in January 1991, my contributions were a staple diet for music-lovers. Not just the miniature interviews on Saturdays (I did hundreds of them over a quarter of a century) but also proper one-hour features where I would talk to Hungarian musicians, visiting artists, and those I met abroad.

Interviewing became a way of life. I made sure I would be well prepared, reading whatever I could find in libraries, but once in a while I also had to improvise. I seem to have had a tape recorder with me as a natural accessory similar to a watch or a pen, ready to switch it on and point my microphone at whoever was willing to talk to me. I became something of an addict. I knew the telephone numbers of all the Budapest hotels where artists would be put up and rang a dozen times, if necessary, before they answered the phone. I would then introduce myself and ask for an appointment.

More often than not, we would meet in the green room after the concert and, having fought my way behind the stage (the Cerberus on duty would invariably be difficult), I would hasten through narrow corridors to reach my next victim. There I would need to take a deep breath and, using my microphone as a flaming sword, would shoo off autograph hunters, get to the door, and close it firmly behind me.

That is how I came face to face with Arthur Rubinstein in Budapest's second opera house and concert hall, the Erkel Theatre. It was October 19, 1966—the date I began my work as an interviewer. I also landed a scoop sometime in 1967 when I persuaded Elisabeth Schwarzkopf to reply to my questions after her lieder recital at the Erkel Theatre. It turned out later that the radio's staff reporter had had no luck. The interview was broadcast both on shortwave and on the home service—after that, whatever I had to offer was taken with no questions asked.

My breakthrough could also have been due to the interview I did with Joseph Szigeti in the presence of the head of the radio's classical music department. Szigeti, by then an old man with a weak voice and opalescent eyes, readily answered my questions coming as they did from a young man nearly half a century his junior.

Slowly, imperceptibly, work in the English Section was becoming rather routine. It no longer presented a challenge. I was ready for something new, even though I never formulated it in so many words in my mind.

One day in September 1971, the telephone rang in my cubicle. It was the secretary of László Sarlós, managing director of Editio Musica Budapest, the Hungarian music publisher. Would I be free and interested in visiting Comrade Sarlós at such and such a time? A new chapter in my life had begun.

CHAPTER 9

EDITIO MUSICA BUDAPEST

László Sarlós's offer was irresistible. He explained that he had succeeded in persuading the Ministry of Culture and Education that a music publisher needed someone to promote its products. The idea that a commercial enterprise should by definition aim at making a profit was wholly alien to his superiors: for ideological reasons, the notions of profit and socialism were mutually exclusive. After all, organizations like the music publisher or theaters could count on state subsidies, they did not need to worry about profits. Editio Musica Budapest (EMB) was therefore in a position to publish anything it considered of value (such as Eric Walter White's book on Stravinsky) regardless of the number of copies it was likely to sell. In return for state subsidies, cultural organizations were dependent on prior ministerial approval of whatever they wished to present to the public.

In his dealings with the ministry, Sarlós argued that in promoting contemporary Hungarian music in the world, the firm would serve a laudable purpose that was very well compatible with the idea(l)s of socialism, for it would demonstrate the cultural viability of our system. That rang a bell and Sarlós was free to look for a promoter.[1]

Eventually, he found me. It sounded like an ideal job: it had to do with music, I could put my English to good advantage, and it involved traveling—a rare luxury for Hungarians. The only thing that worried me was whether I

---

1 László Sarlós had spent a few years in London as representative of a Hungarian cultural export firm. He will have gleaned some of the ideas he was to implement in running Editio Musica from his experiences in Britain.

could continue with my radio programs. Thanks to Sarlós, I could carry on; he had enough trust in me to know that I would not misuse my freedom.

It was with a sinking heart that I told Charlie I wanted to have a word with him. "This was bound to come sooner or later," he replied. He had in his mind given me six years in the section and the six years were now up . . . To put off my departure, he made me stay on for two more months.

I took a tearful departure from my colleagues. It upset me to be leaving Charlie in the lurch and I vowed to never again say a formal good-bye if I should ever change jobs—I would just walk out, without looking back. It was a promise I have more or less kept since.

Sarlós and I embarked on something new—certainly new to Hungary. The very word "promotion" was a novelty; it has no Hungarian equivalent. Logically, the activity it covers was also unknown. We ourselves had very little notion of what I needed to do, so Sarlós asked me to write monthly reports on what I had accomplished. We would then get together and discuss it.

My mandate was the promotion of contemporary Hungarian music in the world. However, the world did not know such a thing existed, nor was it aware that it was a commodity it had been sorely missing. Worse than that: I was a newcomer to this field, I had not met any of the composers who were to be my charges, and my only experience of contemporary music had been *Pezzo sinfonico* by Attila Bozay as well as the same composer's solo cello piece *Formazioni*. I had heard it played by a then prominent artist, László Mező, and it struck me as a more or less hopeless struggle of the soloist with the apparently superhuman technical requirements of the music. I heard noise and saw perspiration.

Actually, it now occurs to me that I had heard another piece of new music, probably in 1959 or 1960. My parents and I attended a performance of Witold Lutosławski's *Musique funèbre* in Memoriam Béla Bartók (composed in 1954–58). We could not make heads or tails of it and my father commented: "If anyone were to shoot the conductor, he would be acquitted on the grounds that he was acting in self-defense."

I spent the first couple of years getting to know the repertoire, the "back catalogue." I listened to LP records (the compact disc was not yet around) released by the Hungarian state record company, Hungaroton. If a piece proved difficult to digest, I heard it again and again, until I was satisfied that I had a rough idea of what the composer meant to convey.

The rest of the time I wrote letters. I mean I typed them: the computer had not yet been invented or if it had, we had not heard about it. The fax machine was also *Zukunftsmusik*. When eventually a telex was installed, we were thrilled to have such an advanced means of communication. International telephone calls had to be booked in advance with the exchange and they took a long time to materialize, so I made use of them sparingly.

I think the very first letter I typed was addressed to John Andrewes, my opposite number with Boosey and Hawkes, the British music publisher with subsidiaries in different parts of the world, who represented Editio Musica Budapest. John was popular and highly regarded in the profession, not only as a "promoter" but also as a conductor, I think mainly of Benjamin Britten's small-scale music theater pieces.

Editio Musica Budapest was the *only* music publisher in Hungary. It goes without saying that it was state-owned, as was every other cultural institution in the country. It had been established in 1950 after the nationalization of prewar private firms, such as Rózsavölgyi, Rozsnyai, and Bárd.[2] The names might ring a bell for Bartók and Kodály scholars: their first works were taken on by those enterprising gentlemen. Nationalization meant that the copyright of those early compositions was transferred to EMB—including Bartók's First String Quartet, his symphonic poem *Kossuth* (1903), the *Scherzo* (1904) for piano and orchestra, and some other pieces, as well as choruses and piano works by Kodály.

EMB's monopoly meant that it had to publish the music of practically *every* composer active in the country. And since Sarlós saw to it that the firm owned a printing press and had an expert staff of music engravers, the overwhelming majority of scores was printed. It proved to be a trump card for me because publishers in the West often preferred manuscript copies, which were considerably cheaper to produce. The scores I took on my travels never failed to impress my customers at least as far as the quality of the engraving was concerned.

o

Zoltán Kodály died in 1967. He was the last great Hungarian composer with an international reputation, one whose orchestral and choral music had acquired a secure niche in the repertoire worldwide. None of the composers who survived Kodály measured up to him in any way. He was more than a great composer, he was a "national institution." He was a living symbol whose authority ensured that music education occupied a prominent

---

2   The founder, Gyula Rózsavölgyi (1822–61) was the son of the celebrated violinist and composer of popular dance music (verbunkos and csárdás), Márk Rózsavölgyi (1789–1848). Márk and his orchestra were invited to play at a feast in honor of Franz Liszt in Pest on May 6, 1846. In his Hungarian Rhapsodies nos. 8 and 12, Liszt used two of Rózsavölgyi's tunes. Between 1908 and 1912, Bartók published his works with Gyula Rózsavölgyi and Károly Rozsnyai.

place in the curriculum. He envisioned a singing nation and had an army of ardent supporters—teachers and chorus conductors—to realize his dream. Kodály also insisted that folk music should feature prominently among the subjects taught at the Academy of Music. The Kodály Method (developed with the help of Jenő Ádám) was to prove a successful export item, with teachers of the method swarming out to different parts of the world, carrying the torch.[3]

Kodály, with his friend Béla Bartók, had created Hungarian art music of world standing. His compositions are deeply national but have an international appeal and are popular without making any concession.

His was a hard act to follow. When I appeared on the scene, there were of course composers of the post-Kodály generation (most of them the master's pupils, with one notable exception: Ferenc Farkas had studied with Ottorino Respighi in Rome), who counted as "grand old men." They were influential teachers—Farkas of composition, Pál Kadosa of piano, András Mihály of chamber music—or played a role in public life (lesser talents joined the Party and furthered their careers in this manner).[4] Those born in the 1930s and early 1940s were also present, composing, teaching, wanting to be heard.

In hindsight, the two most outstanding composers, both pupils of Farkas and Kadosa, were György Ligeti and György Kurtág. The former left in 1956 and accomplished something none of his colleagues had managed to do: he represented for the world new Hungarian music as such, which was highly respected and widely played. He became something of a guru for some of his colleagues in Hungary who sent him their scores for his comments. "What did Ligeti say?" was a recurring question. Kurtág's career was much slower to unfold but he, too, has outgrown his colleagues, has left the pond and arrived in the ocean.

Yes, Hungarian musical life was a small pond positively teeming with fish. I do not think they were carnivorous—in other words, composers were not really out to harm one another, jealousies and conflicts notwithstanding—but there was certainly a great deal of jostling for the bait thrown in by the National Philharmonia, the state concert agency—bait standing for performance opportunities.

---

3 A pupil of Zoltán Kodály, Jenő Ádám (1896–1982) was a composer, professor, and chorus conductor.

4 Pál Kadosa (1903–83), composer, pianist, and professor of piano, with György Kurtág, Zoltán Kocsis, András Schiff, and Dezső Ránki among his pupils. András Mihály (1917–93), composer, conductor, professor of chamber music, and director general of the Budapest State Opera House.

Composers in Hungary were not dependent for a living on income deriving from performances. Many of them had jobs (such as teaching at the Music Academy) but the salaries were not particularly generous. Composers lived off scores ("points" we called them) allotted by Artisjus, the Hungarian collecting society. From this point of view, composers in Hungary were better off than creative intellectuals in other walks of life, such as writers. Each year, a committee would convene, made up of composers, and decide on the number of additional scores to be given to their colleagues (and themselves, of course). Over the years, enough scores—each worth so many forints—were amassed to ensure that composers could live free of material care. The system was done away with by Hungary's right-wing government in 2012, depriving composers of their livelihood.

My appearance was supposed to build a canal linking the pond to the ocean—a hazardous undertaking, if anything, from a psychological point of view. Before 1971, all composers were equal, that is, they were unknown beyond the country's borders. Some composers may have been more equal than others: Rudolf Maros (1917–82), for instance, published his works with Peer Musikverlag in West Germany. He was paid $2,000 or so a year to deliver a certain number of compositions. He lived comfortably off that fee and dutifully produced one piece after another—what happened to all that music, whether it was ever played, I do not know. As a result of my promotional activities, however, the lukewarm balance was upset: unavoidably, a process of selection set in, with some composers receiving more performances and commissions than others. No wonder I was to blame, and blamed I was with increasing ferocity.

It is high time I came to the point and got down to discussing the activity to which I devoted nineteen years of my life in Budapest, followed by over fifteen years with Universal Edition in Vienna. Indeed, I might as well give it a chapter within this chapter and call it

Promotion

A music publisher is a financial enterprise like any other: it has to produce an income in excess of its spending. What makes it different from other firms in the business world is that it is built on an extremely fragile phenomenon: taste. Its catalogue *must* include a sufficient number of composers whose music appeals equally to concert organizers and the public at large; it is played in their lifetime and also after their deaths with a regularity that guarantees a financial basis ensuring the firm's survival and allowing it to be adventurous in its artistic policy. In other words, a music publisher must be constantly on the lookout for new talents, invest in them in the hope that one day they, too, will contribute to the firm's profitability, but must accept the very real possibility that it has backed the wrong horse. The composer will probably never make it, the money invested in him has been lost.

The problem with Editio Musica Budapest was that its catalogue did not include a single "hit" of a composer. (Bartók and Kodály published the main body of their work with Universal Edition and subsequently with Boosey and Hawkes.) It earned its money from the sales of its publications of school music, that is, educational items, as well as sales of scholarly editions, such as the *Complete Piano Works of Franz Liszt*.

László Sarlós employed me in an attempt to reverse that situation against rather heavy odds: he expected me to try to make the publishing of contemporary Hungarian music profitable—or, at least, less of a financial loss. Also, of course, Sarlós was aware that promotion was part and parcel of the infrastucture of any self-respecting music publisher. His ambition was to establish EMB's international reputation and once that was achieved, to further it.

I must hasten to add that he never put pressure on me, he supported and appreciated my efforts, was happy with the results and comforted me in my disappointments. In fact, he was an ideal boss. In his own way, he gave me what Charlie had, for both were good psychologists and realized, I think, that what I needed was recognition and encouragement.

o

Promotion managers are the publishers' ambassadors, their faces for the world outside. You must be utterly dependable, inquiries must be answered, scores and recordings posted immediately on receiving requests for them. Also, you must have—as far as possible—a winning personality. Your customers should look forward to your visits, take time for and have faith in you: if you suggest that a composition is worth listening to, they must take you seriously.

Promotion is based on contact. You may meet a young man or woman in a subordinate position with a small orchestra or in a provincial theater, and follow their careers over the years as they rise to ever more responsible jobs. You may meet someone your age, a director of this or that institution, find that you have a great deal in common and become friends. Promotion then becomes less easy, for you do not want to misuse your friendship, but you will have exchanges of ideas that may spontaneously lead to performances.

A promotion manager is the composer's impresario. Rather like that of a performing artist, the reputation—and much more important, the oeuvre—of a composer has to be built up. You have to identify yourself wholeheartedly with your charges, so that their success becomes yours as well. You work for them with the same dedication as if you were working for yourself. The composer and his promoter are one team. This is essential for the composer's psyche, his morale: he must be sure in his mind that he is the most important thing in your life. The promoter is a friend, a confidant, a father-confessor.

Their interests are identical: both want to have as many performances as possible. Obviously, this is not merely a question of economy. A composer writes music to be heard. The more a work is played in different interpretations, by a range of performers, the likelier it is to develop a tradition over the years. The ultimate goal is, of course, for it to become part of the international musical consciousness, the standard repertoire.

Composers usually write for commissions. It is the promotion manager's job to secure them. Commissions provide composers with money they can live on (especially in the West where many of them prefer to freelance), they evoke in them the reassuring sensation that their music is needed, and they keep their names in the news. World premieres are newsworthy events.

As everyone in the music business knows, there is a positively unhealthy demand for first performances and an inordinate number of pieces disappear after their premieres without a trace. Second performances are far more difficult to organize than world premieres. One solution is to secure co-commissions with the result that if you are lucky, you have a series of two, three, or four concerts in as many countries; the composer receives a higher fee but the individual commissioners have less to pay.

The addiction to world premieres also leads to an overproduction of music. Successful composers are inundated with requests for new pieces and very often they do not have the strength of character—or the courage—to say no. It is the promotion manager's job to protect the composer, to warn him of the danger inherent in taking on yet another commission and to ensure that deadlines remain realistic. A young composer is usually overjoyed to receive a commission and the more prestigious it is, the more it serves a publicity purpose as well: a world premiere by the Berlin Philharmonic attracts the attention of festival directors, conductors. and orchestra managers; they will be easier to convince that they should program it or ask the composer for a new work. It cannot be the promotion manager's role to kowtow to the composer after every single premiere and assure him that he has written a masterpiece. I never hesitated to be critical (perhaps not right after the event), always stressing the possibility that I might be wrong.

To jump forward in time: in the course of my book-length interview with Berio I told him that I found *Coro* too long (he said in that case the performance must be to blame);[5] following the first performance of what was supposed to be the final version of *Dérive 2*, I told Boulez that I had some problem with the bassoon solo in a particular section (he agreed and said the player had had little time to practice that bit and he, Boulez, was going to revise it anyway).[6]

Neither can you be expected to love each work in your catalogue. I think my critical observations surprised some of my "customers" but also contributed to developing relationships based on trust.

O

My very first trip as EMB's promotion manager took me to Prague, to visit the Music Information Center (Hudební Informační Středisko). The time was early 1972, that is, just over three years after the combined armed forces of the Warsaw Pact countries had put down the Prague Spring.[7] The atmosphere was sombre, enhanced probably by the gray winter skies and snow covering the streets, and the Information Center was depressing: the director, a sympathetic, cultured lady who did *not* look like a comrade was about to be replaced by someone more reliable: she was married to a government minister who had fallen afoul of the Party. (It is amazing the extent to which devoted party members wore their ideological convictions on their faces in whatever country I may have met them. They seemed mass-produced on purpose-built conveyor belts. Comrade Dunai in the Hungarian Ministry of the Interior was one of them.)

I had arrived in another pond, slightly larger than the one I had come from but just as teeming with fish who had absolutely no chance of release into the ocean. It was claustrophobic. I shall never forget my clandestine meeting with Miloslav Kabeláč (1908–79) in a café: he gave me to understand that he was under a cloud with the authorities and the Information Center was not supposed to know of our conversation. On parting, he gave

---

5 Luciano Berio (1925–2003), *Coro* for forty voices and forty instruments (1975–76).
6 Pierre Boulez (b. 1925): *Dérive 2* for eleven instruments (1988–2006).
7 The Prague Spring (January–August 1968) was an attempt of a group of Czechoslovak communists headed by Alexander Dubček to liberalize the communist system and grant more rights to the citizens.

me some of his scores and suggested I turn the title pages inside: I could have problems if people saw me carrying his music under my arm. Pathetic.

Another composer whom I never saw in the Information Center was Marek Kopelent (born 1932). After 1968, his music was banned by the government for twenty years. I believe he was nevertheless allowed to conduct the ensemble he had cofounded: the Musica Viva Pragensis drew its repertoire from avant-garde music and was thus suspect.

For several years in succession, I visited Prague for a festival of contemporary Czech music held in March. It never failed to be dreary. The music was drab: colorless, predictable, products of another conveyor belt. It was all sham—the applause, the speeches, the smiles. Eventually, I was relieved of the burdensome duty of attending.

I was just as anxious to put an end to my visits to the Soviet Union. It was not only claustrophobic—it was frightening. Not that I had any reason to be afraid. I daresay I was slightly hysterical in fearing that I should not be allowed to return to Budapest. If you remember my worries in the English Section that one day I should be exposed as a bourgeois reactionary, my angst in Moscow and Leningrad was even more acute.

I met with a great deal of genuine kindness and human warmth among Russians, they made me feel welcome. On the other hand, I also experienced their famed misuse of authority, their position of power, however slight it may have been.

Of my very last visit to the Soviet Union I can only remember my departure. Once again it was a bitterly cold winter and I had to get up at the crack of dawn to be driven to the airport. It was dark and sinister outside and I hardly dared to look forward to my flight, which took me to Athens. The sun was shining on my arrival in Greece, the air was balmy and I felt liberated. In the hotel, I peeled off my warm clothes, took a shower in the bathroom, washed my hair, and felt as though I had gotten rid of the last reminders of my time in Moscow. I stepped outside into the sun and was happy.

My first visit to Britain as a representative of Hungarian composers took place in April 1972. I cannot say I was thinking in terms of ponds and fish in those years but it was clear to me that there was simply much more space, figuratively speaking, in the United Kingdom—there was plenty of fresh air to breathe.[8] I also sensed that I was in a different culture.

---

8   In later years I gained the impression that perhaps there very well were several smaller ponds in Britain—in Cardiff, in Edinburgh, at universities—and perhaps a larger one, a lake even, in London. In some cases communication between London and those in the country appears to be blocked, and some composers would found an ensemble (such as Gordon Downie in Cardiff) so that they could at least hear their own music played live.

People communicated with each other more formally than in Hungary or Czechoslovakia (I had not yet been to the Soviet Union); they were polite but also noncommittal. It took me some time to adapt.

My base was 295 Regent Street, the Boosey and Hawkes (B&H) head-quarters. As I mentioned earlier, that prestigious firm was EMB's representative in the United Kingdom, the British Commonwealth, Germany, and also in the United States. The terms of their contract provided for the promotion of EMB's catalogue in B&H's territories. I was too green in those years to realize that publishers rarely observed those terms literally. I was naive enough to expect them to actively work for our composers year in and year out as well as to carefully prepare my visits. My missionary zeal must have been an embarrassment for them.

John Andrewes, a gray-haired, kindhearted gentleman of boyish charm, did introduce me to some of his contacts who in the long run proved to be of little if any help. However, I was allowed to use an office and a telephone, indispensable tools during my stays.

Gradually I made the acquaintance of some important people in British musical life whose interest in Hungarian music was genuine. The first event of some significance I was able to organize was an all-Hungarian concert under the auspices of the Park Lane Group. My regular visits to John Woolf had paved the way for that event, which was eventually made possible thanks to a financial contribution provided by EMB. The jubilation in Budapest was tremendous and we turned up in large numbers, including the composers, of course, as well as a music critic.

Next, Sir Charles Groves took pity on me.[9] If I remember correctly, it was his wife who suggested that he ought at last to give in to my stubborn request over the years. Sir Charles programmed Zsolt Durkó's (1934–97) violin concerto *Organismi* (1964) with his orchestra in Liverpool. Saschko Gawriloff was the soloist. Once again, an event of national importance (I am exaggerating a bit . . .), for it belied the prophecy of pessimists in Hungary that no orchestra in the West would ever be willing to invest money in a work by one of our composers.

And so it went on. Boosey and Hawkes complimented me for putting Hungarian music on the map. It was certainly true that having started with a blank, I had succeeded in attracting some attention to our composers. I was—and am—particularly grateful to Robert Ponsonby (born 1926) who in his capacity as "Controller, Music," decided to put on a Hungarian

---

9 Sir Charles Groves (1915–92), music director of the Royal Liverpool Philharmonic Orchestra from 1963. He was highly regarded for his support of both contemporary composers and young conductors.

concert with the BBC Symphony Orchestra under Pierre Boulez. The date has stuck in my mind: February 6, 1976. He asked me to submit some scores and Boulez chose *Iris* (1971) by Sándor Balassa (born 1935). The rest of the program consisted of Bartók and Ligeti.

In the same year, Raymond Leppard (born 1927) performed with the English Chamber Orchestra *III. Concerto* by András Szőllősy, and a few years later the composer's *Trasfigurazioni* in Manchester, where he was principal conductor of the BBC Philharmonic Orchestra.

Rather than continue with my list of "triumphs," I would like to take a step back and draw two conclusions.

Prestigious performances of unknown composers can turn the spotlight on their music overnight. Edward Greenfield suggested in his review of Boulez's concert that Balassa was the strongest talent to emerge from Hungary since Bartók. Later, after Durkó's oratorio *Burial Prayer* (1967–72), once again with BBC forces under Lionel Friend, Durkó took over, temporarily, the position of what we call in Hungarian "the genius on duty," only to relinquish it eventually to György Kurtág. Balassa, Durkó and Szőllősy were to receive commissions in Britain and elsewhere. One key figure in arranging those commissions and programming a range of compositions was the radio producer Stephen Plaistow (born 1937). He was also credited with inviting to the studio Hungarian musicians living in Britain and recording with them chamber pieces, such as works for violin and piano by Pál Kadosa (1903–83).

On a memorable day, I had a call from the Boston Symphony Orchestra asking whether Balassa would be willing to take on a commission for a work to be premiered by Seiji Ozawa. Needless to say, the answer was yes. However, Balassa canceled his trip to attend the world premiere at the last minute. A fatal mistake: his absence deprived the event of a basic ingredient and it failed to make a mark, even though the piece was not bad. That call from Boston was memorable nevertheless because it had been inspired by news of the composer's successes in Britain and elsewhere—it only had indirectly to do with my promotional efforts. Artistic administrators and their ilk do read concert reviews.

The other conclusion is rather negative, I am afraid. No composer and no publisher should let themselves be misled by success, however resounding it may seem in the short term. Balassa, Durkó, Szőllősy, and the rest of them have since disappeared from the international scene almost without a trace. Indeed, all my efforts over nineteen years in Budapest have evaporated—with one exception: György Kurtág appears to have made it into the canon.

Actually, the only performances that count in the long run are those that come about *without* a promoter. It is imperative for a piece of music to create a void that no other work can fill. It cannot be substituted by another one because it has a quality, a message all its own, and precisely *that* quality and *that* message are wanted.

Music history can be seen as a giant sieve. It lets most compositions drop through its holes and only an infinitesimal number survive. Some may keep a tenuous hold on the edge, their future uncertain, often depending on the whim of a conductor.[10] I shall have more to say on this subject in a later chapter about my time with Universal Edition in Vienna.

I really did devote myself to promoting Hungarian music with a missionary fervor. I inundated the world with my letters and recordings, and turned up with stubborn regularity in the offices of potential allies. One, the German choral conductor and radio producer Dr. Clytus Gottwald, also took pity on me eventually—I had visited him in his office year after year, and eventually he put on an all-Hungarian concert in Stuttgart, on October 1, 1977.

On a visit to Nuremberg, I walked in the streets and studied concert posters. I noticed one that looked promising: it advertised an organ recital with several contemporary works on the program, performed by one Werner Jacob. I found his name in the telephone directory in the next booth, rang him and soon enough found myself in his home.

Werner Jacob (1938–2006) was a powerful advocate of new music and received my offers with open arms. In the ensuing years he introduced quite a number of Hungarian organ works in Germany, commissioned and premiered some, and even arranged for the Generalmusikdirektor in Nuremberg, Hans Gierster, to conduct the first German performance of Balassa's *Requiem for Lajos Kassák* (1969). In return, I was able to have him invited to Budapest where he would appear a number of times at the Academy of Music.

I forget how I got wind of the new music concerts organized by the Dutch pianist Ton Hartsuiker (born 1933). I turned up one day in the corridor of the conservatory where he was teaching, waited outside until his class was over, and introduced myself. Ton became a friend. Not only did he play numerous Hungarian piano pieces in Holland, he also commissioned

10 The German conductor Michael Gielen (b. 1927) took a fancy to Josef Suk's (1874–1935) fifty-minute symphonic poem *Sommermärchen*, op. 29 (1907–9), and programmed it over a period of several years. He also recorded it on CD, as did the Russian conductor Kirill Petrenko (b. 1972), as part of his integral recording of Suk's oeuvre. It was a wholly unforeseeable piece of luck for Suk.

a work from András Szőllősy for piano and ensemble, which he premiered himself, with Otto Ketting (born 1935) conducting the Ensemble M of The Hague. The ensemble eventually also appeared at the Budapest Academy of Music. The commission afforded Szőllősy the possibility of expressing his admiration for Igor Stravinsky. He named the composition *Pro somno Igoris Stravinsky quieto* (1978) and had the musicians quietly recite the Requiem text in Latin while playing. I attended a rehearsal and saw tears flowing from Szőllősy's eyes.

I discovered early on how important it was for Editio Musica to reciprocate. Very often the artists who agreed to play music by Hungarian composers would expect to appear in Budapest in recognition of their services. The National Philharmonia was reluctant to invite them: their names were unknown. Eventually, László Sarlós agreed to subsidize a concert series and secured the cooperation of Artisjus, the Hungarian collecting society.

I was now a concert organizer. One event I remember with particular fondness was a recital by the English soprano Jane Manning with Richard Rodney Bennett at the piano.[11] Their program included Luigi Dallapiccola's (1904–75) *Quattro Liriche di Antonio Machado* (1948)—wonderful music by that remarkable Italian composer who unaccountably enough is being unfairly treated by the "sieve" of music history.

I also convinced my boss that we should invite music critics from abroad so that in reviewing a composition in their papers, they could place it in its context within the work of the composer as well as within Hungarian music in general. Paul Griffiths, Dominic Gill, Stephen Walsh, and David Murray all came from London and became regular visitors. It makes all the difference if you can put a face to a name and a title, and some lasting relationships sprang up between critics and composers. I remember Paul Griffiths even presented Kurtág with a haiku he had written. Kurtág proceeded to set it; he might return to it one day. Stephen Walsh became friendly with Attila Bozay and Zsolt Durkó and has written extensively on Kurtág.

A selection of my radio interviews came out in 1972 in cooperation with a small publishing house; all future books appeared with Editio Musica Budapest. In the same year, I was asked by EMB to translate Aaron Copland's (1900–1990) *The New Music* into Hungarian. I complied only to realize soon enough that translation requires an above-average command of your mother tongue. My sentences limped, they would not get off the ground. The text simply would not read as if it had been written in

---

11 Jane Manning (b. 1938), English soprano. A critic has aptly described her as "the irrepressible, incomparable, unstoppable Ms. Manning—life and soul of British contemporary music." Sir Richard Rodney Bennett (1936–2012), English composer and pianist.

Hungarian originally—which is a sine qua non of translation. Eventually I had to ask a friend to help me.

The Hungarian edition of Copland's book, however, became a memorable event through Aaron's appearance in Budapest in 1973. László Sarlós arranged with the National Philharmonia for him to conduct a concert of American music, including his own clarinet concerto. I attended some of the rehearsals and witnessed the orchestra's difficulties with the jazzy rhythms of Aaron's music. He had to positively dance on the podium to convey to the musicians brought up on the Austro-German (and Hungarian) repertoire what they were supposed to be playing. I realized that music was not necessarily an international language.

Aaron Copland and I became friendly. I do not think I knew at the time that he was a national figure in the United States, perhaps somewhat akin to Kodály in Hungary, thanks to orchestral works such as *El Salón Mexico* (1936) or *Appalachian Spring* (1944). He did not put on airs, so he was easy to talk to. I took him out to some restaurants in Budapest. The first such occasion was not much of a success: a gypsy band was playing and Aaron said he could not help concentrating on the music. It was not a question of liking or disliking it: he had no other choice but to listen. He did his best, of course, to carry on a lively enough conversation, but next time I made sure we went to a place without a band.

There was no such problem in New York where we met in the same year. Aaron invited me to the Russian Tearoom near Carnegie Hall and treated me to my first borscht.[12] It was delicious. Our meeting, however, was not devoid of an embarrassing episode. Aaron had handed me his fee in Budapest: it was in the Hungarian currency and he did not know what to do with it. He asked me to buy an antique for him in Budapest and bring it to him in New York. My father was at home in antique silver and I asked him to purchase something suitable. He found an early nineteenth-century ashtray, small but beautiful. Aaron looked at it and was obviously disappointed. "Is that it?" he asked, before putting it in his pocket. I did my best to explain that it was well worth the money it had cost, but I turned rather hot as I was doing so. It did not sound convincing.

Aaron and I exchanged many letters in the years to come (my last one was answered by an assistant). He also helped with a commission for Sándor Balassa from the Koussevitzky Foundation. As I pointed out earlier, promotion is based on contact.

---

12 A soup of Ukrainian origin, the main ingredient of borscht is beetroot, which lends it its deep purple color.

CHAPTER 10

INTERVIEWING

An Obsession

I wonder if parents realize that a remark they happen to drop at one point makes a mark on their children's minds for life. My mother suggested that I should not talk too much about myself. Nobody will be really interested—people prefer to do the talking and want listeners. She was right. On the few occasions I have for some obscure reason misinterpreted signals coming from other people and launched into a subject that was occupying my mind, I soon noticed their eyes wandering as though looking for help. Their nods were automatic, though meant to signify agreement or the fact that they were following what I was trying to say.

Over the years and decades, I have become a good listener. Asking questions is my way of conducting a conversation. In a way, I do interviews all the time. Otherwise I am quiet; I sit in silence and feel comfortable. Knowing what questions to ask and timing them well have proved helpful as a means of avoiding awkward silences. Far more important is the attitude behind it: the curiosity to find out about lives, to learn what makes people tick.

Hitchhiking appears to be more or less obsolete now but I used to enjoy taking a young person with me on a longer ride and asking them about their lives. I had never seen them before and was unlikely to meet them again—perhaps that is why many of them opened up and told me things they probably would not have had we met socially. I was particularly fascinated by a young man who worked in a slaughterhouse. He was quiet and looked as if he could not harm a fly—and yet he spent his time, every working hour of the day, killing animals.

Once I was joined by a microphone and a tape recorder as my permanent companions, interviewing became something of an obsession. Asking questions was no longer a private pastime; I imagined I represented radio listeners on whose behalf I was trying to draw out potential interviewees.

I recorded my first interview of any length with the American violinist Ruggiero Ricci (1918–2012). I had expected him to be Italian and was stunned by his thick American accent. He was small, had unattractive features with a boxer's nose, walked if not exactly with a limp but in a curiously clumsy manner—and was a delight to talk to. He really seemed anxious to tell me in great detail about his childhood. It had obviously been one of drudgery: his father had taken it into his head to turn his son into a child prodigy and positively forced him to practice. Ricci saw himself, even in middle age and with a glowing international career behind him, as his father's victim. Unforgivably enough, I did not keep the tape but Ricci's story influenced the way I listened to his concert—he was, of course, playing a Paganini violin concerto—having watched him enter onstage and walk with his odd gait to the middle. His breathtaking virtuosity impressed me, but I could not forget all the suffering that had gone into his masterly technique.

The other reason for my obsession with interviewing is my conviction that everything an important personality says about his work or even minor details about his life is an irreplaceable document. Starting a recording is reaching out to posterity. It is like writing a colon—you place it after a word and open a gate to whatever comes after.

Before embarking on my book-length interview with György Kurtág, in November 2007, I happened to read a study on the composer by a Hungarian musicologist. He raised the question of whether Kurtág had ever come into touch with folk music and considered the pros and cons of replying in the affirmative. I was stupefied: why did he not simply lift the receiver and ask Kurtág directly? I did so in his stead and the reply was fascinating.

Of course, you cannot do interviews incessantly. My alternative solution has been a diary where I have entered whatever Kurtág, and some others, said during our conversations over nearly three decades now (I am writing in 2011). The diary is like an interview without the questions. Perhaps I am some kind of a James Boswell or Johann Peter Eckermann, except that the frequency, length, and depth of our conversations cannot be compared to those conducted with Dr. Johnson or Goethe.

My interviews, especially those that centered on identical questions I put to composers (published in English by the University of Rochester Press in 2011 under the title *Three Questions for Sixty-Five Composers*), were guided in part by the principle of *audiatur et altera pars*.[1] I was particularly thrilled by being able to confront Witold Lutosławski with Earle Brown's claim that the former had learned his notation from him, or by asking Morton Feldman and John Cage to comment on statements they had made regarding each other.

It is imperative, of course, to thoroughly prepare for an interview (always allowing for the spontaneous give and take of the actual conversation, which may throw up questions one did not consider before), but I have also found that improvisation can produce remarkable results. As I described in the *Three Questions* book, I arrived in Vienna to meet Feldman with very little background information, but his unique personality evoked a reaction in me, incredulous and intrigued as I was, that no amount of preparation would have influenced.

If I were younger, I would approach artists and writers with the three questions, suitably adapted. Having finished the set of interviews with composers back in 1985, I found I could not call a halt to the momentum that had kept me going for eight years. I had to carry on.

I approached three of Hungary's major artists and the interviews convinced me of the validity of my questions for any creative activity. That recognition satisfied me, I forgot about the artists and I got down to turning the sizable material of what were originally eighty-two interviews with composers into a book.

There was one missed opportunity which I regret to this day. My head was positively teeming with questions I wanted to put to Ella Fitzgerald. It was sometime during the 1960s and I made an appointment to see her in Budapest's Hotel Royal. I rang her room from the lobby and was put off by her curt reply. Eventually she materialized in the lift door and I was all raring to begin, microphone in hand. Miss Fitzgerald, however, preferred to talk to somebody else and carried on so long that I was ready to explode. I circled around them like a bird

---

1   Let the other side also be heard.

of prey about to pounce, until I could bear it no longer. I went up to her again and was on the point of addressing her when she suddenly snapped: "Can't you see I am busy?"

I gave up, hurt and bitterly disappointed. I had such wonderful questions . . . But if you consider that in so many years of interviewing that was my only defeat, I have not been doing too badly.

CHAPTER 11

I C H   W A R   E I N
B E R L I N E R

J ohn F. Kennedy declared himself to be a Berliner two years after the construction of the wall that had sealed off the only remaining open space between East and West Germany.[1] The Berlin Wall saved the German Democratic Republic from gradually losing its population and thus its very existence; it also turned West Berlin into an island within a Soviet-controlled communist German ocean. President Kennedy's declaration of solidarity with the plight of West and East Berliners alike (on his own behalf as well as on behalf of the free world) met with tremendous enthusiasm by those attending the rally on June 26, 1963, and I think it was a high point in his presidency. Within less than half a year, Kennedy was assassinated in Dallas.

I moved to Berlin in January 1991, just over a year after the wall's demolition, to take up my position as deputy director of the Hungarian Cultural Institute. I stayed until May 1992, so I have some justification to call myself a onetime Berliner.

After nineteen years with Editio Musica Budapest, I had realized that unless I cut the umbilical cord that tied me to the publisher and to Hungarian musical life—one that I had felt for sometime to be slowly

---

1 President Kennedy was addressing a mass meeting of West Berliners in front of the Schöneberg City Hall, to mark the fifteenth anniversary of the "Luftbrücke": the Soviet occupying forces of East Germany had barred all roads leading to West Berlin in June 1948, whereupon an "air bridge" was initiated by US Military Governor Lucius D. Clay. Until the lifting of the blockade in May 1949, 200,000 flights transported 1.5 million tons of goods for the West Berliners, with planes landing every two or three minutes.

coiling round my neck—I would have to stay until retirement. I found the world I was moving in (even though I continued to travel regularly all over Europe and sometimes also overseas) increasingly claustrophobic, while the enthusiasm that had kept me going was flagging. I needed a change of job and a change of country.

Leaving Hungary had been on my mind since my first visit to Britain in 1964. The contrast with the West was too obvious, too painful to ignore. However, my parents were alive and, with my brother in Australia, I felt I could not turn my back on them. Defecting, then, was out of the question. The dilemma remained a nagging one for several decades and I could never make up my mind for one reason or another until the autumn of 1990 when emigrating no longer represented a crime with far-reaching consequences. I told my wife I was not young enough anymore to wait for Hungary to become a livable country. More than twenty years on I believe I was right.

o

Starting a new life outside Hungary has been an alternative for its population from time immemorial, up to the present, when university graduates, especially young doctors, are seeking jobs abroad and many people in Western Hungary commute daily to neighboring Austria to work as waiters, cooks, and agricultural laborers.

Millions, mainly peasants, left between the two world wars to find a better life in the United States. New York Governor George Pataki's parents may have been among them: he was born on their farm in America in 1945.

Many Jews left for political and racial reasons (you cannot of course separate the two), making a name for themselves in the United States and Britain as well as in other countries. They gained a foothold in Hollywood where Adolph Zukor (who had left Hungary as an adolescent in 1889) founded Paramount Pictures. Michael Curtiz (director of *Casablanca*) was born as Manó Kertész, Peter Lorre as László Loewenstein, Bela Lugosi as Béla Blaskó, and Zsa Zsa Gabor as Zsuzsanna Gábor. Tony Curtis (Bernard Schwartz) was born to Hungarian parents in New York.

Sándor Kellner acquired world fame as a film director, and producer Sir Alexander Korda was a political émigré in 1919, having taken an active part in Béla Kun's Republic of Councils. That most British of British actors, Leslie Howard, was born László Steiner in London.

The playwright Ferenc Molnár left in 1937 and eventually arrived in New York in 1940; Melchior Lengyel (Menyhért Lebovics) left his native country in the same year. He was the author of the pantomime *The Miraculous Mandarin*, which has kept his name alive thanks to Bartók's score; his successful film scripts such as *Ninotchka* have also endeared him to his fans.

Then there were all the Hungarian musicians, with Béla Bartók, Sándor Veress, Mátyás Seiber, and Géza Frid among the composers. The conductors Ferenc Fricsay, Eugene Ormandy (Jenő Blau), Antal Doráti, George Szell, Fritz Reiner, Georg Solti (György Stern) emigrated at different times before or immediately after World War II, and so did scientists such as Edward (Ede) Teller, Eugene (Jenő) Wigner, and John (János) von Neumann.

There was another wave in the 1940s. George Soros, the American billionaire made it over the frontier at the age of sixteen, in 1946. Congressman Tom Lantos left in 1947. Some 200,000 fled in the wake of the Hungarian Revolution in 1956, and so it has been going on ever since.

o

When I arrived in Berlin in January 1991, both the city and the Hungarian Cultural Institute were in a state of transition.

Berlin had been united on paper but you could not yet telephone from East to West: there were perhaps two or three cables in operation. You either dialed West Berlin as if it were in a foreign country, starting with 0049 30 and then the number you wanted to reach, but even that solution proved mostly unworkable in practice. If I had an urgent call to make, I took Bus 100, which linked the two halves of the city, and got off at the Brandenburg Gate. On the far side, there was a telephone booth from which I could make my call. If I remember correctly, the underground lines still stopped at the former frontier and you had to change to travel to the West.

The contrast between the two halves was still stark: you cannot change the character of a city overnight—even over years. With one exception, perhaps: the Trabants and Wartburgs had more or less disappeared and were replaced by Western cars. Their presence not only reduced the air pollution considerably but also improved the atmosphere of the streets. Of course, houses were still depressingly drab, with Western-style neon signs gradually lending them some color. More immediately affecting the everyday lives of East Berliners was the mushrooming of Western food stores and other chains with the corresponding replacement of GDR goods by their West German counterparts.

It was tremendously thrilling to take a bus and watch from the window as the cityscape changed abruptly beyond where the wall used to stand. It was particularly so for me. After all, I used to fly from Budapest to East Berlin's Schönefeld Airport and board a coach right there that took me to the West. It was but a short ride; soon enough it reached the frontier marked by cement blocks, which forced the bus to zigzag before reaching the guards. East German uniforms struck me as disconcertingly similar to Nazi ones—but perhaps I was being overly sensitive.

Hungarian Cultural Institutes had been established in major European countries along the lines of the British Council, the Goethe Institut, the Institut Français, and the Istituto Italiano as prolonged arms of the embassies, which are, by their very nature, not suited to reaching out to the public at large. Cultural institutes obviously serve a publicity purpose: they offer language courses and books from their more or less well-stocked libraries and do their best to attract audiences to their programs, such as film presentations, concerts, exhibitions, and discussions with major politicians or scientists from their countries.

Jobs in Hungarian Cultural Institutes were highly coveted. They meant that you could spend four or five years abroad with decent pay in the Hungarian currency at home, most of which you could save. You also drew a salary in the currency of the country you were working in. It may not have been generous but if you were willing to live frugally, you could save enough to buy an Opel Vectra on your return, which counted as a status symbol back home.

No wonder I detected intense dislike tinged with envy in the eyes of my predecessor who was about to depart when I was moving in.

The director, Comrade Hegedűs, was roughly ten years my senior. He had the looks and accent of a peasant, with an agile mind and a respectable record to look back on. Also, he was reserved and did not interfere with what I was trying to do. He spent his time in his office reading newspapers. When I knocked at his door, I would find him ready to listen but without any particular interest in what I had to say. Eventually, I realized that Comrade Hegedűs knew perfectly well that his time in Berlin was soon to end. A sword of Damocles was suspended above his head and the gray-haired director, who kept his thin lips firmly closed so that they became almost invisible, was also aware who was maneuvering to cut the thread: the Cultural Attaché, Gyula Kurucz.

Kurucz would turn up now and again and visit me in my office. He never hinted at what he was after; I suppose he wished to gain a feel of the place and get to know his future deputy. He was jovial, arrived and left with a smile, and never asked if I had read any of his novels.

Mr. Kurucz (no longer a Comrade!) was a man of postsocialist Hungary, determined to make a career under the new regime. He was or pretended to be an ardent nationalist who in his public statements never failed to emphasize his love for and devotion to his native country. His was a language I was not used to and I did not feel at ease with the ideology it reflected.

Soon after Gyula Kurucz took over—Comrade Hegedűs had been right—the atmosphere of the institute underwent a gradual change. I had gotten on well enough with my colleagues without becoming intimate with them by any means, but I sensed that something was going wrong. I had left my job in Budapest because I had felt increasingly claustrophobic, and had now landed in a Hungarian colony in Berlin where the air was being siphoned off until I felt I was choking.

I became isolated, for my colleagues were, understandably enough, keen to get in Kurucz's good graces; their smiles were no longer genuine. All of them were heavy smokers, incidentally, and they would get together with the new director in a small room, chatting and gossiping, filling the air with smoke, so that I had no other choice but to take refuge in my office. Closing the door behind me was more than a physical gesture.

By the end of the year, I was on the verge of a nervous breakdown. I could only carry on thanks to an incredible stroke of luck, which took the form of a telephone call from Vienna. It must have been sometime in September or October 1991 that the phone rang: the music publisher Universal Edition was on the line. They had heard that I had left Editio Musica Budapest and were wondering if I felt like returning to the world of publishing. My yes burst from me like a cry for help. I had been saved.

O

The biggest single challenge facing cultural institutes is to find a means of breaking out of their isolation. Who would want to spend an evening listening to the recital of a nondescript musician from Hungary if it was possible to go to an established venue to hear an international star from the same country? I mean, a pianist with the reputation of Zoltán Kocsis did not need the meager publicity offered by a concert at the institute; he had the Philharmonie or the Konzerthaus at his disposal.

As long as the German Democratic Republic was enforcing its iron discipline over every aspect of life, the Hungarian Cultural Institute was thriving. Its programs were well attended because to attend was regarded as a sign of opposition to GDR cultural policies. Films banned in East Germany were projected; writers frowned upon by officialdom were provided a forum under the pretext that they had translated Hungarian literature into German. People flocked to their readings. You could breathe some fresh air in the sultry rooms of the Hungarian Cultural Institute.

When I arrived, the institute's onetime public were driving to West Berlin to quench their thirst for the stupendously rich cultural offering they had until recently been deprived of. (In fact, I think the word *drüben* [over there], which had been synonymous with "in West Germany," was disappearing from daily use, to be replaced by *Ossis* and *Wessis*—short for East and West Germans—each with its negative connotations. With the passage of time, they, too, have gone out of use and been replaced by the factual *Ostler* and *Westler*.) Gone were the days when the institute was a refuge for the opposition. Try as I might—and I really did my very best, carrying packets of monthly programs and placing them wherever I thought potential visitors would pick them up—I suffered defeat night after night. Three, four, or five people would turn up for my film presentations, perhaps out of nostalgia or loyalty, and a few more for the concerts.

Once in a while I succeeded in attracting a crowd. The American pianist Alan Marks, for instance, gave a recital at the institute with a program made up exclusively of a selection of Bartók's *Mikrokosmos* juxtaposed with Kurtág's *Játékok*.[2] If you did not follow the printed program, you soon lost your bearings and were hard put it to identify which piece was composed by whom. Kurtág has never denied—indeed, has always gone out of his way to emphasize—the influence Bartók's oeuvre has exercised on him. Alan Marks's fascinating compilation was an audible proof.

Alan was a highly intelligent pianist. Born in 1949, he moved to Germany in 1989 and by the time I met him, he was a Berlin resident. He was really interested in music more than in money and only demanded a symbolic fee of 2,000 marks. I forget whether he or I had wheedled it out of the Berlin Senate—in any case, his recital was one of the few high points

2 *Játékok* (1974–) is a work in progress for piano, eight volumes of which have so far been published by Editio Musica Budapest. It consists of mostly short pieces for two hands, piano duet, and two pianos, many of them homages to living or dead composers. They may have acquired their title because Kurtág found after finishing a piece that it bore some kinship to the spirit or a particular work of a composer or that it was a conscious, sometimes humorous, tribute. *Játékok* has also served for Kurtág as a quarry of material to be built into larger-scale compositions.

of my time with the institute. Sadly, Alan was diagnosed with cancer and died far too young, in 1995.

Leslie Howard (born 1948), the British pianist—no relation to the actor of the same name—best known for his recordings of Liszt, actually appeared for free. I think he was anxious to attract some attention in Berlin and had hoped that critics would turn up for his concert. In the event none did—but I met a genuinely friendly and modest man with whom it was a joy to talk. His recital was fine, despite the less than ideal quality of the institute's piano. The hall was full and I was happy.

The Canadian composer and flautist Robert Aitken (born 1939) drew an audience of a different kind: he played contemporary music including a work of his own. Another worthwhile event.

I also invited the Budapest New Music Studio, which comprised the composer-performers László Sáry, Zoltán Jeney, László Vidovszky, and their musicologist-propagandist, András Wilheim. Their concert also lives on in my memory as a success.

The major event during my stint was the festival Grenzenlos (Without Frontiers), which the Hungarian government organized in cooperation with the Berlin Senate. It was on an altogether different scale from the institute's own efforts, with well-designed posters appearing all over Berlin to advertise it. I believe it was on the occasion of the opening festivity that the then president of Hungary, Árpád Göncz (born 1922), visited the institute. I was waiting for him outside the building and as he got out of his car and walked toward me with quick steps, he reached out his hand and said "Szervusz." It is the way friends greet each other in Hungary, presupposing the familiar "te" (Du, toi). I was instantly won over and was filled with warmth for this wonderful man, Hungary's first and to this day most popular president (1990–2000) since the collapse of socialism.

O

If I was desperately unhappy in the Karl-Liebknecht-Strasse where the Hungarian Cultural Institute had its headquarters opposite the Rotes Rathaus (Red City Hall) next to Alexanderplatz (it is now in a more elegant part of former East Berlin, in an attractively designed new building, and bears the name Collegium Hungaricum), living in Berlin was a real treat.

With my family, we went on tours of discovery every weekend, eagerly absorbing whatever Berlin had to offer. We were aware of being eyewitnesses of the early stages of a historical process: the welding together of two separate worlds that decades before had been one. It was brought home to us how the city had drifted apart under two different political systems, and we were amazed by the extent to which two ideologies had put their distinct stamp on every aspect of life.

We were experiencing the way the consequences of that artificial separation were being slowly reversed, the West adapting the East to its own image. Doing it in the opposite direction would have been unthinkable. I alluded to changes in East Berlin in the wake of reunification earlier in this chapter. Apart from the appearance of Western shops and the vanishing of GDR cars with their foul-smelling two-stroke engines, scaffoldings went up all over the place, temporarily obliterating from sight some of the major historic buildings that the Marxist regime had sinfully allowed to fall into disrepair. West Berlin was like a different country. Since the districts that make it up used at one time to be self-standing villages or towns, passing from one to another gave one an added sense of crossing frontiers. (East Berlin was no different, of course, but the postwar decades had cast a veil of uniformity on its districts, which, likewise, originally had characteristics of their own.) Visiting the city's museums, attending concerts and opera performances, driving to towns in the vicinity—it all helped me to survive those months in the Karl-Liebknecht-Strasse.

Since leaving Berlin in April 1992, I have visited it innumerable times and have been able to follow up on the astounding growth of the capital, with the Potsdamer Platz having been the single biggest construction project not only in Germany but also in Europe as a whole. I feel at home there, as much as I do in Vienna. I was and to a certain extent still am a Berliner.

CHAPTER 12

MOVING TO VIENNA

he invitation from Vienna and my eager acceptance of it set a process in motion that was to introduce a new chapter in our lives: leaving Hungary behind, in other words emigrating, and settling permanently in Austria.

Austria, like Hungary, had been an ally of Nazi Germany, with a large section of the population enthusiastically welcoming the *Anschluss*, the country's takeover by Hitler in 1938. Like Hungary, it had lost World War II, but the State Treaty of 1955 ensured its independence, ending the occupation by Allied forces. *Österreich ist frei!* "Austria is free!" Foreign Minister Leopold Figl announced on May 15, 1955, from the balcony of Belvedere Palace. The Soviet foreign minister, Viacheslav Molotov, who was standing right next to him, did not so much as bat an eyelid.[1] The Soviet troops left Austria but they stayed on in Hungary for more than three decades; there was no knowing how much longer we would be playing host to what was officially described as the "Soviet army temporarily stationed in Hungary."

Ever since 1955, Austria has been a neighbor much envied and admired from the Hungarian side of the border. Austria's development into a prosperous neutral country in the middle of Europe demonstrated the alternative that remained out of reach for Hungary, separated as it was from the free world by a barbed wire fence and landmines. Austria was and is a country Hungary might have become but has not.

I first arrived in Vienna in 1964 on my way to London. It was at the Westbahnhof (Western Railway Station), where I changed trains, that I

---

1   The United States was represented by John Foster Dulles, Great Britain by Harold Macmillan, and France by Antoine Pinay.

caught my first glimpse of the world beyond the barbed wire fence. I was absolutely bowled over and sent an enthusiastic postcard home. Today, it makes rather pathetic reading.

On my way back from Britain, I spent a few days in the city and instantly felt at home. All Hungarians do: Vienna and Budapest have a great deal in common as far as their architecture is concerned. In fact, architecture is one aspect of our shared past that lends cities and towns familiarity for citizens of the former Dual Monarchy, whether they are visiting Ljubljana in Slovenia, Zagreb in Croatia, or, say, Lemberg, the capital of the former Austrian province of Galicia (Lviv in today's Ukraine). Much of the cityscape in the former multiethnic Monarchy is marked to this day by the eclectic style of the 1860s and later, an expression of the newly rich bourgeoisie's desire to demonstrate its wealth. Around the turn of the twentieth century it was supplanted by *Jugendstil* (art nouveau), in Lemberg as much as in Vienna or Budapest.

Vienna and Budapest have particularly close ties in this respect, since many architects were active in both cities in the late nineteenth and early twentieth centuries. Coming from Budapest, you are bound to come across buildings or certain features of buildings that look familiar. There is, for instance, a church near the Westbahnhof that sports the dome of the Houses of Parliament in Budapest—both were designed by the architect Imre Steindl (1839–1902).

Universal Edition's invitation meant that the gates of Vienna were opened for the Varga family to come—and to stay. For us to step over the threshold, however, a number of hurdles were to be cleared first. For one thing, a labor permit had to be obtained, with the publisher explaining to the Austrian authorities that my work was indispensable and that in employing me they were not putting native Austrians at a disadvantage.

Meanwhile, in Berlin, I paid a visit to the Austrian consulate and applied for a visa valid initially for three months. The office was walking distance from the Hungarian Cultural Institute. In opening the door and entering (a moment to which I attached something of a symbolic significance), I found myself in an altogether different world. I was made to feel welcome and was much relieved by the matter-of-fact way in which my document was granted within a short period of time.

I was acting in secrecy, of course; my colleagues had no idea that I was busy preparing my departure. On two weekends, I flew to Vienna from Berlin's Tempelhof Airport. Opened in 1924 and closed down in 2008, it was practically in the middle of the city, within easy reach by public transport. Its Bauhaus-style buildings exuded a rather special historical aura: it was at Tempelhof that airplanes transporting food and other goods landed in short intervals to help West Berliners ride out the Soviet blockade in 1948 and 1949.

In Vienna, the airport bus took me to the Hilton Hotel. I walked past the Museum of Applied Arts and found myself in the Ringstrasse, one of the city's main thoroughfares built after the demolition of the medieval city walls under Emperor Franz Joseph in 1857. Beyond palaces in eclectic styles, there rose, in the 1860s, in place of the ramparts, elegant mansions built in neoclassical, neogothic, and neo-Renaissance styles. This harking back to the art of the past is usually referred to as *Historismus*. The Ring, together with the capital's inner city, is now part of UNESCO's world heritage.

I took a quaint red streetcar and alighted near the State Opera House, a stone's throw from the Musikverein, home of Universal Edition (UE).

O

The people seated around a table in the Café Imperial were to play an important role in my life over the next fifteen years and beyond. Dr. Johann Juranek, a leading expert in copyright law, has been Universal Edition's chief executive for the past several decades and is still active in 2012, the year in which I am writing, at the age of eighty-two. Dr. Otto Tomek (1928–2013), a key figure in European music history over the past sixty years, had only worked for UE for a short time around 1953, but was closely associated with the firm, in various functions, until the end of his life. Marion von Hartlieb, born in Wiesbaden, Germany, had joined the publisher at twenty-four in 1971, and steadily worked her way up in the hierarchy, eventually being elected to the board. As such, she oversaw promotion and I reported to her.

Over lunch, Dr. Juranek offered me the artistic directorship. I declined without a moment's hesitation: not being a musicologist and lacking any experience whatsoever in running a company, there was no question in my mind that I was wholly unsuited for the job. "That's all right," Dr. Juranek said, "then let's try a rung lower. How about the promotion department?"

O

Back in Berlin, I sent a fax to the Hungarian Ministry of Culture, announcing my resignation. I knew my decision to leave would come as no surprise. Officials in the lower echelons were well aware of my plight and took my side; they viewed Kurucz with suspicion, even disgust.

With the fax in hand, I knocked on Gyula Kurucz's door. Our brief exchange was surely frustrating and infuriating for the director: there was nothing he could do but to take note of my announcement. After all, I had been appointed by the ministry; he had had nothing to do with it. Kurucz swallowed and replied in a hoarse voice: "Well, there have been tensions . . ." It transpired sometime later that, to his mind, in going to Berlin I was only looking for a springboard to help me find a job elsewhere.

My resignation was announced at a staff meeting. It was greeted in total silence and a lowering of heads—I had never seen a demonstration of shame and remorse in such a picture-book manner. Walking out of the institute was almost disconcertingly simple. I only met one of my colleagues, a technician with whom I had gotten on reasonably well. He said he was sorry and he would never forget me.

A year and a half's ordeal was over.

○

The story of finding a home in Vienna, transporting our chattels from Berlin and from Budapest to the new apartment is nothing to write home about. It took place in May 1992; I drove my wife and children to our summer house at Lake Balaton in Hungary, and I settled down to my job in the rooms of Universal Edition.

Then, on September 4, I set out from Vienna in my East German, two-stroke Wartburg car to fetch the family and embark on a new life in a new country.

On September 6, we had just about reached the spa town of Sárvár in Western Hungary when I saw an Audi with a German number plate suddenly change direction and move straight toward us. I remember muttering, "What on earth is she doing?" then lost consciousness.

When I came to, I was sitting by the side of a ditch. My wife was lying next to me in the grass, groaning. I also vaguely heard the noise of a helicopter as it was taking off from the other side of the road. I was unaware at the time that it was carrying my daughter Fanni who had suffered brain injury, in addition to breaking a leg and losing four teeth. Where my other daughter, Flora, was, I cannot remember.

We were taken by ambulance to the hospital of the nearest city, Szombathely. The German couple also landed there. They admitted freely that the wife had fallen asleep at the steering wheel.

At the hospital, doctors took stock of our injuries. Fanni was worst off: she was in a coma and remained unconscious for a week. Flora's face was swollen out of all recognition, and she had deeps cuts on her forehead and a leg, but basically, she was all right. Except, of course, that as the only one of us who had not lost consciousness, she was fully aware of the details of the accident and of what had happened to us. My wife had a bad fracture of her right leg; a cut just above her left eye was a near miss. It was a matter of millimeters for her to lose her eyesight. I lost a tooth, broke a finger in my left hand, broke my nose (which went unnoticed; by the time they realized what had happened, the bone had set again and my face had become the richer for an asymmetry). Also, I had internal bleeding and injuries that made any movement of my body a forbiddingly painful exercise. An auspicious start to a new life . . .

As soon as the pain had subsided to a tolerable degree, I asked for a wheelchair and Flora trundled me to see my wife and my other daughter. Fanni was lying by herself in an intensive-care ward, linked to machines whose sign language I could not interpret. Her eyes were amazingly large and beautiful and as long as her mouth was closed, her missing teeth were not apparent. She was clearly unaware of the outside world. It made no sense to talk to her, but her twin sister (they were eleven at the time) chirped and chatted away to her nevertheless, pretending that all was well. It was a heartrending scene. I was then trundled back to my wife and I reported to her on what I had seen. She must have been sedated, for she took it all in her stride, something that under normal circumstances would not have been her way of accepting even the slightest illness of our children.

News of our accident spread like wildfire. Composers, my former charges at EMB, kept on calling to ask about our well-being, and so did my former boss László Sarlós; even the Hungarian Institute in Berlin asked somebody to telephone to find out how we were doing.

Then, one day as I was lying on my bed, I saw an apparition. It was a tall, white-haired gentleman, with a box of *Mozartkugeln* in each hand.[2] Incredulously, I recognized Otto Tomek. To see him in the Szombathely Hospital ward was as unexpected as it was joyful.

I was deeply moved by this gesture of Universal Edition: after all, I was still an unknown quantity, I had not had time to prove myself—but they reached out to me, I was obviously considered one of them. It was to be the first of many gestures of support over the years, which have won the firm my unswerving loyalty and enduring gratitude.

Dr. Tomek cannot have been impressed by what he saw, for soon enough we received another visit: Dr. Elena Hift, a former leading light of

---

2   *Mozartkugeln* are Austrian delicacies created by the Salzburg confectioner Paul Fürst in 1890. They consist of pistachio marzipan, nougat crème, and dark chocolate coating.

UE, by then in retirement, came by and arranged with the hospital management that we would be taken to Vienna before any of us was operated on. (Months later, she admitted it had been the most difficult assignment of her life.) An ambulance was sent from Vienna. My wife and Fanni (still in a coma) were lying on stretchers; Flora and I were sitting in our pajamas. Behind the scenes, Universal Edition had meanwhile found a place for us in the capital's best specialist hospital, the Lorenz Böhler Krankenhaus. We were all examined; my wife and Fanni were placed in a ward by themselves, Flora and I were sent home. There was nothing they needed to do for us, except put my left hand in a new, more professional cast and offer me regular physiotherapy to teach me to move my fingers once the cast was ready to be removed.

Austrian surgeons know their jobs, as I suppose do their colleagues in other mountainous countries where skiing is a national pastime: broken legs are the order of the day during the winter season. My wife's was a particularly complicated case, in that her leg had sustained multiple fractures and had to be assembled together from many bits and pieces. Thanks to Universal Edition's generosity, she (and Fanni) can now walk without a limp—the mind boggles at the idea of an operation in ski-abstinent Hungary—even though my wife's leg has since been a more reliable source of weather forecast than the media.

Soon enough, I was impatient to resume work and reported back for duty, if only for a few hours per day. I was still in need of rest and also wanted to see my wife and daughter in the hospital. Fanni's brain was gradually healing but it was quite a long time before we were reassured that she would be fully normal.

CHAPTER 13

UNIVERSAL EDITION

I had a quick look around, took off my hat having made sure no one saw me (after all, you never know, especially if you are a newcomer and a foreigner to boot), and began to mount the well-worn stone steps leading upward. A small sign said that the offices of Universal Edition were on the first floor. If you continued your way up, you eventually reached the Library and the Archives of the Society of the Friends of Music. Those very steps had also been trodden by Gustav Mahler and Anton Bruckner, Hugo Wolf and Johann Strauss, Johannes Brahms and Archduke Eugen. I was still holding my hat in my hand. A feeling of reverence overcame me. In the evening, however, as I descended those steps with my hat on, the ghosts had vanished. If in the morning I had been guided by Bruckner and Brahms, my mind was now filled with Schoenberg, Bartók, and Janáček. A single day at Universal Edition, even in the humble position of an intern, had changed my life and put a stamp on it once and for all.

The young man who had just arrived in Vienna from his native city, Karlsruhe, to take up his internship at UE in 1923, was Hans Heinsheimer (1900–1993). Shy as he was to begin with, only a year later he was entrusted with running the Opera Department. Until his emigration to the United States in 1938, he was to play an important part in the publisher's affairs. The quotation above has been taken from his reminiscences recorded for the Austrian daily newspaper *Die Presse* in 1970.

The well-worn stone steps were only replaced a few years ago and as I mounted them in June 1992—with no hat on—I was filled with a similar feeling of reverence. It has stayed with me right up to the present.

I sensed the presence of music history even more keenly in the spacious conference room that had been the office of the firm's first director of international standing, Emil Hertzka, once UE had moved into its present premises in the Musikverein in 1914. The walls are still lined with period bookcases, the old tomes on their shelves so many silent witnesses of the past. Hertzka watches his successors from his portrait hanging on the wall.

It was in that room that Hertzka introduced Heinsheimer to Alban Berg, an encounter that the young man was to recall in numerous articles after his retirement as vice president of the New York music publisher Schirmer. The power of Berg's personality caught him unawares and turned him into a lifelong admirer and friend until the composer's untimely death in 1935.

It was also in that office that Alfred Schlee (a year younger than Heinsheimer, he joined UE in 1927 and stayed until 1985 or so) introduced Janáček to Webern; there he received Szymanowski, whose perfumed scent—as he told me later—continued to waft in the rooms well after he had left. But all the other composers of that legendary catalogue had no doubt also come by to visit the director and the employees who looked after their works; with a little bit of extrasensory perception I might have picked up whatever the walls had soaked up of their presence.

But not just theirs: before UE moved into the Musikverein, those rooms had belonged to the conservatory, with Bruckner among the professors (he used to teach in a corner room, which now houses the License Department). This means that Mahler and countless others were students within those walls. Heinsheimer had every reason to take off his hat, and, in my mind, so do I.

O

Universal Edition was founded in 1901 as a publisher of the standard repertoire of *universal* music literature. Six years later, the director's chair was taken over by Emil Hertzka, whose visionary publishing policy exerted a defining influence on music history in the first half of the twentieth century.

Hertzka was born in Pest-Buda in 1860. His roots were identical with those of Theodor Herzl (1869–1932), born next to the Dohány Street synagogue: the Hungarian Jewish middle class. Herzl's dream was the creation of a modern state of Israel; Hertzka summarized his in a preface to the book brought out in 1926, to mark the twenty-fifth anniversary of the firm's foundation:

Our goal lies in the distance and we have a long road ahead of us. We march, however, with light and carefree steps, for we are in the company of youth. We let them lead us and make our mistakes together, embarking without hesitation on unmapped, thorny paths. We feel that youth will always find the right way forward. The faith in youth, the pleasure that we have already accomplished something for it and the hope that we shall achieve even more, give us the strength to march forward.[1]

Hertzka needed the instinct of someone with a divining rod to predict a promising future for many of the composers he placed his faith in. Two years after taking over the helm, in 1909, he signed up Gustav Mahler, Arnold Schoenberg, Franz Schreker, Richard Strauss, Max Reger, Josef Bohuslav Foerster, and others.

Mahler was of course no unknown quantity, but he wrote symphonies of giant proportions, which he kept on revising. The number of performances was unlikely to produce the income to cover the costs. Hertzka had the power of conviction to take Mahler, by then no longer director of the Opera House, under contract.

Schoenberg, with *Verklärte Nacht* (1899) and *Pelléas und Mélisande* (1902/1903) to his credit, had also composed the *Kammersymphonie* (1906), which indicated that he was about to set out on a voyage to alien lands where only a fraction of the public was prepared to follow him. Hertzka remained loyal even when this young man—and his pupils—became the object of ridicule, his music and public appearances triggering scandals.

Franz Schreker was less of a risk: he had composed late-romantic music, such as the *Phantastische Ouverture* (1902), *Nachtstück* (1906/1907), and *Valse lente* (1908). Hertzka's uncanny instinct must have intimated to him that, with the opera *Der ferne Klang* (premiered in 1912), Schreker would compose the first of several music-theater pieces that would prove enormously popular and lucrative for some twenty years. (*Nachtstück* might have provided a clue: it was actually an orchestral interlude from the third act of *Der ferne Klang*.)

Richard Strauss was clearly a safe bet: by 1900 he had already composed a range of symphonic poems and some exquisite Lieder, such as "Zueignung" (1885), "Ruhe, meine Seele" (1894), and "Morgen" (1894/1897).[2] Sadly, in

---

1   Hans Heinsheimer and Paul Stefan, eds., *25 Jahre neue Musik* (Vienna: Universal Edition, 1926), 7.

2   Richard Strauss's works had actually been acquired by Universal Edition in 1904, with the purchase of the Joseph Aibl Verlag of Munich. In 1909, UE concluded a contract with Strauss for his new compositions.

1932, the year of Hertzka's death, Universal Edition was forced—because of dire finances resulting from the world economic crisis—to sell the rights of the symphonic poems, including *Till Eulenspiegel, Also sprach Zarathustra,* and *Tod und Verklärung,* to C. F. Peters.

By 1917 when Hertzka invited Bartók to entrust his compositions to UE, the publisher was an established player on the international music scene: Bartók was elated, as we know from his correspondence with his family, and did not hesitate to say good-bye to his publishers in Budapest, including Rózsavölgyi and Rozsnyai.

Bartók's decision may have been motivated by UE's promotional activities on behalf of its composers. The same considerations had led Karol Szymanowski to seek contacts outside Poland where none of the music publishers entertained any international contacts. Szymanowski was well aware that, if he wished to make his music known beyond the borders of his native country, he needed relevant professional support.

Each year, new names were signed up, in a consistent effort to expand the catalogue. They included the twenty-one-year-old Ernst Krenek, a brash youth who produced one large-scale symphony after another. Hertzka must have sensed the makings of an international sensation, which came six years later, in 1927, with the "jazz"opera *Jonny spielt auf.* However, before *Jonny,* UE had had to invest money in music-theater pieces that were far less promising: *Die Zwingburg* (1924), *Der Sprung über den Schatten* (1924), and *Orpheus and Eurydike* (1926). Krenek continued to produce at an impressive rate and in every genre. He was clearly a man of exceptional talent and was even his own librettist. But Hertzka, perhaps because of his innate optimism, could not foresee that Krenek would never again be able to match the success of *Jonny.*

In 1924, Hertzka followed the advice of Ferruccio Busoni and took on his twenty-four-year-old pupil Kurt Weill. The young man—Krenek's exact contemporary—had a few chamber pieces to his credit, such as a string quartet (1923) and *Frauentanz* (1923/1924) for soprano, flute, clarinet, bassoon, horn, and viola as well as a remarkably original concerto for violin and wind ensemble, with double bass and percussion (1924). They showed talent, but once again, a dowser's instinct was needed to predict *Die Dreigroschenoper* only four years later. Like Krenek, Weill had composed a number of pieces leading up to that evergreen, which, unlike *Jonny,* has lost none of its popularity in nearly a century since then. Perhaps it was not until the one-act opera *Der Zar lässt sich photographieren* of 1927 with its hit "Tango Angèle," and, even more so, with the *Mahagonny Songspiel* of the same year that it became apparent that

Weill's radical change from an expressionist musical style toward a popular one was permanent.[3]

Leoš Janáček was sixty-two years old in 1916 when he signed a contract with Universal Edition. *Jenůfa* had been premiered in Brno twelve years before, but the actual first performance that launched the opera's international career, albeit in an arbitrarily altered form that Janáček could never make peace with, took place in Prague in the same year, 1916. Once again, Hertzka's instincts served him well: all of the Moravian composer's masterpieces on which his fame rests—*Káťa Kabanová* (1921), *The Cunning Little Vixen* (1924), *The Makropoulos Affair* (1926), and *From the House of the Dead* (premiered posthumously, in 1930) were composed in the few years under UE's aegis, prior to his death in 1928.

With his long beard and mane, Hertzka may have looked like a relic from the nineteenth century. In actual fact, he was aware of the latest technical developments in the music industry and recognized their implications for publishing. In June 1930, he spent three weeks in the United States, "to arrange for sound film and radio productions of some of our operas. There is a tremendous future along that line, and the importance of such productions in the development of a more widespread interest in opera in America cannot be overestimated," he said in an interview for the *Musical Courier* (published on June 21, 1930). Hertzka continued: "The vast number of radio stations and film houses in your country will bring opera home to many millions. Do you know that New York City and its direct environment has about two dozen broadcasting stations, as against two for Berlin, one for Vienna, and four for all of Austria? Some 700 stations are scattered throughout the United States. What a medium for the education of the masses!"

It would be idle to speculate what he could have accomplished, if he had not died in 1932: Nazism would have driven him out of Austria, but at sixty-three, he would probably have been too old to gain a foothold in a foreign country.

○

Emil Hertzka also possessed the talent for picking young people to work for him who understood his goals and were anxious to help him realize them. After his death, they proved worthy successors.

---

3 I trust that the adjective "popular" is not misleading. Weill was consciously seeking an idiom "whose appeal will be unusually broad," as he wrote in his letter to Hertzka on August 25, 1927. Elsewhere, he described his music as one that had "found its way to the masses."

As early as 1910, he employed Alfred Kalmus, twenty-one at the time, who was to stay until his death sixty-two years later. Kalmus must have been an extraordinarily ambitious young man who consciously planned his future career: he studied copyright as well as musicology at the University of Vienna, in addition to taking courses in book printing and art design. Also, he was clearly quite proficient on the violin, for he devoted much of his free time to playing chamber music.

Alfred Kalmus was called up in the army at the outbreak of World War I and was taken prisoner by the Russians in 1916. He turned the three years in Russia to good use by learning to speak the language fluently. At the end of hostilities, his courage and competence stood him in good stead in helping thousands of fellow prisoners of war find their way home.

Back in Vienna, Kalmus took up his duties at Universal Edition and stayed until 1923. It was in that year that he realized a long-standing plan of his by founding a music publishing firm of his own. He called it "Philharmonia" and specialized exclusively in pocket scores. Four years later, he returned to UE, bringing his catalogue with him. Until recently, the Philharmonia pocket scores with their dark gray cover, known and respected the world over, remained part of UE's publishing program. Composers regarded it as an honor for their works to be published in the series alongside the classics from Haydn to Bartók. This legacy of Kalmus now lives on in a somewhat larger format but marked by the same high standards of scholarship and publishing excellence.

It makes you feel dizzy to consider that Alfred Kalmus met Mahler in person; he worked with composers of the generation who came after Mahler, and in his last years helped the young generation: Boulez, Berio, Stockhausen, and Halffter as well as many British composers such as Harrison Birtwistle.

He achieved what he did against heavy odds: he had to flee with his family to Britain in 1936, before Nazi Germany posed a threat to Jews holding an Austrian passport. Kalmus was forced to start life anew at the age of forty-seven. He founded Universal Edition (London) Ltd. and turned it into an important center of contemporary British music.

I touched on Heinsheimer's work at the start of this chapter. As head of the Opera Department, he was deeply involved in that golden age of music theater (including opera and more popular forms) in the 1920s. The extent of his role can be measured by his correspondence with Kurt Weill.

Hertzka and Heinsheimer between them took an almost fatherly interest in the young man's development (of course, they were also mindful of the financial aspects of his projects).

Their admonitions and doubts expressed in their letters inspired Weill to formulate statements—much quoted in relevant musicological studies ever since—that throw a revealing light on his motivations for working with Brecht or on his conscious break with his expressionist style in an effort to write music of popular appeal.

Admirably enough, Hertzka and Heinsheimer were not blind to the danger of Weill's getting stuck in the *Dreigroschenoper* and *Mahagonny* idiom. In a letter of October 10, 1929, for example, Heinsheimer warned him that this highly accessible new style "could not be copied indefinitely": "If I judge its place in your development correctly, it is, as it were, the breakthrough to a popular, simple musical style that radically liberated you from the style evident in, say, *Frauentanz*. But in the long run this song style can serve only as a basis for your return to more profound and substantial musical creations."[4]

It was this responsible attitude to the work of a young composer of exceptional talent that justifies Christopher Hailey's opinion that the correspondence between Universal Edition and Kurt Weill was "a dramatic chronicle of one of the most striking publishing successes of the Weimar period."[5]

Hans Heinsheimer happened to be visiting New York in 1938 when Austria was gobbled up by the Third Reich. The *Anschluss* convinced him that it was wise not to return home but to seek employment in the United States. His work for Boosey and Hawkes as well as for Schirmer was no less significant than his years with UE: he helped Bartók in his years of emigration and promoted Aaron Copland; as vice president of Schirmer he looked after the compositions of Leonard Bernstein, Samuel Barber, and others.

Erwin Stein's (1885–1958) career was similar to that of his colleagues Kalmus and Heinsheimer. He found employment with Universal Edition as a young man, was appointed to head the Orchestral Department (in which capacity he went out of his way to persuade Weill to "make another appearance as an absolute musician"—that is, a composer of symphonic or chamber works) and was forced by political developments to flee to Britain.[6] In London, he joined the staff of Boosey and Hawkes and promoted the music of Benjamin Britten.

---

4   Christopher Hailey has kindly revised his English translation for the present book. "Creating a Public, Addressing a Market: Kurt Weill and Universal Edition." In *Essays on a New Orpheus: Kurt Weill*, ed. Kim Kowalke (New Haven: Yale University Press, 1986).

5   Hailey, "Creating a Public, Addressing a Market," 22.

6   Erwin Stein's letter to Kurt Weill is dated May 16, 1930. Zemlinsky was also persuaded to compose an orchestral work without soloist to enhance the chances of promotion. He responded with

However, there was a difference. Between 1906 and 1910, Erwin Stein studied with Schoenberg—an encounter that gave his life a new direction. He dedicated much of his energy to furthering the music of his master as well as that of Webern and Berg, both in Vienna and after his emigration to London. His name will be familiar to those who have read a selection of Schoenberg's correspondence that he edited.

The only member of Emil Hertzka's legendary team I actually met in person was Alfred Schlee (1901–98). As mentioned earlier, he spent an extraordinarily long time with UE and as an "Aryan," he ran no personal risk in staying and salvaging whatever he could of the catalogue.

Born in Dresden, Schlee was twenty-six when Heinsheimer's invitation reached him. Mahler was no longer alive but all the other composers who defined UE's profile were around for him to get to know and to work for. Initially, he was seconded to Berlin to represent Universal Edition. In his autobiography of 1954, Schlee commented: "Under the national-socialist regime, my assignment was as important as it was delicate. In view of the fact that I was employed by a foreign firm which, in addition, was known to be Jewish, I could avoid membership of the *Reichsmusikkammer* [Reich Chamber of Music]."[7]

After the *Anschluss*, Schlee was asked to return to Vienna and work at UE's headquarters in the Musikverein.

> Although for the outside world I worked in a subordinate position, in actual fact I was able to influence the leadership of the publisher in a meaningful manner. I could induce the National-Socialist directors to take measures that helped former directors of Universal Edition to establish themselves in England and the USA. . . . My endeavors served on the one hand to save the firm's possessions and on the other, to make preparations for the time after the war. I could conclude contracts in those years which would become effective after the defeat of the National-Socialist regime.

Schlee "saved the firm's possessions" in a literal sense: he hid the printing plates of the Second Viennese School in his garden, so that the scores could be made available as soon as the war ended.[8] He had absolutely no

---

his *Sinfonietta* in 1934.

7 From an unpublished autobiography, dated 1954, found as a typed transcript in the Universal Edition offices.

8 Erwin Ratz (1898–1973), a member of Schoenberg's circle, hid behind flour sacks at his home two scores of Hanns Eisler's written to antifascist texts before the Nazi occupation of Austria. The world premiere took place after the end of the war.

doubt in his mind that the Third Reich would be defeated, a conviction that inspired the promise he made to the Swiss-Jewish composer Rolf Liebermann (1910–99) that he would be signed up after the war.

The spring 1946 issue of the periodical *Modern Music* carried an article by Alfred Schlee under the title "Vienna Since the Anschluss."[9] It gives a fascinating insight into the spirit of liberation that was experienced by progressive representatives of the capital's musical circles once the hostilities had ended. Schlee wrote:

> The Saturday afternoon private concerts which I have held at the Universal Edition for a small group of invited guests have been particularly well received, since they offer an opportunity for explanation and discussion.
>
> We eagerly await the scores of works which were heard in other countries during the war. Some material has already been supplied through the kind cooperation of the musical members of the armies of occupation. This includes records of some of the new major works of Schönberg. Unfortunately, the apparatus on which these giant records must be played lies behind the line of demarcation, so we can only admire the silent grooves with faithful respect.
>
> In May we intend to make a unified stand; we shall take the initial steps toward contact with the outside world by means of the first Vienna festival. We dream that Toscanini, Walter and Kleiber will conduct, that Schönberg, Stravinsky, Milhaud, Martinu, and Krenek will stretch out their hands to us. Our faith is strong and we have in this country a boundless love of music.

That last sentence could have been written by Hertzka—indeed, the will of renewal that imbues the article is true to the old director's heritage.

Alfred Schlee expanded the catalogue with the bright young composers who emerged during the postwar years: Boulez, Stockhausen, Berio, and the rest of them. He told me how, after attending a concert featuring Stockhausen's music, he had gone up to the young composer and announced to him: "I am your publisher."

Clearly, with his sensitive antennae, he picked up the rebellious spirit of the period exemplified by the composers of Darmstadt and espoused the aesthetic ideals embodied in the music of Stockhausen and Boulez. In later years, Schlee discovered György Ligeti, György Kurtág, and Wolfgang Rihm for UE, and did not hesitate to welcome Arvo Pärt, even though the Estonian composer had no truck with the European avant-garde.

---

9   Alfred Schlee, "Vienna Since the Anschluss," *Modern Music* 23 (Spring 1946), 99.

Was Schlee endowed with Hertzka's instincts? Did he foresee that one day Pärt would have an international cult following and his music would be performed all over the world practically on a daily basis?

Schlee's personal taste certainly led him in a particular direction that—luckily for Universal Edition—ensured that the firm has continued to flourish as a torchbearer of new music up to the present.

On one occasion, however, I was witness to a revealing conversation between him and György Ligeti. In my first year with UE, Schlee would come by every now and again and go through the catalogue with me, commenting on each composer and each composition. One day, Ligeti turned up in my office when Schlee was on a visit. The two greeted each other in a polite and rather reserved fashion. Presently, Schlee said: "I still regret that you never wrote that book on Webern." Whereupon Ligeti said: "I preferred to compose."

I think Schlee's comment can be explained in a historical context. Universal Edition was the publisher of the famed musicological journal *Die Reihe* (1955–62), edited by Herbert Eimert with Karlheinz Stockhausen as his assistant. Three of the issues carried analyses by György Ligeti, each of which count today as classic examples of musical scholarship at its highest level: book 4, titled *Junge Komponisten* (Young composers, 1958), printed Ligeti's essay "Pierre Boulez: Entscheidung und Automatik in der Structure Ia" (Pierre Boulez: Decision and automatism in structure Ia]; book 5, published a year later under the title *Berichte—Analyse* (Reports—analysis, 1959), had Ligeti's "Zur III. Klaviersonate von Boulez" (On the Piano Sonata no. 3 of Boulez); and book 7, *Form—Raum* (Form—space, 1960), published the article "Wandlungen in der musikalischen Form" (Changes in musical form).

No wonder Alfred Schlee was impressed by Ligeti the musicologist and in the early sixties placed his scholarly qualities above those of his compositions.

There was another thing as well: Schlee had been close to Webern and had hoped that a musicologist of Ligeti's stature would write an authoritative book on him. He was, I believe, ninety-two years old when that chance encounter in my office took place, and what he meant to convey was that his disappointment had not diminished with the passage of time.

When UE sounded me out about whether I was interested in returning to publishing, Alfred Schlee and György Ligeti had been among those consulted. Both were in favor. I have every reason to be grateful to both of them.

o

It would be logical at this point to get down at last to my own history with Universal Edition. Still, I feel I must make a detour and pay tribute to the victims of those tragic twelve years between 1933 and 1945. Universal Edition itself was a victim, with its dedicated directors fleeing for their lives, the firm taken over by one Johannes Petschull, a Nazi stalwart. Alfred Schlee alone was left to guard the flame.

Hans Krása, Erwin Schulhoff, Pavel Haas, Viktor Ullmann, László Weiner, and many others were murdered in concentration camps.[10] Their luckier colleagues emigrated before it was too late: Béla Bartók and Ernst Krenek for political reasons; Schoenberg, Zemlinsky, Weill, Korngold, Max Brand, Egon Wellesz, Vittorio Rieti, Wilhelm Grosz, Karol Rathaus, Eric Zeisl, and others, on "racial" grounds.

Franz Schreker's calvary began in 1932 when he was forced to renounce the world premiere of his opera *Christophorus* in Freiburg. Next, he was divested of his position as director of the Berlin Music Academy—it was in fact his fellow UE composer Max von Schillings who ordered his compulsory retirement. His masterclass was also taken away. Schreker could not get over the humiliation: he suffered a stroke, and died of a heart attack in 1934.

Manfred Gurlitt's is a pathetic story: he resorted to lies to cover up his part-Jewish background and went to considerable lengths to curry favor with the National Socialist regime. He even joined the party in 1933 but was ejected in 1937 because of his "contaminated" blood. Eventually, in 1939, he settled in Japan and introduced many works of the standard opera repertoire to that country.

Walter Braunfels and Heinrich Kaminski went into internal exile: both were half-Jewish and their music was taken off concert programs. Nevertheless, both went on composing. Emil Nolde, Kaminski's friend, comes to mind: his *ungemalte Bilder* (unpainted pictures) emerged in the years when he was under a cloud as a "degenerate artist."

Nightmare years.

o

The vestiges of 1950s brainwashing ensured that I was somewhat apprehensive about working in the West. Capitalism and exploitation, hard work and insecure existence—what was I letting myself in for? The future

---

10 Haas, Ullmann, and Weiner were not published by Universal Edition.

of my family depended on whether I would meet the expectations of my new employers.

On one of my very first days in the office, I sat in on a discussion that concerned Stockhausen's *Punkte*, Feldman's *For Flute and Orchestra*, and Brand's *Maschinist Hopkins*.

I was all at sea. I simply did not know the catalogue.

O

It is a catalogue for all seasons.

In my Budapest years I used to receive UE's quarterly *Musikvorschau* (Music Preview) with its interminable list of performances. Each time it was an impressively thick booklet and I would study it incredulously and with envy. My *EMB NEWS*, in which I reported my own harvest, ran to four pages, sometimes to as many as six.

Universal Edition has a catalogue of major works. It features history-making compositions from every decade of the twentieth century, with one notable exception: not a single work by Stravinsky. Of course, there are other gaps as well, such as Britten or Hindemith, but you cannot have everything. As far as Shostakovich and Prokofiev are concerned, Universal Edition has the rights of their entire oeuvres for the territory of Austria; Shostakovich's early opera *Nose* is a UE copyright and so is the orchestral suite from the ballet *The Golden Age*.

It is a favorite pastime of mine to study festival programs and mark "our" works in it. I happen to have the Aldeburgh Festival program book of 2011 at hand. UE is respresented by Mahler's *Das Lied von der Erde* and Second Symphony; Kurtág's Eight Duos; Reich's *Clapping Music*; Berg's Vier Stücke, op. 5, and *Lyric Suite*; Szymanowski's String Quartet no. 2; Messiaen's *Oiseaux exotiques*; Webern's Sechs Bagatellen, op. 9; Stockhausen's Klavierstück VII; Berio's *Sequenza VIIb*; Boulez's *Messagesquisse* and ... *explosante-fixe* ... ; as well as Kodály's Sonata, op. 8.

I think that program is fairly representative: in putting together concerts of twentieth-century music, it is difficult to get around including at least a couple of pieces published by Universal Edition—usually more.

My job as promotion manager was threefold: making sure that living composers were getting their fair share, both as regards their existing pieces and receiving commissions to produce new works. It was also my responsibility to represent the back catalogue from Mahler through Frank Martin to Kurt Weill. Finally, I went to considerable lengths in an attempt to resuscitate compositions of the first half of the twentieth century, which for some reason had fallen into oblivion. All three aspects of my job became something of an obsession; indulging them gave me enormous pleasure as well as a sense of frustration in equal measure.

"Making sure that living composers were getting their fair share" is something of an understatement. The ultimate goal of promotion by a music publisher such as UE is to embed works by contemporary composers in the international repertoire. In other words, to ensure that program makers select particular works *as a matter of course*. It is easier said than done, but that is what you should aim for. Ligeti's *Atmosphères* has made it, I believe. So have, in an altogether different context, Pärt's *Cantus in Memory of Benjamin Britten* and Luciano Berio's *Folk Songs*, both in its original version of 1964 for mezzo-soprano and seven instruments and the one for mezzo-soprano and orchestra of 1973.

As I gradually got into my stride, I met composers and heirs of composers: widows, children, grandchildren, and foundations. All of them expected me to do my duty as promoter and deliver the goods in the way of performances and commissions.

The one exception was Pierre Boulez: he needed no promotion, certainly not to get new commissions. He had more than enough to keep him busy. If only he got down in earnest to compose, and canceling rather than accepting conducting engagements!

I had known him since 1968 when he brought his Residentie Orkest of The Hague to Budapest. We did the first of many future interviews on that occasion and I used to visit him wherever our paths crossed: in New York in 1973 or at IRCAM in Paris when I happened to be passing through the city. Boulez has always been friendly; he can be ironical in a paternal way ("you are a *filou*," he said once. I suppose he meant "rascal"), but he is not one to open up. He does, however, show emotion on occasion.

After a concert of his at the Salzburg Festival, I accompanied Alfred Schlee—by then well into his nineties—to meet him. Boulez's smile, the warmth in his eyes, the way he raised his arms to embrace his old mentor, supporter, and publisher, were expressions of genuine affection.

Years later, once again in Salzburg, I presented Boulez with a copy of his *Dialogue de l'ombre double* (1984) for clarinet and tape, straight from the printers. The happy smile, the glint in the eyes, the welcoming gesture were once again there. It is a complicated score that needed lengthy and careful editing and had been rather long in coming. It was at last there and the composer was happy with the outcome.

I am basically an emotional person, so, obviously, I respond to *Rituel* more strongly than, say, to his iconic *Le marteau sans maître*. I have been impressed by *Répons* (not only under his own baton but also with Péter Eötvös and Jonathan Nott) as well as by *sur Incises* more than by *Pli selon pli*, which is universally regarded as a chef d'oeuvre. The reason could lie in Boulez's treatment of the human voice. For me, it remains a vehicle to express human emotions; I need to discern a sense underlying the succession of notes, whereas abstract compositional computations raise a barrier I cannot pass. In *Répons* and in *sur Incises*, I have been bowled over by the sumptuous sonority, in the former also by the music coming from different directions. I am as well a great "fan" of *Notations* and still have not despaired of Boulez's adding to the existing five pieces at least a couple more, which are supposed to be almost ready.

I have heard *Notations* quite a few times with Boulez conducting; each time, no. 2 had to be repeated as an encore. If there is such a thing as a hit in contemporary music, *Notations II* certainly is one. With the composer in charge, all five pieces pulse with tremendous life, they have a throbbing energy.[11]

I am absolutely convinced that a conductor, or indeed a soloist, does disservice to the composer if he cannot render his works in an authentic manner. A composer is at the mercy of his interpreters; there is nothing he can do to prevent performances from taking place. Ligeti showed his disapproval by refusing to take a bow onstage. On one occasion, he was so incensed by a production of his opera *Le grand macabre* that he made a noisy exit.

I am grateful to Boulez, the conductor, for rehabilitating compositions for me that I had doubts about after hearing them in mediocre renditions. The music ranges from Karol Szymanowski's Third Symphony, a piece he had never conducted before and, as he told me after the concert, he felt he had not quite done justice to, through Berg's Chamber Concerto (with the wonderful soloists Mitsuko Uchida and Christian Tetzlaff) right up to György Ligeti's Chamber Concerto. Not to speak of Janáček's *From the House of the Dead* . . .

Luciano Berio I knew since the 1970s. We grew quite friendly in January 1981 when I stayed at his house in Radicondoli, Tuscany, to record a booklength interview to be published in time for his portrait concert in Budapest in October of that year.[12] Three weeks after our farewell, my

---

11 On hearing one of the early performances of *Notations VII*, György Kurtág commented: "I have had a lesson in instrumentation."
12 The concert took place on October 26, 1981, at the festival Korunk zenéje (Music of Our Time). Two works made up the program: *Ritorno degli snovidenia* (1976–77) with the cellist Miklós Perényi playing the solo part and *Coro* (1974–76). The conductor was Péter Eötvös.

twins Fanni and Flora were born, an event greeted by Luciano and Talia in a telegram: "to you four from us four."

When the nature of our relationship changed, that is, after I turned from his interviewer into his manager, the chemistry did not work quite as harmoniously. I do not think there is any rational explanation, for Luciano was aware of my admiration for his work. By the time I moved to Vienna, he had been universally recognized as a major figure of postwar music and I knew I was in an extremely privileged position to be able to witness the emergence of his new compositions, and also the way he continued to work at some of them in the wake of their world premieres.

I remember, for instance, *Alternatim* for clarinet, viola, and orchestra. I attended the first performance in Amsterdam on May 16, 1997, but I believe it was not until after the Paris concert that he decided the viola was rather overshadowed by the clarinet, especially at the beginning. He added a wonderfully lyrical, expressive solo passage that greatly enriched the piece. In the Concertgebouw, he had conducted himself, whereas in Paris, where he was sitting in the hall and Michael Gielen was conducting his Baden-Baden orchestra, he had a better chance to hear the music from the outside, as it were, and make a judgment about it. (The concert in Paris took place on December 13, 1997; the soloists were the same as in Amsterdam: Paul Meyer, clarinet and Christophe Desjardins, viola.)

An episode also comes to mind, which, I now realize, might provide some explanation for the malfunctioning of the chemistry between us. I was aware of Luciano's fascination with music history, his treatment of certain compositions of the past as objets trouvés. Beyond integrating them into his own works (the *Scherzo* from Mahler's Second Symphony in his *Sinfonia* of 1968–69), or filling out gaps with his own music (fragments from Schubert's "Unfinished" Symphony in D Major D 936A in his *Rendering* of 1989), he also enjoyed arranging and orchestrating them. The list is long—from Purcell, Boccherini through Brahms, Verdi, Mahler, and de Falla right up to the Beatles.

Hence the idea I put to Luciano: how about arranging for chamber ensemble three of Arnold Schoenberg's Six Songs, op. 8 (1904)? He showed initial interest, but then asked who the arrangers of the other three songs were. "Erwin Stein and Hanns Eisler," I replied. On hearing Eisler's name, Luciano lost his temper. He would certainly not dream of touching anything having to do with that composer. Could it have been Eisler's political views that put him beyond the pale? The storm my idea reaped (I am still convinced of its merits) intimidated me and of course I let the subject drop immediately. Luciano could be gruff and it made me draw in my horns.

When Eric Marinitsch joined the Promotion Department, he took over Berio (and Arvo Pärt) from me and developed a partnership that worked without a hitch.

Toward the end of his life, my relationship with Berio grew closer once again, thanks perhaps to my organizing two German premieres: those of his music theater works *Passaggio* (1961–62) in Mannheim and *La vera storia* (1977–78) in Hamburg.[13]

Berio did not live to hear reports of *Passaggio*'s production but he knew it was in the pipeline. I attended the premiere and found it an interesting sociological as well as musical experience. Defined by Berio and the librettist Eduardo Sanguineti as a *Messa in scena* and premiered in Milan in 1963, it is scored for solo soprano, two choruses, and instruments. Chorus A is placed with the orchestra in the pit, Chorus B is distributed in the theater, with singers seated among members of the public. Composer and librettist had anticipated loud shouts of protest coming from the audience in true Italian fashion—after all, *Passaggio* represents a radical break with the traditions of music theater—and made sure that those shouts would be repeated, imitated, and reinforced by Chorus B. No wonder the world premiere was something of a scandal.

Just over four decades later, in the medium-size German city of Mannheim, the audience meekly accepted what it was being presented with. No one dreamed of shouting—except for members of Chorus B who did their job as required, attracting stunned or amused looks from their neighbors. The provocation did not work as such, *Passaggio* proved a relic of a past era, but the music made an impact quite independently from the production, for it was Berio's music and it never fails to delight.

He was anxious to have a detailed report on the German premiere of *La vera storia*; his joy on hearing of the production's success gave me much satisfaction. *La vera storia* is not easy to bring off. It reflects, I believe, Berio's recurring reluctance to pin himself down, to be unequivocal in questions of genre (cf. *Passaggio* above). Hence, I suppose, the definition of the work as *Azione musicale*. The live encounter with the piece (I had only heard a recording of it) certainly convinced me that it was not an opera. Or rather, I thought that I was seeing one in a dream where the characters were all acting *as if*. They went through the motions of entering into conflict, they displayed passion or desperation in arias and duets; there were choruses

---

13   The German premiere of *Passaggio* took place in Mannheim on October 3, 2005. The conductor was Frédéric Chaslin, with Joachim Schlömer directing. *La vera storia* received its first German performance in Hamburg on September 15, 2002. Ingo Metzmacher conducted, and Henning Brockhaus was the director.

and so on, but it all did not *quite* make sense. You know that it is remotely related to *Il trovatore*, but I, at least, could not detect any connection. For all that, the work was received with resounding applause in Hamburg, for the music is beautiful and Milva was a magnificent ballad singer, a role Berio had created for her.[14]

I also had a part in getting *Epiphanies* (1991–92) for female voice and orchestra programed by the Wiener Konzerthaus in 2000. Luciano was present and acknowledged the applause standing onstage like a sovereign. He did not take a bow, just stood there, faintly smiling and occasionally nodding. Backstage, I felt it was insufficient just to tell him how much I loved his music: frustratingly enough, the words that come to your lips when you really mean them are identical with those you think up as a polite gesture. On an impulse, I embraced him—the first time since knowing him—and Luciano laughed. I should like to think of that embrace as our reconciliation. It was also, I believe, the last time we met.

Soon after taking up my job, Friedrich Cerha and his wife Gertraud invited me to their beautiful house in a garden suburb of Vienna and treated me to dinner. Here I was, yet another promotion manager at UE, yet another man to get to know, to win over, in the hope that he will work more successfully than his predecessors.

Cerha (born 1926), of the Ligeti–Boulez–Berio–Xenakis–Nono–Kagel–Stockhausen–Pousseur generation, is a hero in Austria, the grand old man of music. He has been around for over half a century now, both as composer and as conductor and his name has become a symbol of his art.

His birthdays are celebrations of music, with series of concerts in both major venues in Vienna, the Musikverein and the Konzerthaus. His music is also featured at many other times, all over the country, including the Salzburg Festival. I do not think a composer can hope to achieve more than Friedrich Cerha has in his native country.

Outside Austria, it is another story. What he and his wife Gertraud expected of me was to help put him on the world map. Friedrich Cerha freely admits that he would be nowhere without Gertraud championing his music. Even in her eighties, her energy and single-mindedness are admirable, enviable, and formidable. They are a unique couple, Friedrich Cerha preferring to stay in the background, confining his verbal eloquence to his

14 Milva (Maria Ilva Biolcati; b. 1939) is an Italian singer and actress. With her flaming red hair reaching below her shoulders and her deep, slightly hoarse voice, she was the ideal choice for the ballad singer. She represented for me *Italianità*, a primeval figure drawn from the Italian folk. In Hamburg, she would appear in the auditorium as if out of nowhere, standing or walking slowly in front of the orchestra pit, facing us, singing and moving her head so that the masses of her hair fell heavily on her shoulders, to the right or to the left of his head.

prose writings on music. Gertraud is his agent in the original sense of the word: she acts on his behalf, she is his mouthpiece, speaking for him even in his presence, but also lecturing and writing on his music.

I did my best to be a reliable partner for Gertraud Cerha, and eventually she came to trust me. I needed no prodding, I was as anxious as she was to get things done, such as organizing performances of the historic cycle of seven orchestral works that go by the title *Spiegel* (1960–61). A performance in the Philharmonie in Berlin with Cerha conducting proved a veritable triumph and Sylvain Cambreling's performances at the Bregenz Festival and in Vienna were celebrated occasions.

Where I failed was in getting at least one of Cerha's operas produced. His *Baal* (1974–79), based on several versions of Brecht's play, was on the program in Vienna in 1992, and I was as impressed by the music as by Theo Adam in the title role. *Der Rattenfänger* (the Pied Piper), composed in 1984–86, also ought to crop up at regular intervals, at the very least in German-speaking countries. Based on the eponymous play of 1974 by Carl Zuckmayer (1896–1977), *Der Rattenfänger* is an expression of the composer's political convictions, his condemnation of dictatorship and total commitment to the idea of liberty. It is a sombre opera, no doubt, but it treats of a subject that is unlikely to lose its topicality. The music casts a spell on the listener and, given a good production (such as the one I saw in Darmstadt and again at the Vienna Festival), makes a lasting impression.

The composers I have listed so far are at least fifteen years my senior. Wolfgang Rihm is eleven years younger, yet, I always felt like his pupil. He is larger than life, a master in the traditional sense of the word: one who seems omniscient in practically every walk of life, marked by a serene calm and an unshakable confidence in his place in music history. Our first contact goes back to 1982 when he replied to the three questions I was in the process of putting to a great many composers all over the world. He answered by hand: he is still averse to using machines such as a typewriter or a computer (he does not drive either) and magnanimously presents his correspondents with handwritten letters, that is, genuine Rihm manuscripts.

Next, I saw him at the National Gallery in London, standing in line at the cashier's to pay for a book he had purchased. I recognized him from his photographs, introduced myself and we exchanged a few words.

In March 1992, his fortieth birthday was celebrated at the Philharmonie in Berlin with the Ensemble Modern playing his *Chiffre*-cycle (1982–88) under Arturo Tamayo. It consisted at the time of nine compositions ranging from three instruments up to chamber orchestra, lasting some seventy-five minutes. I knew by then that Rihm would soon be one of the composers I would be promoting in Vienna, so I got a ticket, even though I could not stay until the end.

Years later, Wolfgang asked me why I had left . . . I was speechless. Could he have remembered my face from that brief meeting in London? And even if he had, how could he notice my absence, with hundreds of people sitting in the hall?

When I "inherited" Wolfgang Rihm from my predecessors in UE's Promotion Department, in June 1992, he had already composed a couple of hundred works. Soon enough, I witnessed the way the body of his music continued to spawn, to bring forth the products of his restless, ceaselessly active brain.

He has created a universe, or let us say, a planet in the firmament of new music. In whichever direction you set out to discover its many different landscapes, you find new ones in the making and by the time you return to any particular spot, you are in danger of losing your way: the landscape has changed, new mountain ranges, new islands, new vistas have been added.

You could also picture for yourself Rihm as Jesse portrayed on medieval genealogical trees as the forefather of a large family with innumerable branches and twigs standing for descendants. Rihm-Jesse is the progenitor of a veritable dynasty, one that grows new branches and twigs all the time. You need to be a Rihmologist to keep track and to be aware of lines of descent. There is, for instance, a work for wind ensemble, called *Et nunc II* (1993). At one point, a piano was added, which turned the piece into the piano concerto *Sphere* (1994). In the same year, the piano part of *Sphere* was weaned to start a new life as the solo piano piece *Nachstudie* (1994). And so it goes on.

Needless to say, I was awed by his prolificacy and very often also by the works he produced. Clearly, I could not be happy with every single new piece and also told him so: ours was a partnership based on sincerity. My criticism could sometimes wound him; my enthusiasm may have pleased him but his reaction would be remarkably modest, almost bemused.

I rang him, for instance, after the world premiere of his *Verwandlung 2* (2005). For some reason, he could not attend the concert in Leipzig, where Riccardo Chailly conducted the Gewandhaus Orchestra. I had arrived in time for the general rehearsal. When it was over, the conductor turned around and said to me: "This piece is here to stay."

He was absolutely right. *Verwandlung 2* is one of those rare compositions that you feel simply had to be written, and once born, they appear to be timeless. I dialed Wolfgang's number and flooded him with my enthusiasm. He was, as I wrote above, bemused, perhaps slightly embarrassed but certainly very pleased.

Because of the sheer size of Rihm's oeuvre, I had to develop a suitable approach to properly promoting it. You cannot "push" 400 compositions simultaneously. I had to become something of a Rihmologist myself to be able to suggest a work when the occasion arose.

Of course, promoting Rihm's music was fulfilling: he commands tremendous respect in his native Germany and in many other European countries as well. He has admirers in important positions, who have followed his career from the beginning and who program his works based on years of experience, knowing their backgrounds, their context, their history of interpretation. Over the years, a new generation of program makers has appeared on the scene who have grown up on Rihm's music—for them, he has been around from time immemorial.

Georg Friedrich Haas, one year Rihm's junior, is an altogether different personality with an altogether different background. He joined the UE stable of composers in 1993, that is, at the age of forty. His life until then had been marked by his faith in his calling and the almost total absence of positive feedback from the outside world. He craved recognition but his pessimistic disposition and his lack of success in the past rendered him apprehensive about any real chance of making his way. To a certain extent, we share the same temperament, which helped me empathize with his vulnerability.

Haas's way as a composer has been determined by his single-minded exploration of a sound world beyond the well-tempered system. With admirable consistency, and helped by an unusually fine hearing, he has built his musical universe out of microtones.

Over the fourteen years of my promoting his music, I derived a great deal of pleasure from witnessing his growing success, which, in its turn, has tempered his pessimism. We became comrades-in-arms; my contribution was buttressed by the emergence of new compositions that truly fascinated me.

One of his works that is very dear to me is *Sieben Klangräume* (Seven sound spaces, 2005). Seven movements, which—interspersed between those of Mozart's *Requiem* fragments—literally took my breath away. One sound space, for instance, is made up of noises produced by the instruments of the orchestra, evoking those of machines in a terminal ward today. It is no foreign body within the *Requiem*, but a shattering reminder of the fragility of the man who had written the score with the last remnants of his physical strength.

Haas's opera *Die schöne Wunde* (The beautiful wound, 2003) contains some of the loveliest music I had ever heard, or indeed, have heard since. It is the passage where the lights have been turned off; in the total darkness you are enveloped by music coming from a chorus as well as orchestra and singers. Heavenly sounds that you absorb not just with your ears but your whole being.

Georg Friedrich Haas is now universally acknowledged as one of the most original and significant composers in the world today.

The American composer Jay Schwartz (born 1965) also became a friend. Transplanted from his native San Diego, California, to Germany, he has not had an easy time of it. I was impressed by his quiet determination to write the music he heard in his head and by the strength he drew from the conviction that the idiom he had developed was genuinely new. "Determination" and "conviction" are strong words; they are offset in Jay's spiritual makeup by a heartwarming, touching vulnerability (something that gave me added motivation to try to help him) and an ongoing struggle with question marks swarming in his mind about the new aesthetic he is trying to create. I have attended some of his performances and have been extremely happy to see him celebrated by the public—in Stuttgart as much as in Vienna—his slight figure almost disappearing onstage, surrounded by the orchestra. Jay's keen intelligence and his modesty are two of his endearing qualities that make him such delightful company.

Discovering a young composer, first for myself and then for the outside world, was one of the most thrilling and gratifying aspects of my job. In the case of Johannes Maria Staud (born 1974), the discovery was actually shared with Otto Tomek. We were attending a concert of the Ensemble Modern in the Mozartsaal of the Wiener Konzerthaus in 2000, and heard two works by composers in their twenties that stood out from the rest: one each by Staud and the German composer Enno Poppe (born 1969). We were intrigued by both and eventually decided in favor of the young Austrian: his music had genuine poetry, a remarkable mastery of instrumentation and a talent for writing new music with the accent on the noun rather than the adjective.

Until my retirement at the end of 2007, I did my very best to build Johannes up and he rewarded my efforts with one new piece after another that, I am convinced, will make their way in the years to come. He has proved worthy of his prestigious commissions: by Simon Rattle for the Berlin Philharmonic, Franz Welser-Möst for the Cleveland Orchestra, the Salzburg Festival for the Vienna Philharmonic, and many others. Our contact has grown into a friendship that has outlasted our professional relationship. I derive great pleasure from observing Johannes's career and listening to his music.

I cannot claim to have discovered Vykintas Baltakas (born 1972): he was recommended to UE by various contacts. This maverick Lithuanian, a pupil of Wolfgang Rihm and Peter Eötvös, speaks a musical language all his own. It has a primal force, informed to a certain extent by the folk-music tradition in which he grew up, a refreshing unpredictability, and an acute sense of timbre. Vykintas is proud, sensitive, and vulnerable, his blue eyes can sometimes look at you with unsettling sharpness; his mind, his thinking have a great deal of intriguing surprise in store for you. We have stayed in touch, although his e-mails tend to be few and far between: he has a wife and two small children to look after.

I have selected a few of the many composers I worked with for more than fifteen years to give an idea of the very close personal relationships that can develop between a publisher and his composers. You identify wholly with their careers and you sense that they need you, sometimes just your presence at a concert, an e-mail or text message wishing them success, a concern for their well-being, or a word of advice.

I was rewarded by my charges' successes and sometimes also by dedications. Several Hungarian composers had dedicated their works to me between 1971 and 1990, and a few came my way also during the Vienna years: Georg Friedrich Haas offered me his Cello Concerto (2004), Johannes Maria Staud his Berlin Philharmonic commission *Apeiron* (2004–5) and its offshoot, the piano piece *Peras* (2004–5), Vykintas Baltakas *Scoria* (2004–10) for orchestra. I cannot think of a finer sign of recognition.

CHAPTER 14

BACK CATALOGUE

The catalogue of a music publisher is an important document of the state of musical creativity at any given time. It also reflects the wisdom or otherwise of the conclusions drawn from it by the firm's decision makers.

If you put yourself in the position of Emil Hertzka and his colleagues and successors, I think you cannot but approve of their artistic policy. Unblinkered by stylistic preferences, they cast their net wide within Europe (later also as far as the United States, Canada, Japan, China, and Australia) and invited to Universal Edition a great many composers who were established figures with numerous performances (such as Alfredo Casella, Gian Francesco Malipiero, and Walter Braunfels) or bright young ones born around 1900 who were writing fashionable music—perhaps music of the future (such as George Antheil, Wilhelm Grosz, or Alexander Mossolow).

Luckily, they put their bets on other figures as well who have actually made it into the canon. It is well-nigh impossible to foretell who will one day count as a classic. May I refer you to the interview with Sir William Glock: he relates how it was not until 1958, forty-seven years after the composer's death, that the BBC launched a Mahler Renaissance in Britain by programming all the symphonies twice over. However late in coming, the proof of Hertzka's faith in Mahler was eventually delivered.

In the 1960s in Budapest, when Claudio Abbado invited me to his performance of the Second Symphony, I declined by saying that it was too long. I ought to have been ashamed: I simply had no idea. I must have heard someone say that Mahler's symphonies outstayed their welcome and without knowing them, I just aped that "opinion." It was only in the early

1980s, during a visit to Los Angeles, that I first heard the Second Symphony in a musician's home, on an LP record conducted by Leonard Bernstein.

In any case, a catalogue builds up over the decades and no promotion manager can afford to ignore it. I certainly derived much pleasure from exploring this veritable jungle of names and titles and came up every now and again with pieces I was anxious to present to the world at large.

Sometimes, the world responded. It really only took a dramaturg in a theater who actually listened to a CD I had suggested. That was the case with Walter Braunfels's opera *The Birds*.[1] I thought it represented a singularly delightful piece of late-romantic music that could not fail to please today's audiences. The dramaturg agreed, she suggested the work to the intendant and *The Birds* carried the day. It was programmed by the Vienna Volksoper, and the success convinced the theater to keep it on its repertoire well into the following season. There followed productions elsewhere, such as one in Cologne that I was able to attend.

At other times, the world failed to respond. I still cannot see why Gian Francesco Malipiero's music (1881–1973) should have been falling on deaf ears. His atmospheric, sensitively instrumented orchestral works composed in the first decades of the twentieth century represent to my mind an Italian version of musical impressionism. Try as I might, I could not interest any conductor—until, close to my retirement, the American general music director in Mainz, Catherine Rückwardt, put *Pause del silenzio II* (1926) on one of her programs. As I thanked her after the concert, she said "I cannot see why this music is not played more often." That was the question I had kept asking myself.

It also happened that the "world" approached Universal Edition of its own accord.

There is an enterprising opera festival at Wexford in the Republic of Ireland that specializes in discovering forgotten operas. In 2002 or so, the artistic director had hit upon a work that few of us were even aware of: Joseph Bohuslav Foerster's *Eva* (alternative title: *Marya*).

The Czech composer Josef Bohuslav Foerster (1859–1951) was Mahler's contemporary and friend who outlived him by forty years. Some of his concert works, such as his *Stabat Mater* (1891–92), his Symphony no. 4 (1905), and his Violin Concerto (1910–11) crop up occasionally in his native country. Composed in 1895–97, the story of *Eva* is related to that of Janáček's *Jenůfa*, inspired as it was by a work of the same Czech writer, Gabriela Preissová (1862–1946). The music is intensely felt, affecting,

---

1 Walter Braunfels (1882–1954), *Die Vögel*, op. 30 (1912–19). Based on the play by Aristophanes.

with challenging roles for singer-actors. I was thrilled by this wonderful score and did my best to bring about another production—to no avail. I trust sooner or later some producer or conductor will think of it again. The Wexford production has been released on CD; there is also a studio recording to be consulted.

And then, there was what has come to be known as the *Bielefelder Opernwunder* (the Bielefeld Opera Miracle): Between 1980 and 1993, the conductor Rainer Koch, the dramaturg Alexander Gruber, and the director John Dew set out to unearth twenty more or less forgotten operas of the Weimar Republic. A promoter's dream come true.

Universal Edition had a field day, or rather, field years, with Krenek's *Der Sprung über den Schatten* (1924) and *Die Zwingburg* (1924), Karol Rathaus's *Fremde Erde* (1930), the nineteen-year-old Erwin Dressel's (1909–72) *Armer Columbus* (1928), Max Brand's *Maschinist Hopkins* (1929), George Antheil's *Transatlantic* (1930), and three operas by Schreker: *Irrelohe* (1924), *Der singende Teufel* (1928), and *Der Schmied von Gent* (1932).

I arrived on the scene in time for the last of the Bielefeld team's production: that of Kurt Weill's three-act opera *Die Bürgschaft* (1931), the outcome of his cooperation with Caspar Neher (1897–1962) as librettist.

Luckily, some of the operas have had an afterlife: Brand's *Maschinist Hopkins* was staged in Vienna, Schreker's *Irrelohe* was a success in Bonn, *Der Schmied von Gent* has been released on CD and so has *Die Bürgschaft*, following a production in the United States. As for the others—at least they have had their chance to prove that they are stageworthy pieces that could be considered for future programming in any theater.

Thanks to a series of CDs released by a Danish label and devoted to the oeuvre of Paul von Klenau (1883–1946), I was able to become acquainted with the music of that forgotten composer. Born in Denmark, von Klenau spent most of his active life in Germany. As a result, he did not come under Nielsen's influence, unlike most of his colleagues, and developed a thoroughly Germanic musical idiom.

I was particularly taken with his *Paolo and Francesca* (1913)—in the subtitle, the composer calls it a "Dante-Fantasy." I set about promoting it, and some other pieces, with a vengeance.

Who was Paul von Klenau? Did he have any heirs? I wondered. A reply to my first question was provided by Soma Morgenstern in his memoirs under the title *Alban Berg und seine Idole* (Alban Berg and His Idols) published in 1995 by the zu Klampen Verlag in Germany.[2] I am not aware of

---

2   The zu Klampen Verlag is in the process of publishing the entire oeuvre of Soma Morgenstern
    (1890–1976). Born in East Galicia, then a province of the Austro-Hungarian Monarchy, which

an English translation of this uniquely interesting book, written by a close friend of Berg. Klenau is also touched upon and is presented in a less than favorable light.

As far as heirs are concerned, our files produced the information that one lived practically next door to Universal Edition. She was also related to the conductor Willi Boskovsky (1909–91), who used to be extremely popular in Hungary, thanks to his New Year's concerts of Johann Strauss waltzes broadcast live from the Musikverein.

I had no trouble arranging an appointment with Ms. Boskovsky. Soon enough, I was climbing the steps of the rather derelict building where the middle-aged lady, whose modest appearance showed no sign of any link to the arts or artists, received me in the company of her dog. Her apartment was no less neglected, but I saw some intriguing works of art on the walls, including a drawing of her grandmother—Paul von Klenau's wife—by Oskar Kokoschka.

She was clearly somewhat surprised by my interest in Klenau: I may well have been the first representative of Universal Edition to have contacted her. She said she had a chest full of the composer's papers in the neighboring room and offered to show me its contents. She opened the door and I followed her. Presently, I was standing right in front of an old lady, sitting motionless, like a statue, in an armchair. Her face was without any expression, her eyes looked dead. "This is my mother," Ms. Boskovsky explained. I was so taken aback that I beat a hasty retreat, I am afraid, letting my hostess pull the heavy chest into the next room all by herself. From it, she produced letters by Schoenberg and Berg addressed to Paul von Klenau. "Does anybody know of the existence of these treasures?" I asked. Ms. Boskovsky was unsure. In a state of excitement, I suggested she visit me in the office and allow me to make photocopies. She agreed promptly. In the next few days, she did come by and the letters were xeroxed.

I immediately got in touch with the Arnold Schoenberg Center and the Alban Berg Foundation, to report on my find. Apparently, both institutions were aware of the existence of those letters but had somehow failed to take steps to actually locate them.

I had my reward: in return for the correspondence, the Alban Berg Foundation invited me to visit Berg's apartment at 27 Trauttmannsdorfgasse in Vienna's 13th district. The building is known to all those who have seen

---

also produced Joseph Roth, Soma Morgenstern was a writer and journalist. In addition to his memoirs focusing on Alban Berg, Morgenstern also wrote a book on Joseph Roth. His autobiography as well as his fiction are also of interest.

the photograph of Berg in the open window and right underneath him in the street, his large portrait painted by Schoenberg, leaning against the wall.

The foundation is in the same house, one floor above the apartment. The door was opened for me—and I found myself in the 1930s. Once again, many photographs have been taken of that room, usually with Berg sitting there. Everything was exactly the same, except for the composer's pale death mask lying on the piano. Words cannot describe the experience. I was also shown the kitchen and the bathroom; it all looked lived-in, although the last occupant, Helene Berg (the composer's widow), had died in 1976.

Soon after, of the many prominent people who had once visited the apartment, I met Lotte Ingrisch, the widow of the composer Gottfried von Einem (1918–96). Ms. Ingrisch, born in 1930, has maintained a low profile lately, but until recently she was often in the news. Her books would be reviewed but her pronouncements of a transcendental nature would attract even more attention. She claimed, for instance, that she continued to be in permanent dialogue with her deceased husband and reported on what he had had to communicate to her.

She came by one day to my office and I told her of my visit to Alban Berg's apartment. It turned out that she used to be a regular visitor there, in the last years of Helene Berg's life. She would be treated to some dessert that Helene prepared specially for her and that she would bring in on a tray from the kitchen. On one of her last visits, however, Helene Berg was too weak to fetch the dessert herself and asked Lotte Ingrisch to do so. She got up and walked to the kitchen; in doing so, she reached a spot in the room that made her feel very peculiar. Having moved on, she felt normal again; on returning to the table with tray in hand, she passed the same spot and once again, the curious sensation overcame her. Lotte Ingrisch told Helene Berg of her experience. Helene was not surprised: "Oh," she said, "Alban is standing there. You walked through him both ways." Lotte Ingrisch had met her match. I cannot say I had a similar sensation during my short time in that room, but I must admit it did have a very special atmosphere.

Visiting museums that were once the homes of people now deceased has for me an element of indiscretion, just as reading correspondence, irrespective of the fact that in some cases the writers of the letters had every reason to suppose that they would one day be published.

I was lucky enough to have visited Frank Martin's house at Naarden in Holland—also a museum by now—with the Swiss composer's widow, Maria, as my guide. She showed me those rooms, the furniture she once owned and had used as a matter of course, at one remove: her relationship to them could not have been more intimate and yet, it was a space she had already left behind and given over to posterity.

My visit to the apartment of Egon Wellesz's daughter Elisabeth also had something of a haunted quality, even though it was not a museum. I felt as if I had traveled several decades back in time, especially in Ms. Kessler's study (she was married to Charles Kessler, a former official at the British Foreign Office). On the wall, she had a photograph of her great love, the conductor Sergiu Celibidache as a young man—strikingly good-looking he was, too—and in a corner, she had an old cupboard with numerous drawers, holding the papers and manuscripts of her father. Egon Wellesz (1885–1974), a Schoenberg pupil, left behind a considerable oeuvre now looked after by the Egon Wellesz Fonds. He was also highly regarded as a musicologist, a scholar of Byzantine music. Ms. Kessler introduced me to her father's world and I did my best to promote his compositions in Austria and elsewhere.

By joining the staff of Universal Edition, I had the privilege of meeting some of the representatives of an earlier era—if not the composers themselves whose works make up the back catalogue, at least members of their families. Through those encounters, as well as of course through the music itself, the back catalogue became filled with life; it was in no way a museum I would occasionally pay a visit to. It was my responsibility to ensure that it continued to be an integral part of musical life today.

CHAPTER 15

THE PSYCHOLOGY
OF PROMOTION

The psychology of promotion is closely linked to an aspect of the psychology of creativity, or rather, the psychology of creators. Creative artists, in whatever field, could not exist without their promoters (agents, managers, publishers, gallery owners): promoters are their link to the outside world, for which they create in the first place.

I am sure that the relationship between Picasso and Ambrois Vollard or Braque and Daniel-Henry Kahnweiler was basically similar to that between Emil Hertzka and Arnold Schoenberg or the American writer Carson McCullers and the publisher Houghton Mifflin, which discovered her talent and continued to publish her books.[1]

Creators need someone they can trust—someone who understands and appreciates their art, who responds to new works intelligently and with empathy, who supports them in crises that are bound to befall those whose life centers on turning themselves inside out and placing their findings for all to view; creators need someone who paves the way for the encounter with those ready, even eager, to absorb newly created works of art, someone who brings the world to the artist and the artist to the world.

---

1 Ambrois Vollard (1865–1939), French galerist and publisher, organized Picasso's first exhibition in 1901. He also represented and supported Matisse, van Gogh, and Cézanne at a time when they counted as controversial artists. Daniel-Henry Kahnweiler (1884–1979), a German-born French galerist, placed Derain, Braque, and de Vlaminck under contract as early as 1907. Carson McCullers (1917–67) published her first novel, *The Heart Is a Lonely Hunter* (New York: Houghton Mifflin, 1940), at the age of twenty-three.

The promoter must be as selfless as the creator must needs be self-centered; both share a sensitivity without which creation and its promotion would be unimaginable. Under no circumstances can the promoter be a failed artist. He must be capable of vicarous joy: as I put it in an earlier chapter, he must experience his protégés' success as his own. The promoter had better not be vulnerable and should not take the failure of his efforts or downright rejection personally. He is a salesman who deals in art. The product he sells has no practical use; its worth is subject to highly diverse and individual assessment. The promoter needs to have a strong physique, so that he can take late nights, little sleep, and jet lag in stride.

Well, that is about as much as I can think of in terms of the promoter's job description.

Whether I meet those requirements, is another question.

Let us take just one criterion: knowledgeability. Right at the start, I had to decide how to go about learning the catalogue. If I had begun with composition A of composer A and systematically proceeded until I reached composition Z of composer Z, actual promotion would have had to wait for at least a couple of years.

I also realized that I could not afford to address myself to any one work the way a musicologist would, submitting the score to thorough analysis, listening to recordings in different interpretations.

I had to resign myself to the fact that initially at least, I would need to make do with scratching the surface. The story has a happy ending: over the years I did master the catalogue to a degree that I was able to suggest pieces for any occasion, in any style and any instrumentation. It gave me much pleasure to talk to an orchestral director, listen to his needs, and list works from the catalogue, not necessarily just ours, that might suit him.

I would also get requests from festival intendants and their ilk for compositions to do with a particular subject. For instance, a festival would be programmed around the theme "metamorphosis" and it would be my job to find suitable works. Drawing up a list, with detailed explanations as to why I thought they were relevant, was tremendously thrilling and fulfilling. Needless to say, I would keep and save such a file for future use. Gradually, I broke down the entire catalogue from a wide range of angles and prepared what I called thematic lists.

As for sensitivity, that was a requirement I met without fail. I do not know about my colleagues, but I certainly possessed what I would call "a promoter's telepathy." I found that no matter how often I may have heard a particular work by myself and formed an opinion of it, this changed the moment I had anybody with me to listen to it. Before they expressed an opinion, I knew what they were going to say, for at that moment, my own impression was wholly different from my usual reaction.

On one occasion, telepathy failed to work, much to my luck. It happened in Budapest sometime in the 1980s. I had persuaded a critic to listen with me to a prize-winning composition at UNESCO's International Rostrum of Composers. Soon enough, he fell peacefully asleep. I felt terribly silly, listening to this music I knew from the first note to the last, accompanied by faint snoring from my immediate vicinity. And he actually expressed an opinion when he woke up! In any case, it is a good job I had not followed his example and joined him in his slumber.

I kept in touch with my contacts by mail, by telephone as well as on my travels, in person. I much preferred face-to-face contact for it facilitated the direct exchange of metacommunicative signals. On my monthly travels, I would visit the orchestras and theaters of a particular region, especially in Germany, where an area like the Ruhr abounds in music centers situated cheek by jowl with one another. Every April, I would visit the Witten Festival of New Chamber Music, which covered a weekend, and would use it as my base to travel to nearby cities once the festival was over.

Donaueschingen in October was less convenient from that point of view. On the other hand, it attracted new music wizards from all over Europe and even overseas. My diary would soon be filled with appointments; each year, I had a rich harvest—unless I was confronted with the all-too-well-known phrase: *wir sehen uns*. That is, "see you later." Usually, the opposite was meant.

I was fond of Donaueschingen, a typical small German *Residenzstadt*, that is, the former capital of a once-independent ministate. The Princes zu Fürstenberg who have sponsored the festival ever since the 1920s, may no longer reside in their palace, but the reception they give after the last concert still takes place in its rooms.[2] Sometimes the prince and the princess receive their guests at the entrance, shaking well over a hundred hands. Dinner is served by waitresses, local women speaking their racy dialect, dressed in folk costume, and you immerse yourself in this enchanting world of chandeliers, Persian carpets, wall hangings, delicious food and wine. You are in the middle of a huge park and the Danube springs just outside the palace.

The *Musiktage* at Donaueschingen traditionally constitute a festival of world premieres. More often than not, little-known composers (either too young to have established themselves or too experimental to have regular

---

2   The first festival took place in 1921, under the patronage of Prince Max Egon II (1863–1941).

access to the concert platform) will be invited to submit new works. Rarely, someone like Lachenmann or Rihm has a new composition performed, or a noteworthy anniversary is observed, such as the fortieth of the premiere of Luciano Berio's *Chemins I* in 2005. In any case, the festival never fails to surprise: you will hear new works by composers you do not know.

Clearly, Armin Köhler, the artistic director, has not set himself the goal to treat his public to masterpieces. It is in the nature of a festival of world premieres that he, too, will be surprised by the works he commissioned. I think he accepts the fact that he may on occasion be disappointed; on the other hand, you cannot fail to see his pleasure when a novelty proves a success.

The artistic director's programming principles have a great deal in common with Pierre Boulez's approach to new works. Interviewed by Peter Heyworth for the *Observer* prior to the start of the concert series of the BBC Symphony Orchestra at London's Round House, Boulez said: "We must try to rid ourselves of the idea that when we listen to new music we are searching for masterpieces of the future." He added that what he wanted at the Round House was "to create a feeling that we are all, audience, players, and myself, taking part in an act of exploration . . . and if something valid and valuable turns up, then we can be pleased."[3]

I must admit that my own attitude was less magnanimous (and this is where the promoter's psychology comes in). At festivals I listened to new music as, let us say, a car salesman casts a critical look at the new models he will have to sell.

Can I identify myself with the new work? Could I promote it with conviction? These questions would occupy my mind whether the pieces were published by UE or elsewhere; they flooded my mind—they were an occupational hazard.

o

Failing personal encounters, I made do with mail and phone calls. Mail is a more polite way of communication, for it can be read anytime; calls may come at an inconvenient moment.

However, mail has the exasperating snag that you may have to wait ages for an answer. I used to bite my nails, figuratively speaking, wondering as to the reason for silence at the other end: did my message get lost

---

3   Quoted by William Glock in his contribution "With Boulez at the BBC," in *Pierre Boulez: A Symposium.*

(which did happen, though pretty rarerly), was it read at all, why on earth was there no answer—any answer? I used to pray for at least a "no," for even that was preferable to the uncertainty about whether a commission or co-commission was going to materialize, a territorial premiere was confirmed, whether a piece I had suggested had been listened to, liked, and accepted for performance or otherwise. My agitation was also part and parcel of the promoter's psychology.

The people at the receiving end of my mail and phone calls, the people I visited on my promotional tours also had their psychology. I never talked to them about it, so I have no evidence to lean on; I can only go by their reactions. There were those who welcomed my offers to keep them informed, treated me as an equal partner, and gave me the reassuring feeling that my services were needed: an ideal situation of give and take.

At the other end of the spectrum, I encountered people, mostly in the Scandinavian countries, who were manifestly averse to being approached. Sooner or later, I had to admit defeat and tell myself: they know I am there to help, they will contact me if they need anything. Usually, they never did.

I think empathy is once again the key word. One has to realize that promoters' "targets" are inundated by suggestions and information of the kind I was trying to share with them. They have had to develop some method of self-defense to be able to work in peace. I had to accept that.

As for having a strong physique: it may not appear to have anything to do with psychology but in a way it does: a postconcert dinner with your business contacts makes for an atmosphere that a discussion in an office cannot hope to match. Sharing a good meal and drinking to each other's health forges friendly ties.

In my last years before retirement, probably because of failing health, I became rather unprofessional from that point of view. I noticed that I was growing weak physically, and a late night out exhausted me for several days. Nowadays, I prefer not to eat after six p.m.

Wolfgang Rihm usually insisted that I have dinner with him after a premiere and of course I could not say no. The two of us would go to a restaurant of his choice—he is a gourmet par excellence—and he would order a hearty meal. It was impossible to sit there and watch him eat, so I would order a salad to keep him company. Rihm never failed to be amused and would tease me about my unorthodox ways. Now that I have retired, my salad days are over.

CHAPTER 16

FAREWELL AND AFTER

I t was all kept a secret until the last minute.

In the autumn of 2007, I was looking forward to retirement. Daily work was becoming something of a strain; I was feeling exhausted and depleted. Early in November, I was casually asked if I would be free on the twenty-ninth. With no travels planned, I said yes. Some time toward the end of the month, I was told to show up at such and such a time in the afternoon and I noted it in my diary without the slightest idea what it was all about.

My wife and I arrived at the stage entrance of the Musikverein, which had been my access to the UE offices, and were confronted with a printed notice placed on a stand: "Konzert für Bálint András Varga. Musikverein, Steinerner Saal. Wiener Klaviertrio, Heinz Stolba, Reciter" (Concert for Bálint András Varga. Musikverein, Stone Hall. Vienna Piano Trio, Heinz Stolba, reciter).

In a state of excitement, we made our way to the hall and there, in the lobby, I caught sight of Friedrich and Gertraud Cerha, Sir Harrison Birtwistle, Cristóbal Halffter, Georg Friedrich Haas, Johannes Maria Staud, Jay Schwartz, and Vykintas Baltakas, as well as the board of Universal Edition and all my colleagues. They were waiting for us, with a knowing smile on their faces: unlike me, they were fully informed—in fact, they had actively prepared the event.

The idea had come from Johannes Maria Staud. He had suggested that UE bid farewell to me by arranging a concert of world premieres, all written for the occasion. And that is precisely what happened. Composers were approached; in addition to those who could actually fly to Vienna to attend, also György Kurtág, Wolfgang Rihm, Mauricio Sotelo, David Sawer, Saed Haddad, and Arvo Pärt.

Amazingly enough, all the pieces had been completed in time for my colleagues to print the scores and the parts and for the Vienna Piano Trio to learn twelve compositions (Baltakas's *Varga-Lied* was an electronic piece. He had recorded our telephone conversations and edited out those bits where I made some sort of sound—a grunt, hm, aha, things like that—and turned them into a composition. He even made me sing by transforming the material electronically—hence the title).

The afternoon started with the managing director, Astrid Koblanck, giving a *Laudatio*, and saying good-bye to me on behalf of UE. She was followed by Johannes Maria Staud, who related the background to the concert and recalled episodes of our work together since 2000, the year he was invited to UE. Finally, I said some words of thanks in English, for the benefit of Birtwistle, whose German is at best scanty. I was then presented with a score of all the pieces bound in a volume with UE's well-known glossy white cover and the logo in the upper left corner.

There followed the concert of world premieres. The Vienna Piano Trio had rehearsed the pieces with the composers present and also, in the case of György Kurtág and others, through the telephone. They are excellent musicians and played the program as if the trios had been on their repertoire for years.

I listened elated and dazed. No music talks to you the way music written for you does. I had to think of a similar event in 1991 when Alfred Schlee's ninetieth birthday had been celebrated in the Mozartsaal of the Konzerthaus. I was still in Berlin at the time, but I was familiar with photographs of the scene where Schlee was standing onstage with his protégés of many decades standing in line to shake his hands. The works written to mark the event were also published and some of them have lived on—such as Kurtág's string quartet *Aus der Ferne III*.

Those of my colleagues who had been present, told me that that concert had been a rather formal occasion: numerous representatives of Austrian cultural life were in attendance, whereas mine was more of a family event—the UE family got together in an unforgettably relaxed and warm atmosphere. My farewell was a welcome pretext for composers, editors, and colleagues working in the various departments to enjoy each other's company and to rejoice in being part of this great publishing house.

Both Cerha and Staud proceeded to expand their trios, turning them into full-fledged concert items. The pieces have since been taken up by other ensembles, as has Kurtág's trio. (He has not given up the idea of adding a fast movement; right now, work on his first opera occupies all his time.) Birtwistle's trio, too, has been played since, as has Sotelo's. An immense pleasure.

O

Five years have passed since. In March 2008, I was diagnosed with cancer—no wonder I had been feeling out of sorts lately. The operation took place in June and the side effects have been singularly faithful to me, up to this day.

Nevertheless, I have been fairly busy. In November 2007, I recorded several hours of conversations with György and Márta Kurtág, and turned that fascinating interview into a book published in Hungarian in 2009. As soon as that was done, I translated it into English; others addressed themselves to preparing the French and German versions. The University of Rochester Press brought out *György Kurtág: Three Interviews and Ligeti Homages* in the same year; the French translation also appeared at that time, the German one was published early in 2010.

The University of Rochester Press has kept me busy ever since. They expressed interest in my *Three Questions—Eighty-Two Composers* that had been published in Hungarian in 1986; I got down to translating it into English, omitting material and adding some newly written contributions.[1] And here I am, writing the last chapter of my third book to be incorporated in URP's prestigious *Eastman Studies in Music* series.

If this one proves to be my last book, I shall gladly devote my free time to my grandson, Leon, born in September 2012. A few hours a week are reserved for Universal Edition, where I work as a consultant. I enjoy keeping in touch with my colleagues, but I also enjoy the luxury of a nap in the early afternoon. I go to concerts in the Musikverein and the Konzerthaus and once in a while attend world premieres abroad—Staud's in Dresden and Munich, Baltakas's in the same series, the Musica Viva, in the Bavarian capital.

Retirement suits me down to the ground.

---

1 Varga, *Three Questions for Sixty-Five Composers.*

N O T E S   I N
R E T R O S P E C T

In a way, this book is a double self-portrait. The *Memoirs* are one by definition, but so are the interviews: a portrait of the young man that I was, rushing around the world with his tape recorder, forefinger ready to press the record button, right hand holding the microphone.

I think I was aware right from the beginning that by starting the recording, I was about to arrest the passage of time, or rather, cut a slice out of it, to keep for the future. I was a collector of self-engendered documents, encouraging the musicians I met to take a look back and thereby help preserve information of use for future generations.

I relished the role of medium-cum-amanuensis, and also the fascinating psychological experiment that interviewing represents: finding the key to a personality, creating an atmosphere of trust, awaking the interviewees' desire to open up, and in making them unwind, releasing memories stored in their brain.

My natural propensity to *look back* has been linked to the keen awareness that each and every one of us, without exception, has exactly the same number of hours per day to spend according to our talents and our circumstances. The outstanding personalities I had the privilege to talk with, had had the single-mindedness, the strength of character, perhaps also the luck, but certainly the gift to make the very best use of their time. It was a lesson for me for life.

I was also fortunate enough to spend decades with composers in real time, so to speak. Rather than induce them to talk *about* their work, I could help them create it by obtaining commissions and thereby creating in my turn an ambience conducive to their work. It was also gratifying to build up their careers from scratch or join them midway, by arranging performances of existing works, in an effort to embed them in the reper-toire in the present and, that was the hope, in the future.

I believe everyone needs a goal in life—something to work for that later gives one the reassuring sense that it was worth the effort. I never made it as a pianist but have been lucky enough to spend a life in music nevertheless. This book is a record of that process.

INDEX

Eastman Studies in Music

Ralph P. Locke, Senior Editor
Eastman School of Music

Additional Titles of Interest

Analyzing Atonal Music:
Pitch-Class Set Theory and Its Contexts
Michiel Schuijer

CageTalk: Dialogues with and about John Cage
Edited by Peter Dickinson

György Kurtág: Three Interviews and Ligeti Homages
Bálint András Varga

Intimate Voices: The Twentieth-Century String Quartet
Volume 1, Debussy to Villa-Lobos
Edited by Evan Jones

Intimate Voices: The Twentieth-Century String Quartet
Volume 2, Shostakovich to the Avant-Garde
Edited by Evan Jones

John Kirkpatrick, American Music, and the Printed Page
Drew Massey

Leon Kirchner: Composer, Performer, and Teacher
Robert Riggs

The New York Composers' Forum Concerts, 1935–1940
Melissa J. de Graaf

Three Questions for Sixty-Five Composers
Bálint András Varga

The Whistling Blackbird: Essays and Talks on New Music
Robert Morris

A complete list of titles in the Eastman Studies in Music series
may be found on our website, www.urpress.com.

Bálint András Varga makes available here nineteen extended interviews with some of the most notable figures in music from the past fifty years, as well as lively snippets from interviews Varga conducted with thirteen other equally renowned musicians. The interviewees include singers Elisabeth Schwarzkopf and Cathy Berberian, pianists Alfred Brendel and Arthur Rubinstein, violinists Isaac Stern and Yehudi Menuhin, conductors Claudio Abbado and Sir Neville Marriner, composers György Ligeti and Karlheinz Stockhausen, and legendary pedagogue Nadia Boulanger. Of special interest is an interview with the reclusive composer György Kurtág, published here for the first time.

From Boulanger to Stockhausen concludes with a poignant memoir by Varga of his experiences growing up in a Jewish family in Hungary during World War II and the early years of Communist rule. Varga's recollections also include details about his many interviews with some of these remarkable musicians, and about his employment at the Hungarian state radio station and then in the music-publishing industry, which brought him to, among other places, Vienna, where he now lives.

Bálint András Varga has spent nearly forty years working for and with composers. His previous books for the University of Rochester Press are *György Kurtág: Three Interviews and Ligeti Homages* and *Three Questions for Sixty-Five Composers*.

"Bálint Varga's books have shown his devotion to the great composers of contemporary music. The interviews in *From Boulanger to Stockhausen*, which he carried out over the past few decades, have today become an important document for new generations of musicians and music lovers."
—Riccardo Chailly, Gewandhauskapellmeister, Gewandhausorchester Leipzig

"This is a book of voices. We hear great musicians speaking with fresh immediacy, each of them introduced by a pen-portrait at once incisive and sympathetic. But we hear also the intimate voice of the one who observes and listens, the author of this astonishing book, in a moving memoir of a childhood in communist Budapest and a working life promoting the music he loves."
—Paul Griffiths, author of
*The Substance of Things Heard:
Writings about Music* (URP 2005)

"Bálint András Varga is one of the great listeners in the recent history of music. In his interviews with composers and musicians, in his work for Universal Edition, in his own writing, he waits for what matters and then pursues it, his attention his passion. Surging toward sound on every silent page, this book is a major document both of the century now past and of the century unfolding."

—Alex Ross, music critic, *The New Yorker*

"This book has given me enormous pleasure. The interviews are full of valuable information about music and musicians. Ligeti, Sir William Glock, and Walter Legge are no longer with us, yet here they are, speaking to us directly. Bálint András Varga is a good listener and a perfect interviewer; he always asks the right questions. The autobiographical part of the book is—at least for me—no less fascinating. Jewish identity, life in postwar Budapest, the world of publishers—Varga tells his story humbly, honestly, and not without a sense of humor. He has helped me to remember my own not too distant past."

—András Schiff, musician

www.ingramcontent.com/pod-product-compliance
Lightning Source LLC
Chambersburg PA
CBHW030811100426
42814CB00002B/78